RE-VIEWING
BRITISH
CINEMA,
1900-1992

RE-VIEWING BRITISH CINEMA, 1900-1992

Essays and Interviews

EDITED BY
WHEELER WINSTON DIXON

State University of New York Press

Published by
State University of New York Press, Albany

© 1994 State University of New York

For information, address State University of New York Press,
State University Plaza, Albany, N.Y., 12246

Production by Marilyn P. Semerad
Marketing by Theresa A. Swierzowski

Library of Congress Cataloging-in-Publication Data

Re-viewing British cinema, 1900-1992 : essays and interviews / edited
   by Wheeler Winston Dixon.
         p.   cm.
      Essays first published as a double issue of the journal Film
   criticism.
      Includes bibliographical references and index.
      ISBN 0-7914-1861-8 (acid-free). — ISBN 0-7914-1862-6 (paper :
   acid-free)
      1. Motion pictures—Great Britain—History. I. Dixon, Wheeler
   W., 1950-   . II. Title: Reviewing British cinema, 1900-1992.
   PN1993.5.G7R4 1994
   791.43′0941—dc20   93-1548
                                                                    CIP

10 9 8 7 6 5 4 3 2

For Mary C. Wheeler

CONTENTS

Acknowledgments xi

CHAPTER ONE 1
Introduction: Re-Viewing the British Cinema
Wheeler Winston Dixon

CHAPTER TWO 11
Frederic Villiers: War Correspondent
Stephen Bottomore

CHAPTER THREE 25
British Filmmaking in the 1930s and 1940s:
The Example of Brian Desmond Hurst
Brian McIlroy

CHAPTER FOUR 41
The Doubled Image: Montgomery Tully's *Boys in Brown*
and the Independent Frame Process
Wheeler Winston Dixon

CHAPTER FIVE 53
Lance Comfort, Lawrence Huntington, and the
British Program Feature Film
Brian McFarlane

CHAPTER SIX 67
Re-Constructing the Nation: *This Happy Breed*, 1944
Andrew Higson

CHAPTER SEVEN 83
The Demi-Paradise and Images of Class in British Wartime Films
Neil Rattigan

CHAPTER EIGHT   95
The Repressed Fantastic in *Passport to Pimlico*
Tony Williams

CHAPTER NINE   107
Revision to Reproduction: Myth and Its Author in *The Red Shoes*
Cynthia Young

CHAPTER TEN   121
The Tension of Genre: Wendy Toye and Muriel Box
Caroline Merz

CHAPTER ELEVEN   133
An Interview with Wendy Toye
Wheeler Winston Dixon

CHAPTER TWELVE   143
The Last Gasp of the Middle Class: British War Films of the 1950s
Neil Rattigan

CHAPTER THIRTEEN   155
Evidence for a British Film Noir Cycle
Laurence Miller

CHAPTER FOURTEEN   165
The Tradition of Independence: An Interview with Lindsay Anderson
Lester Friedman and Scott Stewart

CHAPTER FIFTEEN   177
The Sight of Difference
Ilsa J. Bick

CHAPTER SIXTEEN   195
Twilight of the Monsters: The English Horror Film 1968-1975
David Sanjek

CHAPTER SEVENTEEN   211
Re-Viewing the Losey-Pinter *Go-Between*
Edward T. Jones

CHAPTER EIGHTEEN 221
Keeping His Own Voice: An Interview with Stephen Frears
Lester Friedman and Scott Stewart

CHAPTER NINETEEN 241
The Politics of Irony: The Frears-Kureishi Films
Leonard Quart

CHAPTER TWENTY 249
The Long Day Closes: An Interview with Terence Davies
Wheeler Winston Dixon

Notes on Contributors 261

Bibliography 263

Index 275

State University of New York Press
State University Plaza
Albany, New York 12246

We take pleasure in sending you this review copy of
RE-VIEWING BRITISH CINEMA,
1990-1992: Essays and Interviews

Edited by: Wheeler Winston Dixon

Publication date:

July 17, 1994

$19.95   ~

Price:

Please send two copies of your review to

STATE UNIVERSITY OF NEW YORK PRESS
STATE UNIVERSITY PLAZA   ALBANY, NEW YORK 12246

C3052-279

ACKNOWLEDGMENTS

"INTRODUCTION: RE-VIEWING THE British Cinema," by Wheeler Winston Dixon; "Lance Comfort, Lawrence Huntington, and the British Program Feature Film," by Brian McFarlane; "*The Demi-Paradise* and Images of Class in British Wartime Films," by Neil Rattigan; "Revision to Reproduction: Myth and Its Author in *The Red Shoes*," by Cynthia Young; "An Interview with Wendy Toye," by Wheeler Winston Dixon; "The Last Gasp of the Middle Class: British War Films of the 1950s," by Neil Rattigan; and "Re-Viewing the Losey-Pinter *Go-Between*," by Edward T. Jones appear here for the first time.

"British Filmmaking in the 1930s and 1940s: The Example of Brian Desmond Hurst," by Brain McIlroy; "The Doubled Image: Montgomery Tully's *Boys in Brown* and the Independent Frame Process," by Wheeler Winston Dixon; "Re-Constructing the Nation: *This Happy Breed*, 1944," by Andrew Higson; "The Repressed Fantastic in *Passport to Pimlico*," by Tony Williams; "The Tension of Genre: Wendy Toye and Muriel Box," by Caroline Merz; "Evidence for a British Film Noir Cycle," by Laurence Miller; "Tradition of Independence: An Interview with Lindsay Anderson," by Lester Friedman and Scott Stewart; "Twilight of the Monsters: The English Horror Film 1968-1975," by David Sanjek; and "The Politics of Irony: The Frears-Kureishi Film," by Leonard Quart are reprinted through the countesy of *Film Criticism*, Lloyd Michaels, editor. These articles originally appeared in Vol. XVI, Nos. 1-2 (Fall/Winter 1991-1992) of *Film Criticism*.

"Frederic Villiers: War Correspondent," by Stephen Bottomore, originally appeared in *Sight and Sound*; reprinted by permission.

"The Sight of Difference," by Ilsa J. Bick, originally appeared in *Persistence of Vision*; reprinted by permission.

"Keeping His Own Voice: An Interview with Stephen Frears," by Lester Friedman and Scott Stewart originally appeared in *Post Script*; reprinted by permission. This article was originally printed in Vol. 11, No. 3 (Summer 1992) of *Post Script*.

"*The Long Day Closes*: An Interview with Terence Davies," by Wheeler Winston Dixon, originally appeared in *Cineaste*; reprinted by permission.

CHAPTER ONE

INTRODUCTION: RE-VIEWING THE BRITISH CINEMA

Wheeler Winston Dixon

> By discarding what they view as monologic and myopic historiography, by
> demonstrating that social and cultural events commingle messily, rigor-
> ously exposing the innumerable tradeoffs, the competing bids and
> exchanges of culture, New Historicists can make a valid claim to have
> established new ways of studying history and a new awareness of how his-
> tory and culture define each other.
>
> —H. Aram Veeser, *The New Historicism*

THIS COLLECTION OF essays began as a double issue of the journal
Film Criticism covering the period in English cinema between 1900 and 1975. The
public response to the issue was immediate and positive. The essays included in
that issue broke new ground in British film history and aesthetics, and they brought
to light the work of a number of important but hitherto overlooked British
cinéastes, including Montgomery Tully and Brian Desmond Hurst. In addition, the
volume featured an outspoken interview with director Lindsay Anderson and Caroline Merz's essay on Wendy Toye and Muriel Box, two British filmmakers who
have never really received the public attention they so obviously deserve.

Editing that issue of *Film Criticism* was a distinct pleasure, but it also
had its downside; there were a large number of essays and interviews that I
would have liked to include but could not, simply because of lack of space.
This volume allows me to reprint the entire contents of the issue and add an
additional ten articles to the existing text, affording an overview of the British
film that ranges from the pioneering battlefield cine-reportage of Frederic Villiers all the way to the most recent work of director Terence Davies. In all cases,
the essays in this volume deal with aspects of the British film that are not considered in other anthologies and with directors and/or films who have all too
often been marginalized within critical discourse. The resultant collection, then,
affords the reader a view of the British film in the twentieth century simply
unavailable elsewhere.

1

There are a number of excellent survey volumes on mainstream British film history, cited at the end of this introduction and briefly considered here. John Barnes's *The Beginnings of the Cinema in England*, for example, offers a comprehensive look at the work of a number of pioneer British filmmakers, notably Robert W. Paul, but doesn't touch on the work of a number of other important early figures in any real detail, including the Frenchman Augustin Le Prince (who did his most important early work in England, before he mysteriously disappeared) and Frederic Villiers. Paul is perhaps the best known of the early British film pioneers, and Barnes's book predictably foregrounds Paul's undeniable accomplishments in the medium. However here, as elsewhere, it is the dominant tale that is being told at the ostensible expense of lesser-known, but perhaps equally important, cinema artists.

George Perry's *The Great British Picture Show* also tells the tale of the dominant order within fictional narrative filmic practice, highlighting the work of Alexander Korda, Alfred Hitchcock, Cecil Hepworth, Maurice Elvey, Anthony Asquith, Victor Saville, Sir Laurence Olivier, and other well-known names in British cinema history. Other figures, notably Lance Comfort, Brian Desmond Hurst, Lawrence Huntington, Wendy Toye, Muriel Box, and Montgomery Tully, get decidedly less attention. These personages have for too long been confined to the margins of the British film canon, yet their work is of great interest to modern scholars and historians. We can see now that "A" films (that is, films with a lavish budget and well-known personalities as principal stars) have for a long time been given an artificial precedence, because of their lavish physical execution, over "B" films of equal or greater thematic interest. Often, these more modest films question the dominant social order in ways that mainstream films would not dare to do, if only for fear of not recouping the substantial investment involved in their production.

Many "Bs" (or "quota quickies") were designed simply as escapist entertainment. But even in the humblest British "programmer," the seeming predictability of the narrative often disguises implicit critiques of the British social, sexual, political, and class order. As the essays in this volume on such established canonical "classics" as *The Red Shoes*, *Passport to Pimlico*, *Peeping Tom*, and other films demonstrate, even those "A" films ostensibly made in defense of the dominant social order often contained the seeds of rupture within their respective frames. A number of the essayists included here have reexamined these seemingly "exhausted" texts and arrived at fresh and insightful reinterpretations that tell us a good deal that is new not only about the films themselves, but also about the British upper classes who brought about their creation.

Charles Barr's *All Our Yesterdays*, Ernest Betts's *The Film Business*, James Curran and Vincent Porter's *British Cinema History*, Roy Armes's *Critical History of the British Cinema*, and other standard survey texts on British film history and practice afford the reader an excellent overview of the general outlines of canonical cinema in the United Kingdom, but, of necessity, they cannot explore every area of the industry without becoming prohibitive in length. Newer texts in film theory and history, such as Robert Murphy's *Realism and Tinsel*, Paul Swann's *Hollywood Feature Film in Post-War Britain*, and Alexander Walker's *Hollywood UK: The British Film Industry in the Sixties*, concentrate on smaller blocks of time and/or thematic material, and they suggest that a reinterpretation of certain periods (or, indeed, any period that one might choose of potential interest) may profitably be pursued within the scope of a more narrowly focused study. Beyond all this are the immensely serious and still largely unexplored questions of British colonialist film practice, racial inequities and stereotypes in British cinema, and social and sexual marginalization within the British film. These are some of the issues explored in this anthology; at least, we can make a start in this direction.

Women have been ruthlessly marginalized from historical British cinema discourse (both critically and practically), and we hope to attempt some small correction in this regard. Although there are now a number of well-known women working in various capacities within the film industry in Great Britain, such important historical figures as Wendy Toye, Muriel Box, and Jill Craigie have never received their proper due. In this volume, I have tried to bring historical British feminist film practice a bit more into the light, through the agency of Caroline Merz's aforementioned essay on Box's and Toye's work, and also a recent interview with director Wendy Toye, whose career has been considerably undervalued by most historians.

Then, too, Brian Desmond Hurst's career as a filmmaker within the British studio system was continually modified by his position as a gay filmmaker within an overall structure of heterosexual patriarchal cinema practice. Brian McIlroy's essay in this volume illuminates the problems and inequities visited upon Hurst both personally and professionally as a consequence of this societal marginalization. In conjunction with this line of inquiry, it is only comparatively recently that questions of British colonialism have been directly addressed within the cinema of the United Kingdom, most notably in the series of films made in the late 1980s by scenarist Hanif Kureishi and director Stephen Frears. These films are also examined in this anthology.

As Michel Foucault notes, "in modern thought, historicism and the analytic of finitude confront one another" (1970, 372). Nowhere is this truer than in the study of twentieth-century filmic practice, in which the spectator and theoretician are both confronted with a series of texts of such spectacular complexity as to nearly defy definitive analysis. Recent critical writings, such as Stam, Burgoyne, and Flitterman-Lewis's *New Vocabularies in Film Semiotics*, give proof to the inescapable fact that there is no "solid ground" upon which the new critical historicist can base her/his work. Rather, it is the continually unfolding dynamic of an utterly flexible spectrum of textual and methodological possibilities that gives the present-day theorist the freedom to explore a nearly infinite series of texts and critical approaches, without genuflecting to canonical precedents of the past.

This is not to say that the works cited at the end of this introductory essay are in any way defective in their scope and/or methodological approach to cinema history, theory, and practice. But it does signify that any study (including this one) defines limits of inclusion and exclusion by the very creation of its textual perimeters. Further, the New Historicist approach suggests that the current "bedrock" of cinematic archaeology is, in fact, only another layer of geologic limestone that needs to be stripped away, perhaps to reveal yet another series of structures beneath it. The reinterpretational essays in this volume, in conjunction with those that break new ground in cinema history, afford an invitation to yet another series of historical and critical explorations into the history of cinema theory and practice in the future.

There is certainly a measure of comfort and exhilaration provided by this historical uncertainty. In cinema theory and history, as in other areas of critical studies, new discoveries lead to newer areas of exploration, and our most important and fruitful task in current critical practice is to investigate activity at the margins of textual and critical production. Thus, this text concerns itself with "the tale not told" (in Mas'ud Zavarzadeh's phrase) by most canonical surveys of British cinema practice, and it concentrates on the women and men whose impact on film in the United Kingdom is real, but often unexplored. As Zavarzadeh notes, "seemingly innocent films—what are usually taken to be neutral aesthetic acts of entertainment—are sites of . . . ideological investment" (1991, 1). Who is to judge the "centrality" of certain forms of discourse or the "marginality" of others? Instead of seeking an artificial center, this volume questions the valorization of certain areas of the British film industry and seeks to suggest new horizons for future critical and historical investigation.

Stephen Bottomore's article on the work of Frederic Villiers, the first British war cinematographer, brings to light the life and career of a person who has been generally forgotten in cinema history. It is more than a little ironic that most casual students of history can recall and readily view the work of Matthew Brady, the justly famous still journalist of the American Civil War, yet the work of Villiers, who brought his primitive motion picture camera to the front of the battle lines, has somehow vanished from our collective memory. Bottomore's essay goes a long way to restoring Villiers to his rightful place in British cinema history.

Much the same might be said about the work of Brian Desmond Hurst, whose work in cinema was filtered through his own personal identity as a gay filmmaker working in a pronouncedly homophobic society, It is certainly correct to see Hurst as an uncelebrated, and often ignored, cinema artist who paved the way for such later film artists as Derek Jarman and Terence Davies. Brian McIlroy does a brilliant job in presenting the complex and often difficult life of this pioneering filmmaker.

My own article on Montgomery Tully's film *Boys in Brown* examines not only Tully's career as a director, but also the difficulties of working within the British studio system. In particular, I discuss the forced use of the "Independent Frame Method," a money-saving system of photographic nonrepresentationalism used by Rank to bring down both the cost and the shooting time of their less ambitiously mounted films. As I note, the Independent Frame Method had consequences far beyond the immediate economic and temporal considerations foreseen by Rank, and it served as a metaphor for the entire enterprise on British colonial rule.

Brian McFarlane's piece on Lance Comfort and Lawrence Huntington deals with the work on those directors who are usually relegated to the rank of "program filmmakers." As McFarlane correctly points out, Comfort, Huntington, and the other directors discussed in his essay often used the genre film as vehicle for their personal concerns. Certainly this is not a new concept, but in examining the life and works of these underappreciated filmmakers, McFarlane opens up a rich new vein of critical study and brings into the existing canon a brace of refreshing and innovative films that tell us a great deal about the social circumstances of their creation. The artificial distinction between "high" and "low" has long ago been profitably done away with by a number of writers; here, McFarlane maps out the territory that is opened up when these synthetic barriers are abolished.

Andrew Higson's essay on David Lean's *This Happy Breed* sees Lean's work as an attempt to pull the nation back together as a war was drawing to its conclusion, to restate the vision of Empire as a reassuring constant in a world that had been utterly changed by the events of the preceding decade. Higson argues that Lean was both successful and unsuccessful in this attempt. Lean's film harkens back to a period of relative political and social stasis within British society but, as Higson notes, this period was marked by a rigidly controlled system of social, sexual, racial, and political hierarchies, all of which were called into question by World War II. *This Happy Breed*'s vision of British society, then, is seen as something both outdated and artificially constructed, something that Lean attempted to "reconstruct" in his film.

Neil Rattigan's piece, "*The Demi-Paradise* and Images of Class in British Wartime Films," takes this exploration of societal stratification one step further, exploring the societal codes and values that led to the rigid separation of one social, political, racial, or economic group from another through a system of clearly defined (but popularly unacknowledged) codes and signifiers. In order for the United Kingdom to survive in World War II, Rattigan argues, this careful partitioning or multileveling of British society was essential for the mobilization of national forces, dividing leaders into one group, followers into another, and spectator/civilians into yet another discrete aggregation. Rattigan's examination of the "images" used to perpetuate and disseminate the rules of class structure during the war demonstrates both the insidious and pervasive aspects of filmic iconography, showing that a series of codes and glyphs swept over the wartime cinema-going audience, lulling them into acceptance of the class system while simultaneously diverting their attention from the rigidity of the roles they were forced to accept.

Tony Williams examines the classic comedy *Passport to Pimlico*, a film that has certainly been written about before. Williams, however, sees in the work a desire to temporally liberate, or perhaps more accurately identify and suppress, the "repressed fantastic" implicit in the subtext of the film. Seen as a series of narrative tropes on postwar British social structures, the film posits the existence of a secessional subset of the United Kingdom. In *Passport to Pimlico*, the residents of the London neighborhood of Pimlico, through a complex series of plot machinations, declare that they are in fact "Burgundians," and thus not subject to the draconian rationing laws of postwar Britain. The artificial release from British rule depicted by the balance of the film's narrative is climaxed with the readmission of the rebels to British society and the restoration of the rationing rules that the inhabitants of Pimlico had sought to escape. In his examination of the film, Williams demonstrates how *Passport to Pimlico* delights in rebellion only to add to the ultimate authority of the system it criticizes; to abrogate existing values is to invite chaos.

Cynthia Young's rereading of *The Red Shoes*, the Powell/Pressburger classic, is another "re-vision" of a film that has long since entered the cinematic canon. In suggesting to its audiences that it was altogether acceptable, even desirable, to sacrifice one's self for one's art, the film also firmly restated the overriding and repressive power of the artistic patriarchy, specifically through the character of the ruthless impresario, played by Anton Walbrook. Young seeks to deconstruct the overarching mythos the film so transparently revels in and demonstrate how the desired coefficient of the film's narrative was continued subservience to a system of values that, as I have already suggested, were rapidly becoming both obsolete and irrelevant. In addition, *The Red Shoes* seeks to reaffirm the primacy of male dominance in all spheres of British commercial and social intercourse, an enterprise made "necessary" by the vast numbers of British women made economically self-sufficient through the agency of wartime munitions employment.

Caroline Merz's piece on Wendy Toye and Muriel Box briefly considers the careers of these two groundbreaking feminist directors; Box began her career as a novelist and writer, while Toye started her work in the cinema as a dancer and choreographer. Unfortunately, Muriel Box is no longer with us; but Wendy Toye is still actively involved in the theater, and she readily consented to a long and detailed interview on her life and work, which I conducted during the summer of 1992. Toye is refreshingly direct in her recollections of working with Alexander Korda for his company, London Films, as well as in those of her later activity as an independent filmmaker, financing her own productions. Interestingly, despite her reputation as a person skilled in the handling of farcical comedy, both on screen and on the stage, Toye reveals that she was always more at home as a director of "fantasy films."

In "The Last Gasp of the Middle Class: British War Films of the 1950s," Neil Rattigan explores the re-visionary process that was already well underway when the events of World War II were still part of the collective public's recent memory. These films attempted to "refight" the conflict that had just been won; they also called into question what exactly had been accomplished between 3 September 1939 (the date that Britain declared that a state of war existed between itself and Germany) and 1945. Further, the events in Korea and the decline of British colonial rule were never far from the narrative concerns of these reconstructional war films. Rattigan demonstrates that while these productions attempted to shore up morale at home, reassuring a restless public that the world had remained essentially unchanged, they also implicitly (and often unconsciously) acknowledged that the values underlying the war had been fatally called into question by the rapidly changing social milieu of the 1950s.

In line with this, Laurence Miller's index of British film noir may come as something of a surprise to most readers, who may have generally assumed that the noir cycle is a narrative enterprise unique to American cinema practice. However, as Miller notes in his catalogue, the noir cycle, which started in Britain in 1940 and lasted into the late 1950s, foregrounded social concerns unique to the English sensibility, coded into a variety of subgenres dealing with motifs of revenge, false accusation, amnesia, flight, betrayal, and other social and personal dilemmas. Miller shows that these films reflected and reinforced the instability of the social structure in Britain both during and after World War II and, in many cases, foreshadowed the collapse of many of the systems of social discourse that had been so fervently embraced by the public for such a long period of time.

Lester Friedman and Scott Stewart's interview with Lindsay Anderson is both wide ranging and surprisingly candid. Anderson discusses his impatience with, or perhaps resistance to, current film theory, particularly the work of Peter Wollen. Anderson also offers direct and anecdotal accounts of working on the set with Bette Davis and Malcolm McDowell, and he implicitly argues for the existence—or at least what he perceives to be the need for the existence—of a uniform system of values for the appreciation of cinema practice. Anderson's voice is that of a no-nonsense practitioner who deals with the day-to-day practicalities of getting a film finished on time and under budget.

Ilsa J. Bick's essay on *Peeping Tom* re-views this well-known and often discussed film by Michael Powell in an entirely new light. The film caused a public and critical furor when first released in 1960, and it brought cinema discourse to a new level of graphic specificity. The film's narrative centers on a young cinematographer who murders his victims while filming their death agonies. Powell himself played the young man's (Karl Boehm's) father, making this an intensely personal and dark consideration of the mechanics of sadism, sexual and social repression, and personal violence. Interesting enough, *Peeping Tom* was made at the height of the reign of the Hammer horror films, such as *The Curse of Frankenstein* (1957) and *Dracula* (1958). While the Hammer films also dealt with admittedly gruesome subject matter and were reviled by many popular critics of the period, they managed to escape general censure as spirited works of Grand Guignol. *Peeping Tom*, however, received a disastrous commercial and critical reception, and for all intents and purposes ended Michael Powell's career as a filmmaker within the British cinema industry. Ilsa Bick suggests some of the reasons why this happened and posits that the male gaze implicit in all patriarchal film practice may have found its most perverse expression in Powell's film.

David Sanjek's "Twilight of the Monsters" examines the more traditional British horror films of the late 1950s to the 1970s and demonstrates that changing values of representational violence, as well as the multivalencies of contemporal societal discourse, led to the collapse of the 1959-65 horror "Renaissance" in England. Sanjek is nostalgic for the more restrained "fairy tale" approach of the production studios Hammer and Amicus, yet he also argues that horror, operating as it does on the margins of cinematic discourse, must continually seek ever more graphic representationalism to appeal to increasingly jaded audiences.

Edward T. Jones's examination of *The Go-Between* discusses this often underappreciated Joseph Losey/Harold Pinter collaboration, exploring the ways in which Pinter, in his narrative structure, is aided and abetted by Losey's penchant for lengthy takes and long tracking shots, a style that can be traced back to Losey's earlier films of the 1960s, particularly *The Servant*. *The Go-Between* represents for Jones a restatement of the values espoused by Losey and Pinter in their earlier work together and an exploration of how these beliefs have been transmogrified by the passage of time and events.

Next, Stephen Frears, who has recently gravitated to mainstream Hollywood with his not particularly successful film *Hero*, is interviewed by Lester Friedman and Scott Stewart. When this interview was recorded, Frears was fresh from his triumph as director of *My Beautiful Laundrette* and would shortly go on to make *Dangerous Liaisons* and *The Grifters*. The freshness of Frears's vision in the mid-1980s, and his ability to work under severe constraints of time and budget (as Lindsay Anderson notes in his interview with Friedman and Stewart, *My Beautiful Laundrette* was shot in 16mm, as a television movie, and only later released theatrically) are effectively conveyed in this interview, even as Frears notes that Friedman and Stewart obviously "expected a younger man" on their first meeting.

In an accompanying essay, Leonard Quart examines the films of Frears and his key scenarist during the 1980s, Hanif Kureishi; this piece offers a number of interesting insights into the ways in which the Frears/Kureishi films serve as mordant social commentaries on the policies of Thatcherism. *My Beautiful Laundrette* and *Sammy and Rosie Get Laid* are both "era-specific" film texts; their evocative landscape of urban decay and social breakdown serves as a compelling backdrop for narratives of social, racial, and sexual displacement. Though the Thatcher era may be officially over, these films serve as reminders of the inequities spawned by her "reign" in office and give proof that political commentary and spectatorial pleasure need not be mutually exclusive, as is often assumed to be the case.

Finally, I had the opportunity to view Terence Davies's most recent film, *The Long Day Closes*, at the Society for Cinema Studies Conference in the spring of 1991 and a chance to briefly meet the director in person. We exchanged telephone numbers, and as this anthology was being readied for publication, it seemed to me that an interview with Davies would be the perfect way to complete this selection of essays. As I discovered during my interview, Davies is moving from a series of intensely personal, autobiographical films to a suspense thriller set in New York, which he hopes to shoot in early 1994. The interview covers Davies's early work for the BFI Production Unit and his international success with *Distant Voices, Still Lives*, as well as the drastic circumstances of his childhood and the enormous influence that American films (particularly musicals) have had on his career as a director.

As editor of this volume, I would like to thank Stephen Hilliard, Lloyd Michaels, Arthur Nolletti, David Desser, Richard Brown, Gary Crowdus, Roma Rector, LeAnn Messing, Linda Rossiter, Gerald Duchovnay, Alan Kibble, Deac Rossell, Wilf Stevenson, Joseph Liggera, the members of the Department of English at the University of Nebraska, Lincoln, and Gwendolyn Foster for their help and support during the long work of compiling and editing this volume. There is certainly much more to be written about the British cinema, as a recent number of books on the subject readily indicate; nevertheless, this volume, I feel, affords both the scholar and the recreational reader a glimpse into critical and creative cinema practice that is simultaneously rigorous, yet hopefully not entirely without textual pleasure.

WORKS CITED

Armes, Roy. *A Critical History of the British Cinema*. New York: Oxford UP, 1978.

Barnes, John. *The Beginnings of the Cinema in England*. Newton Abbot: Charles, 1976.

Barr, Charles, ed. *All Our Yesterdays: 90 Years of British Cinema*. London: BFI Publishing, 1986.

Betts, Ernest. *The Film Business: A History of British Cinema, 1896-1972*. London: Allen and Unwin, 1973; New York: Pitman, 1973.

Curran, James, and Vincent Porter, eds. *British Cinema History*. Totowa, NJ: Barnes and Noble, 1983.

Dixon, Wheeler Winston, ed. "British Cinema: 1900-1975." *Film Criticism* 16.1-2 (1992).

Foucault, Michel. *The Order of Things: An Archaeology of the Human Sciences.* New York: Random House, 1970.

Murphy, Robert. *Realism and Tinsel: Cinema and Society in Britain 1939-1948.* London: Routledge, 1989.

Perry, George. *The Great British Picture Show from the 90s to the 70s.* New York: Hill and Wang, 1974.

Stam, Robert, Robert Burgoyne, and Sandy Flitterman-Lewis. *New Vocabularies in Film Semiotics: Structuralism, Post-Structuralism and Beyond.* London: Routledge, 1992.

Swann, Paul. *The Hollywood Feature Film in Post-War Britain.* London: Croom Helm, 1987; New York: St. Martin's, 1987.

Veeser, H. Aram, ed. *The New Historicism.* London: Routledge, 1989.

Walker, Alexander. *Hollywood UK: The British Film Industry in the Sixties.* New York: Stein and Day, 1974.

Zavarzadeh, Mas'ud. *Seeing Films Politically.* Albany: State University of New York Press, 1991.

CHAPTER TWO

FREDERIC VILLIERS: WAR CORRESPONDENT*

Stephen Bottomore

IT IS COMMONLY assumed that the first war films (i.e., filmed records of warfare) were taken in 1899-1900 during the Boer War. The only earlier claim is that put forward by Albert E. Smith, who said that he, with his partner J. Stuart Blackton, filmed action in Cuba during the Spanish-American War in April 1898 (though this was denied by Blackton in his unpublished memoirs). But whatever the truth of Smith's account, it would appear that there was someone taking war "newsreels" almost a year before the Spanish-American War had even started. In an article by Kenneth Gordon of Associated British Pathé in the BKSTS journal of August 1950, there appears the following sentence: "The story of the late René Bull, the great war artist, building a rostrum of bamboo poles in order to film the charge of the Dervishes at the battle of Omdurman, and the London *Times* report of filming the action in Crete in 1897 by the war correspondent, F. Villars [*sic*] constitute the first coverage of war news."

Neither of these men is listed in any of the standard works on early cinema. From Gordon's information, however, it was fairly easy to find René Bull: he was a correspondent for *Black and White* magazine during the battle of Omdurman; but, although he took many still photographs of the battle, I have found no record of his having taken ciné pictures either there or elsewhere.[1] But for "F. Vilars" [*sic*] the story is different. Unable to find any reference in the *Times*, I eventually located him through *Who's Who*.

It turned out that his name was in fact Frederic Villiers. He was a war artist and special correspondent for the *Illustrated London News* and the *Standard* (among other papers) in what might be called the "golden age" of British war correspondents. In the last thirty years of the nineteenth century, this profession was followed almost exclusively by Britons. A group of men—among them

*I am indebted to Patrick Hickman-Robertson for giving me the initial quotation on Villiers and to Kevin Brownlow for his encouragement and help. Thanks also to the staff of the National Army Museum and the Film Institute.

George Steevens of the *Daily Mail*, Bennet Burleigh of the *Telegraph*, Melton Prior of the *Illustrated London News*—would regularly risk their lives to obtain up-to-the-minute reports and drawings of (mainly colonial) wars. Of this group, Frederick Villiers was both the most colorful and the best known. Dick Heldar, a war correspondent in Kipling's *Light that Failed*, is said to have been based on him, and Forbes-Robertson came to Villiers for advice when playing the role on stage.

By 1912, Villiers had covered more campaigns than any other correspondent and seen more battles than any soldier living and endured more privations. (See F. Lauriston Bullard's *Famous War Correspondents*, 1914). His obituary in the *Times* said: "Although not one of the best, he was one of the most prolific and ubiquitous of the old school of war correspondents, and he always carried with him into the lecture room that air of the swashbuckler which was at one time considered the correct comportment for the soldier of the pen." Pat Hodgson, in *The War Illustrators* (1977), is more candid, describing him as a "poseur," contributing much to his own legend. Villiers would normally appear at his lectures in full battle dress with his collection of medals and ribbons prominently displayed. His friend Forbes complained that in the field Villiers would go to bed wearing his spurs, believing that this "contributed to his martial aspect." As an artist he was only "of moderate ability" (the *Times* obituary); he found figure drawing "tiresome and uninteresting." None of Villiers's war sketches was published in a magazine as it stood—it was always redrawn by a staff artist. But despite—or perhaps because of—this limitation, Villiers pioneered what was to become a far more important means of reportage than the drawing.

Villiers started as a war correspondent in 1876 for the *Graphic*. By 1897 he had covered some seven campaigns, two in the Balkan region. When Greece raided Turkey in April 1897, the region was again at war, and Villiers, representing the *Standard* and *Black and White*, found himself at the port of Volo in Thessaly. Perhaps because he knew the area and anticipated only a minor war, Villiers felt that he could afford to take chances. Whatever the reason, he had included in his luggage two novel pieces of equipment: a bicycle, for the first time in a European campaign; and a cinematograph camera, for the first time in *any* war. ("The cinema camera was then in its infancy," he recorded, "so at considerable expense I took one to the front.")

He wrote: "When this little war broke out I had ingeniously thought that cinema pictures of the fighting would delight and astonish the public." His life at the front line seems not to have been unpleasant: "I was well-housed during the fighting in front of Volo, for the British Consul insisted on my residing at the consulate. To me it was campaigning in luxury. From the balcony of the residence I could always see when the Turks opened fire on the Velestino plateau; then I would drive with my cinema outfit to the battlefield, taking my bicycle with me in the carriage. After I had secured a few reels of movies, if the Turks pressed too hard on our lines I would throw the camera into the vehicle and send it out of action, and at nightfall, after the fight, I would trundle back down the hill to dinner."

But this cozy state of affairs could not last long. Early in May, Volo was abandoned by the military. In order to save the Greek population, Villiers, with customary enterprise, suggested to the British Consul that they "go boldly into the Moslem lines to intercede with Edham Pasha on behalf of the remaining population." The mission succeeded, and, returning to Volo, Villiers met the newly appointed governor, Enver Bey, who granted him a safe conduct to Athens. Not content with this, Villiers asked the governor for confidential information: "I want to know when and where the next fight will take place. You Turks will take the initiative, for the Greeks can now be only on the defensive." Not surprisingly, Enver Bey was staggered by his request. Looking at Villiers steadily, he said at last: "You are an Englishman and I can trust you. I will tell you this: Take this steamer . . . to Athens, then get another to Lamia, the port of Domokos, and don't fail to be at the latter place by Monday noon." Villiers arrived in Domokos "on the exact day and hour to hear the first gun fired by the Greeks at the Moslem infantry advancing across the Pharsala plains." On 20 May, his telegraphed report of the engagement appeared in the *Standard*.

Villiers's account of his experiences is certainly dramatic, but is it true? There are several reasons why we should take his claims with a pinch of salt. First, his early autobiography, published only five years after the war, though mentioning that he had a movie camera and bicycle at the front, contains none of the anecdotal material about these innovations. Second, Villiers seems to imply a scoop in being at Domokos for the hostilities. In fact he arrived with the Reuters correspondent W. K. Rose (see the latter's *With the Greeks in Thessaly*), and several other correspondents were also present. Third, Villiers was not alone in possessing a bicycle at the front—René Bull, who was also covering the war, had one, and the *Morning Post* correspondent, Wilfred Pollock, wrote a book, *War and a Wheel*, detailing what he in turn implied were *his* unique experiences with a bicycle during this campaign. Fourth, none of the other eight accounts of the campaign that I have examined mentions Villiers's movie camera (though, to be fair, most do not mention Villiers himself either). The only contemporary corroborating evidence is Villiers's entry in *Who's Who*, which, from the 1899 edition onwards, states that he "used the cinematograph camera for the first time in history of campaigning during the war."

So *was* Frederic Villiers the first war cinematographer? He undoubtedly exaggerated parts of his account, but would he actually have invented basic pieces of information? Unfortunately, there is no way of knowing with certainty. The written sources reveal nothing, and I have failed to trace Villiers's descendants. There is, however, confirmation of Villiers's account of filming at the Battle of Omdurman in 1898. And if he is telling the truth about one campaign, why should he falsify details of another?

Figure 2.1. Frederick Villiers, ca. 1897. Courtesy: Stephen Bottomore Collection.

But whatever one's doubts on the matter, there is no denying the fascination of the next part of Villiers' account:

> It was a laborious business in those early days to arrange the spools and change the films; and I sweated a good deal at the work, but managed to get touches of real warfare. It was a great disappointment, therefore, to discover that these films were of no value in the movie market, for when I returned to England, a friend, generally of ordinary intelligence, said to me: "My dear Villiers, I saw some wonderful pictures of the Greek war last night."
>
> By his description I knew they were certainly not mine. I wondered at this, because my camera was the only one to pass the Greek customs during the campaign. Then he described one of the pictures: "Three Albanians came along a very white dusty road toward a cottage on the right of the screen. As they neared it they opened fire; you could see the bullets strike the stucco of the building. Then one of the Turks with the butt end of the rifle smashed in the door of the cottage, entered and brought out a lovely Athenian maid in his arms . . . Presently an old man, evidently the girl's father, rushed out of the house to her rescue, when the second Albanian whipped out his Yataghan from his belt and cut the old gentleman's head off." Here my friend grew enthusiastic. "There was the head," said he, "rolling in the foreground of the picture. Nothing could be more positive than that."

Villiers added that the film had been made by "a famous firm outside Paris . . . and since then many others of similar nature have delight the movie 'fan.'"

There seems little doubt that the "famous firm" was that of Georges Méliès. He had been making films since 1896, and his studio was in Montreuil-sous-Bois, an eastern suburb of Paris. But even if Villiers had not given the firm's location, the film's subject would immediately have revealed its author. As Paul Hammond has noted in *Marvellous Méliès*, decapitation was a recurrent theme in Méliès work (and in the stage acts of various magicians before him). At least a dozen of his films involve heads being severed from bodies, and many more are concerned with other kinds of maiming.

On 22 March 1897, Méliès moved into his new Montreuil studio, where he believed he would "rendez-vous avec mon destin." In *Méliès l'Enchanteur*, his granddaughter, M. Malthête-Méliès, writes: "C'est en tout cas, pour le moment, le rendez-vous de l'Histoire car Méliès a l'idée de reconstituer en studio les faits saillants de l'actualité. La guerre gréco-turque ayant éclaté au mois de février 1897 et continuant avec rage, Méliès en reproduit les épisodes les plus sanglants."

These "bloody events" were among the first reconstructed scenes ever filmed. They were, with their Star Catalogue numbers: 103/104: *Episodes de guerre*; 105: *Les Dernières Cartouches*; 106: *Prise de Tournavos par les troupes du Sultan*; 107: *L'Execution d'un espion*; 108: *Les Massacres de la population Crétoise*; 110: *Combat naval en Grèce*. Of these, 105 is a reconstruction of the famous events at Bazeille in the Franco-Prussian War of 1870; 103/104 is also known as *La Défense de Bazeille* and—despite what Sadoul and, more recently, Paul Hammond suggest—is clearly also to do with the war of 1870 and not the Greco-Turkish War. A detailed description of the remaining films (106-10) is contained in an advertisement of an early film distributor, Philipp Wolff, in the *Magic Lantern Journal Annual 1897-8*: "18. Mohammedan inhabitants of Crete massacring Christian Greeks; 19. Turks attacking a house defended by Greeks (Turnavos); 20. The Greek man of war 'George' shelling the fort of Previsa; 21. Execution of a Greek spy at Pharasla." The descriptions closely match 106-10, and it seems clear that it was film number 19 (or 106) that roused the enthusiasm of Villiers's friend. Villiers attempted to disillusion him by describing how a movie camera was operated:

> You have to fix it on a tripod . . . and get everything in focus before you can take a picture. Then you have to turn the handle in a deliberate, coffee-mill sort of way, with no hurry or excitement. It's not a bit like a snapshot, press-the-button pocket Kodak. Now just think of that scene you have so vividly described to me. Imagine the man who was coffee-milling saying, in a persuasive way, "Now Mr. Albanian, before you take the old gent's head off come a little nearer; yes but a little more to the left please. Thank you. Now then, look as savage as you can and cut away." Or "You, No. 2 Albanian, make that hussy lower her chin a bit and keep her kicking as ladylike as possible." Wru-ru-ruru-ru!

Villiers here neatly sums up the problems of obtaining "dramatic" film of real warfare. (It was a problem that D. W. Griffith was to face while making *Hearts of the World* during the First World War—eventually, he abandoned most of the footage he had shot at the front and faked it on Salisbury Plain.)

Villiers's films were on a subject that was headline news, and yet he found them unsalable. The public wanted action, not truth. Méliès was eager to supply such action, the Greek war fakes being the first films produced in his new studio. In light of the subsequent dominance of studio production, it is interesting that these films should have scored such a notable victory over (Villiers's) undisturbed reality at such a early stage in cinema history. As Villiers ruefully observed: "Barnum and Bailey, those wonderful American showman, correctly, averred that the public like to be fooled."

In 1898, the intrepid Villiers was again in action, when he joined Kitchener's march to Omdurman as correspondent for the *Globe* and the *Illustrated London News*. He was not new to the Nile region, having been there twice before as a correspondent in the 1880s, and had clearly grown fond of the area, describing it as a "happy hunting ground for the war correspondent," a somewhat inappropriate description considering that no less than seven correspondents were killed during these campaigns. At the Battle of Omdurman alone, one was killed and two were wounded.

But it was not in Villiers's nature to be worried by such details. As in the Greco-Turkish War, he was again experimenting with novel campaign equipment: his tent was "a new idea for the desert, a glorified umbrella that could be put up in less than five minutes by tugging at a cord"; and again he had his bicycle. Despite his setbacks in the Greek war, Villiers had again decided to take a ciné-camera: "I thought that in this case I might get some of the real stuff before the fakers set to work, because it would be hard for them to vamp up the local colour of the desert, dervish costumes, and so forth."

Villiers kept the camera secret from his colleagues, since he wished to be the "first in the field." Unfortunately, the sheer size of the apparatus gave his secret away. When some of Villiers's fellow correspondents learned of this remarkable device they all "wanted to take movies as well." Villiers continues:

> Why they imagined they could get the necessary camera and spools simply by writing to Cairo, as one would for a packet of tea, I have no idea; but anyway, the whole thing caused no little excitement in our mess. The two who were going to upset my little plans would occasionally look at me with a kind of pity for the "beat" they were making. Presently their box arrived, and the look of triumph quickly died out of their faces when they found that instead of a camera it contained a lantern projector and quite an amusing series of films of a racy terpsichorean nature to please an Egyptian audience.

By the end of August, the Anglo-Egyptian Army had reached Omdurman, and it became clear that the showdown with the Khalifa's forces would take place here. On the night before the battle, Villiers—suffering the aftereffects of a scorpion sting—slept fitfully: "Shortly before dawn I woke up, remembering that I had forgotten to fix up my cinematograph camera with films, and there might be a chance to get some action in the coming fight." But the moon was out, and "charging the camera could only be done where darkness reigned; so I aroused my servant, got the apparatus together, and took it down to the gunboat the 'Melik,' where I found darkness enough for the purpose in her stifling forehold."[3]

He was there for a while ("the films for movies were difficult to fix in a hurry in those days"), and by the time the camera was loaded dawn had broken. They had received sailing orders, and it was now too late for Villiers to go ashore. "This was annoying but Gordon [Major Stevely Gordon, captain of the *Melik* and nephew of Gordon of Khartoum] told me I could erect my tripod in the aft battery, which had been put out of action the previous day . . . I thought it was a good idea, for I had a level platform and a wonderful coign of vantage."

The boat took up its position and prepared to give supporting fire to the right flank of Kitchener's army. Villiers hurriedly set the camera on its tripod, ready to start cranking. The scene was everything a cameraman could ask for:

"The Dervishes were now streaming toward us in great force—about ten thousand spearmen—just as I wanted them, in the face of the early sun and in the face of my camera." But fate, alas, was against him:

> I had just commenced to grind the coffee pot when our fore battery opened fire. The effect on my apparatus was instantaneous and astounding. The gunboat had arrived on the Nile in sections and had evidently been fixed up for fighting in a hurry, for with the blast of her guns the deck planks opened up and snapped together, and down went my tripod. The door of the camera flew open and my films were exposed. However, I had not time to weep over spilt milk, for the fighting had commenced. I pulled out my sketchbook, and my only comfort was that from my vantage point I saw many thing I should have missed ashore and that no camera of my kind could have registered.

As with his experiences in Greece, the question again arises of Villiers's credibility. It might seem suspicious that his camera should overturn so "conveniently." Writing of another war in 1898, that between Spain and America, Terry Ramsaye describes in *A Million and One Nights* old-timers "telling tales of photographic desperation and film-making amid the shock of clashing battle lines and bursting shrapnel. But all these tales end with, 'And then a big shell came along and blew up my camera and I never got back with any of the film.'" But descriptions by early cameramen of such misfortunes occur too frequently to be mere excuses. (Kevin Brownlow quotes several cases in *The War, the West, and the Wilderness*: Jessica Borthwick, Tracy Mathewson, and Urban's *Britain Prepared* cameraman). Further evidence of Villiers's veracity is to be found in his contemporaneous reports in the *Globe*, reports that tally closely with the account of the battle in his autobiography written more than twenty years later. (On the night after the battle, Villiers remained on the *Melik* and, he reported with telling exactitude [the *Globe*, 4 October 1898], "my bed was the platform of the fore battery, and my camera my pillow.")

On page 174 of the *Optical Magic Lantern Journal* for December 1898 there appears the following paragraph titled "A New Military Cinematographic Picture":

> When at the offices of Mr Philipp Wolff, of 9, Southampton Street, W.C., a few days ago, Mr Hessberg, the manager, informed us that they were about to publish a remarkable cinematographic picture taken in the Sudan by a well-known war correspondent. We give, with permission, an extract from an explanatory letter written to Mr Wolff: "The cinematograph film which you have was taken by me on the battlefield of Omdurman the day before the battle. It is the only genuine Sudan film as nobody else had a cinematograph with them. There was a rumour that the Dervishes were advancing to attack us, and all the men were told to lie down and be

in readiness to fall in for anything. I therefore fixed my camera on the Grenadier Guards (Queen's Company) and when the brigade trumpeter, whom you see in the photograph, sounded the call, I took the man standing up, fixing bayonets, and marching off . . ." Mr Wolff is to be congratulated on having the publicity of this valuable film.

It might seem that this "explanatory letter" was from Villiers. However, the following appears in *Chambers Journal for 1900* in an article about George Albert Smith, the film pioneer: "Mr Smith has a copy of one real battle-picture which he developed—the earliest one, he believes, in existence . . . The original film is the property of Mr Bennett-Standford [*sic*], the war correspondent, by whom it was taken, and it represents a portion of the English army springing from bivouac, forming up, and running forward to join in the annihilating of the Dervishes at Omdurman." The film sounds very much like the one described above. But whether or not it was, Villiers's claims to exclusivity must again be challenged: he was not the only person with a ciné-camera at the Battle of Omdurman.[4]

Like many other correspondents in the Sudan, Stanford does not seem to have believed that his role was that of a mere observer. In *The Khartoum Campaign 1898*, Bennet Burleigh relates: "Mr Bennett Stanford [*sic*], who was splendidly mounted, with a cocked four-barrelled Lancaster pistol aimed deliberately at the Dervish, who turned towards him. Waiting till the jibbah-clad warrior was but a score of paces or so off, Mr Stanford fired, and appeared to miss . . . for the Dervish without halt rushed at him, whereupon he easily avoided him, riding off." Burleigh himself eventually killed the Dervish. Burleigh mentions that Stanford was "formerly with the Royals"—from contemporary Army Lists I can add that his full name was John M. Bennett-Stanford. From 1892 he as a lieutenant in the prestigious Royal Wiltshire Yeomanry. In March 1897, he joined the First Dragoons as a *reserve* lieutenant—hence he was free the following year to act as a war correspondent at Omdurman.

In an interview with Rachael Low, G. A. Smith said that Stanford was a wealthy amateur (from Brighton, as was Smith) who "took up kinematography as a hobby" and sent back the first film of the Boer War. In his *Chambers Journal* interview, Smith describes a film taken by Stanford while under heavy fire: "That film . . . was manifestly left off in a hurry. It looks as though he had snatched up his machine and run for it." Stanford was eventually wounded while filming action in the Boer War.

W. K. L. Dickson, Edison's former assistant, was also present as a cameraman during the Boer War, shooting on an early form of 70-mm film. On the ship to South Africa he met young Winston Churchill, who had also been the *Morning Post* correspondent at Omdurman. Like the *Times* representative (who was killed), he took part in the famous Charge of the Twenty-first Lancers. Villiers wrote that he had always "envied that intrepid young officer, Mr Churchill, who . . . received his baptism of fire that day." Churchill was known in later life as a fervent cinema fan. To judge from his description of the battle, films were already a preoccupation. "The whole scene flickered exactly like a cinematograph picture, and besides I remember no sound. The event seemed to pass in absolute silence" (*The River War*, 1899). Considering the short time that it had been in existence, the level of interest in cinematography among the correspondents at Omdurman does seem truly extraordinary.

In 1902, Villiers was married to Louise Bohne, and they moved into a small mill house in Hampshire. But domesticity could not change such an adventurous nature, and in 1904-5 Villiers again saw action as a war correspondent, reporting on the Russo-Japanese hostilities and specifically on the siege at Port Arthur. Though he did not have a ciné-camera with him, there *was* a cinematographer present.

This was Joseph Rosenthal, who had obtained much of the action footage of the Boer War on behalf of the Warwick Trading Company and was perhaps the most famous of early news cameramen. At Port Arthur, he was again working for the Warwick Company. (Villiers wrongly states that it was the Bioscope Company.) In Villiers's account of the events there, he (somewhat patronisingly) describes Rosenthal doing the cooking for the other correspondents, who apparently called him "Rosy." "He has the gentleness of the fairer sex, unless some outsider steps into the focus of his bioscope when he is churning out films; then his language belies the sobriquet." The name seems to have stuck, for some years later Rosenthal started an enterprise named "The Rose Film Company." The films he obtained at Port Arthur were shown in England in April 1905 and are said to have been "the most spectacular series of war films so far seen." (Rosenthal had managed to get close in to the fighting, thanks to the bullet-proof shield he had for his camera.)

Villiers's next reference to his cinematographic activities concerns his work in the Balkans in 1912. It was in this area that he had first experimented with a ciné-camera in 1897, and perhaps it was his failure then that prompted him to take a movie camera again fifteen years later. This time he was with the Bulgarian Army. The Bulgarians were allied to the Greeks and Serbians, the common enemy being the Turks. Villiers writes:

> The Bulgarians sent word to the correspondents assembled at Mustapha Pasha that the execution of two Turkish spies was to take place the following morning. Execution of spies is always brutal and not particularly a happy subject for illustration, and I thought I would not go. But my servant told me that all the other correspondents intended to be there, and then I felt bound to show up, as I was for the moment directing a moving picture operation called "Kinemacolor."

Villiers made his way to the place of execution (an orchard) and there:

found the two spies being harangued by a Bulgarian officer who was reciting their appalling deed to them while they stood bound by the wrists under the shade of some fruit trees, over the stout branches of which were slung two ominous looking ropes . . . Then followed a scene that was indescribably disgraceful. The cameramen—and there were legions—crawled up the trees, mounted the roof of the barn, and occupied every coign of vantage. Bulgarian children, dressed in gala attire and accompanied by their fathers and mothers, crowded up to the gallows trees to gloat over the misery of those wretched men. I became so nauseated with the disgusting sight that I closed down my machine and fled.

In the *Kinemacolor Supplement* to the *Kinematograph and Lantern Weekly* (14 November 1912) appears a report headed "War in the Balkans." Speaking of "the Kinemacolor staff distributed at various strategic points in the Balkans," it continues: "Mr Charles Urban, the head of the Kinemacolor organisation, has been fortunate in obtaining the services of Mr Frederick [*sic*] Villiers, the famous war artist, who is now directing the efforts of Kinemacolor operators at the front." In his autobiography, Villiers describes what happened after he fled from the execution: "Within ten minutes after this wretched experience I was called to the bridge over the Maritza to see King Ferdinand, who had just arrived."

In his description of their conversation which follows, Villiers does not mention filming the king, but apparently he did, according to the *Kine* report, which both confirms and adds to Villiers's version: "While King Ferdinand was in Adrianople a few days ago, His Majesty alighted at the bridge near the church to examine the spot where the Turks made an attempt to destroy the bridge in their retreat. Mr Villiers asked the King's permission to make a Kinemacolor record of the incident and the request was immediately granted, an excellent and lifelike portrait of this important figure in the great struggle being obtained." In the catalogue for a 1916 private exhibition of Kinemacolor there appears, with other records of the Bulgarian forces, a film entitled *Ferdinand the Former King of Bulgaria.*

Villiers's final venture with a movie camera was during the First World War. His and most of the correspondents' complaints at this time were to do not with the war itself but rather with officialdom. Censorship of war reporting had of course take place before 1914—war artists had been arrested as early as the Franco-Prussian War of 1870. Villiers himself had met the problem at Omdurman where, for the first time in a British campaign, all dispatches and drawings had to go through a military censor. He considered this a minor inconvenience at the time; but in the early years of the twentieth century, censorship by the military was to increase dramatically.

The culmination came during the First World War when correspondents and cameramen were actually being banned from the front. Villiers wrote bitterly:

At times I resented being so scurvily treated by my own folk, when through forty years of British warfare I had been *persona grata* with generals like Wolseley, Roberts, Methuen, Brown and Buller [significantly, Kitchener of Omdurman is not on the list]. Time and again during the early years of the war I called at the War Office in London to ask for an explanation of this extraordinary fiat against the artists, but with a shrug the officials told me there was no explanation. The only reason I could find to account for this silly restriction was that the War Office itself was trying to make a corner in the pictures, for it eventually produced some wonderful films . . . The powers at the War Office were so sour with their own countrymen of the "fourth estate" that even after the ban was raised and we were allowed to go to the front, I have seen Englishmen sent back by the escorting officer while foreign representatives of the press were given extended time in the war zone . . . Everything that could be done to annoy, irritate and delay English correspondents in the execution of their duty in the early days of the campaign was done by the War Office officials.

Villiers did get to the front eventually (without permission) and thereafter regularly sent back drawings to the *Illustrated London News*, some of which were scoops. But it must have been hard for a man of sixty-five to be continually dodging the military police, and it came as a relief when he was invited by the French to act as war correspondent with their forces.

By the beginning of the First World War, except for Villiers all the famous war correspondents—Forbes, Steevens, Prior—were dead. And by the end of the war, Villiers had become something of an anachronism. Sir Philip Gibbs wrote: "When Frederic Villiers began his career it was a different way of life. War was always terrible, but not so mechanical as this last war and the correspondent was a more romantic figure, more dependent on his own resources, initiative, daring, imagination and audacity . . . It was a sporting life and a hard one."

After the war, Villiers spent most of his time lecturing, writing and travelling to see the "great wonders of the world"—one of these he considered to be Hollywood. While there he met Chaplin, whom he described as "a daintily well-groomed slender figure of a man."

On 3 April 1922, after a long and painful illness, Villiers died. If he is remembered at all today, it is as an adventurer and magazine correspondent. His activities as an innovating cameraman have been forgotten. And this is only partly due to bad luck and the consequent lack of tangible results in his ventures. The main reason for his eclipse is, perhaps, that Villiers was essentially a man of the nineteenth century.

The year 1899, in terms of warfare, was the dividing line between the nineteenth and twentieth centuries. Omdurman in that year was the last of the traditional colonial battles. The Boer War in the following year introduced a new factor to the British experience of war, guerrilla tactics. When one thinks of Kitchener and the Sudan campaign one thinks of a nineteenth-century colonial conflict; the Boer War, by contrast, was the prototype of the less formalised twentieth-century pattern. In the popular consciousness, Omdurman is as far removed from the Boer War as the war artist's drawing is from the cinema newsreel. How much easier it is to think of this change in the *character* of warfare coinciding with the change in the *means of reporting it*. How much more simple to imagine a youthful cameraman surreptitiously filming guerrilla soldiers than a middle-aged character out of Kipling cranking away at "Tommy Atkins" and "Fuzzy Wuzzy" with General Gordon's nephew beside him and the sun that never sets over his shoulder. (In the case of the United States, a change in the character of warfare did coincide with the first alleged filming of it: the Spanish-American War was the United States' first colonial military intervention.)

But events do not always fit into such neat conceptual pigeonholes. In this case military history and media history are "out of sync" by two years. Frederic Villiers is forgotten simply because he was before his time. Villiers met many of the early news cameramen and worked for Urban, one of the best-known pioneers of British cinema. In the light of these connections, it might still be thought strange that Villiers's contribution to cinema history has not been recorded. In reply I can only reiterate what so many people have said before—that the early days of cinema are shamefully poor in documentation. Indeed Villiers's case might be taken as a symptom of this poverty—a man who was a legend in his lifetime, the most famous war correspondent of them all, who was taking war film before anyone else and still filming nearly twenty years later—yet today this man is not mentioned in a single film textbook.

NOTES

1. I now believe that this report of cinematography at Omdurman is confused with Villiers's activities there. (Bull described his still photography at the battle in *Captain* Apr. 1899: 66.)

2. The Villiers quotes in this article are taken from his autobiography, *Villiers: His Five Decades of Adventure* (1920).

3. From Villiers's report written 8 Sept. 1898 and published in the *Globe* on 26 Sept.

4. The *Era*, 17 Sept. 1898, advertised film of "A Charge of Lancers." In the *Optical Magic Lantern Journal* (Oct. 1898: 143), a distributor, Fuerst Brothers, advertises film of "the Charge of the 21st Hussars (now the 21st Lancers)." An early exhibitor, Albany Ward, mentions scenes of fighting in the Greco-Turkish War and at the Battle of Omdurman (*History of the British Film*, vol. 1). According to the *Chambers Journal* article on G. A. Smith, these films were not genuine: "As soon . . . as there was a demand for the Charge of the 21st Lancers at Omdurman, pictures were forthcoming which had been taken at Alder shot a year or two before."

5. The information on Kinemacolor comes from the Urban files at the Science Museum. (Incidentally, Kenneth Gordon, the early newsreel cameraman through whom I traced Villiers, was also in the Balkans at this time; it seems likely that it was here he heard of Villiers's film exploits in 1897-98.)

CHAPTER THREE

BRITISH FILMMAKING IN THE 1930s AND 1940s: THE EXAMPLE OF BRIAN DESMOND HURST

Brian McIlroy

JEFFREY RICHARDS, IN a series of articles and in his book, *The Age of the Dream Palace: Cinema and Society in Britain 1930-1939* (1984), argues that the films of the 1930s, emanating as they do from a set number of studios, are best viewed as "product" rather than "art." Richards draws attention to the personal strength of producers Michael Balcon, Alexander Korda, Basil Dean, and Herbert Wilcox, their close association with the views of the Censorship Board, and the fact that most of their films came from tested literary material (many of them successful novels, stage plays, or musicals), all of which ensured that the films produced and distributed kept within the bounds of the dominant ideology of the period. This ideological framework included the following: the admiration of law, order, and the monarchy; the undesirability of class movement by underhand means or by ignoble intentions; the need for women to serve (and to sacrifice for) men; and the privilege of sexual repression as a "middle-class achievement ethic (Richards 1984, 323). The social system is generally sound; necessary improvements in the system could almost be summed up as the need for compassion for the poor. For the most part, a similar catalogue of ideological constructs typifies 1940s Britain.

In his recent book *Realism and Tinsel: Cinema and Society in Britain 1939-1948* (1989), Robert Murphy regrets not having the space to consider lesser-known directors. Murphy devotes much of his survey to the generic forms of British cinema in the period under his purview, and, given the scope of his endeavor, it is natural that the discussion of individuals should be dispersed throughout his text or omitted. One of the directors that Murphy mentions is Brian Desmond Hurst (1896-1986), a filmmaker who worked on at least twenty films in the 1930s and 1940s. It seems to me an interesting point whether or not the general statements about the film scene in 1930s and 1940s Britain are fully validated by the close look at one of its most prolific directors. Such an investigation problematizes the relationship

between the individual and the studio system. These tensions may appear contradictory on a theoretical level, but I would argue they bring us to a richer, and more
thorough, analysis of the phenomenon of a film culture.

In the 1930s, before the increasing dominance of Rank in the 1940s, five
studios were important: Associated British Picture Corporation (ABPC), Gau-
mont-British/Gainsborough, British and Dominion, London Films, and Ealing.
The producers associated with these studios were, respectively, Walter Mycroft,
Michael Balcon, Herbert Wilcox, Alexander Korda, and Basil Dean. These five
men were forceful personalities who shaped the British film industry in the 1930s.
An alleged fascist, a liberal Jew, a socially adept entrepreneur, an Hungarian emi-
gre, and a man from the theatre with high cultural expectations provided together
a curious and fascinating mixture of British movie moguls. Why did these men
produce material that was so clearly conservative in nature? They did, after all,
employ people who were by no means conventional, but a combination of British
reserve, censorship, and a need to please the financiers of the studios—as well as
the government—contributed to this lack of distinctiveness. Nevertheless, we
should not be carried away by this 1990s wave of pessimism, for, as Tony Aldgate
has written in an essay on the British domestic cinema of the 1930s (1983), British
films were well attended and clearly contributed to the national culture.

Brian Desmond Hurst in his career worked for ABPC (Mycroft), London
Films (Alexander Korda), the Government's Ministry of Information, Gainsbor-
ough (Josef Somlo), RKO British (William Sistrom), and two Rank Subsidiaries,
G & S Films (Josef Somlo) and Two Cities (William Sistrom, W.P. Lipscomb, and
Hugh Stewart) before working specifically for Rank in the 1950s and sometimes
acting as his own producer (*Tom Brown's Schooldays* [1951] and *Scrooge* [1951]).
His working life is fascinating as a snapshot of the free-market dynamics in con-
tracts in the 1930s and 1940s and of the various limitations cast upon a director.

How did an Irishman from a poor Belfast background, who was also
homosexual, achieve a respected status in the British film industry? Clearly, part
of the answer lies in Hurst readily agreeing to take on projects that producers
asked him to direct. This compliance has meant that his filmography is one that
appears to be without individuality, as pointed out by an anonymous *Sight and
Sound* reviewer in 1958. Although concentrating on his 1950s work, the critic's
comments could equally apply to Hurst's films of the 1930s and 1940s:

> This director's work has covered an almost bewildering range of themes: his last
> half dozen pictures have been a comedy-with-music, a Dickens adaptation, two war
> stories, a Mau Mau drama and a costume romance; and his subjects before that
> were equally varied. Such versatility makes it difficult to pin down any one aspect
> of a shifting talent. His films are rarely less than competently handled, but the
> unevenness of the scripts and subjects he has tackled has been such as rather to blur
> his own individuality.

If we believe the core elements of Hurst's autobiography, "Travelling the Road" (1986), the British film industry was quite an *insular* establishment in the 1930s. After working with John Ford in Hollywood as an unofficial, though presumably well-paid, assistant art director on some of American's silent films, he returned to Britain to seek a living through filmmaking. Hurst recounts:

> When I came back to England in 1932 I had letters of recommendation from Irving Thalberg, then head of MGM, Jack Warner and John Ford, but they were so glowing that nobody believed them. Although I said to one producer, "Send a telegram to America at my expense to verify these," I was still unable to get any work. (1986, 91)

Rejected by the studios, Hurst looked to a wealthy acquaintance, Henry Talbot de Vere Clifton, who put up the finance for his first two films made in 1934, *The Tell-Tale Heart* and *Irish Hearts*. Both of these seem to be unavailable for viewing today. Hurst recalls:

> With the money, I made my first film, "The Tell-Tale Heart," based on the Edgar Allan Poe story of the murderer who betrays himself because he is convinced that he can still hear the heart-beats of his victim. I selected this story because it was sensational film material, and was in the public domain (i.e. no copyright to pay for) and would call attention to me. I hired a cameraman. There were no professional actors in the film. The detectives were played by two electricians, the old man by a painter, the brother of Sir Johnston Forbes-Robertson, and the lead by Norman Dryden. I used for music records of Tchaikovsky and what the film people called "De-*Buss*-y" as we could not afford composer or musician. At the big Elstree Studios nearby, they said, "There's a fellow over at Blattner's Studio who's making practically a silent picture."
>
> Walter Hutchinson, the head of Fox Films, saw the film and bought it for quota. He said to me, "The critics at the press show may not like your film. It is strange and artistic but don't be upset. They are always bad-tempered in the morning, having to walk to work." . . . "Tell-Tale Heart" was sold for 4,000 [pounds] at 1 [pound] a foot so we managed to make a profit of 800 [pounds], having gone 200 [pounds] over budget. (93-94)

For a film that was clearly within the cheap "quota-quickies" bracket, it was still accorded high praise for its technical competence. The *Variety* reviewer was particularly impressed:

> Importance of the film is two fold. First it is photographically a gem, some of the shots being reminiscent of Harry Lachman and Rouben Mamoulian at their best. The shadow photography is especially apt and successful. Secondly, the film's

importance comes from its use of dialog. It seems to the audience as though there were barely a dozen or so speeches in the entire film, and all of them clipped. Hurst maneuvers his dialog in such fashion as to employ an absolute minimum, using pantomime and silent screen technique to manage it. (Rev. of *The Tell-Tale Heart* 1934, 27)

Irish Hearts is certainly one of the main contenders for the first Irish sound feature film. Set in a small seaside town, it depicts a doctor who fights a typhus epidemic with the help of two nurses who fight equally for his affections. Many of the smaller parts were filled by actors from the Abbey Theatre.

The first Hurst film to be readily available for viewing today, at least at the British Film Institute, is *Riders to the Sea* (1935), an adaptation of the famous play by J. M. Synge. The money for this production came from Gracie Fields, whom Hurst had met through a painter friend John Flanagan. The director laments:

> The film cost about 6,000 [pounds] to make and, although we tried to sell it for quota, Gracie never got her money back. Though it was shown publicly in both Dublin and America, the film was never shown publicly in London, only privately, until the first English public showing at the National Film Theatre in April 1977, some forty years after the film was made. (Hurst 1986, 103)

Hurst captures in this forty minute film the extreme desolation of the womenfolk of Ireland who must watch and wait for their husbands and sons to return from fishing in the tempestuous Atlantic waters. While it appears at first viewing to be a simple, rather stagy, reconstruction of the play onto film, on second viewing one is struck by the Arabesque quality of the harsh landscape photographed, the women's keening, and the mourning attire. Recent books and films, such as Bob Quinn's *Atlantean* (1986), have suggested that the classical view of inhabitation of Ireland by movement overland from the continent of Europe is inaccurate; and they argue instead for a *seabased* theory, where merchants from Africa and Spain travelled to and fro with relative ease. When one reads Hurst's memoir that he spent time in North Africa during the First World War, one senses that he made good use of his experiences.

As luck would have it, Walter Mycroft, chief of production at British International Pictures (BIP; later ABPC) attended one of the private screenings of *Riders to the Sea* and sent a letter stating that he wanted to meet him. Hurst explains his contact and tenure with Elstree studios very briefly:

> BIP had begun work on an Irish picture called *Ourselves Alone* (a translation of "Sinn Fein") and Mycroft asked me to take a look at what the other director had done. I watched what had been shot and then I said to him, thinking I was talking myself out of a job, "Nobody talks like that in Ireland. The dialogue is impossible."

They asked me to read the script. I took it away and throughout the script opposite each shot I made a little sketch, perhaps 300 small drawings in all. When I brought this back, they looked at it and Mycroft asked, "Could you direct this film?" I said, "With my eyes blindfolded and my hands tied behind my back."

To help with the script, I brought over Denis Johnston, the Irish playwright famous for "The Moon in the Yellow River." Robert Clark, the chief accountant at BIP told me, "of course, all our money has been allotted already and there's nothing left to pay you. Not very much, anyway."

"Well, how much is there left for me?" I asked.

"One hundred and fifty pounds."

I thought it over and told him, "Well, it's 150 [pounds] more than I've got. But you musn't use any of the other director's work because it won't match what I will do at all." BIP agreed and I finished the film. Before it came out, I had been given a contract by BIP. I got 40 [pounds] a week, which was the top salary for a director then, plus 500 [pounds] every time I made a film. So within one year, I made not only *Ourselves Alone* but also *The Tenth Man*, based on a Somerset Maugham story, and *Sensation*, a sensational newspaper story, all three of them starring John Lodge, and *Glamorous Night* written by Ivor Novello. We really had to go at it then. Making films was rather like scrubbing and washing in the tub. (104-6)

What we can glean from the above is Mycroft's willingness to interfere with a director's work (in this case, Walter Summers) when he thought that the production was not proceeding as it should. Bringing in Hurst as an Irish consultant revealed his cautious nature, and offering him the job showed his commercial and entrepreneurial sense. Rachael Low, in her magisterial *The History of the British Film 1929-1939* (1985), has little time for Mycroft, "a bitter man with fascist views . . . [who] operated a policy of cut-price window dressing, trying to make cheap films which looked like expensive ones" (116-17). The concern for films coming in under budget is certainly indicated by Hurst's recall of films appearing to have been produced as if on automatic. BIP produced more than two hundred features and shorts in the 1930s, with Mycroft credited as producer on at least sixty. These facts tell us that while he was an important guiding hand, Mycroft's personal views when it came to serious drama may not have been particularly crucial. He certainly left Hurst to get on with directing the jobs he had been assigned. Of course, Hurst's war record (he had fought for the British army at Gallipoli) may have implied that he was a "politically safe" director.

Ourselves Alone (1936) is important today because it is a rare specimen of a British film directed by an Irish Protestant on the War of Independence period in the South of Ireland. It concentrates on Inspector Hannay (John Lodge) of the Royal Irish Constabulary, his fiancée Maureen Elliott (Antoinette Cellier), her brother Terence (Niall MacGinnis), who was an IRA leader, and the English captain

Wiltshire (John Loder). Hurst seems to be concerned that the point is made that Irish Protestants can be on opposite sides of the conflict, as Hannay says to Terence "I'm as Irish as you are." Hannay implies here that he does not need to be an IRA revolutionary to feel Irish. The film seems to have avoided censorship, though it had a limited distribution in Ireland and did not appear to reach the North. John Lodge's Hannay is one of extreme self-sacrifice. When Terence is shot by Captain Wiltshire, who clearly has the love of Maureen, Hannay takes responsibility for the killing so that the two can leave Ireland for a new life together. While it appears that this film could be seen as a form of personal therapy for Hurst—an Irishman who nevertheless fights for the British—the fact that our sympathies lie with Inspector Hannay, the figure of local policing, is important to conveying a sense of the need to retain the status quo as well as the need to respect law and order.

By contrast, John Lodge's next two roles for Hurst in *The Tenth Man* (1936) and *Sensation* (1937) are leading ones of extreme selfishness and concern themselves with more complex areas of human experience. The former film is an adaptation of a Somerset Maugham story, where we enter the world of Lodge's George Winter, a ruthless and ambitious investment broker who works out of Liverpool. One of the first shots is a close-up of Winter signing a cheque for one hundred thousand pounds. Money, however, brings little happiness to the financier, who hectors his wife curtly, "I married your social position and you married money." The title of the film refers to Winter's belief that nine men out of ten are fools, but, as his wife foresees, he proceeds to meet the tenth, a man who will not be bribed into any underhand financial chicanery. The film is thus extremely cynical about the asset-stripping activity of business and about politics, since we see Winter win a parliamentary election through sheer opportunism. Once found out that he has not the financial resources to cover his muddy tracks, he commits suicide. Hurst directs us to this man's unworthiness less through his financial scams than through his severe treatment of his wife, who loves another man. But again the underlying theme is a conservative one: the class mobility achieved briefly by Winter is reversed by his exposure as a crook and by his forced suicide.

Sensation also lacks warmth. John Lodge's portrayal of Heaton, a crime reporter, resembles (some might say "apes") the American newspaperman films of the era, particularly *The Front Page* (1931). We are presented with the parasitic, competing community of reporters, who talk at great speed. Furthermore, we are shown the dilemma that their working lives leave little time for "normal" human relationships. Heaton is played as an unscrupulous reporter who worms his way into the home of the suspect under false presences and even steals photographs from the family album. His only redeeming act is a small one: after the murderer is sentenced to hang, Heaton returns stolen love letters to the convicted's wife. It is Heaton's girlfriend who seems to be the only route out of dubious moral and ethical issues. The production is interesting, for the reporter film usually allows serious subjects to be explored, and more often usually than not it fetishizes the individual who undermines both the police and the criminals. Yet in this film, the success of the reporter turns him into an emotionless monster. Hence, one assumes the idea of the return of love letters and the more important pulling power of acceptable heterosexual relations with the girlfriend, which will prevent him from probing society's institutions or the consequences of them.

Hurst's next film, *Glamorous Night* (1937), is a musical with contemporary relevance. Originally adapted from the Ivor Novello stage success about a king in love with a commoner, the film for some became an ambivalent look at the Edward VIII and Mrs. Simpson "event" of 1936, which culminated in the royal abdication. The film opens with an English geologist, Anthony Allan (Barry Mackay), witnessing Romany dances and songs in the forest where he has found a reservoir of oil. On learning of the find, the gypsy Melitza (Mary Ellis) remarks with an almost 1990s wisdom, "Oil means War." This undefined kingdom in the world, here called "Krasnia," has its own constitutional crisis. King Stefan (Otto Kruger) is in love with the gypsy queen. An ambitious and rather fascist-looking (often black-shirted) First Minister Lyadeff (Victor Jory) arranges for an attempted assassination of the king, but the Englishman foils the enterprise. Lyadeff takes full control of the state, however, and forces King Stefan to make an abdication speech on radio. At this juncture, the British viewer can only see parallels between this scene and London in 1936, but Stefan instead makes a bold renunciation of Lyadeff on the radio. The first minister is soon displaced, and the world is set to rights with the reuniting of Stefan and Melitza. It comes across as a musical Robin Hood story, a fantasy world where real-life problems are almost solvable by love and trust alone. The film defends the monarchy, wishing the ruler to be understood as only human and often misguided but intrinsically good. And it is the role of the middle-class geologist and the lower orders to defend the monarchy from extremists. Based on this film alone, it is difficult to believe Rachael Low's contention that Walter Mycroft, the chief of production, favored fascism, at least not that of the Oswald Mosley kind. What is not in doubt is the overall conservative nature of these productions and how tight a rein Mycroft kept on finances.

A more opposite experience could not have been found in England at the time than with Alexander Korda at London Films, where Hurst was invited to work in 1937. Hurst recounts the experience:

> I went over to see Korda and we liked each other. He then staggered me by the proposition he made for directing three films. For the first, I was to get 3,500 [pounds], for the second 5,000 [pounds] for the third, 10,000 [pounds]. All in one year. I don't know how I got out of his office without fainting. I went back to BIP and said, "If you'll give me half of what I've been offered, I'll stay with you." They wouldn't so I moved over to Denham Studios, which Korda had built, paid for by the Prudential.

> After six weeks of doing nothing, I went to Korda and said, "Look, I've been here for six weeks and I've not been working." "Take it easy, my boy, something will come up for you." A wave of economy hit Denham. It manifested itself in a coarser grade of lavatory paper and the decision that no windows were to be cleaned. We all ended up bringing in our own toilet paper and moving about in a fog. At this time they were filming *Knight Without Armour* for which Alex was paying Marlene Dietrich 70,000 [pounds].
>
> After another six weeks, I went back to Alex and said, "Look, I've now been there for three months and I haven't done a stroke of work." "Have another little rest," he said. Four more weeks went by. I returned to Alex again. "This is absurd. You're paying me all this money and I still haven't done any work for you." Korda was still calm. "Have a holiday. Go to the south of France." I did. (1986, 107-8)

Korda was keeping Hurst in the hopes of using his Arabic language skills in the making of a film on Lawrence of Arabia, but in the end the Governor of Palestine would not allow large gatherings of Arabs, even for an imperialist-influenced film. Hurst's first of only two films for Korda's company was not assigned without some personal acrimony, but what emerges is the liberal-mindedness of Michael Korda. Hurst writes:

> There was a meeting of very high executives at Denham and my name came up as replacement director for *Prison Without Bars*, a remake of a French film about an open prison for women. One of the executives remarked, "Oh yes, Desmond Hurst is a very fine director, but I hear he's a bugger." I was later told this by someone who was present. The next day, I met this man walking along with the studio heads, including Korda, in front of the studios. I stopped in front of them and said to him, "Oh, I hear that you said at a public meeting that I was a bugger. Well, that may or may not be true. Just ask your brother what happened between us a week ago."
>
> Later Korda came down to see me on the stage. He never visited any of his directors there without first sending a message to see if he could come. When he arrived, he said, smiling, "You are a terrible young man to talk like that to one of my senior executives." (109)

Prison without Bars (1938) on the surface is an extremely unusual film in that it concentrates on a "State Correctional Institute for Girls," a few kilometers from Paris. It dwells, however, on the importance of love and trust in human relationships. It also poses problems similar to those outlined in *The Tenth Man* and *Sensation*, in particular the toss-up between a career and a successful relationship. What makes the film intriguing is the emphasis on the professional woman who brings new techniques of personnel management to the Institute by preferring to make the incarcerated girls feel wanted rather than punished. Visually, Hurst makes a clear statement at the opening of the film that the current institute practices are cruel. We watch the girls in long shot walk in a circle in the courtyard as part of their daily exercise. The image is a strong one, clearly suggesting the Dantesque circles of hell. Breaking that circle is the responsibility and aim of Yvonne (Edna Best), the new superintendent, who ostensibly has come to be with her fiance George (Barry Barnes), the doctor serving the institute.

The duties facing Yvonne, however, allow little time for a relationship. By the end of the film, as of a newly released girl departs, she says, "They go and we stay. We're the prisoners in this house." The flirtation between the doctor and one of the girls, Suzanne (Corinne Luchaire), is really a side issue to this general theme of self-sacrifice, which links the film to *Ourselves Alone*. Overall, *Prison without Bars* takes an equivocal position with regard to the role of women in society. The film clearly shows the abuse of power by female attendants, and the title may refer to the domestic chores of women inside the home in a more general metaphorical way. The difficulty of a woman to have a career *and* a relationship is posed, but no preference for either or a combination of the two is indicated in the film text.

The question of falsely acquired money, raised in *The Tenth Man*, is brought up again in Hurst's most celebrated film of the 1930s, *On the Night of the Fire* (1939). This production came together under the auspices of an early Rank-influenced company, Gilbert and Sullivan Films (G & S). Here Ralph Richardson plays Will Kobling, a barber, who is tempted one day to steal money from an office desk near an open window. The decision to steal and to use the money to pay off his wife's debts to a local shopkeeper turns an innately decent man into an enraged and paranoid killer. The shopkeeper, Pilleger (Henry Oscar), begins to blackmail Kobling; this drives the latter to commit murder on a night when the streetfolk are occupied with a dangerous fire. The plot develops slowly and teasingly, giving Richardson an opportunity to show his range of talent. Although reviewers found it hard to be totally convinced as to the authenticity of Richardson and Diana Wynward as lower-middle-class cockneys (a reservation shared by Hurst when Richardson declined to accompany him to an East End barber shop to savor the atmosphere, claiming his acting skills were all that were required), the choice of subject, from an F. L. Green novel, is a remarkable departure from the decadent sets in *The Tenth Man* and *Glamorous Night*. The focus on an "Everyman" figure undoubtedly fueled the film's popularity. The scenes of fire fighting were to prove prophetic, since the blitz was only a year away. From the above summary, it may appear a simple "crime does not pay" production, but Hurst spends considerable time on the main character——his desire to please his wife, his hopes to escape the back streets, his gradual deterioration, and his decision to let himself be killed by the police, once he learns his wife has died from injuries in a car crash (escaping newspapermen who are following her husband's story)——and

Figure 3.1. Brian Desmond Hurst in 1939. Courtesy: Brian McIlroy.

the result impresses the viewer as an intense psychological analysis of the first order. But again, the denial of class movement by underhand means is strongly underscored, however needy these lower-middle-class characters are.

When Britain went to war in 1939, its film industry started to make a contribution to the war effort, and Hurst was no exception. He was credited second behind Michael Powell but before Adrian Brunel in the rather hastily put together Korda propaganda film *The Lion Has Wings* (1939). The film educates the audience on the background of Hitler's aggression and the reasons for the declaration of war. No criticism or appearance of Neville Chamberlain is shown. Instead, Hitler is personalized in the narration as "one man who seeks to destroy civilization." Britain's war machine is described as capable of any task. Reconstructed air raids on the Kiel Canal are glorified, and clumsy montage is employed between shots of the German bombers and those of a Spanish Armada, which looks suspiciously like models in a water tank! Merle Oberon appears as a nurse who speaks of women's "sacrifice" in the war, claiming that the British are fighting for "Truth, beauty and fair play and kindness." It was a film to legitimatize the war.

The female role in wartime Britain is taken up by Hurst in the short propaganda film *A Call for Arms* (1940), which features an all-female cast. Two chorus girls decide to join the war effort in the munition factories after seeing a woman faint in the street from tiredness after a long shift. The film touches on the fear of bad news, when one worker reveals her husband has been reported missing in action. The munition workers volunteer spontaneously to work on an even longer shift when there is a sudden call for more ammunition. Many glances are exchanged, emphasizing female camaraderie, in what seems an attempt to strike a balance between the necessity of offering service and the sense of community gained by doing so.

Another Ministry of Information film concerned with promoting a sense of community is Hurst's *A Letter from Ulster* (1942). In response to propaganda emanating from the Dublin German embassy, Hurst was given a brief to produce a documentary to show that American and British troops stationed in Ulster were more than content with the welcome from Northern Irish residents. Concentrating on American GIs, Hurst was able to persuade one Catholic and one Protestant soldier to write letters home, explaining their impressions of their stay. From these letters, Terence Young, the scriptwriter, was able to construct a sequence of activities that revealed the differing traditions in Ireland. One unusual scene for the time was a recording of an actual Mass, where in a slow tracking shot down the aisle we see a number of GIs. The producer Bill MacQuitty recalled in an interview with this writer in July 1990 that the soldiers visible were actually inmates taken from the local military prison. None of them was very happy to be marched to church early on Sunday morning!

Returning to more conventional drama, Hurst made in this early part of the war one of his most famous films, *Dangerous Moonlight* (1941). Hurst was not freelancing and was taken on by RKO British to make a film about the sinking of a German submarine, but his assistant, Terence Young, came up with a better script about the Polish pilots who flew with the RAF. RKO liked it, and production started. Anton Walbrook stars as Stefan Radetzky, a Polish musician and pilot who sees his country overrun and seeks refuge in the United States, touring as a renowned pianist. He marries an American journalist (Sally Gray) whom he had previously met in Warsaw. He is torn, however, about his departure from Poland, and when the RAF creates a Polish squadron, he sets sail for England. Interestingly, his Irish friend Mike Carroll (Derrick de Marney), who describes himself as one of the "Wild Geese" (an historical reference that Hurst may have considered apt for his own exile from Ireland), is the catalyst for Radetsky to seek reconcilement with his wife. On a more grand scale, although the film achieved notoriety for Richard Addinsell's *Warsaw Concerto*, it is important to Hurst that our heroes are a Pole and an Irishman, showing the international mix fighting fascism. Whereas Radetzky is caught in his feelings of conflict—"I'm like a man riding two horses at the same time"—Carroll seems used to the situation, noting humorously, "We must preserve the English, so we have someone to fight against when it's all over." The film serves the same overall purpose of *The Lion Has Wings* but is decidedly more sophisticated and genuine in conception and execution, allowing through comedy some critique of the status quo.

As the war took hold and developed a pattern and rhythm of its own, Hurst turned to stories of a diverting nature, *Alibi* (1942) and *The Hundred Pound Window* (1943). The latter film, centering on betting activities at an English race course and starring Richard Attenborough in a small role, does not seem to be readily accessible today for viewing. Set in pre-war France, *Alibi* gives free range for performances by James Mason, Raymond Lowell, and Margaret Lockwood. It was the only film that Hurst made for Gainsborough, and the melodrama for which the studio was noted creeps into this crime film.

Hurst's interest in decadence or excessive extravagance is again present, with Lowell taking on the role of Professor Winkler, a mystic who claims psychic powers and performs in a sumptuous Paris cafe. Lockwood's Helene is desperate for money and accepts too readily from Winkler a sum of francs. In return, she gives him a solid alibi by confirming to the police that he stayed the night with her, thereby eliminating him as a possible suspect in a murder case. Gradually, Winkler is undermined by the underground detective work of Mason's Andre who proceeds to fall in love with Helene. The money-love tussle, present in other Hurst films, is more starkly developed here. This time love wins. The exploitation of women by figures in crime is conveyed strongly, but the main theme is that of respect for and confidence in law and order. The police may have to resort to a certain level of deceit, but it is all in a good cause. It all smacks of a metaphorical approach to justify war in a nominally Christian society.

In the latter part of the war, Hurst seemed to expend an inordinate amount of his energies on Gabriel Pascal's *Caesar and Cleopatra* (1945), and his contribution rises and falls depending on whom one reads or to whom one talks. By all accounts, it was a stormy period for each participant. A much happier working atmosphere was to be found in Hurst's next two postwar films, *Hungry Hill* (1946) for Two Cities and *Theirs Is the Glory* (1946), financed from private and governmental sources.

The former film, adapted from the Daphne du Maurier novel, is surely Hurst's most direct investigation (with the possible exception of *Ourselves Alone*) of his own country's history and problems. Raymond Durgnat (1971, 20) is one writer who finds it a bold class-conscious film that was very timely, given the new Labour government of 1945. Exploring the Protestant Brodricks versus the Catholic Donovans over three generations offers an Irish specific historical theme. Hurst's approach is not sentimental; he reveals both sides with their warts and all. Inherent in the Protestant roles played by Cecil Parker, Dennis Price, and Margaret Lockwood is a sense that wealth carries responsibilities and sacrifices. Miscommunication is blamed for much of the agony. Religion is not foregrounded at all, but the religious conflict between "planter" and "Gael" is. To a modern viewer, the casting of the Irish Protestant roles by English actors confuses an historical interpretation. The necessity to do so no doubt came from the need to raise the requisite "package" to sell to distributors. Gate and Abbey Theatre actors are "relegated" to minor roles. The key answer to the Irish question, it seems from this film, is in sharing the land and in wiping the slate clean of personal grudges. This socialist theme periodically provokes a critique of class in English society, although it is suppressed in the adaptation as a whole. Interestingly, the film curtails Du Maurier's five-generational conflict to three, and where she sees the Protestant estate more or less in ruins by the turn of the century, Hurst prefers to give out an inkling of hope, a possibility of reconcilement.

Theirs Is the Glory was Hurst's personal favorite. Apart from the director and producer, no credits for the film were given out. This may have been because it depicted a reconstruction of such a serious subject, the disaster at Arnhem in 1944. As the *Variety* reviewer remarked, "This is a war documentary to end all war films" (Rev. of *Theirs Is the Glory* 1946, 14). For this reconstruction, Hurst gathered together troops who had actually fought at Arnhem. Perhaps *Hungry Hill* was on his mind, as of the three or four "ordinary" soldiers the narrator discusses at the beginning of the film, one comes from Ballymena in the North of Ireland and one from Waterford in the south. Later on in the film, one of these Irish men is killed and asks his countryman to take a message to his mother. Hurst movingly reinforces the loss of many soldiers by a slow, eerie, pan across the empty beds of a previously full dormitory. The full dramatic developments of the Arnhem operation are followed with precision and with outstanding verisimilitude.

From the gritty realism of these two films, Hurst turned back to high society in *The Mark of Cain* (1948) and *Trottie True* (1949) both for Two Cities. The first film begins in France in 1898 where, in the midst of palatial surroundings, John (Patrick Holt) and Richard Howard (Eric Portman), brothers from the north of England who own an overseas cotton plantation, meet the beautiful Sarah (Sally Gray) for the first time. The two brothers seem equally besotted with Sarah, who chooses to marry John. When their marriage seems on the rocks and John becomes ill, Richard poisons his brother. But when the plan backfires and Sarah is condemned to hang instead of her supposed lover, Jerome Thorne (Dermot Walsh), Richard finally owns up. What is of interest to the audience is less the courtroom drama, which seems to take up a good third of the film, than the gradual disintegration of Richard into a conniving killer. This psychological study rivals that of Richardson's Kobling in *On the Night of the Fire*. The film also provides a gentle critique of colonialism, but it seems that the major attack is on the nouveau riche—"vulgar" northerners who aspire to southern and European sophistication. In this sense, the emphasis on the familial strife and jealousies would seem merely to confirm that these upwardly mobile brothers are unfit for class "promotion."

Trottie True was Hurst's first film in Technicolor, and the explosion of color evident here tends to coincide neatly with the general unreality of the musical. Jean Kent takes the leading role and unquestionably delivers the strongest performance in the film. Her rise from Camden Town to a Mayfair residence and marriage to Lord Digby (James Donald) is not without its digressions and serious traps, but Trottie's breeziness allows her to court but ultimately reject other eager suitors. On the surface, the film is a light entertainment that, nonetheless, criticizes severely the institution of marriage as overly restrictive. It also *supports* (unlike *The Mark of Cain*) class mobility and the *right* of a lower class to bring its attitudes and values along with it.

I set out in this essay to test the assumptions of Richards and Murphy about 1930s and 1940s British filmmaking by reference to one typical filmmaker of the period. On the whole, I have to agree that they are correct to argue that the constraints of the studio system, despite the free-lancing possibilities for directors and some producers, led to films that more often than not helped to define and defend the British status quo. On closer inspection, however, I would also like to argue that while Hurst's full filmography is, indeed, mixed, we can find "progressive" or "countercurrent" themes being explored.

From my own viewing of his films, I find it interesting, firstly, that at the height of the 1930s Depression Hurst was making films like *Riders to the Sea* and *Ourselves Alone*, both of which emphasized the limited choices available to people in times of poverty and political crisis. Secondly, his concentration on the changing role of women in society is explored unsentimentally in *Prison without Bars*, *A Call for Arms*, and even, behind a comic guise, *Trottie True*. Thirdly, he seems very aware in such films as *Sensation*, *Glamorous Night*, *On the Night of the Fire*, and *Hungry Hill* that Britain's social mix determined by money and class is always teetering on small, if not large, revolutions. Hurst and his work can serve, therefore, as a tension-packed paradigm of the problematic relationship between the auteur and the studio system in 1930s and 1940s Britain.

WORKS CITED

Aldgate, Tony. "Comedy, Class and Containment: The British Domestic Cinema of the 1930s." *British Cinema History*. Ed. James Curran and Vincent Porter. London: Weidenfeld and Nicolson, 1983.

"Brian Desmond Hurst." *Sight and Sound* Autumn 1958: 257.

Durgnat, Raymond. *A Mirror For England: British Movies from Austerity to Affluence*. London: Faber and Faber, 1970.

Hurst, Brian Desmond. "Hurst [Travelling the Road]." Unpublished ms. British Film Institute, 1986.

Low, Rachael. *The History of the British Film 1929-1939: Film Making in 1930s Britain*. London: Allen and Unwin, 1985.

McIlroy, Brian. "Appreciation: Brian Desmond Hurst 1895-1986: Irish Film-maker." *Eire-Ireland* Winter 1989-90: 106-13.

MacQuitty, Bill. Personal interview in London. July 1990.

Murphy, Robert. *Realism and Tinsel: Cinema and Society in Britain 1939-1948*. London: Routledge, 1989.

Quinn, Bob. *Atlantean*. London: Quartet Books, 1986.

Rev. of *The Tell-Tale Heart. Variety* 19 (June 1934): 27.

Rev. of *Theirs Is the Glory. Variety* 28 (Aug. 1946): 14.

Richards, Jeffrey. *The Age of the Dream Palace: Cinema and Society in Britain 1930-1939*. London: Routledge, 1984.

CHAPTER FOUR

THE DOUBLED IMAGE: MONTGOMERY TULLY'S *BOYS IN BROWN* AND THE INDEPENDENT FRAME PROCESS

Wheeler Winston Dixon

IN THE LATE 1940s, as England emerged from the wreckage of World War II, the Rank Organization, a giant British film production company, strove to get assembly-line film production back on track at prewar levels. However, Rank's chief problem in this endeavor was a problem also faced by England as a whole. The blitz bombing of London not only destroyed churches, houses, schools, factories, and other essential buildings, but also seriously damaged film studio production facilities in the United Kingdom. Warner Brothers, for example, had several of their main sound stages destroyed during nighttime Nazi bombing raids. In addition, the shock waves of wartime rationing of film stock and other essential film-production materials were still being felt. Rank, along with such smaller British firms as Hammer, Exclusive, Renown, and other film production units, were constantly seeking ways to decrease the considerable expense of film production, hopefully (but not necessarily) without a noticeable sacrifice in quality.

One method that was briefly considered and implemented during this period by Rank was a system of "process shooting" known as the Independent Frame system. Basically, Independent Frame productions relied heavily on intense preproduction planning of all phases of the film's actual shooting period, with an unusually detailed storyboard for the period, coupled with the use of an enormous number of process shots, using rear-projection, mattes, and other special effects techniques, to eliminate weather delays and transportation problems and to minimize shooting time. The ideal Independent Frame film thus utilized an extensive number of "background plates" and rear-projection shots, in which stand-ins, doubling for the stars of the film and disguised through the use of hats, veils, raincoats, or other items of clothing, would appear in location background shots. Many "exterior" shots (castles, ancestral homes, country cottages, prisons) were in fact simply "matte" paintings, a practice that persists to this day. The stars of the film would then play out their parts against a series of rear-projection screens or, in "Schüfftan process," glass shots, with a few simple props foregrounded in the frame (a railing, or a telephone kiosk) to preserve the illusion of space and depth. Once location background shooting had been accomplished, the stars of the film could shoot all their scenes in a matter of days, all within the confines of one studio, and never have to venture outside. In this manner, there would be no need to expose the unit to production problems typically found when filming in the outside studio "back lot."

The Independent Frame process is interesting for a number of reasons, although, as will be seen, it failed to catch on as a standard method of film production. First, one is struck by the *displacement* afforded by the Independent Frame process, allowing the protagonists of a given film to complete their work without ever coming into contact with extras, subsidiary actresses and actors, or members of the general public. In this respect, the Independent Frame method affords a considerable degree of privilege to the stars of a film while relegating the other performers to the status of shadows, whose rephotographed movements serve as a backdrop to the metatext of the film's linear narrative structure.

Second, the Independent Frame method assumes that cinema audiences will accept this degree of glyphic substitution as a perfectly satisfactory alternative to the use of "natural" sets, actual locations, and conventional outdoor shooting. Rear projection, and other trick shots are, of course, a part of nearly every film production; some films, particularly in the science-fiction and horror genres, depend almost entirely upon a systematic substitution of synthetic, or prosthetic imagery in the place of genuine manifestations of external reality. However, Rank proposed to make even films of a "social documentary" nature with the independent-frame system. This required a considerable leap of faith on the part of audiences, who had already been exposed to *The Bicycle Thief, Shoeshine*, and other films of the Italian neorealist movement. Then, too, even the other small British studios of this period seemed to embrace a certain degree of naturalism in their productions. Hammer, for example, shot many of their films during the early 1950s in a converted manor house near Cookham Dene and later at Bray. While this practice did not work well on certain projects (such as director Terence Fisher's science fiction films *Spaceways* [1953]), it served admirably for more intimate films, including *Murder by Proxy* (1953) or *The Stranger Came Home* (1954). In this light, Rank's cost-cutting strategy with the Independent Frame process developed in direct contradiction to contemporary cinema practice as pursued by independent producers, and it can be seen as a metaphoric extension of Rank's reliance on the traditional, large-scale studio as the optimal supplier of cinema product.

Third, and perhaps most intriguing, was Rank's belief that, through the intense preproduction planning afforded by the Independent Frame method, all the elements of a given film production might be assembled in one large shipping crate for export to other nations, enabling citizens of other cultures to produce versions of a Rank film in their own languages, without the use of "foreign" location shooting, props, or large groups of extras. This metaphoric packing crate would include not only all the necessary near-projection materials used in the film, but also all the free-standing props placed in front of the screen to anchor the protagonists within the frame. A complete script, matte plates, and a storyboard completed the package. Rank would thus export not only the physical materials needed to, essentially, reproduce their film for non-English-speaking audiences; it would also impart to foreign audiences the social values encoded in the background plates for the film, thus inviting production companies in other, often colonial nations to further identify with the representational values then espoused by the British cinematic patriarchy. No matter what the secondary film's ultimate language must be, and even considering the double "removal" of location encoded in the prefabricated backgrounds, the subsidiary film would be seen by local audiences as precisely that: subsidiary. The new film would thus derive its authority not from the culture of its adoptive nation but from the hegemony of the British commonwealth, as presented in the original production. While this colonialist cinematic practice never, in fact, took place (because of the abandonment of the Independent Frame process itself), the informing instinct behind the system remained an attempt at cultural supremacy, with English societal modes of behavior and class structure firmly centered as the desired model of the endeavor.

As one might imagine, Rank moved cautiously to introduce this rather radically stylized system to the public. After a series of exhaustive tests conducted by the Rank art director Frank Rawnsley (whose more distinguished work included the art direction for Nöel Coward and David Lean's *In Which We Serve* [Perry 1974, 119]), Rank produced a short children's feature, *Under the Frozen Falls*, in 1948 (Larsen 1950, 216). Directed by Darrel Catling under Rawnsley's close supervision, the film was adjudged acceptable by the trade and was a modest success at the box office. Accordingly Rank went ahead with the creation of the first full-length Independent Frame feature, *Boys in Brown*, which went before the cameras at Pinewood Studios, Iver Heath, Bucks, from 4 May through 17 June 1949 (Tully 1990, 1991). The film, which was written and directed by the British studio veteran Montgomery Tully, starred Jack Warner, Richard Attenborough, and Dirk Bogarde. The relatively long production time for *Boys in Brown* was due to the fact that many of the technical details still had to be worked out for this first "large-scale" feature; most of this extra time was spent in preparing the necessary background materials and process plates. The actual shooting with Warner, Bogarde, and Attenborough was accomplished in slightly less than two weeks (Tully 1990, 1991).

Attenborough and Bogarde were, at the time, members of Rank's "Charm School" for aspiring cinema actresses and actors. Interestingly, Paul Swann cites Bogarde as "perhaps the quintessential example of a British star who was 'manufactured' by the [studio] system . . . [Bogarde's] insider's view of the star-making process reveal[ed] the way in which the Rank organization carefully led the fan press material about the stars and manipulated personal appearances to develop public interest in certain stars" (1987, 77). Swann here makes reference to Bogarde's autobiography, *Snakes and Ladders*, which clinically depicts the way in which Rank promoted Attenborough, Bogarde, and other up-and-coming performers, just so long as they adhered to company policy.

Boys in Brown was, in many respects, a perfect choice for the first Independent Frame feature. Set in a boy's prison, specifically H. M. Borstal Institution at Portland and Dorset, much of the film necessarily took place indoors. The brown uniforms worn by the inmates readily lent themselves to easy "matching" of close and distant shots, and they made substitutions between actors and stand-ins extremely easy to accomplish. *Boys in Brown* was designed to simultaneously publicize the "humane and decent" conditions of British prisons while still allowing the viewer to participate vicariously in the lives of those who would seek to subvert the dominant order so fervently embraced by the film. As the film states directly in its opening titles:

> In fairness to the Borstal system, the producers wish to make it clear that improvements in methods and conditions are being made every year and that several have been made since the period of this story.
>
> In an average year there are 5000 boys undergoing Borstal treatment. On an average of 100 of these attempt to run away and 300 commit new crimes while they are at liberty.
>
> But six out of every ten boys who pass through Borstal never appear in a criminal court again—and two more appear only once. In other words, 80 per cent of all Borstal boys reform and become decent citizens. (Tully 1949, i)

Thus, this first Independent Frame production can be seen as a "corrective" film in nearly every aspect of its construction. Not only does it seek to place the British societal system as the dominant (if not only) mode of discourse within the film; it also seeks to undermine opposition to that system (or any questioning of the British hierarchal patriarchy) by featuring, as the film's protagonists, a group of young criminals. This approach "de-narrates," as Mas'ud Zavarzadeh notes, the legitimacy or even the possibility of any "deviant" approach to social intercourse other than that of the monarchy (1991, 7). The metaphoric exportation, then, of the box of implements that would enable and empower the replication of *Boys in Brown* in other cultures and in other languages is an act that not only foregrounds the primacy of the British film industry, and the iconic models embraced by that system, but also encodes the social, sexual, political, and narrative structures embodied in this "program" picture into the cultural diegesis of the host country. Further, it sets standards of representationalism founded upon the duplication of the image within the image, or the "doubled image," inherent to the Independent Frame process, and it posits the repetitive falsification/actuality replacement structure of the Independent Frame system as a model to be emulated and desired.

While economy was, of course, the foremost aspect of the process that appealed to Rank, it is interesting to note that alternative methods of speeding film production that were being explored during this period were seen by some British industry observers as "a step back on the road of the long and laborious emancipation of the film from the theatre" (Larsen 1950, 215). Critic Egon Larsen, for example, found Alfred Hitchcock's *Rope* (1948) seriously lacking in visual imagination, while he simultaneously misdocumented Hitchcock's actual method of shooting the film. Larsen wrote that *Rope* was shot "in the Spring of 1948 . . . with five or six cameras trained upon the rooms or parts of the set, one taking over from the other as the actors move about" (215). In fact, Hitchcock conceived and executed *Rope* as a series of ten-minute takes from one continuously mobile camera.

On the other hand, Larsen embraces the Independent Frame system wholeheartedly, likening it to an intriguing "jigsaw puzzle." In view of the intricacy of the process, Larsen's description of the Independent Frame production method is worth quoting in some detail:

> There was no single item in the I.F. system which had not been used before. What was new was the intelligent use of all these processes, together with the purpose of speeding and facilitating production without losing quality.
>
> There are four main elements in I.F., namely:
>
> 1. Pre-planning to the n-th degree.
> 2. Pre-staging—i.e., shooting in advance of actual production on the floor—of all scenes where the faces of the principal actors are not recognizable. These scenes are shot with doubles in the principal actors' clothes. Furthermore, "plate"—still or moving shots for background projection—are made for all scenes which would normally have to be shot on location, as well as plates as backgrounds for most interior shots, vistas out of doors and windows, etc.
> 3. The maximum possible use of all forms of process work: background, projection, hanging foreground miniatures, foreground transparencies (shooting through a glass pane on which part of the set is reproduced in painting or photography), matte shots, glass paintings as backgrounds and side portions of the set, etc., so that only a bare minimum of settings has to be built.
> 4. The building of all sets on wheeled rostrums.

From points 2 and 3 can be gathered why this system is called "Independent Frame": an independent framework consisting of all backgrounds, etc., is built for each scene before production starts on the floor. This framework, plus the

Figure 4.1. The Independent Frame Process at Work: Shooting *Boys in Brown*. Courtesy: British Film Institute.

clothes worn by the doubles and a few props, can be packed into a box and sent to any foreign country that may wish to shoot its own version of the film in its own language! If suitable actors can be found there to fit the doubles, there is no reason why foreign versions of the film should not be produced, even with very limited studio space . . .

On the technical side, camera positions and lens angles are calculated mathematically. Plans showing the date, positions of plate screens and projectors, exact measurements of built self-parts and rostrums, etc., are drawn. All these preparations ensure that no waste footage is shot. When production starts at last, everything falls into place: the projectors take up position, the camera moves to its set-up, the artistes—who have been rehearsed for one or two weeks in special rehearsing-rooms—move from mark to mark. It all dovetails like a jigsaw puzzle: for instance, the doubles are first seen on a moving background plate, crossing from right to left until they disappear behind a piece of built rock; and a second later the real actors emerge from behind the rock, walking on in front of a still background plate—thus uniting the action in a single flow as the camera pans from background screen to background screen. After the shooting, the rostrums are wheeled back to their assembly bay, so that no studio space is taken up longer than absolutely necessary.

In a country like England, with its unpredictable and unstable weather, the I.F. system saves an enormous amount of time and cost on location alone! By taking only doubles and extras on location for the shooting of the B.P. plates there are no expensive actors hanging around waiting for the sun. When the story of a big picture calls for a "cast of thousands," with the principal actors in the foreground, these thousands will be employed and filmed in a few days' work, and the foreground action, which demands a longer schedule, is then shot in the studio against the background of the mass scenes. If one of the principal actors falls ill the shooting schedule can easily be switched—another plate is put on, another rostrum wheeled in with bits of the set on it, and work continues with other actors.

I.F. reduces the normal shooting time by a third. It reduces the necessary studio space by more than half, and electricity consumption by 90 per cent. Only a fraction of the normal amount of building material is used. Moreover, as much as one-third of the cost of an I.F. production is invested in shots which become permanent library material (as there are no main artistes on the plate shots) (1950, 216-21).

While numerous aspects of this scheme bear scrutiny, it is the quality of mechanistic replacement and utilitarianism that dominates Larsen's discussion. Not only are extras and bit actors relegated to shadowland status; even "one of the principal actors . . . can easily be switched" (219). In short, the Independent Frame process removes a good portion of creative and/or aesthetic *power* from the hands of both the director and the actors. They are always, if the need arises, easily replaceable. We are told that the system "reduces normal [a telling use of the word] shooting time by a third . . . reduces the necessary studio space by more than half, and electricity consumption by 90 per cent . . . Moreover, as much as one-third of the cost of an I.F. production is invested in shots which become permanent library material" (221). This is the ultimate triumph of the Rank/Gainsborough combine over any of the individual participants in the film, and it is the cultural displacement of the human agency in deference to the corporate spirit. Dennis Kinlaw, in his 1991 study of "work teams," cites several differences between a "superior work team," and one that simply carries out the tasks set by the company in a routine manner. Perhaps the most telling characteristic in a "superior work team" relevant to this discussion is Kinlaw's assertion that satisfied workers operate in a relatively "informal" atmosphere in which their input is encouraged by management (1991, 19). With Independent Frame, workers became as interchangeable as the anonymous extras and stand-ins they photographed.

Larsen acknowledges that "to many 'old-fashioned' film-workers and film-lovers this technical [system] may sound like a nightmare . . . but the tendency to save time and cost through extensive 'trick work' has come to stay" (1950, 221). In short, if humanist concerns are to be sacrificed, then sacrificed they must be, particularly since any who might oppose the Independent Frame system are "old-fashioned" or "film-lovers" and thus not realistic in their judgments. The continual war between the commercial and artistic sides of the film production equation are nowhere seen more clearly than here, in a call to progress that seeks to decenter the actual and substitute the rephotographing of images under utterly artificial circumstances for location shooting. It is certainly telling that Donald Wilson, a producer at Rank who made six films in the Independent Frame method, later went on to produce *The Forsyte Saga* for the BBC, a production both artificial and cost-conscious in the extreme and one that featured the use of videotaped interior shots intercut with exterior filmed sequences, entirely for purposes of economy (Betts 1973, 222).

Paradoxically, this revisualization of the real may also be seen as one of the Independent Frame system's paradoxical strengths, in that the system strips down visuals to such an extreme that shadows, props, and backgrounds seem to be (and in fact are) part of an overall system of imagistic substitution. Even at the time, this was not lost upon the technicians who had created the system. David Rawnsley wrote that "an oblong patch of light on the floor, for instance, immediately indicates the presence of a window in the vicinity, while shadows of various shapes imply the nature and position of objects by which they are projected" (Perry 1974, 119). Critic George Perry agrees with this contention, noting that in Independent Frame films "settings were simplified to the point of symbolism . . . actors would stand in a room that wasn't really there at all, perhaps only a table and a chair with the rest back-projected" (Perry, 1974, 119). And in the opening sequence of the script for *Boys in Brown*, director/scenarist Tully specifies that

The MAIN AND CREDIT TITLES are superimposed on a high angle shot looking down on the inner Courtyard of a Borstal Institution. There is no movement in this background—no officers or inmates are visible—only the grim prison buildings.

As the last of the CREDIT TITLES FADES OUT this background picture remains on the screen, until suddenly, from the door abutting on to the Courtyard, a crowd of Boys in Brown comes out and starts to walk around the Courtyard. Soon the whole area is teeming with life. The CAMERA MOVES BACK a little and we find we are looking down on this scene through the symbolic bars of a Borstal window. (Tully 1949, i)

These images anchor the narrative within the locus of Borstal, seen from the vantage point of an omniscient observer. The sterility of this concrete landscape is further underscored through the conspicuous lack of any human agency in the beginning of the shot. When the "Boys in Brown" finally do appear, "teeming" about the courtyard, we maintain our superior vantage point. Tully enhances this with a pullback, reframing the courtyard through "the symbolic bars of a Borstal window." In these opening seconds of the film, Tully has effectively suggested the emptiness and implacability of the Borstal setting and demonstrated that, even with the introduction of human presence, it is the architectural trap of the prison that remains the supremely informing structure.

The stylization of this sequence is, in a peculiar manner, further enhanced by the inherent artificiality of the rear-projection screen, which flattens out perspective to an even greater degree than one normally anticipates in a filmic text. The only objects *directly* photographed by the primary camera in this scene are the prison bars; the rest of the shot (courtyard, buildings, and young men) is entirely rear projected. Thus, if properly utilized, it would seem that the Independent Frame method had potential for effectively stylizing certain films under carefully controlled conditions.

In the case of *Boys in Brown*, the audience's participation in the film *depends* upon the skillful and immediate introduction of the dialectic of the rear-screen projection system; these intensely processed images must be seen as "real" from the outset. As the narrative begins to dominate the syntactical structure of the film, the members of the audience are led to an acceptance of the signified object in place of the directly recorded photographic image. When properly implemented, the illusion is seamless, carefully crafted into a consistent tapestry of almost entirely synthetic signification.

Yet according to George Perry,

Independent Frame was disliked by directors because it was an inflexible system, removing a great deal of spontaneity from their work . . . A great deal of pre-rehearsal would take place and, in order to save time, every movement of the scenery was carefully plotted in advance with the aid of charts, every line of the script, every bar of the music, was timed exactly in advance . . . There was also a rigidity in the positioning of the actors, a feeling of artificiality, and the system was detested by those who had to perform with it. (Perry 1974, 119)

It is worth pointing out that Rank never proposed to use the Independent Frame method for their "A" productions. The introduction and implementation of the system was to be confined solely to "Quota" or program films, films aimed at working-class audiences. These audiences, Rank supposed, were less likely to object to the (from Rank's point of view) inherent artificiality of the process, presumably because these viewers were more intent upon following the narrative line of the film than critiquing the imagistic construction of the text. However, Rank may have misjudged their audiences in this respect. A 1943 survey of working-class cinemagoers included this comment from a Mrs. E. Howarth: "I much prefer seeing American films, as you get the real thing. They spare no expense when making a film to get the real scenery and it isn't faked like the English films . . . English pictures always remind me of someone being hard up, afraid to spend" (Richards and Sheridan 1987, 125).

The intelligent or aesthetic use of the Independent Frame process was a matter left by management solely to the discretion of the individual director. If Tully, for example, was able to effectively employ the Independent Frame system in the making of his film, all well and good. Rank's interest in the process was strictly economic. Then, too, Independent Frame films were always strict genre films, in this case a generic "hot-wiring" of the relatively recent "youth gang" genre, as arguably introduced by Val Lewton and Mark Robson in *Youth Runs Wild* (1944), with the venerable "men in prison" genre. The film industry in both Britain and the United States has traditionally seen the familiarity of genre as offering an immediate economic advantage over such disparate films as *The Lost Weekend* (1945) or *Open City* (1945), which are not as easily reduced to a series of pre-ordained constructs. Further, Rank's use of the Independent Frame process was confined to Gainsborough Films, Rank's wholly owned corporate subsidiary, whose avowed purpose as a production unit (under the studio chief, Sydney Box) was to make cost-conscious films with rigidly defined thematic content.

All Independent Frame films would be shot in black and white, thus relegating these productions to the bottom half of the "double bill" in first-run theaters. Rented to theaters on a "flat fee" basis, Gainsborough films were constrained by numerous economic and aesthetic considerations. They cost a certain amount to make, were produced in a preset number of days, and generated a certain specific amount of income from rentals. Since these "B" films never received a percentage of the theater receipts, the possibility of a "sleeper," or unexpected hit film, was nonexistent. Every aspect of a Gainsborough Independent Frame production, from script to final release, was thus predictable and entirely preplanned, with no variation either desired or allowed for (Petley 1986, 108).

In *Sex, Class and Realism*, John Hill notes that "in the social problem film, it is characteristically a crime or a 'deviant' action which represents the 'force' which initiates the plot . . . it is in the nature of the conventions of narrative that these 'problems' be overcome" (1986, 55). The Independent Frame system, in a sense, enclosed the problems represented by social "deviance" within a studio enforced embrace of the artificial, thus "doubling" the adherence of the image to the narrative. The "problems," and the "solutions," are confined by the production process to a single narrative structure and location. Seen in this light, *Boys in Brown* risks nothing, exposes nothing, critiques nothing, and seeks only to uphold the status quo.

At least one critic has been favorably impressed with *Boys in Brown*: Raymond Durgnat finds the film "ahead of its time in criticizing the running of the Borstals," and while he thinks the film on the whole "superficial" and "the execution [of the film] less convinced," Durgnat still sees *Boys in Brown* as socially, if not aesthetically, admirable (1970, 51). Robert Murphy, however, calls *Boys in Brown* "dull and conventional" (1989, 93); this last criticism, as we have seen, is certainly true on a number of levels. The societal and iconographic "conventions" espoused by the Independent Frame system and *Boys in Brown*, for better or worse, informed the current television assembly-line production system used in hour-long television shows shot on film and video. Rank finally abandoned Independent Frame in the late 1940s after only a few productions, with the considerable loss of six hundred thousand pounds (Perry 1974, 119). The process, in the final analysis, was both too complex and too costly for widespread adoption at that time.

Yet, the narrative conventions and stylistic inhibitions imposed by Independent Frame are still with us, implicit in any system of imagistic production that values quantity over quality and a saving of time over the benefits of personal investment. Tully and his compatriots were the first to try to rise above the inherent shortcomings of such a system of values, and, in their struggle against Rank's corporate vision as well as in their limited victory in this regard, we are given one more proof of the inevitable and continual battle between the individual creative act and the motion picture production and distribution monopoly that remains in force with even greater global impact in 1992.

WORKS CITED

Betts, Ernest. *The Film Business: A History of British Cinema, 1896-1972*. London: Allen and Unwin, 1973; New York: Pitman, 1973.

Bogarde, Dirk. *Snakes and Ladders*. London: Chatto and Windus, 1978.

Durgnat, Raymond. *A Mirror for England: British Movies from Austerity to Affluence*. London: Faber and Faber, 1970.

Hill, John. *Sex, Class and Realism: British Cinema 1956-1963*. London: BFI Publishing, 1986.

Kinlaw, Dennis C. *Developing Superior Work Teams: Building Quality and the Competitive Edge*. San Diego: Lexington, 1991.

Larsen, Egon. *Spotlight on Films*. London: Max Parrish, 1950.

Murphy, Robert. *Realism and Tinsel: Cinema and Society in Britain, 1939-1948*. London: Routledge, 1989.

Perry, George. *The Great British Picture Show: From the 90s to the 70s*. New York: Hill and Wang, 1974.

Petley, Julian. "The Lost Continent." *All Our Yesterdays: Ninety Years of British Cinema*. Ed. Charles Barr. London: BFI Publishing, 1986.

Richards, Jeffrey, and Dorothy Sheridan. *Mass-Observation at the Movies*. London: Routledge, 1987.

Swann, Paul. *The Hollywood Feature Film in Post-War Britain*. London: Croom Helm, 1987; New York: St. Martin's, 1987.

Tully, June Montgomery. Correspondence with Wheeler Dixon. 31 Dec. 1990, 15 Feb. 1991.

Tully, Montgomery. "Boys in Brown." Unpublished screenplay, 1949.

Zavarzadeh, Mas'ud. *Seeing Films Politically*. Albany: State University of New York Press, 1991

CHAPTER FIVE

LANCE COMFORT, LAWRENCE HUNTINGTON, AND THE BRITISH PROGRAM FEATURE FILM

Brian McFarlane

IF AUTEURISM IS not exactly a dirty word in 1990s film culture, the critical standing with which the likes of Andrew Sarris once imbued it has long since been rendered problematic at best, romantically irrelevant at worst. Nevertheless, there could be real value in the application of Sarris's (1968) archaeological work on the American cinema to the comparable undergrowth of the studio years of British cinema. Somewhere between the critical acclaim that greeted the postwar flowering of David Lean, Carol Reed and the late blooms of Anthony Asquith, along with Olivier on Shakespeare and the Ealing comedies, and the decades-later canonisation of Michael Powell, a whole slew of interesting if minor filmmakers has been neglected. It would probably require a Sarris-like dedication to sift through the studio output from the thirties to the sixties, and there would certainly be a lot of dross to be viewed. However, without there being any need to erect a Sarrisian hierarchy, such a sifting would uncover a number of films and directors worthy of anyone's attention.

This is not to suggest that there are mute inglorious Fords and Renoirs waiting to stun us with hitherto unregarded *oeuvres*. It is in fact a characteristic of the directors I have in mind that the body of their work is radically uneven. Some like Charles Frank (*Uncle Silas*, 1947) may have made only one film of real interest. Others made several very attractive pieces before their careers tailed off in the stagnating waters of mid-fifties British cinema and (to muddy the metaphor) the wake of early television. Others responded to particular studio setups or stars or other shifting circumstances. They do not typically exhibit the staying power of those director-producer teams (e.g., the Boulting Brothers, Launder and Gilliat, Ralph Thomas and Betty Box, Basil Dearden and Michael Relph) that weathered studio shifts and changing public tastes to maintain a steady output of more-or-less even quality over a couple of decade or more. A director like Arthur Crabtree grabbed his moment in the mid-forties, made a handful of popular melodramas, which benefited from his origins as a fine cameraman—and found nothing else to interest him or his audiences until a couple of surprisingly vicious horror films a dozen years later.

A taste for melodrama is, in fact, one of the distinguishing marks of the directors with whom this essay is concerned. This taste does indeed distinguish them from the two more respectable strands of British cinema of the forties and fifties, that is, the literary and the realist. There are of course melodramatic elements in such critically acclaimed films as *Great Expectations* or *Oliver Twist* and *It Always Rains on Sunday* or *Seven Days to Noon*, but in them these elements are, as it were, validated or rendered respectable by their origins in literary classics in the former pair and by their apparent subordination to social realism in the latter. And of course there are literary and realist elements in the films made by the directors in question. However, their real strengths most often lie in their assured handling of melodramatic plots and their subtextual interests in the discourses on sexuality/gender and class that these plots display.

Who, then, are these directors for whom claims of neglect might be made? Among those who may be said to have made at least one film that deserves more than passing respect are Charles Frank, Lewis Allen, Bernard Knowles, Quentin Lawrence, Alfred Roome, and Fergus McDonell. Frank's *Uncle Silas* is a rare example of British cinema of a full-blooded excursion into the Gothic. Based on Sheridan LeFanu's mid-nineteenth-century novel, it offers a full panoply of endangered heiress (Jean Simmons), deranged guardian, scheming housekeeper, upright squire, contested will, and attempted abduction—and it has a visual style to match all this. It has some memorable images (decaying mansion, dead birds hanging in the yard), and its use of swirling montage sequences creates a world of seductive excess. Lewis Allen made some charming films in Hollywood, including the ghost story *The Uninvited* (1944), but only one of the films he made in his native Britain rewards attention. This is the sumptuous melodrama *So Evil My Love* (1948), starring Ann Todd in a role that makes very skilful and ambiguous use of her chiselled blond beauty. She plays a missionary's widow who returns to Victorian London, where she is seduced into shedding her widow's weeds and her sexual inhibitions by an artist-conman played by Ray Milland. The conflict of passion and respectability is articulated through a series of very well written and acted scenes of confrontation, especially between Todd and the chillingly effective Raymond Huntley.

Of the other one-offs cited, only Knowles had so long a directing career as Allen's. He had been a distinguished cameraman (on such films as *The Thirty-nine Steps* [1935] and *Gaslight* [1940]) before he turned director, as so many British cameramen did (such as Ronald Neame, Arthur Crabtree, Guy Green, Jack Cardiff, and Freddie Francis). It is his first film as a director, the Gainsborough ghost story, *A Place of One's Own* (1945), that is his claim to distinction. Marcia Landy has argued convincingly for the film's significance in its "redefinition of paternal and conjugal roles" and for the way in which "the house . . . presents the crushing

Figure 5.1. Ray Milland and Ann Todd in Lewis Allen's *So Evil My Love*. Courtesy: British Film Institute.

weight of the past, which must be exorcised to make room for new life" (Landy 1991, 303). Knowles's other dealings with Gainsborough lack the visual and melodramatic flair of Asquith, Crabtree, or Leslie Arliss, and his career declined rapidly and steeply in the 1950s.

Alfred Roome had a career as an editor that spanned nearly five decades and includes such films as *The Lady Vanishes* (1938), Carol Reed's *Kipps* (1941), and many films of the "Doctor" and "Carry On" series throughout the fifties, sixties, and seventies, but he made only two films as a director. I have been unable to see the comedy *It's Not Cricket* (1948), described by David Quinlan as a "funny second-feature with a riotous climax" (Quinlan 1984, 221), but Roome's other film as a director, *My Brother's Keeper*, made in the same year, is interesting enough to make one wish he'd tried again. Predating Stanley Kramer's socially ambitious melodrama, *The Defiant Ones*, by a decade, *My Brother's Keeper* centers on the escape attempt of two criminals handcuffed together: Martin, a hardened old lag (Jack Warner, whose homely image has tended to efface a couple of excellent villains), and Stannard, a slow-witted youth (George Cole). In their dealings with the people they meet on their way and with each other, the film is consistently interesting, and particularly unsentimental in its view of the Warner character.

As Robert Murphy has noted, *My Brother's Keeper* "is marred by a silly sub-plot involving a reporter . . . roused from his honeymoon" (Murphy 1989, 175-76). The tense climax as Martin defiantly risks his death on a minefield owes something to Roome's background as an editor. In its oddly literary touches (Martin quotes Longfellow and the Bible); in its overt criticism of the constraints of English life (Martin wants "to get right away from this country—to somewhere like South Africa or Australia where it's new and young"); in its sharp discrimination between Martin's careworn wife (played by Beatrice Varley, archetypal drudge of forties British cinema) and his independent-minded ex-mistress (Jane Hylton): in these and in many other touches, *My Brother's Keeper* quite tantalisingly suggests a directorial sensibility one would have liked to see more fully extended.

It is hard to find out much about Quentin Lawrence, who made one admirably taut little thriller, *Cash on Demand* (1962), among a handful of justly forgotten films, including a science fiction piece, *The Trollenberg Terror* (1958), a lugubrious spy story, *The Man Who Finally Died* (1962), and a war film involving female/male impersonation, *The Secret of Blood Island* (1965). *Cash on Demand* is set wholly in a country town bank, whose prissy manager, Fordyce (Peter Cushing), is trapped by a suave but ruthless criminal (André Morell) into emptying the bank's vaults of cash. The thriller element is executed with precision and tension: in fact, it is hard to think of a British film of the fifties that rivals it in this respect. The accompanying action of Fordyce's being terrified into a more likable humanity is equally compelling.

In this respect, *Cash on Demand* is immeasurably assisted by what may be Peter Cushing's finest performance, subtly suggesting the inner changes in the man while the outward demeanour scarcely alters. In fact the whole cast is excellent, especially Richard Vernon, Edith Sharpe, and Norman Bird as members of Fordyce's unappreciated staff, playing with a quiet concern for the minutiae of everyday behavior that is unusual enough at any time, let alone in a sixty-six-minute second-feature from Hammer. Perhaps Lawrence simply got started too late; if he'd started a decade earlier, he might have racked up a string of creditable films comparable to those of Roy Ward Baker, whom—on the basis of *Cash on Demand* in its study of man under intense pressure—he resembles.

Those who worked with Fergus McDonell, including producer Anthony Havelock-Allan and actors Valerie Hobson and Kathleen Byron (interviews with the author, 1990), speak of him as a conscientious craftsman but as being perhaps too diffident to inscribe his films with a strongly personal signature. Like Alfred Roome, he began his career as an editor in the thirties (e.g., on Roy Kellino's *I Met a Murderer* [1939]), and his output as a feature director seems to have exceeded Roome's by only one. *The Small Voice* (1948) is a tense thriller that anticipates Joseph Hayes's novel and play *The Desperate Hours*, and William Wyler's subsequent film version, by several years. If McDonell's film lacks the social dimension of Wyler's, in which middle-class values are more closely scrutinised when the home is invaded by a gang of escaped convicts, it is no less proficient in the creation of suspense. It is also sensitive to the tensions between the husband and wife (James Donald and Valerie Hobson), tensions that the external threat will inevitably affect in one way or other. The threat is not just of violence but in the sexuality of the virile criminal Boke (Howard—then Harold—Keel's first film role), beside whom the symbolically lame husband at first seems ineffectual.

McDonell's 1950 film, *Prelude to Fame*, is more strident melodrama than he is perhaps comfortable with. However, it has the advantage of a strong central performance from Kathleen Byron as the obsessive Signora Bondini, who wrenches a young boy's life out of its course by turning him into a world-famous conductor. She mines in the character not just the elements of culture-vulture patroness of the arts but veins of frustrated maternal feeling, as well. The film also merits attention as a study in a range of parent-child relationships and of notions of the married state. McDonell's other film, *Private Information*, is a quiet little piece of social realism about a council house tenant (Jill Esmond) who takes a stand against a corrupt local government. Maybe the strengths of McDonell's films are as much those of his collaborators as his; he at least orchestrates these strengths to achieve some modestly pleasing films.

The foregoing has by no means exhausted the list of those who have at least one or two films that deserve to be known. There are others who have more wide-ranging achievements and of whom too little is heard. The rest of this piece will focus on the two who seem to me particularly ripe for reappraisal—Lance

Comfort and Lawrence Huntington—but others who have a sufficient body of interesting work due for reassessment include Harold French, Roy Ward Baker, Compton Bennett, David McDonald, Ken Annakin, Anthony Pelissier, and Philip Leacock. If none of these ever made an incontestably great film, they all have their names on some of the most attractive entertainments of the British cinema in its most productive years. The reasons for their neglect are interesting to ponder. In many cases, they worked in popular genres such as thrillers, romantic dramas, and war films, which meant they received less critical attention at the time than would have been accorded the more obviously prestigious products of the period like those named early in this essay.

They are on the whole not auteurs with a strongly individual signature, so the *Movie* generation of the sixties would not have taken them up. Some of them, it must be said, do not exhibit a vivid visual sense, relying on strong casts, well-written if rather theatrical dialogue, and plotting rich in incident. In some cases, too, the very uneven nature of their careers suggests that they were heavily reliant on the contribution of this or that collaborator; none of them had the long ongoing associations of the director-producer teams cited earlier. The studio system that their Hollywood comparators might have counted on for support was never as firmly established in Britain and was certainly losing what energy it once had by the mid-fifties. And some of them came into British films just when the industry was losing the impetus the war had given it.

LANCE COMFORT

Lance Comfort (1908-67) worked in films up until his early death, but all his most notable films were made in the forties. David Quinlan has an opposing view: "after a run of poor films in the 1940s, he fell into second-features. But, iron-ically, some of these contain his best work" (Quinlan 1983, 57). From what I know of these later programmers, including a frantically old-fashioned and unfunny piece with Arthur Askey, *Make Mine a Million*, I find this view hard to sustain. And the forties films—especially *Hatter's Castle*, *Great Day*, *Bedelia*, *Temptation Harbour*, and *Daughter of Darkness*—are all interesting, all exhibiting real melodramatic panache, all offering lively enactments of sexual and/or social issues, and all marked by acting of unusual intensity. The later films may well deserve reclamation, but "a run of poor films" will not do as a summary of his for-ties work. *Hatter's Castle* (1941), based on A. J. Cronin's novel, offers the spec-tacle of melodrama in full cry, greatly abetted by an appropriately bravura per-formance by Robert Newton as the tyrannical patriarch, Brodie.

Brodie is the first of Comfort's obsessively driven protagonists. He has built a grandiose Gothic-looking mansion that has led to talk about his aspiring to be more "important" than a mere hatter in 1879 Scotland should be. Later his banker rebukes him for erecting a "sham castle," but Brodie defends it as "the realisation of a dream," though his son Angus (Anthony Bateman) has told him that his schoolfellows have made fun of "hatter's castle." Angus is, in fact his other obsession: Brodie alternately cossets and bullies him. "There's still my boy," he cries when his business has failed, and the film dissolves from him smashing up his shop to Angus desperately studying for a scholarship. The two patriarchal obsessions—the castle and the son—are linked in a climax in which the boy blows his brains out, unable to live up to his father's expectations or to face his tyranny, and Brodie sets fire to the castle, a burst of maniacal laughter accompanying the leaping flames. As well as this strand of action that renders Brodie's wild ambition, he hounds his downtrodden, cancer-ridden wife (Beatrice Varley, in another care-worn victim role) to an early death and literally casts his pregnant daughter (Deborah Kerr) out into the snow.

It is always possible to outline to plot of a melodrama and make it sound ridiculous. However, one can do the same with tragedy: try, for example, a synopsis of *King Lear*, in which Shakespeare's insight and verbal virtuosity transform an unlikely story into a tragic masterpiece. Comfort's sensibility, greatly assisted by the stylish chiaroscuro of Max Green's black-and-white camera work, endows the feverishly plotted action of *Hatter's Castle* not just with real melodramatic *élan*, but also with persistently interesting discourses on class and sexuality. The film offers a strong critique of Brodie's patriarchal bullying, not only of the favored son he drives to suicide, but also of the women he demeans and ill-treats: the wife he neglects, the mistress he uses to humiliate his wife, and the daughter whom, with sexual hypocrisy, he accuses of "wallowing in the mire."

Though in line with the usual procedures of melodrama, characterization is conceived in largely polarised terms. An interesting complexity is introduced by presenting Brodie not merely as a megalomaniacal bully, but also as the victim of local snobbery. At a county ball, there is applause for Lord and Lady Winton (Stuart Lindsell and Mary Hinton), purely on the basis of their position, and, when Lord Winton rebuts Brodie's claims of kinship, there is a clear sense of the upper class using its clout to put down bourgeois aspirants to their eminence. Comfort negotiates the diverse strands of narrative and thematic interest with a vigor and panache that he perhaps never outdid. However, many of its strengths are to be found in his other 1940s films.

Robert Newton is again the protagonist in *Temptation Harbour* (1947). Bert, a railway signalman, is a basically decent man who falls into moral danger from the twin temptations of money and a *femme fatale*. The latter is Camellia (Simone Simon), the "disappearing mermaid" in a carnival, and as in Comfort's next film, *Daughter of Darkness* (1948), the carnival is represented not as essentially festive but as potentially disruptive. It offers the occasion for the loosening of decorums, especially of the sexual kind. By intervening when the show's master of ceremonies bullies Camellia, Bert opens himself not merely to sexual temptation (the end of which will be *Scarlet Street*-style humiliation for him) but to the lure of stolen money. The film ends on a sombre note as Bert delivers himself up to the police for the accidental killing of a man who knows about the money. The main arena of conflict in the film is in Bert's own mind, and there is some use of voice-over/interior monologue to render this.

Temptation Harbour seems totally different from *Hatter's Castle*; it may well be because of the crucially divided protagonist, and this, in turn, may be symptomatic of the period. Unsurprisingly, British cinema was influenced by Hollywood's film noir cycle for the mid-forties onward, and in matters of narrative structure, characterization, and iconography, *Temptation Harbour* is a prime example. A decent man's life is wrenched awry, ironically as a result of acts of unpremeditated kindness; the gold-digging heroine ends by taunting him for his sexual clumsiness, when his inherent honesty spells the end of her chance of wealth; and visually the film has a strangely grey, murky look, uncommon in British films, reflecting a mixture of film noir and, perhaps as a gesture to the Simenon novel on which it is based, those French films of the thirties and forties in which people on the fringes of life are found haunting railway yards and fog-shrouded quays.

Daughter of Darkness and *Bedelia* (1946) are more unequivocally melodramatic in their orientation. They also have in common narratives driven by a "wicked" woman, though in each case the films invite audience empathy with these women rather than with the pallidly respectable types who stand in their way. Like Brodie the hatter, these two women—Emmy Baudine (Siobhan McKenna) and Bedelia (Margaret Lockwood)—are examples of the driven protagonists who propel the narrative in Comfort's best films, and they have allegiances with the film noir heroines of 1940s Hollywood melodramas. *Daughter of Darkness*, derived from Max Catto's play, *They Walk Alone*, is remarkable in British cinema for its confrontation of women's sexuality. Emmy, the Irish servant girl (and the Irishness is a way of distancing her impulses from respectable British life), is a nymphomaniac whose capacity to disturb the everyday world leads her from her Irish village to an English farm, where she seduces the men and rouses the hostility of the women.

I have written elsewhere that "the film would perhaps be tougher if Emmy were merely sexually aggressive . . . but she proves to be homicidal as well and the film responds with Gothic intensity as she cuts a swathe through the men she meets . . . What makes the film so interesting is the way in which, cutting across the narrative grain, one retains a sympathy for Emmy and spares little for the law-abiding opposition" (McFarlane and Mayer 1992, 218-19). This is partly because Emmy is aware of the power of the sexual impulse, whereas the other women suppress it in various ways and use the weapons of class and education to try to *oppress* Emmy. The use of the carnival as a signifier of, and catalyst for, disruptive forces (cf. *Hatter's Castle* and *Bedelia*) remind us of the film's predecessors and that Comfort is not a director to eschew the bold visual and aural effect in the interests of forging a melodramatic climax.

Though *Daughter of Darkness* is certainly a fervid melodrama, it is not as generically clear-cut as that tag suggests. It has overtones of the US wicked-woman genre, though *Bedelia* is more obviously out of this stable, and, although Emmy comes to an apparently deserved and grisly end, even the most perfunctory reading across the grain will qualify melodramatic notions of guilt and innocence being given their just deserts. The good are too self-righteously sure of themselves, and Emmy's otherness commands sympathy in spite of some of its more dangerous manifestations. *Daughter of Darkness* has elements of the Gothic (the wild organ-playing, the dog howling for revenge); of the moody French romantic thriller (e.g., Renoir's *La Chienne* or *La Bête humaine*); and of the British pastoral with sour undertones (cf. Comfort's own *Great Day*). The film failed to establish Siobhan McKenna as a major star, but as one of Comfort's obsessives she is undeniably a strange and compelling presence at the film's center.

Bedelia, starring the British screen's reigning wicked lady, Margaret Lockwood, is a more conventional piece, of the same lineage as, say, *Temptation* or *Ivy*, or the homegrown *Dear Murderer*. In terms of narrative structure, it is more single minded than the other Comfort films under discussion. Bedelia, with several mysteriously dead husbands behind her, marries and attempts to poison her latest, Charlie (Ian Hunter), an architect, for his insurance, but as a result of the efforts of a detective, Ben (Barry K. Barnes), Charlie's devoted partner, Ellen (Anne Crawford), and the nurse (Jill Esmond) engaged by Ben, she is thwarted and is herself brought to suicide. If there is nothing very remarkable in this narrative, Comfort nevertheless imbues it with a more interesting texture than the above synopsis suggests. Much is made of the deceptiveness of appearances: the film opens on a portrait of the beautiful Bedelia, light gradually crossing it and a voice-over describing her as being "like a poisonous flower," and it closes with the voice-over, again accompanying the portrait, this time with words about "the enigma of a human being who could caress and—with those soft hands—kill."

Bedelia doesn't like having her photograph taken, and she is very unwilling to sit for her portrait to be painted; there are narrative reasons for these attitudes, but the film seems also to be implying that one skilled in rendering beautiful surfaces might, in doing so, hint at darker, more dangerous depths. Further, Ben, posing as an artist, is really an insurance investigator whose appearances in Bedelia's life are far from coincidental; and Nurse Harris is also not what she seems. And overhanging this appearance/reality motif, manifested at several levels of the film's narrative/narrational strategies is the figure of Bedelia herself. On the surface, she is another of Lockwood's wicked women, those sexual transgressors who meet bad ends; her Bedelia is given an extra dimension of interest through her obvious distaste for men ("I hate men. They're rotten beasts. I didn't choose them," she cries hysterically), despite her seeming attraction to and for them. There is also a suggestion, wicked as she may be, that the county set into which her marriage to Charlie places her is morally scarcely her superior (one couple is "not divorcing because Allan's making too much money").

Very different in tone, though still recognisably a Lance Comfort film, is *Great Day* (1945), one of his most attractive works. The "great day" of the title refers to a visit to the Women's Institute of the representative village of Denley, in a gesture of Anglo-American friendship, of Eleanor Roosevelt. During the twenty-four hours of preparation for this occasion, Mrs. Ellis (Flora Robson), hard-working vice-president, has also to deal with the arrest of her World War I veteran husband (Eric Portman) and the romantic problems of her daughter, Meg (Sheila Sim). It is a busy little film, but as in his other films, especially *Hatter's Castle* and *Temptation Harbour*, Comfort shows a capacity for keeping several narrative strands in hand at once. What is particularly interesting about *Great Day* is its clear-eyed awareness of the constraints of village life. Arthur Ibbetson's handsome black-and-white photography deals well with the quiet rural beauty of Denley *and* with objectifying the sense of inner anguish of Captain Ellis for whom nothing has gone right since the previous war and for whom the village is no more than a source of imprisonment.

In a way, Ellis's situation prefigures the plight of those film noir protagonists of the (chiefly American) post-World War II cinema who have difficulty adjusting to the demands of peacetime living; and the striking alternation of Ellis's tormented face and its fractured image reflected in the river as he contemplates suicide is the climax of this aspect of the film's drama. He is saved by Meg, whom previously he has warned not to get trapped, as of course he has allowed himself to be: he is trapped in the net of his own self-aggrandising memories certainly, but equally it is clear the village offers no challenge to his imagination. Meg, fearing to repeat the insecurity of her mother's marriage, has become engaged to a well-to-do local farmer, whom she "likes," rather than commit herself to the soldier she loves. The film is rich in detail about the situation of the Ellises, setting them against the gossiping lives of the village women, and is saved from melodrama by astute individualising touches which enrich the texture of the dramas of class and gender conflict at the film's heart.

The brief commentaries above do not exhaust the possibilities or even do justice to Comfort's best films. Writing about them, one becomes aware of making a sort of auteurist case for them, though this wasn't the original intention. However, in their preoccupation with obsessed protagonists (and in the striking performance these attract), in their confident deployment of the strategies of melodrama, in the use of certain recurring motifs, in their implied critiques of aspects of British society, and in their more than usual visual boldness, it is hard to resist the idea that Comfort is a director who, in favorable circumstances at least, created a body work of enough distinction to warrant attention for that reason. The films do of course invite genre study, and some of them do indeed receive this in Landy's groundbreaking study. Deborah Kerr, who made two films for him, called him "underrated" (see interview in McFarlane 1992)—not, one hopes, for too much longer.

LAWRENCE HUNTINGTON

Lawrence Huntington (1900-1968) cut his teeth on low-budget crime thrillers in the thirties, and this experience stood him in good stead when he began his "A"-feature career in the next decade. His range is wider than Lance Comfort's: it includes farces (*Women Aren't Angels*), spy thrillers (*Night Boat to Dublin*), psychological dramas (*The Upturned Glass, Mr Perrin and Mr Traill*), social problem stories (*When the Bough Breaks*), mysteries (*The Franchise Affair*), and romantic comedy-thrillers (*There Was a Young Lady*). None of these is a remarkable film, and Comfort achieves more in his more limited range, but, until—like Comfort's—his career declined in the mid-fifties, he made some compelling entertainments. He shares with Comfort a narrative flair that carries him through some hectically plotted films, though his control of tone and atmosphere is less secure than Comfort's. Like many of the directors referred to in this essay, he responds well to the challenges of melodrama; his best films are structured around clearly articulated conflicts. Like Comfort, he has a preference for obsessed protagonists, and his visual style, favoring very tight compositions and low-key lighting, intensifies our sense of their obsessions and highlights the nature of their conflicts.

All his films move swiftly, none more so than the 1945 thriller *Night Boat to Dublin*. Hearty rather than subtle, this offers a marriage of convenience between an endangered European refugee (Muriel Pavlow) and a British intelligence agent (Robert Newton) against a background of atomic secrets competitively sought by the British and the Germans alike and involving German agents in Dublin. The film maintains a balance between comedy (the marriage leads, inevitably to something more romantic and allows for a comic anticlimax) and a series of breathless excitements. Huntington, in his first "A" feature, is aiming at no more than a lively entertainment, and, abetted by a very good cast and Otto Heller's camerawork (which does justice to both studio set and location shooting), he establishes his proficiency in the chosen genre.

It is too long since I saw *Wanted for Murder* (1946) to remember reliably anything about it except that, in Eric Portman's performance as the mentally disturbed descendant of a public hangman, it offers the first of Huntington's obsessed protagonists (this Portman persona had been honed in such films as Michael Powell's *49th Parallel* and *A Canterbury Tale* and Comfort's *Great Day*). The next three were played by Rosamund John (*When the Bough Breaks*), James Mason (*The Upturned Glass*), and Marius Goring (*Mr Perrin and Mr Traill*). *When the Bough Breaks*, one of the early Gainsborough films made under the regime of the Box family, whose avowed aim was to produce films of contemporary relevance as distinct from costume melodrama, centers on the battle for the custody of a child. Working-class Lily (Patricia Roc), unwitting victim of a bigamous marriage, surrenders her child to middle-class Marjorie (John) but without formalising the arrangements. Marjorie, rejecting her husband's counsels for caution, pours out all her stifled maternal feeling on the child, her own child having died a year before. When Lily marries and wants the child back, the conflict, dramatized with some power, is not simply between the two women but between the two classes that they represent and that are rendered through the details of *mise en scène*, diction and accent. The conflict, also heightened by Huntington's predilection for tight framing, is too easily resolved, and criticism of this has perhaps led to the rest of the film's being undervalued or, indeed, scorned.

The Upturned Glass, like *When the Bough Breaks* and *Mr Perrin and Mr Traill*, opens sombrely on a long shot of a large building, a university medical facility. Like the other two films, which feature hospital and public school respectively, the film quickly narrows its focus on to the individual. In this case the focus is on Michael Joyce (Mason), a brain specialist who lectures about a "perfectly sane valuable member of society" who acts madly, murdering the person he believes responsible for the death of the woman he loves. Through extended flashbacks it is clear to us that he is presenting his own case history for his students' consideration, and, through his characteristic tight compositions and his use of high overhead shots, Huntington draws his audience into the mind of a man in the grip of a monomania. The growth of Michael's love for the woman (Rosamund John) is narrated through one of those montage sequences that forties British cinema is so rich in, here underscoring the unexpected growth of feeling in Michael.

Huntington, like Comfort and several other directors of the period, is refreshingly free from the inhibition about melodrama that characterises the "prestige" films of the day. *Mr Perrin and Mr Traill*, perhaps his most fully achieved film, has an almost literally cliff-hanging climax. Traill (David Farrar), the popular games master of Benfield Public School, falls back over a cliff onto the beach, and the frantically jealous Perrin (Marius Goring) watches in horror as the sea starts to wash over him. Huntington's use of the overhead camera, incorporating Erwin Hillier's ominous contrasts of black and silvery white, and Alan Gray's pounding musical score perfectly understand the scene's demands yet though this is melodrama in full cry, the film's effectiveness lies in the way it grows out of character and its reversal of our expectations in this matter. It is the timid Perrin, who had been ousted by Traill in the affections of the boys and the school matron, Isobel Lester (Greta Gynt), who rescues the manly athletic war hero, lifting him to safety before being washed away himself.

Leading up to this climax, Huntington's version of Hugh Walpole's study of the closely confined milieu of a boys' boarding school has been marked by his typically swift storytelling and an observant eye for the way the milieu generates conflict. There are tightly shot and lit scenes in the common room that economically sketch the allegiances and antipathies inseparable from such close quarters and the sharply edited confrontations between the sadistic head-master (Raymond Huntley) and Perrin. Marius Goring as Perrin creates a complex, detailed study in frustration. He is a dull but efficient teacher, with a touch of Rattigan's Crocker-Harris about him, but with a slightly more robust, polysyllabic wit.

A very expressive composition shows the headmaster dominating the right side of the screen as Perrin enters left to receive a rebuke; and the composition is repeated shortly afterwards when Traill enters the headmaster's study, except that this time the lighting favors Traill, putting him at significantly less disadvantage. Later, again in the study, Traill, at low center screen, watches appalled as the headmaster humiliates Perrin. (Again and again, Huntington's sure sense of frame composition becomes a key signifier in our reading of the meaning of the scene.) Perrin's furious rejection of Traill's sympathy alerts the viewer to the extent of his mounting jealous frenzy. The film resists the easy explanation of mother-domination for Perrin's neurosis, and in fact the scenes between him and fondly concerned but not possessive mother (Mary Jerrold) are touching in the exactness of the feelings delineated.

There were some very poor films for Huntington in the later fifties, as there were for Lance Comfort, but his best films, like Comfort's, deserve much closer analysis than has been possible here. They cover some of the same territory: they belong essentially to British genre filmmaking, which until recently has received scant attention; they imbue their genre films with an edge of anxiety and melancholy that is peculiarly characteristic of forties British (and American) cinema; and they sometimes subvert the expectations of their genres with complexity and compassionate insight that might have won them more attention if they had been working in the more respectable realist modes of the period. And, as suggested above, they are not alone.

WORKS CITED

Aspinall, Sue, and Robert Murphy, eds. *Gainsborough Melodrama: BFI Dossier 18*. London: BFI Publishing, 1983.

Byron, Kathleen. Interview with author. 1990.

Hobson, Valerie. Interview with author. 1990.

Landy, Marcia. *British Genres: Cinema and Society 1930-1960*. Princeton: Princeton UP, 1991.

McFarlane, Brian. *60 Voices: Celebrities Recall the Golden Age of British Cinema*. London: BFI Publishing, 1992.

McFarlane, Brian, and Geoff Mayer. *New Australian Cinema: Sources and Parallels in American and British Film*. Cambridge: Cambridge UP, 1992.

Murphy, Robert. *Realism and Tinsel: Cinema and Society in Britain 1939-1948*. London and New York: Routledge, 1989.

————— . "Riff-raff: British Cinema and the Underworld." *All Our Yesterdays: 90 Years of British Cinema.* Ed. Charles Barr. London: BFI Publishing, 1986.

Quinlan, David. *British Sound Films: The Studio Years.* London: Batford, 1984.

————— . *The Illustrated Guide to Film Directors.* London: Batford, 1983.

Sarris, Andrew. *The American Cinema: Directors and Directions 1929-1968.* New York: Dutton, 1968.

CHAPTER SIX

RE-CONSTRUCTING THE NATION: *THIS HAPPY BREED*, 1944*

Andrew Higson

During the War British producers have been able to provide less than a sixth of British programme needs, but the product of their studios has reached such a remarkable artistic standard in so many films that it is obvious there has been a renaissance of the cinema of Britain and that we have founded a national school which can take its place in film history.
—Roger Manvell, *Film*

Undoubtedly, it is the influence of realism on the British film in wartime which has given it its new and individual character and which has weaned it away from being an amateur and clumsy pastiche of its Hollywood counterpart.
—Michael Balcon, "The British Film during the War"

DAVID LEAN AND Noël Coward's film *This Happy Breed* was released in Britain in mid-1944—that is, at a key historical moment, as World War II was drawing to a close and peace was in sight. The film should thus be understood as one small facet in the process of ideological reconstruction, an attempt to renew the nation's self-image. It does this by adopting a self-consciously populist mode of address and by working with the traditions of a conservative and nostalgic urban pastoral to construct an image of an organic national community, the British people as one large happy family, and nationhood as a timeless and invariant category. The film tells the story of an "ordinary" lower-middle-class family, the Gibbonses, who live in the suburbs of Clapham, South London. Several parallel narrative threads detail the various trials and tribulations, romances and argu-

---

*This article is adapted from "Constructing a National Cinema in Britain," by Andrew Higson.

ments that attach to each member of the family over the twenty-year period between the two world wars, as the children grow up, marry, and leave home. This private narrative is placed in the broader public context of a popular history of the nation over this same period, presented in montage sequences inserted into the gaps between the episodes in the private drama.

The film was a major success both at the British box office and with contemporary reviewers, the latter treating the film as yet another example of the growing strength of the national cinema. As such, *This Happy Breed* was part of a cycle of films that might be called "melodramas of everyday life" and that were central to the formation of a national cinema in the mid-1940s and that have remained central in most historical accounts of British cinema. This cycle of films draws on a variety of cultural traditions, but in particular, it incorporates certain features of the documentary idea and its concern with the public sphere into the conventions of the domestic woman's picture, with its focus on the private sphere. It is this particular articulation of the public and the private that makes it possible for these films to construct such a powerful image of the nation as a secure and self-sufficient community (see Anderson 1983).

This Happy Breed and other films of the cycle clearly owe a great deal to the documentary idea; they seek to authenticate their fictions by drawing on the rhetoric of documentary and its connotations of responsibility and realism, and they establish a relatively expansive narrative space—the space of the nation—by employing certain of British documentary's montage strategies. But British reviewers admired such films because they resisted what was seen as the "pure" documentary's most worrying aspect, its emotional distance. On the other hand, the films were also acclaimed because they did not go too far in the opposite direction and become too personal, which was seen as one of Hollywood's main failings. But it is undoubtedly the case that such films share much with the woman's picture and its discourse of the feminine: their characteristic narrative space is the space of the home; their dominant thematic material that of the family, personal relationships, and romance; and they tend to foreground emotion rather than either rational thought or aggressive action. All this would seem to fit ill with the more self-consciously masculine realm of documentary and its world of work, of dignified manual labor, placed within a rational framework (see Colls and Dodd 1985).

How does the contemporary critical discourse respond to these features? There are three points worth noting here. First, the home is remarked upon not as a feminine space but as a national metaphor. The response to *This Happy Breed*, in particular, is to read the Gibbons family home as a bulwark of the nation; implicit here is the symbolic figure of the mother—that is, an ideal version of the feminine—as the center point of the family/community/nation, but this symbolism is rarely dwelt upon in the critical discourse. Second, if a female point of view is articulated, it is admired not because of its femininity but because of its humanity, in an abstract, generalised, universal sense; the point of view is significant for its sincerity, its emotional truthfulness, its mature balancing of desire and responsibility. This leads on to the third point: it is not emotionality, or romance as such that is admired in these films but the *restraint* with which it is handled (see Barr 1977, 1986).

It is perhaps this fact above all else that enables the critical discourse to avoid the issue of popular melodrama in these films. They may occupy the thematic territory of the woman's picture, but these films tend to underplay melodramatic effect. The potentially excessive characteristics of melodrama, its overblown qualities, the passionate intensity, even hysteria, with which it deals with the subjective, are constantly offset here by the details of realism. It is films like Gainsborough's *Madonna of the Seven Moons*, released at the same time as *This Happy Breed*, that are melodramatic in these terms, not films like *This Happy Breed*, that seek always to authenticate their fictions, and to understate the pleasures of fantasy. *Mise en scène*, camerawork, performance, and use of music are all tastefully restrained. What *is* excessive about such films is the emphasis on the social, not the exploration of the subjective. The potential melodramatic intensity of any particular drama is constantly displaced by shifting focus to another drama. Individuals are present in these dramas as representatives of the social, and their capacity to resist social responsibility by pursuing an individual wish is explored less than their capacity to play an allotted part within a consensual social formation. The social constantly exceeds the boundaries of any particular narrative lines. These films are, then, stories of the everyday life of the nation, not melodramas of wish-fulfillment: "The number of good films about English life has been mounting up; *Millions Like Us*, *The Demi-Paradise*, quite recently, have explored the unexplorable; and with *This Happy Breed* we shall no longer be able to keep up any pretence of not knowing ourselves. It would be hard to overpraise the skill, the feeling, and the enhanced fidelity of this film" (Whitebait 1944a, n.p.).

"Knowing ourselves" with "enhanced fidelity": this is typical of the way the film was taken up as a realistic impression of the ordinary life of the nation, with numerous of the middle-class critics of the "quality" daily and weekly press somewhat condescendingly celebrating the fact that "this film about the suburbs has gone out into the suburbs, and the suburbs have taken it to their hearts" (Lejeune 1944). While reviewers acknowledged the part that documentary films had played in enabling these realist dramas to exist, the secret of *This Happy Breed*'s critical success was the way in which it was felt to have superseded the perceived coldness of the documentary idea:

> [It] is not just a photographic and microphonic record of suburban life. If it were, nobody would care to see it. Art does not consist in repeating accurately what can be seen and heard around us. (Lejeune 1944, n.p.)

> Not only is *This Happy Breed* true to life, to emotions as well as exteriors,
> but here [in the opening shot of the film] is the camera magic woefully lacking
> from so many documentary-inspired stories. (Whitebait 1944b, n.p.)

It was these moments of magic, these "instants of poetry" (Whitebait 1944b) that
distinguished the film from the mere document: "A Mass Observation report on
'Sycamore Road, Clapham' would no doubt provide us with the same detail,
exhibited under glass; Mr. Coward sees it very much alive" (Whitebait 1944a). But
the film is superior not only to documentary; it is superior also to the standards of
the Hollywood film:

> In point of photography and direction and acting few recent films from Amer-
> ica . . . have approached it. This technical confidence, accompanied by a native
> warm honesty and an increasing sureness in the defining of atmosphere, marks
> the progressiveness of the British cinema as opposed to the backward trend of
> Hollywood, gripped in a deadly paralysis of self-imitation. (Winnington 1944,
> n.p.)

This was a national cinema, but it was also a serious, responsible, and
intelligent cinema. The marks of this cinema, despite the derisory criticisms of the
documentary idea, were its restraint, its sense of reserve—once more elevated to a
national characteristic during the war period and here being used to praise the
acting, the emotional quality of the film, and even its use of color—"so discreet
that one almost loses sight of it" (Whitebait 1944a, n.p.):

> The flavour of *This Happy Breed*, with its accumulation of *clichés* and small
> touches, is as subdued as the admirable Technicolor . . . Miss Celia Johnson's
> performance is a miracle of unstressed vitality and charm that makes one wonder
> how English audiences can ever have wept over a pasteboard Miniver. (Whitebait
> 1944a, n.p.)

The distinction between the Hollywood melodrama of *Mrs. Miniver* (1942)
and the down-to-earth qualities of *This Happy Breed* can be seen as an attempt to
mobilize a *true* sense of national identity over and against Hollywood's vision of
Englishness. The representation of the nation and the national character in *This
Happy Breed* should—as I have suggested—be seen in terms of urban pastoral: the
imagined community of the nation is an extended family, consolidated here in
the image of the Gibbonses, who, as one reviewer put it, "are a large family: they
are found all over the British Isles . . . [and] the special quality of [this film is that
it] finds in a house in a row the symbol of a nation" (Lejeune 1944, n.p.). The text
seeks to establish that this community is knowable to itself—and that the nation is
an organic body—even in the context of a massively urbanized and heavily pop-

ulated environment. It does so for the most part by focusing on the relationships that exist among the members of one family (and between that family's one set of neighbors); but it also tries to make the metaphorical relationship between individual family and the nation as a whole as solid and as visible as possible by developing the history of the family alongside a history of the recent national past. The shots that open and close the film are also crucial in establishing the family / knowable community / nation relationship in as fluid and seamless a way as possible. The first shot of the film is a high-angle panoramic shot of London; the camera pans across this landscape and appears to move down toward a particular, immaculately ordered neighborhood, then one street within this neighborhood, and eventually the house in which the action is set. This movement in, via the pans, a crane movement and a series of dissolves, continues through the window of the house; the camera moves down the stairs and to the front door, which the Gibbons family is just entering for the first time. The final scene of the film shows, from inside the house, the Gibbonses now *leaving* the house for the last time and shutting the door behind them; virtually the same movements and dissolves with which the film had opened are now repeated in reverse, as the camera leaves the particular detail, to place it once more within the general view of the city.

The film is also concerned, at least implicitly, with the form the nation should take after the war, coming down on the side of stability, or at the very least, gradual evolution. In order to be able to foreground the family so conclusively, but also to be able to place a *complete* family at the centre of the narrative, *This Happy Breed* has to situate itself outside the war, in the interwar years of peace. The narrative place of *This Happy Breed* is resolutely the home, and its protagonists are, in the end, all members of one extended family, which enables the film to establish the family as the stable and secure cornerstone of the nation in peacetime.

Thus the film returns again and again to scenes of the family gathered together for moments of celebration—a wedding, Christmas, or just a pot of tea. The family and the home exist as a secure, stable, virtually unchanging sanctuary from the hectic and threatening outside world. This narrative focus on the family and the home also reaffirms woman's place as firmly within the domestic sphere, her role being to transform house into home. The figure of the mother—and there are few more ideal than Ethel Gibbons—is thus placed right at the heart of the nation-as-family (Gledhill and Swanson 1984, 61). While in some other films of the period, such as *Millions Like Us* and *The Gentle Sex* (both 1943), there is some effort to show women involved in traditionally masculine occupations, away from the home, at least for the duration of the war, *This Happy Breed* explicitly shows women in their place, in the home, and never releases them from it. The film is, in this way, able to acknowledge the strength of women in processing the domestic sphere and maintaining the home—and thereby the nation—but in the film's terms, the discourse of women is constructed as both trivial and comic:

Figure 6.1. David Lean's *The Happy Breed*. Credit: British Film Institute.

the invitation is to laugh at, rather than to laugh with, the women and their domestic quarrels. The image of the mother is thus no more than symbolic for the nation as a whole: outside the domestic space, within the public sphere, she has no real power.

Where other films like *Millions Like Us* quite self-consciously play on progressive forces within the conjuncture, *This Happy Breed* tends to close down those very issues. Both films confront historically specific ideological and political problems of national life, and both work to forge some sort of unity of the popular forces of the moment. Neither attempts to be class-specific; rather, they attempt to construct a popular consensus outside class distinctions, above class antagonisms. But where *Millions Like Us* directly questions the stability of that consensus, *This Happy Breed* posits it as the natural and essential product of the national character: it seeks to articulate national character as the backbone of England/Britain, as a timeless quality forged in the past.

This Happy Breed is thus decidedly nostalgic for the settlement, the security, and the stability that it finds in its representations of interwar domestic arrangements and family life; it may propose that this should be the social basis for the postwar world, but it also seems to suggest that such a society belongs only to fond memory. The film is invested with a powerful sense of loss throughout its course, but particularly in the closing moments. This is achieved narratively, in the gradual dispersal of the family via marriages, deaths, and the final move to a new flat, the relentless emptying of the home that has been so carefully and lovingly established. It is there too in the constant knowledge that this film, which so carefully sets itself up as taking place in the aftermath of "the war to end all wars," is being watched while a new war is being waged. This sense of loss in relation to the plenitude of the family in peacetime is finally brought home as the narrative moves toward a close just as this new war opens. It is achieved too in the camerawork, in its preference for the distance of the medium shot and the group shot (rather than the proximity of the close-up) and in the way that, on a number of occasions at the end of a sequence, the camera pulls back to an extreme long shot, as if the image, and the time that it documents, were fading from memory.

The narrative form of *This Happy Breed* is fairly typical of films of this cycle: there is not one dominant, goal-directed storyline but several interweaving plots made up of a series of almost self-contained episodes—many of the scenes are markedly inconsequential. There is no central disruptive force that sets the narrative of the film in motion and no real narrative enigma to be solved—the family is already intact, in place, at the start of the film, which simply plots its development. Insofar as there is any narrative enigma at all, it is situated outside the film, in terms of the course of the ongoing war—we cannot determine the real ending of the film until we know the outcome of the war. In many ways, this film provides the model for the British low-life television soap opera, and, like soap opera, a lot of the narrative work is carried in talk, with much cutting between interlocutors to provide visual interest. The film remains very restrained for the most part, with the most dramatic and eventful incidents taking place offscreen, providing the motivation for yet more talk. Other dramatic or spectacular incidents are taken up in the montage sequences of public rather than private life; they constitute almost a separate diegesis to that of the family and its home. The film as a whole thus betrays a bourgeois fascination with the exotic, trivial details of the lives of the lower classes, renewing the pastoral concern to dignify the common people, but always from a perspective that maintains a safe distance between observer and observed, subject and object (see Stallybrass and White 1986).

Although there is a certain linearity to the film's episodicism, the form of the narrative is more circular and repetitive, which can imply not so much the development of a narrative across time as a sense of timelessness and a refusal to move forward, once more invoking a nostalgic relation to the drama. Repetition is there, for instance, in the ceaseless reworking of numerous similar "trivial," domestic situations and personal relationships, without any of these being developed into a *substantial* narrative trajectory. The circularity—another form of repetition, of course—is particularly evident in the reverse rhyming of the ending with the beginning, discussed above. Movement is the natural flow of time, and closure is thus the poetic closure of turning full circle, the end of an era, time running out, rather than the resolution of disrupted forces, the fulfillment of a wish or the achievement of a goal.

This suggests that it is the diegetic space of the family and the home (and, metaphorically at least, the nation)—rather than a strong, causally motivated, narrative linearity—that binds the various disparate dramas of the film together and organizes the work of the film. If there is a sense of time passing in the narrative of the family, it is achieved above all by the device of the montage sequences; but running against this experience of temporality is the opposite experience of timelessness, of lack of development, of time standing still. The synchronic placing and relating of events and people within the family is then explored diachronically in the context of historical progress. The latter is a narrative of the nation—but it too is marked by a lack of causality, given the way in which the montage sequences are built up out of a series of discrete moments from the recent national past, a sort of rummage through the diegesis of national history.

Although *This Happy Breed* can be seen as an effort to re-construct the nation after the disruptions of war, it does not really seem to know how to conceive of the postwar society: it has no profound vision of the future, it can only return nostalgically to the beginning of the cycle, as if it wants time to stand still, as if to imply that things should continue as they were "before," while at the same time recognizing that this cannot be. As one reviewer noted, "*This Happy Breed* adduces no evidence of better times to come" (Anstey 1944), preferring the apparent stability of class difference and deference, rather than any more democratic settlement.

There is really only one aspect of the film which looks beyond this nostalgia for an untroubled and mundane family life. It is interesting that this is also the one area in which the script allows for the development of a more substantial and causally moving narrative line, one that threatens to break out of the circularity of the text. This narrative focuses on the individual desires of one of the daughters of the family, Queenie, who finds the domesticated life of suburbia utterly unfulfilling and elopes to France with a married man. This emphasis on the individual and her desires puts Queenie at odds with the responsibility of the family and the needs of the community and the nation. In a conventional Hollywood woman's picture, it would surely have been Queenie who was of most narrative interest; in *This Happy Breed*, however, her desires are always marked off as deviant and problematic. We are never in any doubt that the unity and stability of the home and the family are the real sources of wisdom, emotional truth, and moral strength; and it is inevitable that Queenie will eventually return to the fold, as she does, safely married to the boy next door. The figure of Queenie potentially offers a profound critique of everything that the film stands for, in her desire for something more than the familiarity of everyday life, the burden of domestic labor, and the claustrophobic repressions of the family. But in the end her difference is contained, defused.

This Happy Breed is resolutely on the side of the social, albeit a social formation that is understood in terms of a highly self-contained and heavily demarcated *private* family. The diegetic space of the film is relatively wide, inhabited by several significant characters forming a network of social relations, rather than dominated by an individual hero-protagonist. Queenie's story can thus never be developed in its full melodramatic potential, since it is constantly displaced by another line of narrative interest.

The most conservative aspect of *This Happy Breed* is the way in which a public history of the recent national past is written into the private story of a family—in other words, the way in which the montage sequences are woven into the narrative web of the film. These sequences—the only occasions in the film on which we leave the Gibbons family home—are made up of a series of discontinuous fragments of activity from the public arena, mostly depicting concrete manifestations of political power and political struggles: the victory marches at the end of World War I, the British Empire Exhibition of 1924, the General Strike, a British fascist haranguing the crowds at Speakers' Corner, crowds cheering Chamberlain on his return from Munich, and so on. There are also a series of newspaper headlines, radio announcements, and street hoardings giving information of important political moments—the end of the General Strike, news of the Nazi successes in the 1933 elections, news of the 1935 general election in Britain, the death of one king and the abdication of another, a "Get Your Gas Mask Now" poster, "Peace in Our Time," and so on.

These sequences are marked off from the rest of the film, and from the everyday domestic life of the family, by the repeated use of not only a different system of editing and subject matter but also by a different use of music: the montage sequences are accompanied by extra-diegetic music, and often there is no dialogue; in the private drama of the family, dialogue is pervasive, and there is no extra-diegetic music. There is also, at the beginning and end of most of the sequences, a brief passage of harp music, which, by Hollywood conventions, would signal the entry of the fiction into a fantasy world, a dream, or a flash-back, and this is indeed the way in which we are invited to relate to this public, political arena. It *is* almost a fantasy world, quite separate from the private world of the family. One of the sequences, for instance, shows the family and their neighbors in the crowds watching but not participating in the victory celebra-tions; another shows them visiting the Empire Exhibition. Later, Vi (one of the daughters) talks of wanting to "go and watch the crowds cheering" after Cham-berlain's return from Munich: in other words, she wants not to participate in the political celebration but to look at it from the position of a spectator. The public sphere is thus reproduced as spectacle, something upon which the fascinated spec-tator can gaze from a distance.

The montage sequences of course serve to authenticate the "people's his-tory" of the Gibbons family and to invoke the wider dimensions of public life and the national community of which they are just one small part. But the pro-cessing of the montage sequences within the fiction serves also to *separate* these "ordinary people" and their private lives from the public arena of "politics and his-tory," to separate them from the public sphere, in which, it implies, they have no part. The spectacle of the public sphere may provoke emotional crises in the home, but it has no real social or political impact on its inhabitants.

"The national and the international background," as one reviewer noted, "is seen always from the point of view of this single home" (Powell n.d., n.p.). Impor-tant though such a perspective may be, it does at the same time effectively block any recognition of the nature of class interests or of the role of "ordinary people" in the relations of power. By focusing so resolutely on the family and the home, and by foregrounding domestic affairs, class power as an issue or a problem is obscured from view. Insofar as power is explored at all, it is entirely in terms of personal relationships, in which, of course, patriarchy is taken for granted. The film thus reaffirms the "ordinary person's" deference to, if at times slight unease with, the traditional forms of political and social power. It is this deference that Tom Nairn has argued is central to the dominant ideology of Englishness, the populist mythology that holds "not a belief that the People can do anything, in the last resort, but the conviction that popular aspirations will always, in the end, be attended to *up there*" (Nairn 1981, 286).

By an allegory of the aftermath of the First World War, *This Happy Breed* addresses its audience in 1944, with the end of World War II in sight, as a people who have played their part in the public, international struggles during the extraor-dinary events of the war period. It suggests, however, that those same people must now return to their real concerns: the domestic, the everyday, the trivial. The film opens with a voice-over that states, documentary-style, that in 1918 "hundreds and hundreds of houses are becoming homes once more." The implication is that now, with World War II moving toward a close, the urgent task facing the "ordinary people" is, once more, home-making, replacing the family at the heart of the peacetime society and woman at the heart of the family.

Various members of the family do make occasional forays into the public arena, but this serves only to reinforce the effective separation of the public and the private. In the montage of the 1926 General Strike, Frank Gibbons appears as a strikebreaker, driving a bus. He justifies his participation by arguing that it is the precious stability of the nation that is under threat—as he says to his son, "it's up to us ordinary people to keep things steady." While this does show a member of the family participating in political struggle, it is significant that it is the male head of the household whom we see intervening; when this montage sequence of the strike dissolves back to the private sphere, a teapot is placed on an *Evening News* bulletin announcing the end of the strike, and the women are seen gossiping and doing the house work: Gran, speaking from the point of view of "Victorian values," roundly condemns the strike, Sylvia goes to wash some socks, and Mum clears the table. The strike is over, normal family life can resume—and the row that unfolds among the women at home is far more dramatic than any scenes of the strike itself.

Reg, Frank's son, and Sam, his communist-sympathizing friend, have meanwhile joined the strikers, but, in a number of ways, this involvement is marked as deviant within the film's dominant discourse. First, the views that we have of the strike are always from outside, from a distance—notably in a high-angle shot of a demonstration. Thus the spectators in the cinema are never placed by the camera as participants in the strike, but always as observers of it. Second, in conversation, Reg and Sam's involvement in the strike is dismissed as mere youthful hotheadedness. Third, there is a significant play on position and point of view when Frank Gibbons decides to have a talk about politics with his temporarily deviant son. In one shot, Dad explains with good common sense that problems arise from human nature, not from governments and systems; Reg is in the foreground, and Dad is visible only under his arm. Reg replies that human nature would change if everyone started with an equal chance, loses his temper, and sits down facing the camera, completely blocking out any view of his father: momentarily, his point of view, his position, wins the day. But then Dad continues, in very reasonable fashion; he stands up, so becoming once more visible, and the camera follows him as he moves away: it is his point of view that dominates. Finally, the two of them are resolved in shot together as authoritative father and once-more-deferential son. It is by devices such as these that difference is contained and the deviant reduced—or elevated—to ordinariness.

The next montage sequence (roughly 1927-29), we are shown the second daughter, Vi, at her wedding to Sam—in other words, the public manifestation of a private romance and the institutional means of containing Sam's communist excesses, transforming him into an "ordinary man." Later, Vi and Sam are shown visiting a cinema to see the latest "all talking, all singing, all dancing sensation," *Broadway Melody* (1929)—which serves to confirm the place of the spectator in the cinema watching *This Happy Breed* as the same as that of the "ordinary people" of the fiction: primarily spectators of rather than participants in the public arena.

In between these two moments, we do, however, see the erring daughter, Queenie, precisely participating in this public arena and in consequence being transformed herself into a spectacle: she is shown doing an exhibition Charleston with her current lover, a married man, having won a dance competition. The audience at the dance hall gaze at her, while the audience in the cinema are afforded the privilege of a soft focus close up of her as she takes pleasure in being the object of the gaze. It is this escape from the private claustrophobic insularity of the family into the exotic, glamorous—and now eroticised—public arena, this crossing of boundaries, that constitutes the extent of her transgression. But in the context of the rest of the film, this scene serves to label her pleasure as irresponsible and to confirm the dangers of entering the public arena and thereby leaving the safety and security of the home.

The overriding emphasis of *This Happy Breed* is a resolute separation of discourse and history: the series of montage sequences constitute an "objective," "real" history, a metadiscourse that places and processes the mundane discourses of the "ordinary people." The episodic narrative of the family consists mainly of gossip, reminiscence, uninformed and brief discussions of "public" events, family arguments, the occasional restrained love scene—in each case, within the film's terms, inconsequential trivia, mere discourse, in relation to the important and real events of a history over which they have no control.

There are of course occasions when explicitly political views are voiced within the confines of the domestic space, but the most outspoken of these occasions serves once again to underline the improbability of the public sphere having any real bearing on the private dramas of the family. The setting is Christmas 1925, and Sam, a communist at the time, is addressing the rest of the young people: it is a set-piece speech, both diegetically, in that he is standing up and speaking in knowingly formal terms, and in terms of the way it is constructed filmically. It is also a potentially powerful speech, noting in no uncertain terms the nature and extent of class difference in contemporary society. But this power is undermined in various ways. First, he is constantly interrupted by "trivial" and uninformed comments from the women present, the gist of which is that politics are irrelevant to the everyday. But second, his speech seems particularly melodramatic within a text that favors restraint: in its performance, it is too evidently a speech, it is obtrusive, rather than knitted into the discourse of the film, such that the *ordinariness* of the women seems much more the position of audience empathy. They are down to earth, where he is over the top. It is thus the (deliberate) obviousness of the performance that separates it out from the rest of the film as deviant.

Although the public events of "national significance" in *This Happy Breed* are presented as contemporaneous with the everyday experiences of the Gibbons family, they are represented as history to the spectators of the film. The particular form that this narrative of national history takes is typical of the public (re)presentation of national heritage, which, as Michael Bommes and Patrick Wright suggest, "appears to involve nothing less than the abolition of all contradiction in the name of a national culture: the installation of a spectacular display in which 'the past' enters everyday life" (Bommes and Wright 1982, 264).

The refusal to explore the class position or the gender relations of the ordinary people at the center of *This Happy Breed* is precisely this abolition of contradiction; at the same time, the difference between the quiet domesticated home and the lavish parade of public history for the cinema spectator serves to install "the past" as a spectacular display within the everyday:

> At the ideological level, "heritage" involves the extraction of history—of the idea of historical significance, process and potential—from everyday life and its re-staging and display in particular coded sites, images and events . . . In order to become spectacular, something which one can stand outside and then reconnect with in regular acts of appreciation—history must be completed and fully accomplished. As a process which is fully accomplished, history, with all its promise of future change and development, is closed down and confined entirely to what can be exhibited as the "historic past." (Bommes and Wright 1982, 289-91)

This is exactly the procedure that *This Happy Breed* adopts in order to impose a prewar vision of the nation, its people, and its political formation on the prospective postwar period. The public sphere has been absorbed into the popular culture of the ordinary people as another form of cinematic spectacle. But rather than this being the democratization of cinema, of public life, and of everyday life, it is instead the transformation of democracy into an image-commodity. The spectators of the film, far from being absorbed through it into the public sphere as participants, are offered a place precisely as spectators both of the national past and of contemporary politics. As *Today's Cinema* put it, "here, then, is memory-stirring spectacle and drama, all subtly introduced as backgrounds to the compelling domestic theme" (1944, 34). History as *aide-mémoire*, familiar and comforting, helps us to place the narrative of the family, but it is rarely of narrative significance in itself; rather, in the national past, national identity even, it exists as an exotic, compelling, fascinating spectacle.

WORKS CITED

Anderson, Benedict. *Imagined Communities: Reflections on the Origin and Spread of Nationalism*. London: Verso, 1983.

Anstey, Edgar. Rev. of *This Happy Breed*. *Spectator*, 2 June 1944, n.p.

Balcon, Michael. "The British Film During the War." *Penguin Film Review* 1 (Aug. 1946).

Barr, Charles, ed. *All Our Yesterdays: 90 Years of British Cinema*. London: BFI Publishing, 1986.

——— . *Ealing Studios*. London: Cameron and Tayleur/David and Charles, 1977.

——— . "Introduction: Amnesia and Schizophrenia," in Barr 1986.

Bommes, Michael, and Patrick Wright. "'Charms of Residence': The Public and the Past." *Making Histories: Studies in History-Writing and Politics*. Ed. Richard Johnson. London: Hutchinson, 1982.

Colls, Robert, and Philip Dodd. "Representing the Nation: British Documentary Film, 1930-1945." *Screen* 26.1 (1985).

Gledhill, Christine, and Gillian Swanson. "Gender and Sexuality in Second World War Films: A Feminist Approach." *National Fictions: World War Two in British Films and Television*. Ed. Geoff Hurd. London: BFI Publishing, 1984.

Higson, Andrew. "Addressing the Nation: Five Films." *National Fictions: World War Two in British Films and Television*. Ed. Geoff Hurd. London: BFI Publishing, 1984.

——— . "'Britain's Outstanding Contribution to the Film': The Documentary-Realist Tradition." *All Our Yesterdays: 90 Years of British Cinema*. Ed. Charles Barr. London: BFI Publishing, 1986.

——— . "Constructing a National Cinema in Britain," Diss. University of Kent at Canterbury.

Hurd, Geoff, ed. *National Fictions: World War Two in British Films and Television*. London: BFI Publishing, 1984.

Johnson, Richard, et al., eds. *Making Histories: Studies in History-Writing and Politics*. London: Hutchinson, 1982.

Lejeune, Caroline. Rev. of *This Happy Breed*. *Observer*, 27 Aug. 1944, n.p.; collated on microfiche at the British Film Institute.

Manvell, Roger. *Film*. Rev. ed. London: Penguin, 1946.

Nairn, Tom. *The Break-Up of Britain: Crisis and Neonationalism*. London: New Left, 1977; London: Verso, 1981.

Powell, Dilys. Rev. of *This Happy Breed*. *Sunday Times*, n.d., n. p. (probably 1944); collated on microfiche at the British Film Institute.

Stallybrass, Peter, and Allon White. *The Politics and Poetics of Transgression*. London: Methuen, 1986.

Today's Cinema, 28 Apr. 1944, 34.

Whitebait, William. "a." First review of *This Happy Breed. New Statesman*, 27 May 1944, n.p.; collated on microfiche at the British Film Institute.

——— . "b." Second review of *This Happy Breed. New Statesman*, 21 Oct. 1944, n.p.; collated on microfiche at the British Film Institute.

Winnington, Richard. Rev. of *This Happy Breed. News Chronicle*, 27 May 1944, n.p.; collated on microfiche at the British Film Institute.

CHAPTER SEVEN

THE DEMI-PARADISE AND IMAGES OF CLASS IN BRITISH WARTIME FILMS

Neil Rattigan

EVEN IF THE film itself did not make it manifest, it would be clear that *The Demi-Paradise*[1] was intended to be propaganda. It was made in a Britain fully engaged for some three years in "total war" and under conditions whereby all British films were, to some degree, "official" inasmuch as the Ministry of Information (MoI) had a whole network of statutory and bureaucratic controls that amounted to approval, direction, and supervision of all filmmaking activity. The film is determined to present an all-encompassing and unarguable perception of British national identity (assumed apparently unproblematically to be *English* national identity), and this is what it does without relaxing for its nearly two hours running time.[2] Given the time and the context of its production, the "overkill" in which the film indulges is explicable and forgivable, especially when one considers that as propaganda it was aimed at both a "domestic" audience and an American audience. For the American audience, the film hoped to create a positive image of Britain/England to encourage Americans to accept the importance and urgency of becoming engaged in the theater of operations and, subsequently, to maintain a positive image in the face of that engagement and the disruptive presence of millions of American servicemen in Britain.

It was a conscious determination of the ruling class, functioning through the MoI and other cultural institutions and structures not necessarily directly government or state, that the theme of a people's war be the dominant one during the war. Examining the reasons for doing so may bring us close to the "political unconscious"[3] and to the concept that the ruling class could not anticipate the subordinate classes' willingness to fight for Britain/England. This position was informed by the ruling-class "belief" that Britain/England "belonged" to them. In this sense, the ruling class definition of England *was* the "real" England. Thus, the ideology that functioned as an unconscious structuring principle in these films was one that defined England within terms that were (1) inherited from a set of perceptions of a mythical preindustrial England, (2) thoroughly imbued with the "natural" class order, (3) certain of the power of English civilization (an amalgam of 1 and 2) to which the existence of an Empire gave concrete evidence, and (4) equally certain that the true exponents and the living evidence of these principles was embodied in the upper and upper-middle classes as "classes" and in the individual members of those classes.

There is no doubt that *The Demi-Paradise* has little to say about and only slightly more to display of the working class. As in other films of the war such as *The First of the Few* (1942), such members of the working class as do exist within the diegetic world of the film exist only to enthusiastically carry out the policies of the enlightened owners of, in this case, the Barchester shipyards. One working-class character in the film, Tom, the attempting-to-be-upwardly mobile young assistant, dreams of a better social system along Russian lines. It is significant that Tom is a marginalized representative of the working class. He is seemingly moving up the social ladder and expresses his chagrin that he is forced by economic circumstances to stay put in his social milieu. If anything, Tom is an intermediary figure. He is a mediator between the workers (he asks Ann Tisdall, the shipyard owner's granddaughter, to give out the prizes as the workers' dance) and the employers (Tom also is the one who initially encourages the workers to even greater efforts to complete a ship being built for the Soviet government *after* the employers have given up). But the film does not endorse this attempt by a member of the working class to move out of his class position. Tom's valorization of the allegedly more egalitarian Russian society is made to look implicitly ridiculous. When he is introduced to the audience for the first time, Tom tells a working-class "brat" who is fiddling with Ann Tisdall's car to "get out of it," while Ann responds that it is "quite all right" and takes the kids for a ride. Tom's naive and possibly misinformed enthusiasm for Russia is both premature and, of course, wrong. Tom feels that things are unsatisfactory in England and he also feels that the existing political system cannot remedy the current situation. We *do* see later that the workers are enthused to express solidarity with "our Russian allies," but only after the lead is given first by Churchill and then by the Runalow/Tisdall family, who own the shipyard.

The film revealingly but incidentally shows some of the conditions of the working class—living in crowded, "slum" dwellings right next to the shipyards, kids playing in the streets—but it seems to accept this environment as natural and beyond comment. It also is silent some time later when bombs are falling on the shipyards during an air raid. Given the proximity of the workers' dwellings to the shipyards, surely some of the workers' homes have been hit. Everybody, workers included, are concerned only about the damage to the yards and the ships therein. Meanwhile at the semipalatial country home of the Runalows, somebody is playing the cello to the nightingales. Indeed, during the raid of the shipyards, a feigned sense of egalitarianism is produced when Runalow, despite his age and position, runs off to take part in the fire fighting. Runalow is slightly but genuinely injured by a bomb, while a nearby worker is "injured" by having one of his "corns" trodden on by a fellow worker.

From the very opening scenes of *The Demi-Paradise*, the working class is portrayed within the stereotyped roles and narrative and thematic functions inherited from prewar British cinema: as comic relief or comic sounding boards for the dominant ideology. Indeed, the two sailors limping into the Russian port quarters might have stepped out of the working-class community much admired by Richard Hoggart (1957), with their encapsulated working-class catchphrases—"Never mind. Makes a nice change any old 'ow"—having arrived by way of the West End theater. One might argue that these two working-class and/or regional "characters" serve to permit the comic exposure of English xenophobia, which for propaganda purposes the film is intending to reverse and deny without implicating the middle class in such a limited outlook. Even so, the film does later repeat this comic "discovery" of English xenophobia, seen now as understandable ethnocentricity rather than as racial superiority, through the character of Miss Winnie, a maiden aunt within the Tisdall family. "Russians spread things," says Miss Winnie with alarm when she learns that Ivan Kouznetsoff, an engineer sent to help with the construction of an icebreaker, is Russian. She hides in her room rather than eat at the same table. The film is constructed around narrative doubling: nearly everything happens twice. There are two visits by Ivan to England, two pageants, two visits to the same theater, two workers' dances, and so forth. The "conversion" of the working-class sailors to an understanding and appreciation of aliens who understand and appreciate *them* is doubled with Miss Winnie's conversion. Hers is, however, the more significant one. It leads to actual positive action: the "adopting" of Ivan's home town, Ninjni-Petrovsk, by the charity committee of the annual Barchester pageant. This annual pageant is of particular importance to the narrative. Although treated humorously, its particular view of *England's* glorious history is a direct representation of the upper-class interpretation the film itself is promoting. Miss Winnie's conversion is also given much more narrative "space" and thereby thematic or propagandistic importance.

It is not only the actual laboring classes that are given limited narrative space as comic relief. *The Demi-Paradise* is presumably intended to be a comedy, and audiences were expected to be amused as much by the representatives of the upper classes as by those of the lower classes, but in rather different ways. The working-class characters seldom have recourse within the diegesis to reinterpretations of their actions in the way in which the upper-class characters do. Representatives of the lower-middle class, fleetingly presented as they may be, are still important to the film's ideology and to its "need" to show all classes working together for the ideology of a people's war to be confirmed. Yet, although the workers seem to have a sense of a self-supporting community that exists parallel to the community that is the true focus of the film (specifically the irresistibly middle-class community of Barchester and the Runalow family as its admirable and admired metonymic symbol), the lower-middle class represents the meeting or touching point of the governing and the governed classes. To this extent, the lower-middle class is shown to be far more dependent upon the upper classes, not only economically but also in terms of authority and function. Two are especially important here: Jordan, the fussy, elderly clerk in the shipyard's London office, and Toomes, the Runalow's butler. Neither, significantly, seems to have a first name or, at least, is never referred to by one. Jordan is seen to be totally unable to cope with the arrival of Ivan, unable to make a simple decision, and then completely at the beck and call of Ann. Moreover, he describes Ann as "a nicer person you couldn't meet," although she has rudely ignored Ivan throughout—when she isn't insulting Russians generally. Jordan is rendered even more pathetic when he speaks at Hyde Park Corner: he is heckled by the crowd and has to be rescued by Ann and Ivan. Toomes is even less effective. On the night of the air-raid, when the nightingales are being broadcast from Runalow's garden, he directs an enquiry to his employer as to whether the participants should sleep under the stairs or the billiard table (only to be told to figure it out for himself, so to speak) and later has to be told by Runalow to turn out the lights before opening the curtains in the middle of an air raid. He also had no idea what a pageant is for—despite a working lifetime in which the Barchester pageant has taken place virtually under his nose in the grounds of the Runalow mansion.

While it is not true that the working class and the lower-middle class are unimportant to the ideology of the film, they are marginalized by its narrative. They are seen to be dependent to a greater or lesser extent upon the upper classes—for employment, for instruction in their duties, and importantly for leadership. But they have little part in the community that the film is intent upon presenting as a metaphor for and image of the living reality of England. There are no discernible members of the working class in the audience of the pageant nor, indeed, as participants in the "reenactments" that make it up. Indeed, it is noticeable that in the "crowd scenes," such as ones depicting the audience at the pageant or the workers at the address by a Russian delegate, their dance, and at the launching, the narrative/camera point of view changes to express differing points of view. The crowds at the launching, assembly, and ball are nearly always shot from a high vantage point; at the launching this is the visual "equivalent" of the point of view of the serried ranks of the upper class on the platform. However, the crowds at the pageant are shot from an eye-level position. Although there is a slightly more flexible set of viewpoints at the Hyde Park Corner sequence, throughout the film the lower classes tend to be literally rendered as being beneath the gaze of the camera in terms of the resultant cinematic image.

The film's dominant focus for its representation of the ideology of Englishness is on the upper classes. Surprisingly, given the uniformly patriotic tone of the film, there is not a little ambivalence expressed about this Englishness and, more specifically, about those whom the film equates with cultural centrality, those who represent the true English national identity—namely, the upper and/or upper-middle classes, the British bourgeoisie. There are no easily determined representatives of the aristocracy, and the gentry are, of course, represented by Runalow, who is a "self-made" member of the gentry. While making a determined effort to construct a unified and unifying monolithic image of the nation, *The Demi-Paradise* actually builds a few cracks into that very image as it does so.

George Orwell described Britain in the 1940s as

> resembl[ing] a family, a rather stuffy Victorian family . . . It has rich relations who have to be kow-towed to and poor relations who are horribly sat upon, and there is a deep conspiracy of silence about the sources of the family income. It is a family in which the young are generally thwarted and most of the power is in the hands of irresponsible uncles and bed-ridden aunts. Still, it is a family. It has its private language and its common memories and at the approach of an enemy it closes ranks. A family with the wrong members in control. (1968, 68)

Orwell's metaphor of the image of England as it reappears in *The Demi-Paradise* (devoid of the implication that "the wrong members [are] in control") was probably close to the way in which the upper class perceived Britain. The previous discussion of the representations of the working class in this film should perhaps give some sense of where they would fit into Orwell's "Victorian family." What of the others?

Runalow is the patriarch of the family in both senses of family: his immediate relatives and the closed community—middle-class rural village and dockyard slums. This familial structure is metonymically England within the film's diegesis—and the film's construction of his character places Runalow almost above reproach. Thus this paragon of capitalist virtue is able to deflect and defend himself from most of the reproaches that Ivan, in his function as "outsider," throws at him. It is interesting that he never really gives a positive answer to the questions that Ivan asks him on why he is a "big businessman." Runalow rather disingenuously denies obsession with wealth as being at the bottom of his actions, claiming in some strange logic by way of mitigation that the firm's motto of "Duty and Service" exempts him from interrogating the employer/employee structure he is at the pinnacle of. What is unspoken in this scene is the assumption that Runalow is "fit" to occupy the authorative position he does and that it is therefore "proper" that he does so. Thus, within the text of the film, Runalow represents the ideology of the proper or natural function of the upper classes, especially the upper-middle class since the Industrial Revolution.

The character of Runalow is constructed by and through the image of his being a paragon of everything that is good and fine about being English. Yet or perhaps because of this, his character is subject to interrogation by Ivan Kouznetsoff. Thus in the scene just referred to, Ivan, in his forthright, foreign way, challenges Runalow to justify his status and position as a capitalist. Each of Runalow's equivocal rationalizations leads only to a further undermining of his position by

Ivan. The scene "declines" to carry itself through to what seems to be another possible, if externally determined, conclusion, that Runalow is an unrepentant if benevolent capitalist/autocrat. This is prevented by the convenient expedient of the arrival of tea ("at once a beverage and a poem"). Given the film's ideology, it is unlikely to arrive at a conclusion that is critical of Runalow's societal position. Nonetheless, a fissure is present in the seemingly immutable ideology being provided in *The Demi-Paradise.*

Ann Tisdall, by her actions and her persona, comes much closer to the unacceptable face of the ruling class. She lacks this kindly feudalism of Runalow, and her possibly unconscious contempt for the working class, or indeed of anyone not of her class or circle, is revealed frequently. The way she treats both Jordan the clerk and Percy the office boy almost as "pets" is revealing, and it makes Jordan's praise of her even more pathetic. Her attitude is revealed particularly when she unfeelingly and unthinkingly dismisses her promise, or feudal duty, to present prizes at the workers' "Benevolent Fund Dance," preferring to have a night out in London at the theater with Ivan. This reflects just as badly on the workers as Jordan's sycophantic "a nicer person you couldn't meet," in suggesting that the workers are pathetically dependent upon "the guvnor's daughter" to grace their communal rituals.

The narrative is at some pains to distance itself from Ann's heartless behavior. Ivan criticizes Ann's callousness and suggests she apologize for it. Her response is to fall back into the sarcasm with which she has shown particular facility from her very first scene. Ivan's criticism is particularly fixed upon the claim that her "Lady Bountiful" act is just that—an act; her apparent "kindness" is nothing beyond mere condescension. It is possible to interpret this as meaning that Ann has not, unlike Runalow, fully absorbed the tenets of noblesse, or bourgeois oblige. The Runalow/Tisdall family are after all, by Runalow's own account, parvenus, so it cannot come as total surprise that some members do not have the appropriate behavior patterns of the governing classes fully "in the genes" as yet.

As a result of Ivan's lesson, she is able thereafter to display the proper upper-class behavior and attitudes in this regard—including presenting the prizes at the workers' dance at which she also intervenes (allied with Tom) to bring the situation of the need to put in extra efforts to complete the Russian icebreaker to the workers' attention and enthuse them to high achievement. Following the commencement of the war, Ann seems much more socially responsible. Ann works at the canteens at the shipyards, and it seems that she is responsible for taking in the two working-class evacuees. Mrs. Tisdall describes them to Ivan as "Ann's evacuees"—the possessive being rather disturbing. When Ann later joins the Wrens, she just leaves "her" evacuees with the family.

One might profitably consider the images of evacuees in this film and at least one other, *Went the Day Well?* (1942, Dir. Alberto Cavalcanti). The evacuation of hundreds of thousands of children, an overwhelming proportion of whom were working class, from the cities at the beginning of the war and again with the commencement of the blitz in the autumn of 1940 had considerable social repercussions, the effects of which are still a matter of debate among historians. These debates are not particularly pertinent here. What is relevant is that on the basis of the evidence of this film and *Went the Day Well?* it might be assumed that the upper classes took the greater part of the responsibility for housing and caring for the lower-class evacuees. Certainly no one else in Barchester or in Bramley Green (the village in *Went the Day Well?*) seems to have any evacuees other than the wealthy Tisdalls and the lady of the manor in Bramley Green, Mrs. Frazer.

The truth seems to be rather the opposite: lower-class families, in fact, took most of the burden of additional children into their already limited facilities, and there is considerable evidence to suggest that those who were better off and thus the more socially influential managed to avoid any responsibility in the matter (Turner 1961, 75-98; Calder 1972, 40-58; Marwick 1980, 217-19). What is important, then, is that most wartime films ignored the matter of evacuees and that those that did not fostered, deliberately as far as can be judged, a false image, one in which the upper classes comforted and succored the lower classes. There is more than an air of feudalism about this; a harking back to the middle ages when a baron's serfs would fly into the safety and security of the baron's fortified castle upon the approach of an enemy. It is intriguing that while nearly all wartime films scrupulously avoid any unnecessary fraternization between the classes, in these two films domestic or familial fraternization—of a carefully prescribed type—is shown favorably and in contradistinction to the observed facts, in the interests of showing the upper classes leading the way by example in the propaganda call for communal action.

In regard to the changes undergone by Ann Tisdall, *The Demi-Paradise* is rather ambivalent: are they the result of Ivan's critique? or are they part and parcel of the hidden qualities of English culture brought to the surface by the advent of war? Ann and Ivan are the only characters to change significantly, to develop through the course of the narrative. Ivan's critique of Ann is not an objection to the upper class as such; his questioning of Runalow's position as a capitalist employer is much more apposite in this regard. In the narrative "doubling" when Ivan repeats his visit to England, although the social structures are still intact, his criticisms have evaporated. Ann's failure to understand that higher or upper social position carries social responsibility to the lower orders does not challenge the basis of that social order—class distinction. The failure on Ann's part (as seen by the film) is to fully realize her allotted duties in and to the social order she inhabits.

This then points to the fact that Ivan is, as a fictional character in a fiction film (an "actant," or function of the narrative), an English creation. That is to say, his characterization within the narrative is not that of a "real" Russian and/or a "real" socialist.[4] The film is not concerned with propaganda on behalf of Russia or with promoting the official sleight of hand over Russia that had been adopted. Ivan is in fact a stalking-horse for the film's true perspective and its ideology. If he was constructed as a socialist and a Russian, he would be consistent and presumably feel the workers were much better off without the presence of the upper classes at their communal rituals. Ivan is set up as a socialist only in order to prove that the English social system is superior to foreign socialism. Ivan is therefore shown favoring Ann fulfilling her role as caring and concerned ruler/owner rather than rejoicing that she has revealed the true face of the class enemy. He is set up as a foreigner for a much more direct propaganda purpose as well: to indicate, as the last speech he makes so eloquently makes clear, that foreigners (i.e., Americans) do not understand the English, not because of what the English *are*, but because of what they *appear to be*. This was an important propaganda point for Britain in light of images of England—quite accurate ones—as class bound and "undemocratic," images that were widely accepted during this period the USA.

The character of Ivan is thus seemingly schizophrenic but is in fact consistent in terms of the ideology of the film. Even so, his criticisms of England, which are intended to provide an agenda by which the English national identity will be (re)constructed within the film, often have a resonance that cannot be adequately explained away as being the miscomprehensions of an outsider, a representative, in other words, of another and alien culture whose narrative function is to motivate the demonstrations of mythic Englishness the film is obsessed with. There are clear structural contradictions in this. Nearly all of Ivan's articulated objections or interrogations of the nature of Englishness, in both concept and practice, go unanswered by the film. The redressing of these criticisms late in the film—the climatic ship-launching sequence during which Ivan makes a speech in which he claims to now understand that the surface of Englishness is deliberately duplicitous (and in which the deeper layers of English culture are affirmed and confirmed)—does not effectively remove some of the validity of the original critique. This is the consequence of the narrative structure of "doubling" to which I have already referred. In essence, the film consists of two "acts," the second of which is a mirror image of the first, with one significant difference. In the first act, the very "Englishness" of the situation and the characters was a constant irritant to Ivan and a source of his "investigation" on behalf of the audience into the nature and condition of "Englishness." In the second act, these selfsame conditions of "Englishness" are embraced by Ivan as essential and sustaining. The war, off screen, serves as the only possible lens that has altered Ivan's perspective.

The Demi-Paradise seems, on occasion, to not fully believe in the strength of its own apparent convictions. Occasionally, it is surprisingly strident to the point of jingoism in ways that suggest satire. I cannot be the only one, surely, to find it difficult to fully comprehend the amazing scene of dinner at the Tisdall's home when Ivan's insistent questioning prompts some claims that can be explained only by reference to the need for this film to function as propaganda in America. In this scene, heated objections are raised to Ivan's claim that England has conquered half the world. It is difficult to accept or really believe a serious intent when Mrs. Tisdall replies, "Conquered? We never conquered anybody. We just happened to get there first." Here, it seems to me, the film is perhaps insufficiently aware of its own ideological position, confirming, perhaps, the unconscious nature of ideology. The film *does* know, in the final analysis, which side of the fence it stands on. It is the side of the fence that understands England to equal Britain and to equal a perception formed of an imagined, preindustrial past, which persists in some fashion into the present of the film. Inasmuch as industrialism intrudes into this cultural image of identity, it takes the form of enlightened paternalism that sees the new upper classes as the natural inheritors of the top of the preexisting social order.

The working-class ritual, the benefit dance, which Ann first blights by her absence but then the second time around, enhances by her presence, is, significantly, seen only once. The middle or upper-class ritual, the historical pageant, is a central component of the narrative doubling of the film. While on the one hand it is clearly meant to be comic, and is successful at that level, it also has considerable significance in the presentation of an image of England that is at once old-fashioned and quaint but also pertinent and firmly embedded in the English character. Thus Runalow, although he disparages it quite openly on both occasions, also attends it as its most prominent patron and provides the location for it to take place. Ridiculous ritual as it seems to be, the pageant is given enormous prominence in the narrative. It is at the first pageant that Ivan's accumulated distaste for English culture finally breaks out: he denounces it as "all piffles" and something done only because it has always been done. The film answers this challenge, not directly, but through the narrative doubling of another pageant, which Ivan again attends. This time he applauds tableaux that are no less ludicrous this second time around. He also takes part by accepting the money raised on behalf of Ninjni-Petrovsk.

To a spectator viewing the film nearly half a century after it was made, the two pageants seem high comedy. It is likely that contemporary audiences did not see them as quite so ludicrously unreal. Indeed, rather than some quaint custom of sleepy rural villages still somewhat lost in the past, it seems that pageants were considered vital and relevant aspects of British culture even during the war. Ronald Howard (1981), in his biography of his father, Leslie Howard, describes in detail a "national" pageant of almost epic proportions staged on the steps of St. Paul's Cathedral, London, in 1942 in which his father, along with a veritable Who's Who of the British stage of the time, took part. It is difficult not to equate almost exactly the Barchester pageants of *The Demi-Paradise* with his description of the historical pageant of 1942 and to conclude that, sent-up though they may have been, the pageants in the film were intended to serve something of the same propaganda-patriotic purpose as the real one on the steps of St. Paul's.

The Demi-Paradise is "about" a people's war without being about "the people," at least to the extent that, using knowledge external to the diegesis of the film, the people of England were not the upper-middle class. It is "about" the people to the extent that it is convinced, or it is trying to convince its audience, that the cultural and national identity of England is not merely implicated in but synonymous with upper-middle-class ideology. In any construction of the film's message as being, in part, *"we* are all in this together" the *"we"* is narrowly defined. Those whom the film cannot disguise, even if it tries, as "other," are thus encouraged to accept this *"we"* construction of British identity.

Ivan Kouznetsoff is the surrogate for those "others," be they foreigners or other classes in British society. The reason he is cheered at the end, as the recipient of a rousing chorus of "For He's a Jolly Good Fellow," is not because he is Russian or because he has solved the engineering problem of the propeller (the external narrative's nominal Macguffin) but because he has fully internalized the understanding of England in the film's ideological construction of it. Thus, the governing and governed, those who have the image, and those outside this image but exhorted to adopt it, cheer Kouznetsoff as one of the "we" the film so fervently embraces.

NOTES

1. *The Demi-Paradise.* 1943. Two Cities Films. Produced by Anatole de Grunwald. Directed by Anthony Asquith.

2. The extent to which there may have been a secondary propaganda purpose in presenting a sympathetic image of Russia and reversing the prewar negative image of the Soviet Union is confused by the selective and fairly inaccurate view provided. That the Soviet Union is referred to throughout as "Russia" and its inhabitants as "the Russian people" suggests deliberate attempts to activate the images of prerevolutionary Russia rather than the communist Soviet Union.

3. A term borrowed from Marxist literary/cultural critic Fredric Jameson (1981) that seems particularly apposite in this context.

4. The government and many of its ministries, including the MoI, were placed in an awkward position when the Soviet Union was invaded by Germany in 1941 because, while wishing to embrace the Soviet Union as an ally rather along the lines of the politically expedient adage, "The enemy of my enemy is my friend," they were almost paranoid about the possibility that support for the Soviet Union might mean an embracing by the greater British public of communism. Another example of the ruling class's failure to understand the lower orders and another example of the fear that the ruling class had of the lower classes. The solution the government adopted and the MoI put into effect was the rather schizophrenic concept that Russian and Communism were not the same thing, that the Soviet Union was engaged in a nationalistic rather than an ideological struggle, and that British support was thus from one country engaged in such a struggle to another similarly engaged (McLaine 1979, 186-216).

WORKS CITED

Calder, Angus. *The People's War: Britain 1939-1945.* New York: Pantheon, 1969. New York: Ace, 1972.

Hoggart, Richard. *The Uses of Literacy: Aspects of Working-Class Life with Special Reference to Publications and Entertainment.* London: Chatto and Windus, 1957; New York: Oxford UP, 1957.

Howard, Ronald. *In Search of My Father: A Portrait of Leslie Howard.* London: William Kimber, 1981.

Jameson, Fredric. *The Political Unconscious: Narrative as a Socially Symbolic Act.* Ithaca: Cornell UP, 1981.

Marwick, Arthur. *Class: Image and Reality in Britain, France, and the USA since 1930.* New York: Oxford UP, 1980.

McLaine, Ian. *Ministry of Morale: Home Front Morale and the Ministry of Information in World War II.* London: Random House, 1979.

Orwell, George. *The Collected Essays, Journalism and Letters of George Orwell.* Vol. 2. Ed. Sonia Orwell and Ian Angus. London: Secker and Warburg, 1968.

Turner, E. S. *The Phoney War on the Home Front.* London: Quality Book Club, 1961.

CHAPTER EIGHT

THE REPRESSED FANTASTIC IN PASSPORT TO PIMLICO

Tony Williams

This was a time, remember, when the expectations of a Labour government, which had been the whole perspective of my childhood, had been not just disappointed but actively repulsed: the priority of the military alliance with the USA over Labour's quite real achievements in welfare, the use of troops against groups of striking workers and so on. So the crisis for me was an early one.

—Raymond Williams

SPEAKING OF THATCHER'S 1987 reelection in one of his last interviews, Raymond Williams associates his 1947 disillusionment with those later periods of reaction in modern British history. The postwar Labour government's retreat from its initial optimistic promise was no isolated instance. Rather, it heralded a continuing feature within British society: a lack of nerve, that is, failure to advance into new horizons from the dead hand of the past, and a retreat into escapist nostalgia or brutal reaction. Both features characterized the Thatcher decade notable for its hegemonic management of the historical seen especially in the Falklands Conflict (Hurd 1984; Williams 1991). In such a situation the cultural becomes a formative material practice blurring rigid Marxist oppositions. As Raymond Williams argued in an influential essay, "we have to revalue 'determination' towards the setting of limits and the exertion of pressure, and away from a predicted, prefigured and controlled content. We have to revalue 'superstructure' towards a related range of cultural practices, and away from a reflected, reproduced, or specifically dependent content. And, crucially, we have to revalue 'the base' away from the notion of a fixed economic or technological abstraction, and towards the specific activities of men in real social and economic relationships, containing fundamental contradictions and variations and therefore always in a state or dynamic process" (1980, 34).

This definition can be usefully applied to the Ealing comedy *Passport to Pimlico* (1949). As the first of those universally loved exercises in national eccentricity, the film emerged in one of the harshest eras in the "age of austerity" during the first term of Britain's postwar Labour government (1945-51). Dealing with the unexpected opportunity of a London borough to escape the rigors of government rationing and claim independence, it exhibited a wish-fulfillment structure undeniably historically grounded. As scenarist T. E. B. Clarke stated, "At the time of *Passport to Pimlico* everybody wanted to share its characters' freedom from rationing and petty restrictions" (Barr, 1974, 96). However, critical examination tends to regard its nostalgic daydream structure as less preferable to the dark visions of Alexander Mackendrick and Robert Hamer. Such a view overemphasizes *Whiskey Galore* and *Kind Hearts and Coronets* to the detriment of a better understanding of the work of Henry Cornelius and Clarke within its social period. Despite Barr's historical approach to *Passport to Pimlico*, there are additional factors substantiating the work's importance. It is a cultural mirror of production, and it also contains several of the dark features Barr finds in the work of Mackendrick and Hamer. The film is an important hegemonic example of British culture and society of that era. Despite its artistic deficiencies, it is a mistake to neglect it in favor of the "tougher" visions of Mackendrick and Hamer.

Raymond Williams's redefinition of Marxist concepts he clearly found inadequate owes much to the work of Antonio Gramsci. A better understanding of social, historical, and cultural issues, essential for understanding any film within its cultural context, emerges. Within any society "in any particular period, there is a central system of practices, meanings and values, which we can properly call dominant and effective . . . the central, effective and dominant system of meanings and values, which are not merely abstract but which are organized and lived" (Williams 1980, 38). This hegemonic process is termed a "*selective tradition*" whereby certain ideas become the dominant norm or "common sense" and other are neglected or excluded. All selected educational, social, and cultural forces are thus "involved in a continual making and remaking of an effective dominant culture, and on them, as experienced, as built into our living, its reality depends" (Williams 1980, 39). Alternative and oppositional forms exist in different historical eras in varying degrees, either combating the dominant norm, as Freedman notes, or banished to the realm of nightmare and "bad taste" (the Hammer horror films).

In any era work may illustrate what Williams has termed a particular "structure of feeling." This notoriously elusive concept (see Williams 1977; Gorak 1988; O'Connor 1989) derived from Lucien Goldmann represents a social process, "a whole body of practices and expectations, over the whole of living . . . our shaping perceptions of ourselves and the world" (Williams 1977, 110). It is a term designed to avoid the reductionist abstractions associated with the older notion of ideology. The concept is thus applicable to both the structure and the content of a work within a particular social situation. Speaking of Goldmann's influence in "Literature and Sociology," Williams states that "it is just this element of organization that is . . . the significant social fact. A correspondence of content between a writer and his world is less significant than this correspondence of organization, of structure. A relation of content may be mere reflection, but a relation of structure, often occurring where there is no apparent relation of content, can show us the organizing principle by which a particular view of the world, and from that the coherence of the social group which maintains it, really operates in consciousness" (1980, 23).

Although Charles Barr does not mention Williams in his examination of *Passport to Pimlico*, he clearly sees it as exhibiting a particular "structure of feeling" in its historical context. The film is "an authentic response to certain forces in post-war Britain as experienced at Ealing," but lacking an appropriate form to accommodate a lack of drive, it represents a breakthrough into a "fantasy which deals with postwar Britain" (1977, 80). However, *Passport to Pimlico* resembles more a daydream than nightmare belonging to the postwar Ealing mainstream as opposed to certain films (most notably those of Mackendrick and Hamer) that "operate outside the mainstream, subtly undermining its norms without ever breaking free of the Ealing framework to the extent of offending the expectations of a loyal audience" (1977, 82).

Barr thus sets up a binary opposition between two groups of work whose qualities are really fairly diffuse and interrelated. Although a text may attempt to impose a monolithic containment, there may be traces of oppositional elements that oppose such a motion. Barr presents a problematic dualism between "daydream" and "nightmare." Although he uses psychoanalytic concepts in examining *Kind Hearts and Coronets*, there is little evidence of appropriate application in the case of *Passport to Pimlico*. Indeed, the rigid definition he sets up between "daydream" and "nightmare" is itself psychoanalytically questionable.

Boundaries between "daydream" and "dream" are fluid throughout Freud's work, certainly from his very early writings. In his classic analysis of Anna O., Freud (1974, 96) notes that daydreaming does not necessarily involve pathological factors; it can provide the ground from which more negative factors such as anxiety and dread can gain a foothold. His colleague Breuer commented that "If during a state of absorption, and while the flow of ideas is inhibited a group of affectively colored ideas is active, it creates a high level of intracerebral excitation which is not used up by mental work and is at the disposal of abnormal functioning, such as conversion" (Freud, 296). Freud's earliest collaborative work revealed to him that there was no rigid division between the daydream and an actual dream. Indeed, the unconscious operates in both conditions. He continued his investigations in *The Interpretation of Dreams*, describing the daydream as a "phantasy."

Phantasies are both conscious and unconscious, the latter having to "remain unconscious on account of their content and of their origin from repressed material. Closer investigation of the characteristics of these deceptive phantasies show us how right it is that these formations should bear the same name as we give to the products of our thought during the night—the name, that is, of our dreams. They share a large number of their properties with night-dreams, and their investigation might, in fact, have served as the shortest and best approach to an understanding of night-dreams" (1965, 530). Indeed, Freud finds the very same properties of the dream—work-wish-fulfillment, secondary revision concepts of condensation and displacement—active within the daydream. In his *Introductory Lectures on Psychoanalysis*, Freud comments that the daydream represents "scenes and events in which the subject's egotistic needs of ambition and power or his erotic wishes find satisfaction (1977, 98). If there is little difference between the daydream and nightdream, it may be possible to find the occurrence of the very nightmarish qualities of power and eroticism that Barr finds active, respectively, within *Whisky Galore* and *Kind Hearts and Coronets* also present in *Passport to Pimlico*. Freud further states, "A night-dream is at bottom nothing other than a day-dream that has been made utilizable owing to the liberation of the instinctual influences at night, and that has been dictated by the form assumed by mental activity at night. We have already become familiar with the idea that even a day-dream is not necessarily conscious—that there are unconscious day dreams as well" (373).

Although Freud's work is commonly criticized for universal and individualist tendencies, there are instances in which it shows an intuitive awareness of the impingement of historical forces. As a product of the imagination, the daydreams or phantasies "go along with the times, so to speak, and receive a 'date-stamp' which bears witness to the influence of the new situation" (98-99). Bearing these ideas in mind, we thus see an important approximation of the phantasy to the historical. This is, of course, similar to Rosemary Jackson's recognition of a fantastic text's relationship to its historical situation and the "number of forces which intersect and interact in different ways in each individual work" (9). However, with *Passport to Pimlico* we have a historically based text that appears, at first sight, to bear little relationship to the fantastic realm. For the latter to receive appropriate recognition it is thus necessary to understand the text in its historic period before commenting on its hidden fantastic components.

Like the general British public, Ealing studios shared in that brief period of postwar optimism following Labour's victory in the 1945 general election (Barr 1974, 103-16; Barr 1977, 50-79). But beneath the euphoria existed reactionary factors that would emerge both historically and culturally. In this regard Raymond Williams's work reflects a spectrum opposite to that of Edward Thompson. Whereas the latter concentrates on those historical periods of opposition and militancy, the former provides many cogent explanations for the blockage and frustration of progressive movements in certain historical eras (Williams 1977, 134-36; O'Connor 1989, 106). That early "brave new world" exhibited many of the tensions revealed in Robert Hamer's "Mirror" episode of Ealing's *Dead of Night* (1945). As Kenneth Morgan writes, "Britain's vision was more circumscribed than it appeared. It was the product rather of a preponderant mood of nostalgic nationalism, heavily anti-communist with escapist overtone . . . If Britain emerged in the years after 1945 as 'one nation', it was a feeling reached not only in accepted social collectivism at home but also in a spirit of complacent nationalism towards a wider world" (1990, 59-60). This was certainly true of accepting the implications of socialism as well as a broader cultural vision. Britain was still a polarized class society. During the 1947 period there occurred not only the negative features Williams described in his last interview but also political and social problems affecting Labour's aspirations. The 1947 summer that Barr sees as the period setting for *Passport to Pimlico* also witnessed a disastrous convertibility crisis. This followed one of the worst winters in recent British history, resulting in a crisis in fuel production and low national productivity. A decline in national unity began that would have adverse effects in the 1950 and 1951 general elections, the latter returning the Conservatives to power. As if these factors were not bad enough, 15 July 1947 saw a monetary crisis caused by conditions resulting from an American loan made in December 1945. This loan necessitated the conversion of the pound into dollars, causing financial instability until the scheme's suspension a month later. This was the first sign of Britain's developing economic dependence on the U.S.A. The concurrent economic crisis led to the resignation of Hugh Dalton, chancellor of the exchequer, in late November and his replacement by Sir Stafford Cripps (Morgan 1984, 334, 342-58). It is thus not surprising that these factors indirectly influence the narrative of *Passport to Pimlico* in several ways. In one scene, a dollar-sterling convertibility chart appears on the wall behind local bank branch manager Wix (Raymond Huntley). This appears immediately after he has declared independence from the main office following Pimlico's newly recognized status as a province of Burgundy. However, the film demonstrates that the inhabitants cannot handle real freedom. In an earlier scene, Wix's boss criticizes his initiative, "If we start giving a free hand to the manager of a minor branch we'll be in queer street. Head Office doesn't regard you as another Montague Norman." The climax of the film sees Whitehall bureaucrat Gregg (Naunton Wayne) applaud Wix's economic solution for returning Pimlico to Britain as "My dear fellow. A second Montague Norman!" Montague Norman was the interwar governor of the bank of England, one of the "ten guilty men" (others included Neville Chamberlain and Lord Halifax, the foreign secretary) condemned by left-wing critics for their role in the disastrous policy of appeasement as well as for covert activities resulting in the fall of the first Labour government in 1931 (Morgan 1984, 12, 89; 1990, 55). In this sense, the film's recuperation of business-oriented Wix into the fold and the expulsion of publican Garland as Ealing's traditional scapegoat is unconsciously ironic (Barr 1974, 102-4). Wix's acclamation, the film's "loss of nerve," and the circumstances resulting in Pimlico's "return to the fold" thus cast a dubious shadow over the film's structure. Rather than expressing a rational desire for independence, the Pimlico declaration has overtones of interwar isolationism. The nostalgic indulgence in the myth of wartime unity has thus negative aspects, both for Ealing in 1949 and afterwards (Hurd 1984). On the political level alone, the benevolent "daydream" has more nightmarish associations than appears at first sight.

Morgan further notes that "the crises of 1947 did nevertheless mark something like the end of an era. The wartime ethos and self-confidence had been seriously challenged for the first time. Britain, like the Labour government itself, felt under siege" (1990, 69-70). Pimlico's residents finally retreat from their independent status. Despite the circumstances leading to Pimlico's declaration as a province of Burgundy, their desires more resemble conservative isolationism rather than any conscious search for a new form of freedom. It is a regressive nostalgic recreation of wartime unity no longer relevant to the new social conditions of the postwar era. Ironically, the Pimlicans later come under siege from their own former government. Its leading figures are no Labour politicians but Whitehall bureaucrats personified by the upper-class figures of Basil Radford and Naunton Wayne. Morgan sees the summer of 1947 as representing the real end of the wartime spirit. The following years saw movements of consolidation and collectivist retreat from wartime ideals of unity and classless solidarity. Britain's growing dependence on American aid involved increasing defence expenditure, involvement in NATO, and eventual involvement in the Cold War philosophy leading to participation in the Korean War. At the same time an increasing climate of sexual repression followed a wartime period of sexual licentiousness. Although the immediate interwar years saw a baby boom, such births remained firmly within the traditional family marital context. For many, the rigid sexual taboos seen in *Brief Encounter* (1945) and Orwell's *1984* were a grim reality. James Hadley Chase's *No Orchids for Miss Blandish* caused a national outrage similar to that concerning the "video nasties" during the second Thatcherite government in the early eighties (Orwell 1971; Barker 1984). A 1984 parliamentary bill resulted in Britain becoming the most censored nation in Western Europe. Repression and cultural stagnation accompanied each other. "An official cult of sexual and cultural puritanism conflicted with the emergent consumer culture, impatience, or plain boredom of young people with a drab welfarised society, and an urge to create a land fit for consumers to shop in" (Morgan 1990, 96). We see these factors operating within the film in several instances. As John Ellis has shown, Ealing was not what we would consider a progressive studio. Its producers shared many ideas we would now find to be conservative. This was certainly apparent in a studio whose films honored ideological concepts of order and respect for one's elders (*The Blue Lamp*). Before Ealing discovered its popular formula, it experimented with different genres. *Saraband for Dead Lovers*, a neglected 1948 costume drama, is an important cultural text illustrating repressive ideological norms. Despite its box-office failure, it is a key work of morbid pathology exhibiting not only iron-clad concepts of sexual repression but also the dead hand of tradition stifling any revolt against the status quo. Indeed, the worlds of Hammer horror and traditional mainstream British cinema are not all that far apart. The Pembertons eagerly check their daughter's expressions of sexuality and independence whenever necessary. Mrs. Pemberton (Betty Warren) warns Shirley (Barbara Murray) about wearing her modest (by 1990s standards) sunbathing attire outside: "You don't go to the door like that!" During the siege conference, Pemberton (Stanley Holloway) curtly rejects Shirley's advice: "You keep quiet my girl. You're not even on this committee." British repression still continues in independent Burgundy. When Londoners invade Pimlico, eager to indulge consumerist yearnings in an era of rationing, the law-abiding Pembertons regard the influx with horror, speaking of it in terms more appropriate to other generic movies (crime; horror). Mrs. Pemberton rails at the "invasion": "In the meantime nobody cares if we get our throats cut." Mr. Pemberton appeals to Inspector Bashford (Michael Hordern): "We're entitled to police protection." Ealing thus views the market economy with distaste. Inhabitants of Pimlico call a "Clean Up Burgundy" Meeting, its clarion call having, from a nineties perspective, undeniable associations with moral majority outcries against seventies sexual representations as well as regarding the economic invasion in terms similar to Count Dracula's incursion into Hammer's village communities. As the police cordon off the area, Pemberton regards all the interlopers as crooks. He refuses to recognize the ordinary person's desire to briefly escape the rationing rigors of postwar Britain: "At last. Action at last. Order at last. That'll keep the spivs out." A daydream yearning for independence from wartime restrictions thus becomes a nightmare.

This cultural intertextual structure appears throughout the film. Although the dark aspects are not as strong as in the films of Hamer and Mackendrick, they are nevertheless present in a work whose semiotic structure of meaning involves repression and retreat. After the film's opening credits, we see a wreath surrounding rationing books above the caption, "Dedicated to the memory of." The opening scene shows us the bomb-scarred Miramont Place area of Pimlico. Then the camera tracks back into a darkened room. A then unidentified man (Wix) opens the blinds and looks out. This opening image is important. It is one of three tracking movements in the film beginning with a view of the outside before the camera removes itself retreating back into a darkened room. This signifier of retreat, present in the opening image, is a visual signifier for the whole's film retreat trajectory. From the very opening scene we obtain a feeling of withdrawal, a refusal to consider the implications of a situation ideologically coded as a negative. Ironically, when Pemberton falls into the pit caused by the unexploded bomb, his first reaction is to withdraw rather than explore. The camera tracks out as Pemberton ascends. It is the younger generation (children playing) who cause the explosion and stimulate Pemberton to investigate the situation again. Naturally, the film presents children as being as under the firm control of their elders so that no real progression is possible. The second retreating tracking shot again shows us the bombed landscape. This time it leads us into the darkened room of PC Spiller (Philip Stainton), Pimlico's representative of law and order. It leads to his discovery of a black market operating openly in Pimlico, where trader's posters ("Forget that Cripps Feeling") openly proclaim freedom from rationing restrictions. Preceding this sequence is the public house celebration scene where the Pimlicans celebrate their independence by tearing up their ration cards, ignoring official licensing hours, and engaging in a "Knees Up Mother Brown" communal dance. However, it ends with the camera tracking back from the pub door surrounding the inside celebration with outside darkness. It is almost as if Ealing casts a disapproving cinematic apparatus eye over the whole proceedings. To the right of the frame an unidentified couple kiss in the darkness, an act impossible to achieve in the daylight of Ealing normality. Even this economic celebration has a dark underside, the sexual being an overdetermined site for representing unwholesome desire. Naturally, the next morning sees the Pimlicans awake from their achieved wish-fulfillment desires to confront the realities of their independence, both economic (free trading, even on Sundays) and sexual ("Nylons, genuine silk nylons"). In this era, nylons had a sexual attractiveness, due to their general unavailability for postwar females. Postwar "nice girls" simply accepted rationing restrictions for the common good. They certainly *would* not wear silk nylons! In the opening scenes of the film, Edie (Hermione Baddeley) and Mollie (Jane Hylton) conspire over evading rationing restrictions for more attractive clothes. They both immediately cease talking when PC Spiller enters. The later introduction of the Parisian "New Look" was condemned in some quarters as involving an overindulgent use of dress fabric. Dark overtones of sexuality are not entirely absent from the text. They are not simply confined to that Ealing *enfant terrible* Robert Hamer. The third retreating camera movement involves the Duke of Burgundy (Paul Dupuis), heir to Pimlico. Due to the charter proclaiming Pimlico as part of Burgundy territory he is in a position of power similar to that of Wix and Spiller, combining in his persona the authority governing finance and law. However, his arrival (as well as his insipid portrayal) presents no European threat of the sexually potent Frenchman to Ealing customs. He becomes simply part of the scenery and is forgotten at the climax. The studio had a firm tradition of removing sexual connotations from the foreign actors it occasionally employed (Simone Signoret, Françoise Rosay).

However, the sexual as the overdetermined site of dark repressed forces does exist within *Passport to Pimlico*, presenting claims that one should regard the film in the same nightmarish light as is found in the works of Mackendrick and Hamer. This is especially so in the opening scenes following the first tracking back camera movement. A very un-British heatwave has occurred. The audience would immediately think of the summer of 1947. We see individual shots of female sunbathers, a rare incursion into sexual voyeurism for Ealing studios. Following shots show Miramont Place. An overhead shot pans right showing citizens and a lone "jogger," who at that time is a figure of eccentricity in a Britain that is not exercise conscious. The camera then tracks into the overhead canopy of a fish and chip shop owned by Frank Huggins (John Slater). Molly puts an overall over her bathing suit and joins Frank. During this sequence, a radio has played Latin American music, usually regarded as foreign and sensual in Britain's insular culture. However, this connotation is undercut. An announcement states the source to be "Les Norman and his Bethnal Green Bambinos" (a play on the Ealing director, Leslie Norman and the Jewish area of London). This is a particular studio enunciative strategy whereby any possible extension into taboo area of otherness and sexuality becomes immediately undercut and repressed by humor. As Shirley arrives, Frank immediately begins a play toward her, to Molly's chagrin. He tempts her with a fish: "It's a treat to see it again. The Bron." Frank's strategy has definite connotations immediately recognizable to the audience of that period. During 1948, rations had fallen far below the wartime average. Once obtainable items, such as dried egg, fish, cheese, fruit, and bread, became either scarce or nonexistent. Things became worse during the food shortages following the bad winter of 1947. To relieve British discontent, the government introduced substitutes such as whalemeat and snoek, the latter being a species of barracuda (Cooper 1963, 51-52). Frank's ploy is a seductive move toward the ration-stricken Shirley. His final words, "I'll pack it in with a nice bit of cream," delightfully escape Ealing censorship.

Workmen are digging a pit searching for an unexploded bomb, "the last one left from the war." The radio reports the name of the bomb as "Pamela." An issue of the *Daily Express* reporting the heatwave floats down to the workmen below. Behind them on the wall is a prominent female pin-up. It still remains (torn) after the bomb's explosion. These scenes occur well before the opening that Barr describes when he says that the "film opens with Arthur Pemberton putting before the Borough Council his lovingly prepared scheme for recreational use of the ground by the people of the neighbourhood" (1977, 98). The film certainly creates "a blend of fantasy and realism, and of wartime and postwar feeling" (1977, 81) but beneath the manifest text of "the daydream of a benevolent community" lurks something else. The text is really one more of tension than of leisure. It strains to hold back forces that will emerge with full vehemence in Hammer films of the fifties.

The dark pit is the counterpart of the mirror of *Dead of Night*. It contains forces and information that the ordinary citizen would rather deny. In 1957 the pit would play a more crucial role in Rudolph Cartier's BBC TV production of Nigel Kneale's *Quatermass and the Pit*, where the contents of an excavation can no longer be avoided, repressed, or treated with Ealing humor. *Passport to Pimlico*'s pit contains information as devastating to the British character as the Martian spaceship in the Quatermass production. Pimlico is not British. It is Burgundian. Within the pit is no mental force aiming to transform the British character but a charter granting the inhabitants freedom from the restrictions, repressions, and petty restrictions of post-war Britain.

Even the Duke of Burgundy presents no foreign sexual threat to the community. As portrayed by Paul Dupuis, he is no virile presence. In Ealing films, the Frenchman is either represented as a comic character (Eugene Deckers) or as a figure of tedious normality. His nighttime attempts to romance Shirley are respectively defeated by Ealing's "comic" defensive strategies of disruptive cat, gargling man, and Pemberton's call interrupting their kiss.

Within the dark pit is a portrait of the Duke of Burgundy. It represents an overdetermined mode of signifier within the text structuring the failure of Pimlico independence. Both the charter of independence and its representative are unacceptable "others" for Ealing's British way of life. The duke's portrait uncannily resembles that of Richard III, last king of the House of York, in the National Portrait Gallery. This monarch was not only a significant representative of a "loser" dynasty in British history but also one who signified in popular consciousness a monstrous sexual beast, the destroyer of communal bounds—in other words the Count Dracula of his era. Despite historical uncertainty (Dockray 1988; Horrox 1989) about his real significance, Tudor historical propaganda and Shakespeare's play would dominate popular understanding of Richard. Furthermore, although Laurence Olivier was on tour in Australia playing Richard during 1948, memory of his 1944 triumphal stage performance (filmed in 1955) would still be fresh. He revived the production during March 1949, a month before the release of *Passport to Pimlico* (Barker 1984; Harwood 1971; Darlington 1968; Hirsch 1979; Kiernan 1981; Bragg 1984; Tanitch 1985; Olivier 1986; Holden 1988). Olivier became *the* evil Richard III of his generation. Professor Hatton-Jones (Margaret Rutherford) describes the circumstances of the Burgundy charter (granted by the Yorkist king Edward IV) and the supposed death of the duke in terms necessitating a revision of traditional accounts of Richard's death. Supposedly killed in battle ("This poor naked body robbed by harpies, bitten by wolves") the duke actually escaped and survived. In this dark parallel to the Arthurian legend, not only has personal history to be rewritten, but also the history of national origins. "Blimey! I'm a foreigner!"

An alternative thus presents itself to a portion of England, one that will not be realized. This Richard III association is by no means an accidental one either for Ealing or for T. E. B. Clarke. One of the earliest Ealing films was *Jane Shore* (1915), featuring Richard, duke of Gloucester (later Richard III) as a supporting character (Low 1949, 206, 212-20). In T. E. B. Clarke's screenplay for *The Lavender Hill Mob* (1951), Stanley Holloway's frustrated artist, Pendlebury, who now propagates "British cultural depravity" has created a bust of himself as Richard III. Richard appears as a signifier for Pendlebury's "what might have been." Pendlebury quotes, "Of all words of tongue and pen—The saddest are these—It might have been . . . me." Mimicking *Richard III*, he intones "Slave. I have set up my life as a cast"—pointing out the moral of his bust to Holland (Alec Guinness)—"I believe it will turn into a self-portrait—the slave." Like *Passport to Pimlico, The Lavender Hill Mob* is a film of a lost alternative—freedom from British stagnation and creative frustration. But the structure of feeling in both cases is one of blockage. In the opening of *Passport to Pimlico*, the 1947-influenced heatwave reminds us of the opening line of *Richard III*—"Now is the winter of our discontent made glorious summer by this sun of York." However, the real sun of independence waits beneath a dark pit waiting for those who will appreciate it. This does not happen. The final image we see of the duke of Burgundy is that of his portrait hanging above a public house, scene of the Pimlicans brief celebration of liberation from postwar austerity. As the rain falls, ending both the heatwave and Pimlico independence, so does the temperature and the duke's portrait. Repression has once again returned to a cinematic text exhibiting classic tendencies of that negative structure of feeling affecting British society. Despite its surface joviality and lack of seriousness, *Passport to Pimlico* has thus compelling claims to be considered along with the works of Mackendrick and Hamer, not below them.

WORKS CITED

Barker, Felix. *The Oliviers*. London: Hamish Hamilton, 1953.

Barker, Martin, ed. *The Video Nasties: Freedom and Censorship in the Media*. London: Pluto, 1984.

Barr, Charles. *Ealing Studios*. London: Cameron and Tayleur/David and Charles, 1977; Woodstock, NY: Overlook, 1980.

———— . "Projecting Britain and the British Character: Ealing Studios Part I." *Screen* 15.1 Spring, 1974: 87-121.

Bragg, Melvyn. *Laurence Olivier*. London: Hutchinson, 1984.

Cooper, Susan. "Snoek Piquante." *Age of Austerity*. Ed. Michael Sissons and Philip French. London: Hodder and Stoughton, 1963. 33-54.

Darlington, William Aubrey. *Laurence Olivier*. London: Hazell Watson and Viney, 1968.

Dockray, Keith. *Richard III: A Reader in History*. Gloucester, Gt. Brit.: Sutton, 1988.

Eagleton, Terry. *Raymond Williams*. Boston: Northeastern UP, 1989.

Ellis, John. "Made in Ealing." *Screen* 16.1 Spring, 1975: 78-127.

Freedman, Carl. "England as Ideology: From 'Upstairs Downstairs' to *A Room with a View*." *Cultural Critique* 17: 79-106.

Freud, Sigmund. *The Interpretation of Dreams*. New York: Signet, 1965.

———— . *Introductory Lectures on Psychoanalysis*. New York: Norton, 1977.

Freud, Sigmund, and Josef Breuer. *Studies in Hysteria*. Vol. 3 of the *Pelican Freud Library*. London: Penguin, 1974.

Gorak, Jan. *The Alien Mind of Raymond Williams*. Columbia: U of Missouri P, 1988.

Gramsci, Antonio. *Selections from the Prison Notebooks*. Ed. Quintin Hoare and Geoffrey Nowell-Smith. London: Lawrence and Wishart, 1970.

Harwood, Ronald. *Sir Donald Wolfit*. New York: St. Martin's, 1971.

Hirsch, Foster. *Laurence Olivier*. Boston: Twayne, 1979.

Holden, Anthony. *Laurence Olivier*. New York: Athenaeum, 1988.

Horrox, Rosemary. *Richard III: A Study of Service*. New York: Cambridge UP, 1989.

Hurd, Geoff, ed. *National Fictions: World War Two in British Film and Television*. London: BFI Publishing, 1984.

Jackson, Rosemary. *Fantasy: The Literature of Subversion*. London: Methuen, 1981.

Kiernan, Thomas. *Sir Larry: The Life of Laurence Olivier*. New York: Time Books, 1981.

Low, Rachel. *The History of the British Film: 1914-1918*. London: Allen and Unwin, 1949.

Morgan, Kenneth. *Labour in Power: 1945-1951*. New York: Oxford UP, 1984.

———. *The People's Peace: 1945-1989*. New York: Oxford UP, 1990.

O'Connor, Alan. *Raymond Williams: Writing, Culture, Politics*. New York: Blackwell, 1989.

Olivier, Laurence. *On Acting*. London: Weidenfeld and Nicolson, 1986.

Orwell, George. "Raffles and Miss Blandish." *The Collected Essays, Journalism and Letters of George Orwell. Vol. 3*. Ed. Sonia Orwell and Ian Angus. London: Penguin, 1971. 246-60.

Tanitch, Robert. *Olivier: The Complete Career*. New York: Abbeville, 1985.

Williams, Raymond. "Base and Superstructure in Marxist Cultural Theory." *Problems in Materialism and Culture*. London: Verso, 1980. 31-49.

———. "Literature and Sociology." *Problems in Materialism and Culture*. London: Verso, 1980. 11-30.

———. *Marxism and Literature*. London: Oxford UP, 1977.

Williams, Raymond, and Terry Eagleton. "The Politics of Hope: An Interview." *Raymond Williams*. Ed. Terry Eagleton. Boston: Northeastern UP, 1989. 176-83.

Williams, Tony. "Remembering and Forgetting History: *The Ploughman's Lunch*." *Jump Cut* 36, 1991.

CHAPTER NINE

REVISION TO REPRODUCTION: MYTH AND ITS AUTHOR IN *THE RED SHOES*

Cynthia Young

THOSE WHO HAVE reviewed the relatively small number of works relating to the films of Powell and Pressburger cannot fail to note the attention that film scholars have also given to these artists' own critics—those writing for film in the 1940s. They were many and vocal, and, for the most part, their responses were skeptical or openly dismissive. But as several critics have suggested, within the textual discourses of Powell and Pressburger's films there exists an ongoing dialogue with the reviewers of their day. For example, John Ellis explores the highly sophisticated manipulation of time as it affects the "realism" of *A Matter of Life and Death* (1946). He suggests that the narrative "seems to begin to criticize the whole equation between cinema and reality that is a tenet of so much British film-making and criticism alike" (Ellis 1978, 79).

The reception of *The Life and Death of Colonel Blimp* (1943) had been even more tepid, if not hostile. Produced during the war years, it provoked those critics and government officials who were setting guidelines for entertainment form and content, guidelines sanctioning methods of propaganda as a laudable means of raising the national spirit. Ian Christie observes that "while incorporating distinct propaganda moments within *Blimp*'s textual scheme, it sets these in play against the relative autonomy of the 'entertainment film'" (116). Hence we can assume that both *A Matter* and *Colonel Blimp* provide a context within their narrative schema whereby critical and government "voices" as well as the expectations of the mass audience are *reproduced* and investigated. In fact, these discourses are woven so intricately into the fabric of the texts, creating pressures, tensions, and contradictions, that it seems impossible to identity any particular ideological principle in the art of Powell and Pressburger.

These "dialogues" themselves are clearly a preoccupation insofar as they are present in the narrative content, but Powell and Pressburger also locate their narratives within a distinctive form. In their films, content and style are wedded in a manner that typically evokes the mythic and the fantastic, characteristically raising the films to the level of spectacle while inviting the spectator to consider the role of myth as a mode of communication or, more important, as a means of persuasion.

As readers of Roland Barthes are aware, myth is a powerful tool for subtly reinforcing the cultural, political, and artistic ideologies to which myth, as an empty yet recognizable form, is especially vulnerable. Added to the claim that myth makes upon reality are the systems of repetition and reproduction that perpetuate myth. Feminist and poststructuralist theories find this activity prevalent in all forms of discourse—the primary medium of reproduction—and the classic realist film is especially prone to the lure of reproduction as it both determines and results from the narrative mode.

Nowhere is the process of discourse reproduction more evident than in Powell and Pressburger's *The Red Shoes* (1948). Over its dramaturgy there always hovers those "myths" that were solidified into "fact" by film reviewers of the 1940s. Their concern was for the quality film. It must be realistic, unified, logically ordered. It must evince a sense of propose. It must appeal to the aesthetic taste yet provide enjoyment. But above all, its art, its controlling principles, its genius, must remain invisible beneath its "overall flow" (Ellis 1978, 28). In short, we might say that, above all, the quality film must not be modernist or anti-realist. It must not carry on a discourse with itself at the audience's expense, nor may myth be allowed to disturb its pastiche of "real life."

In *The Red Shoes* myth does not merely serve as an element of concept or structure; it is established from a union between the two and emerges as theme. In its presentation of myth through the fairy tale form, the film's discourses demonstrate how our artistic and cultural "texts" are reproduced, or "revised," beneath the guise of the "normal." By focusing on the effects of cinema, stage, and performance, Powell and Pressburger explore the manner in which mythic texts participate in a production of meaning that can influence the subject's relationship to an essentially patriarchal community.

Roland Barthes designates myth as a "semiological system," a "metalanguage" "whether verbal or visual" (1957, 111). And, accordingly, its most significant feature is its form, which constitutes a "second order semiological system" (114). In other words, a myth carries the signification imprinted upon a sign (the product of the first order of signification), yet the sign itself, by long usage, has already lost its meaning, its content, and its "history." In consequence, this sign is empty and infinitely adaptable to whatever ideological message one cares to convey by it. Yet its form misleads because it is recognizable—it reassures. The signs of myth become "innocent and indisputable" (118). They become fact or Nature.

The fairy tale, by its very form, its very history, serves as a second-order semiological system. How could it be otherwise when we know that a single tale, its original intent often forgotten or discarded, is revised over and over again, as its particularly open form is adapted to the sentiments of each passing generation. The

tales of the Brothers Grimm provide the most obvious example of this phenomenon. D. L. Ashliman has observed that many of these tales had originally represented female desires and the triumphs of these desires over patriarchal control.
However, the Grimms "reversed" (or revised) the narrative content so that females
were punished for their transgressions. Furthermore, these revisions were often
used as standard tools of instruction in nineteenth-century German schools (Ashliman 1986, 193). The moral codes that they outlined were accepted as fact.

We can only conclude, therefore, that a tale's content is infinitely nego-
tiable, that it is the narrative *structure*, or basic "plot," that never changes. And this
structure is based solely on the principle of transgression. Whether a male or
female, a youth pursues his or her desire by means of an itinerary of rebelliousness
that poses a threat to the conventions and ideologies of the community. But it
should be noted that there is almost always a return to community order at the
tale's conclusion. Hence, the fairy tale is both a site of transgression and a "safe
form" (Jackson 43). As readers, we may indulge in these transgressions—safely.

In *The Red Shoes*, a film that evokes myth and the fairy tale throughout,
Powell and Pressburger explore this process of revision, or reproduction, while
repoliticizing the "factual" language of myth: those discourses that reaffirm sanc-
tioned ideologies and tie men and women to the essentially repressive codes of a
patriarchal community.

The film's basic organizational principle relies on a play upon the concepts
and structures that determine the fairy tale form. Furthermore, the form itself
appears to operate at three distinct levels of revision (or reproduction), each level
carrying its own unique mythic signification. But these levels continually overlap
in a distinctively recursive mode, calling attention to a motif built from fairy tale
references, allusions, and images, creating a tension between the escapism that the
form provides and the realism to which it pretends.

The first level of revision in *The Red Shoes* seeks to replicate the essential
narrative structure or plot-line of the traditional fairy tale, a strategy that closely
approximates what Barthes calls "mythifying myth" (1957, 135). He asks, "since
myth robs language of something, why not rob myth?" In other words, why not
"mythify" a myth by appropriating its rhetoric and creating a second, or "artificial," myth. Barthes says that "the power of the second myth is that it gives the first
its basis as a naivety which is looked at" (135). In other words, the rhetoric of the
original myth is forced to expose itself as such. In *The Red Shoes* this process is
effected through the appropriation of ideological rhetoric at multiple levels of
narrative reproduction.

It is the rhetoric of the traditional fairy tale, the somewhat saccharine, but
pleasing, convention of the happy-ending plot that is revised into the modern
melodrama that serves as *The Red Shoes'* most obvious level of reproduction.
Julian Craster (Marius Goring) and Vicky Page (Moira Shearer), both artists (and
both British), abandon their home (land) to pursue their fortunes under the tutelage

of the ballet Lermontov. First, Julian and Vicky must earn their way into the company—Vicky by means of her aunt's maneuverings and Julian by virtue of his aggressive persistence. After they both endure a series of trials and hardships, Lermontov rewards them with primary roles in the creation of the Red Shoes Ballet. Lermontov (Anton Walbrook), as the film's dialogue reminds us, plays the part of "father" to the company's "children."

Already it is apparent that this surface narrative has demarcated the means to success along the lines of sexual differentiation, just as does the conventional fairy tale of the nineteenth century. Whereas Julian enters the company as assistant to the conductor, Vicky wins her place as prima ballerina through obedience, subservience, and compromise. Her personal itinerary is analogous to that of Cinderella's. This famous fairy tale heroine falls from a station of privilege to one of drudgery, and her patience and ability to serve are tested by abuse and hardship until she is finally rewarded with marriage.

Similarly, Vicky Page, a London debutante, is not only treated with indifference by the members of Lermontov's company, but throughout the first half of the film the narrative concentrates upon her relatively unimportant place there. It is in accordance with the rhetoric of the fairy tale that she be shown stripped of her upper-class distinctions: she works assiduously at the barre—one among many other hopefuls, just as she must ask for permission before dancing a part at the Mercury Theatre. Ostensibly, Vicky's "reward" takes the form of the primary part in the Red Shoes Ballet, a reward that would both affirm her individual selfhood and confirm her triumphant passage of initiation. However, at this level of narrative reproduction, the special action of the film apparatus joins with the structure of the fairy tale form to privilege the love and romance plot *instead*.

The effects of the film apparatus are evident in the film's opening scene, and the initial pattern that it establishes adds to the sense that *The Red Shoes'* narrative movement will be one of continuity—the kind of unified structure so admired by the 1940s critic. When the film opens in the interior of London's Covent Garden Theatre, Vicky and Julian are strangers, just as they will remain until roughly midway into the film. Both occupy different positions in the theater, and as the performance of the Heart of the Ballet begins, the camera movement is initiated by Julian's gaze as he watches the members of the orchestra below. But quickly the focus of the camera's interest cuts to Dr. Palmer and Lermontov's position and then to Vicky's. Finally, shots cut back and forth between Vicky and Julian while Lermontov's position serves as the central locus.

This rapid alternation of shots sets up a network that intricates Vicky and Julian in the type of logic that is essential to the rhetoric of the fairy tale—that of cause and effect, a form that Barthes describes as Natural (1957, 132), myth masquerading as destiny. Thus, as the narrative proceeds from the first scene, the relationship represented in the alternation of shots generates a sense of imminent fate. We expect these two young people to meet and marry. They do, of course, but

The Red Shoes does not culminate in a "happy ending." The logic of fate and destiny in this first level of reproduction will be interrupted by a seemingly endless play of repetitions, all pointing to the myths that are played and replayed in the classical realist text. As Barthes asserts, "it is the insistence of a kind of behavior which reveals its intention" (120). Hence, each consequent level of reproduction becomes the "naivety which is looked at"—a mask peering at its own reflection.

Because myth confirms a "natural order," one might expect it to close off discourse. However, Barthes insists that "myth does not deny things, on the contrary, its function is to talk about them; simply it purifies them, it makes them innocent, it gives them a natural and eternal justification" (143). In *The Red Shoes'* first level of reproduction the "natural and eternal justification" of love, romance, and the happy ending appear to dominate the narrative. The traditional love story insists upon its innocent realism, relying upon discourses that promote the sovereignty of the heterosexual union. But at the second level, Powell and Pressburger emphasize the production of the very texts (librettos, scores, dances and operas) that justify masculine logic. More specifically, the textual revisions in *The Red Shoes*, both diagetic and nondiagetic, locate and emphasize the act of patriarchal authorship, an act that perpetually "re-writes" the subject according to its logic of repression. This second level looks at the reproduction of the text that constitutes the subjects' place in the social order. Psychoanalytic theorists call this the "Symbolic Order," or the "Law of the Father."

As Lacanian analysis has demonstrated, the entry into the Law of the Father is conditional upon the subject's recognition of himself as "other." This process is inaugurated by the child's sudden awareness of error—that he and the mother are not joined as a unified and omnipotent being but that, rather, he is subject to her control, that she may disappear and reappear according to *her* will.

According to Lacan, the child discovers game playing as a compensation for his lack of control, comforted by the ability to hide things himself and conjure their reappearance. Finally, language enters into this process as the eventual correlates of his own enunciations as they accompany the game. As Nelly Furman in "The Politics of Language" explains:

> The child's verbalizations and game-playing enact his frustrated desire for his mother and his anticipated pleasure at her eventual return. Symbolically, language stands in lieu of the absent mother and is equivalent to her death: [Quoting Lacan] "the symbol manifests itself first of all as the murder of the thing, and this death constitutes in the subject the eternalization of his desire." (1985, 72)

This theory attempts to explain the correspondence between language as a mechanism of control and the view that discourse excludes women from the sources of power, just as it seeks to locate her as "difference." As outlined by the Bellourian school of psychoanalytic criticism, texts, particularly the classical realist text, found their narratives upon woman as sign, the "other," who as original site of power provokes both desire and the fear of castration in the male subject. According to the logic of the text, the male subject must claim the legacy of the Law or Word of the Father but can only do so through the agency of the female, whom he then idealizes (as a remedy for the threat of her sexuality). Thus he attains the proscribed heterosexual union and is able to come to terms with his own anxiety. The implication is that he must prove able to regulate his desire by regulating hers. Bellour asserts that this constitutes "the logic of masculine desire" (Bergstrom 93), a logic perceived as Natural, as 'fact,' since it generates a perpetual repetition of the same basic narrative in many male-authored texts.

Thus, sexual difference is ordained by the text in order that the text may be recovered, passed on: in order that the male subject, in his turn, may further reproduce the logic of the text.

This process of textual reproduction, along with its concomitant assignment of women as guarantor of the male's appropriation of the Law, constitutes the structure and significance of the second level of reproduction/revision in *The Red Shoes*. Revision, quite literally the reclamation and revision of one author's (the Father's) text, is the act that assures the son's entry into the symbolic order. As he represents the son, Julian Craster functions as the primary subject at this level, therefore it is necessary to trace the movements of his trajectory as it reflects his transformation from student (son) to author (Father).

Julian's role as son, an outlaw beyond the scope of the Law, is foreshadowed in the opening scene of the film, coincidental with the forecasting of his role as Vicky's lover. Yet they are two functions that are not complementary. Rather, this duality will later contribute to the most basic contradiction in the text. But here he is the first primary character who appears, and his first words as he rushes up the stairway to the Covent Garden Theatre are "Down with Tyrants!" As the performance of *Heart of Fire* proceeds, we discover that, in fact, Dr. Palmer (another father figure) will earn the designation of "tyrant" since he has "stolen" pieces from Julian's own fledgling score, revised them into the accompaniment for the ballet, and affixed his own name to it. This scene exemplifies the first instance of authorial revision/reproduction in this level of the narrative. The remainder of the film follows Julian's effort to overcome the author who wields this form of power and, finally, to "revise" himself into the image of the Father, even as he reproduces the Father's text. Indeed, it is Lermontov's advice to Julian (who storms Lermontov's private sanctum in order to demand satisfaction) that confirms the truth of authorial counterfeiting. After offering Julian a position as coach to the orchestra, he instructs the youth to tear up the letter of protest and "forget about it," saying that "it is more disheartening to have to steal than to be stolen from." Thus, Julian receives his first lesson on the fact of patriarchal Law.

Julian's arrival "behind the scenes" of the Ballet Lermontov serves as his formal introduction to the symbolic order as it is clearly manifest in every feature of the company's activities. Throughout the film, the dancers, as well as the chief artistic collaborators, refer to themselves as "children" who cooperate obediently in order to maintain the operations of this "happy little family." As Father, or "author," of this structure, Lermontov legislates all procedures in matters "domestic," artistic, and administrative. But Lermontov's small utopia of peaceful international integration is a guise for his most immediate concern—production and profit, the harnessing of family, of the "community," toward the goal of commercial supremacy. The numerous *mise en scène* in which he figures reflect the insularity of this legendary impresario, just as his small rule-bound world mirrors the insularity of a postwar England threatened by the turmoil of cultural and political recovery. He spends more time behind a desk in his private sanctums, surrounded by the artifacts of his "religion," that he does managing dance or orchestration. He is *The Red Shoes*' most ingenious "sign"—emptied of history or any personal past, he is filled with myth, the significance of the wise patriarch.

Likewise, Lermontov's ballet repertoire is fixed, a model of reproduction. *Swan Lake*, *The Sleeping Princess*, *Les Sylphes*—all texts that re-play the narrative of female suffering and transcendence—provide the essential discourses that support this patriarchal order. The reproduction of these highbrow texts guarantees box-office success, just as they have inscribed their discourses within the company. The female dancers, for example, remain "silent" (a placard above the stage entrance reads Silence), and the male collaborators defer to Lermontov's authority. As Julian wanders among the backstage props, searching for Lermontov, he encounters two middle-aged women who sit placidly knitting. "Don't ask us any questions, young man," one of them snaps, "we're just somebody's mother, and that doesn't mean much around her, I can tell you!" Clearly, the threatening figure of the mother, the rival authority, is kept at the periphery of this community.

In light of these textual features, as they correspond to a Lacanian scenario, it is no surprise to find that repression—particularly of sexual desire—is fundamental to this community's stability. The chief artistic collaborators (Ljubov, Boleslawski, Livey, and Ratov) characterize the principle of strict male exclusivity (or perhaps even a homosocial community), while the female dancers are warned against marriage—viewed as a form of tyranny. Lermontov declares unconditionally that love is "adolescent nonsense," that he permits "no dreaming" in his company. As a functioning unit of production, the company's Law demands that its members channel desire back into the product of "reproduction." The discourses of sexuality and desire must be submerged where they can later reemerge in the "safe forms" of the fairy tale discourses that compose the material of the repertoire.

It is the command of this text, and its discourses of authority, control, repression, and authorship, that Julian must seize, and the film's narrative charts the consequent stages of this seizure. His first faltering attempt is dramatized in his second encounter with the orchestra. In defiance of Livey's authority, he calls the orchestra to convene earlier than usual in an attempt to reclaim his lost text (*The Heart of Fire*). As they rehearse the piece, he attempts to revise it, to alter the notes as he conceived them. But Livey discovers this transgression and calls Lermontov to effect a reprimand. The impresario does so, yet he also acknowledges Julian's developing authorship. In this scene, Lermontov actualizes the paradigm of the controlling but interested father, exercising the firm but gentle patriarchal hand.

The first suggestions of Julian's successful entry into the text (i.e. the symbolic order) occur in the scene that Powell himself called "the heart of the picture" (657). The setting is Lermontov's villa situated among the hills of Monte Carlo, and the occasion is the assignment of Vicky and Julian to the creation of the Red Shoes ballet. By now, Julian has already received the Red Shoes score, authored by another composer but given into his hands so that he may revise those passages "marked by a blue pencil." After Vicky's interview with Lermontov, Julian hears strains from the Red Shoes drifting from the studio and rushes in to claim the text that is now *his*. Most significant here is the approval that Julian wins from Lermontov and his colleagues, an approval that Vicky was denied. For, as this "revision" is developed into a full-scale narrative, it becomes apparent that it is no revision at all. Despite the fact that Karen, the little dancer of Andersen's fairy tale, is to be redrawn as a twentieth-century heroine (630), this "Freudian film ballet" (628) quite effectively reproduces the trauma of male anxiety as it is enunciated in the traditional fairy tale, in the classical realist text, and even in the typical film noir of the 1930s and 1940s. In short, it evokes the text that theorists believe supports the essential structure of Western civilization—the text that encourages heterosexual relations as a form of exchange and that punishes women who refuse to participate as a source of exchange.

Thus, although Julian enters the world of *The Red Shoes* as a comparatively radical artist, he has, himself, been "revised" into the patriarchal author. In reclaiming the text and reproducing it according to its original *concept*, he enters the symbolic order. As Julian demonstrates during this crucial scene, the tune and rhythms, the parole or "speech," of the text may have changed in the twentieth century, but the language is the same. The symbolic language of patriarchal discourse still determines the text. The basic terms and the empty yet recognizable form of Andersen's fairy tale are replicated in Julian's version of the Red Shoes.

But here we find, perhaps, a *third* significant level of reproduction. Andersen's tale is, of course, the prototype that inspired Powell and Pressburger's film, just as it serves as the original "myth" from whence the film's revisions and reproductions project. As the centerpiece of the film, the ballet version approximates Andersen's basic plot and narrative quite closely: an indigent little girl (Karen) is adopted by a blind woman who buys her ward the pair of red shoes that she so desires. After Karen dons them, a crippled soldier caresses the sole of her shoe, at which point she begins to dance and cannot stop. Driven to exhaustion, she begs an executioner to chop off her feet, and, afterward, she kisses the hand that wielded the axe. Although clearly a moral lesson on female vanity, critics have already recognized the heavy sexual connotation of the red shoes (a symbol for the female genitalia) as well as the significance of Karen's uncontrollable dancing. Yet Karen is not simply "castrated" for "dancing" excessively. The eternal involuntary dance is itself a punishment. In Andersen's tale, female castration is posed as a healthy solution to an unhealthy excess of desire.

Here, Andersen has created a myth that describes female sexuality as dangerous not only to the community but also for the woman as well. Karen's initiation into sexuality is presented by Andersen as a drive to "exhaust" any and all partners. By definition she is a "horror." Therefore we might call this fairy tale a myth of the "gendering" of the female form a patriarchal point of view. Karen's sexuality must first be fictionalized as a source of danger before the text can justify her punishment. As Nelly Furman maintains, "while sex is an anatomical fact, sexuality is culturally devised; it is the manner in which society fictionalizes its relationship to sex and creates gender roles" (1985, 73). So it is the fiction of "The Red Shoes" to which Julian aspires, but before his entry into the Law can be concluded, he must revise Vicky into Karen's delegate. Vicky must "read" the text of the Red Shoes ballet, and, by virtue of her participation in it, she must adopt the role accorded her by the Law of the Father. Before she can arouse anxiety in the male subject, she must accept the image that "the logic of masculine desire" ordains.

That the presence of Vicky's sexuality is vital to Julian's transformation is evident from the fact that, until the ballet occurs, it is quite clearly *absent*. Unlike the Hitchcock heroines in films such as *North by Northwest, Psycho, Notorious,* and *Rear Window,* Vicky is not introduced to the narrative as dangerous or dangerously sexual. Indeed, her initial relationship to Julian is depicted as asexual, and she is markedly indifferent to anything but her career, as compared to most heroines in films of the 1940s. Her reason for being, as it were, depends not on a relationship but on self-fulfillment, a quest for self-definition. Hence, it is this that provokes anxiety in Julian—her *lack* of sexual desire, the absence of differentiation. She is not only his equal as an artist: she also surpasses him in terms of professional conduct. Her gender must be created as it is imagined by patriarchal logic.

Although the first scene in the Covent Garden Theatre foreshadows Vicky and Julian's union, it also forecasts their rivalry. For this rivalry (both artistic and for the attentions of Lermontov) is the threat that influences Julian's reproduction of the Red Shoes text. The dialogue that follows the rewarding of the two with the ballet demonstrates the drastic change in Julian's tone after his triumph with the collaborators. Merely an assistant before, he is now an author, and he loses no time in making his superiority clear. On a balcony in Monte Carlo:

Julian: (steals up on Vicky and shouts) Why aren't you in bed!
Vicky: Oh! You gave me a fright!
Julian: I meant to. Why aren't you in bed?
Vicky: I was ordered to, but I was much too excited to sleep.
Julian: I haven't seen you.
Vicky: Thank you.
Julian: By the way, you haven't seen me either.
Vicky: Did he send you to bed too?
Julian: (cavalierly) I'm just working on the score of *my* new ballet, the Red Shoes.
Vicky: Isn't that my ballet too?
Julian: (offhand) Yes, I suppose it is.
    (They lean on the balcony)
    I wonder what it's like to wake up in the morning and find oneself famous.
Vicky: You're not likely to find out if you stay here talking much longer.
Julian: Ha, ha.
Vicky: Well, good luck.
Julian: Good luck. (They shake hands and part, Julian whistling a strain from his score as he watches her retreat).

The sense of rivalry here is explicit, and Julian's tone carries a distinct note of hostility. Additionally, the demand to get into "bed" connotes Julian's increased opinion of his own status in the company as well as the confidence he has gained with patriarchal authorship. All that remains is to get Vicky "into the text." If, as Bellour suggests, the solution to the anxiety that the feminine provokes is the heterosexual union (and the consequent repression of female desire), then Julian is successful. Julian and Vicky do marry, but as a result she relinquishes her desire. Her dancing career ends only so that she may become his "inspiration." It is ironic that the opera he eventually composes with the help of this inspiration is entitled *Cupid and Psyche*, the myth that dramatizes female transgression and its punishment. The scene on the balcony shadow their eventual "love" and is analogous to the ill-starred love of Romeo and Juliet. But the steam that engulfs them as a train passes below also hints at the violence that underlies this "solution." Vicky leaps into the path of this very train at the film's conclusion.

The dance sequence, or Julian's revision, demonstrates a masterful depiction of the impact of such texts on the female "reader." Reproduction in this fourteen-minute episode is sharply cast against the more "realistic" fantasy of the other two levels of reproduction. Its excess of sound and movement, and its abundant and impressionistic atmosphere of fantasy, infused with a shadowy and sinister grotesque, all evince a gesture of parody and imitation. Luce Irigaray calls this manner of presentation "mimicry." Like Barthes's notion of the "mythified myth,"

Irigaray's mimicry is "the playful reproducing of a discourse—that undermines the privileged position of the first or original discourse and initiates a displacement through repetition which allows for the emergence of the repressed" (Furman 1985, 74). Or as Nelly Furman suggests: "Through disruption of the symbolic function of language, we are able to give expression to the repressed, or to detect traces of repression, but in so doing we are, even if only momentarily, in breach of the Law-of-the-Father" (1985, 74). In the dance sequence, this disruption takes the form of a shift in point of view. Although the basic narrative, structure, and plot development of the Red Shoes ballet reflects Julian's authorship, a series of three highly symbolic process shots are conveyed through Vicky's subjective point of view. These shots constitute a disruption: they clarify the presence of the symbolic order in *The Red Shoes* text while uncovering the layer of myth that conceals repression and that calls itself "Nature."

The primary purpose of the "camera tricks" is to communicate the movements of Vicky's unconscious. Thus, just as the "realism" at the other two levels is broken by fantasy, in this sequence fantasy surrounds the realism of Vicky's desires and fears. And, as these shots occur, Moira Shearer is clearly acting as Vicky, not as the fairy tale heroine. Or, rather, person and persona are fused into one. Furthermore, as combined with the rapid, even poetic editing, the special effects in this sequence reveal a process by which the female "reader" might be drawn into the text and "rewritten."

The first significant process shot occurs after the Shoemaker invites "the girl" to buy the red shoes. Immediately Vicky sees her own image, her "double," superimposed upon the background. The image is a rendering of masculine desire. Poised upon the red shoes, the image smiles mysteriously, her eyes flash with desire, and her arms beckon seductively. She represents the fantasy of female sexuality with both its attendant promise of pleasure and its threatening power. Responding to the invitation of this masculine construction, "Vicky" leaps into the shoes, an act that begins her own initiation into the symbolic order. Vicky Page accepts the role of the uncontrollable seductress, herself seduced by this image of power and desire.

After a series of tableaux in which "Vicky" exhausts her many dance partners, she is confronted with the second crucial image. At this point she is, herself, overwhelmed with exhaustion and fears her own wild abandon. Unable to enter her mother's house, she turns to find the menacing approach of the impish Shoemaker. First Lermontov's and then Julian's images are superimposed upon the figure of the Shoemaker, their arms are raised in a gesture of entrapment, of condemnation mixed with desire. A reverse close-up of Vicky reveals her sudden awareness of the text's duplicity and her realization that by donning the red shoes she has colluded with this text. Significantly, this close-up foreshadows the film's later close shot of Vicky's maddened gaze before she leaps to her death.

The third special effect characterizes the patriarchal solution to the myth of woman's dual nature—that of the sexual miscreant as posed against that of the idealized object of worship. Before the dance episode Julian had promised Vicky transcendence, that she would hear his music as she is "lifted into the air by her partner." This is the very gift awarded the heroine of the typical nineteenth-century fiction just as it is inscribed within the figure of Andersen's little dancer. Woman is raised from her suffering, from her basely sexual condition, to a position of eminence. In Andersen's fairy tale, little Karen earns her place in heaven by means of the stern tutelage of a priest and her own silent suffering. Near the dance's conclusion "Vicky" accepts this transcendence. Julian literally enters the stage from the orchestra pit, is transformed into Vicky's lover, and lifts her into the air. A series of superimpositions transform her into a flower, a cloud, and a bird—symbols of beauty, etherality, and innocence. Accepting this reward of patriarchal redemption, "Vicky" later suffers the languid and picturesque death of the nineteenth-century heroine.

Vicky's adoption of Julian's revision is later confirmed during the scene that follows Lermontov's discovery of the new "alliance" between his two proteges. As she and Julian embrace within the privacy of a horse-drawn carriage, Vicky claims that she does, after all, "believe in fate." This denial of self-determination is reflected in the *mise en scène*, the carriage rolling along steadily under the guidance of a sleeping driver, the road flanked by a moonlit sea—the symbol of eternal reoccurrence. But then, resuming her former self-possession, Vicky shouts up to the driver because she wants to know "where we are." Upon her second attempt, Julian embraces her with unprecedented aggression and silences her with a kiss. He then tells Vicky his own coercive "fairy tale." He describes a future day upon which he will relate the story of their love affair to a "young girl." According to his tale, Vicky will abandon him for the sake of her career. However, his implicit message is that she will *lose* him as a *result* of her ambitions, therefore she must give up her career. And she does. Vicky meets her "destiny" in the decision to play the part that Julian's revision has ordained: she silences her own desires and becomes his sole "inspiration," just as she has guaranteed his place in the symbolic order.

The mythic elements in the *Red Shoes*, as they occur in the *mise en scène*, in indirect and direct allusion, and through analogy, create a chain of signification whose source can be identified as the patriarchal author and whose function is to engage the participation of the female toward its aim of repression and further reproduction. Furthermore, the reproduction of the ballet's melodramatic conclusion (Vicky's death) within the "realistic" frame story ties together the levels of myth and authorship with a startling coherence and unity. Clearly, this structural coherence pleased most quality film critics and audiences alike. Yet the very neatness, the simple cause and effect logic of this modern fairy tale pushes narrative coherence to the very limits of belief. In response to the deceptive simplicity of narrative "realism" Powell and Pressburger have preserved the very element of transgression that many nineteenth-century revisions eliminated from the fairy tale form: its element of explicit horror, the transgressive narrative disruption of "suture," the broken seam of logic that alerts us to the presence of a controlling ideology. In the case of Andersen's fairy tale, the horrifying amputation of little Karen's dancing feet serves as a correlative to this symbolic "severance." Similarly, Powell and Pressburger evoke this tradition in the film's concluding sequences.

As the film's mythic and authorial signification overlap and fuse, the chain of signification accelerates along with the narrative, the shifting scenes gathering a momentum born of the dramatic tension between Vicky, Julian, and Lermontov. This "chain reaction" finally erupts in the sequence that leads to Vicky's suicide. Her death is a literal rendering of the sign's symbolic destructivity, just as her excessively stylized plunge proves the failure of the mythic feminine, as mythic sign, to sustain a discourse of repression after she has achieved awareness of the text's duplicity. Powell and Pressburger illustrate a definitive moment of narrative self-reflexivity in the single, prolonged shot of Vicky gracefully posed above the railroad tracks. Within this figure resides a host of conflicting dualities: frenzied movement lapsing into a beautifully languid collapse, silence rebuked by excessive gesture, the smiling exultant face bowing under the humility of transcendence. As an instance of filmic dialogy, the discourses that inform the patriarchal text, the quality film, and the mythic/fairy tale forms are stamped upon Vicky's figure. Her pose is a climactic parody of the romantic heroine's languid death and provides a moment of severance in which masculine desire is unmasked. The fulfillment of this desire is confirmed by Vicky's self-annihilation, but the logic that its discourses support is shattered by her death's essential absurdity. The masculine imagination achieves its unconscious desire—the feminine, literally, as "absence." Julian confirms Vicky's mythic transcendence as he kisses her bloodied, broken feet. Lermontov, captured within the cinematic frame, watches the spectacle of The Red Shoes performed without her, his anguish over her loss apparent. Just as patriarchal logic seduces Vicky into its own text, it denies the author an alternative text—a fairy tale—through which he might "revise" himself fully. Like Lermontov, a text's author is also imprisoned, made "spectacle," by the limitations of narrative reproduction.

WORKS CITED

Ashliman, D. L. "Symbolic Sex-Role Reversals in the Grimms' Fairy Tales." *Forms of Fantasy*. Ed. Jan Hokenson. New York: Greenwood, 1986. 193-98.
Barthes, Roland. *Mythologies*. New York: Hill and Wang, 1957.
Bergstrom, Janet. "Alternation, Segmentation, Hypnosis: Interview with Raymond Bellour." *Camera Obscura*, 3.4, 70-103.

Christie, Ian. *Powell, Pressburger and Others*. London: BFI Publishing, 1978.

Ellis, John. "Art, Culture and Quality: Terms for a Cinema in the Forties and Seventies." *Screen* 19.3 Fall, 1978: 9-49.

———. "Watching Death at Work: An Analysis of *A Matter of Life and Death*." *Powell, Pressburger and Others*. Ed. Ian Christie. London: BFI Publishing, 1978. 79-104.

Furman, Nelly. "The Politics of Language: Beyond the Gender Principle?" *Making a Difference: Feminist Literary Criticism*. Eds. Gayle Green and Coppelia Kahn. New York: Routledge, 1985. 59-79.

Jackson, Rosemary. "Narcissism and Beyond: A Psychoanalytic Reading of *Frankenstein* and Fantasies of the Double." *Aspects of Fantasy* 19: 43-53.

Powell, Michael. *A Life in Movies: An Autobiography*. London: Heinemann, 1986; New York: Knopf, 1987.

CHAPTER TEN

THE TENSION OF GENRE: WENDY TOYE AND MURIEL BOX*

Caroline Merz

SUCCESSIVELY NEW YORK, Paris, and now—belatedly—London have been discovering the riches of British film history. Major retrospectives, like the one mounted recently by the Paris Cinémathèque, have covered not simply one *auteur* like Hitchcock, not simply one genre like Ealing comedy, not simply one producer like Michael Balcon, but British cinema across all its periods, genres, and personnel. Never again will it be possible to dismiss the British cinema in the way made notorious by (to speak only of France) the critics of *Cahiers du Cinéma*. However, this rediscovery has not—so far—involved much attention being paid to the role of women within Britain's rich and diverse national cinema. It is this gap which our program of homage begins to fill.

Like Hollywood, the British cinema has afforded a surprisingly large number of points of entry to women. Contrary to evidence available from the standard works of reference on British cinema, women have had an input into cinema in Britain from its beginnings. Research by feminist film historians during the 1970s brought to light unknown films and demonstrated women's significant influence and intervention into past cinema. Their work on American cinema "discovered"—and made available to audiences worldwide—the work of early filmmakers like Lois Weber, as well as that of Hollywood directors like Ida Lupino and Dorothy Arzner. In France, the fascinating and prolific output of Alice Guy was another revelation.

It's only quite recently, however, that attention has begun to turn toward the women of British cinema. Alongside Lois Weber and Alice Guy we can find the forgotten figures of Dinah Shurey and Ethyl Batley (who, under her own pro-

---

*This article was originally published in French in the Catalogue of the Twelfth International Festival of Women's Films in Créteil, Paris, held in April 1990. It was commissioned to accompany a retrospective of films by Muriel Box and Wendy Toye at that festival.

121

duction company, made sixty-seven films in the four years between 1912 and 1916). And what of Alma Reville, whose long and important career in the British film industry has been effaced by the fact of her marriage to Alfred Hitchcock (on many of whose films she worked)? Even before the opening up of opportunities to women filmmakers in the 1970s, concurrent with the rise of women's movement and the independent film workshop movement in Britain, there were several women regularly working in Britain as directors. Most of them, however, were operating in the field of short films and documentaries; and, despite all the talent and professionalism they had demonstrated, women like Jill Craigie and Kay Mander found it impossible to cross over and establish themselves in feature production, such was the strength of the ideology that confined women to their more "natural" roles as scriptwriter, editor, continuity "girl"—and, of course, star.

There were, however, two pioneers who overcame this stereotyping and made a sustained career as directors within the mainstream British industry during the period after the war when cinema was still the dominant popular medium. They are Muriel Box (Lady Gardiner) and Wendy Toye.

It is significant that both of them emerged as directors shortly after the end of World War II. The war gave an impetus to new talent in the British cinema in general, and—as in many other countries caught up in the war—it enhanced opportunities for women in many fields of professional life. Both Box and Toye worked primarily in the mainstream of the film industry. They were both employed by large, male-dominated organisations, making genre films (particularly comedy) without, at the time, being much remarked upon for being women directors. In common with other "prefeminist" filmmakers like Dorothy Arzner, they observed the male-oriented rules of quasi-factory film production. Yet, looked at in retrospect, their films do emerge very clearly as expressing and anticipating legitimate feminist concerns.

But although Box and Toye have much in common in terms of the broad timespan of their careers in cinema and their involvement in commercial, studio-based production, their work is also significantly different, the one from the other. Muriel Box worked her way up slowly and gradually through the industry. Her formation was as a writer, mainly of plays (later, she wrote novels)—all of which were essentially mainstream, generic and middlebrow. Wendy Toye, on the other hand, came from the "avant garde" of ballet and of a more experimental theater: she came to filmmaking completely inexperienced, but as an acknowledged artist. Muriel Box worked in the film industry for most of her career, whereas for Wendy Toye film and television represented an interlude between working as a choreographer and producer in theater and opera. And Muriel Box, unlike Wendy Toye, was explicitly a feminist.

For the first part of her film career Muriel Box worked under her maiden name of (Violet) Muriel Baker, even after marrying Sydney Box in 1936 and forming a writing partnership with him; but her main work in features (as a writer from the mid-1940s and as director from the early 1950s) is as Muriel Box. She was born in 1905 in Surrey, close to London. In her autobiography, *Odd Woman Out*, Muriel recounts how her earliest memories were of her parents' quarrels about money. Her father was fond of gambling; her mother was a teacher. Muriel always knew that she would have to earn her own living. By the time she left home at the age of seventeen (leaving behind her a terse farewell note for her parents, reading "gone to the devil"), she had already decided that she wanted to work in moving pictures. She loved dancing and singing, but particularly acting, and although her ambition to act professionally was never realized, she took part in many amateur productions before turning to playwriting herself. After working occasionally as an extra in silent films, she managed to get her first real job in the industry at British Instructional Films—as a typist.

Muriel thus found herself in the traditional place for the ambitious young film worker: inside a studio, working in the humblest of roles. For ambitious young men, the conventional career structure was to start as teaboy—carrying messages, doing menial jobs, but above all bringing the indispensable British cup of tea to his seniors at frequent intervals—and then to work his way up through the role of assistant director or assistant cameraman or assistant editor toward, one day, if he was lucky, the chance to direct. Women's opportunities for promotion from typist were much narrower. Their best chance was to show by their own initiative that they could do more than type, but could write, suggest ideas, organize schedules. Soon, Muriel was moving from company to company, acting as personal assistant to bright young directors, like Anthony Asquith and Michael Powell, and picking up the skills of budgeting, scheduling, and continuity. She began to read and edit scripts for her various employers and, meanwhile, to involve herself in the theater as a knowledgeable spectator and as a writer of plays herself.

Muriel's work as a playwright forms a fascinating prelude, and counterpoint, to her work in cinema—in several ways. First, it gave her an invaluable professional apprenticeship as a popular storyteller, writing with great speed and economy; she was not writing for an intellectual elite, or even for the prestige theatres of the West End but producing texts to be played by repertory groups and by amateur dramatic societies. The fact that these groups used her work enthusiastically and asked for more testified to her craft and to her understanding of the needs of unpretentious popular audiences. Second, it cemented her partnership with her husband and cowriter Sydney, a journalist and film publicist. This was to be carried over into cinema work: undoubtedly, this partnership made her progress in the film world more quickly than she could have managed as a woman on her own, at least at that period. Third, it engaged her in writing specifically for women. There was a strong demand for plays for women casts, particularly from the many theatrical groups that existed in organizations like the Women's Institute and the Townswomen's Guild, and the Boxes were expert at meeting it, producing several all-women scripts that earned them gratifyingly large revenues from performance—a striking anticipation of their work a decade later at Gainsborough Films, with its dominant roles for women stars and its strong appeal to women audiences.

This was the basis of Muriel's life until the outbreak of war in September 1939; working intermittently in a film studio and writing both on her own account and in partnership with her husband. So far, they had only one screenplay to their credit (*Alibi Inn*, a not particularly successful cheap thriller of 1935). As for so many people—as for the British film industry generally—the war broke up the old pattern and brought new openings. Many film workers were called up for military service: meanwhile, there was a huge increase in the government's need for short films to fulfil urgent wartime needs equally of information, instruction, and inspiration. Sydney Box formed a company, Verity Films, which rapidly obtained contracts and increased its output and its workforce. Muriel was involved full-time in this company's work, even though her name—still Muriel Baker—appears on the credit titles of relatively few of the films. It was for Verity that she had first solo credits both as writer (e.g., of the road safety film *A Ride with Uncle Joe*, commissioned by the Ministry of Information), and as director (e.g., of *The English Inn*, a short documentary commissioned by the British Council).

Like her prewar work as a playwright, this wartime experience was valuable preparation for her feature-film career. It, too, put a premium upon economy and craft; the films could not afford to waste time or money, and they had to put over their message to audiences in an effective way. It gave her priceless practical experience and industry contacts. And, importantly, it did not, as it might have done, detach her from "popular" conventions and divert her into the drier practices of documentary. Many of the short-film companies that flourished in wartime were dominated by disciples of John Grierson, founder of the British documentary movement of the 1930s, who were hostile to the practices of entertainment cinema and sought to use the film for austere social purposes. Many of these companies and individuals did useful, even memorable, work in the special conditions of wartime—one thinks not only of men like Humphrey Jennings and Paul Rotha but also of such women as Jill Craigie, Kay Mander, and Margaret Thomson. None of them found it easy to sustain the momentum of their work after the war, or to find their way into commercial production. Verity, in contrast, always foregrounded the entertainment factor even in their instructional films, refusing to associate themselves with the ideology and practices of the documentary movement. They preferred to work with experienced actors rather than with "real people" and to get across any necessary information or message by involving audiences with characters to whom they could relate, caught up in an interesting story line. By the end of the war, Verity had evolved a distinctive kind of vivid mini-feature film, exemplified by *Jigsaw*, a warning against the dangers of careless talk, told through the emotional experience of a bereaved woman. The natural way forward for those who made these films, after the war, was into the feature industry, and that is indeed where they went; directors like Henry Cass and Ken Annakin, players like Dinah Sheridan (star of *Jig-saw*)—and of course the Boxes.

They had already moved into independent feature production, in a speculative way, before the war ended. Shrewdly, they chose the path of melodrama, and in 1945 their production of *The Seventh Veil*, with its memorably sadistic role for the young James Mason, had a big success on both sides of the Atlantic. It was not surprising that the long-established Gainsborough company, seeking a new head of production, invited Sydney to take over. Muriel went over with him as script editor, a job that occupied her intensively for the next five years.

No company could have suited her better than Gainsborough—just as she suited them. Gainsborough had become a household name during the war for its vigorous melodramas, which were more popular with audiences than with intellectual critics and were especially popular with women, who identified with their romantic, lustful, often transgressive heroines. Muriel supervised, and often herself wrote, a series of woman-centred postwar melodramas, both historical (e.g. *Jassy*) and contemporary (e.g. *Good Time Girl*). Recent commentators have reclaimed such films as eloquent, even subversive, documents of their time, contrasting them with the more tasteful middle-class products of Michael Balcon's Ealing. Significantly, it was Balcon—not exactly a misogynist, but one of the typical patriarchs of British cinema—who had told Muriel that women were unsuited to film direction. Very soon now, she was to prove him wrong.

In the early 1950s, then, her career as a feature-film director began. Her four-stage preparation—studio apprenticeship, play-writing, wartime short-film production, and scripting for Gainsborough—had equipped her admirably for it; and, as a director, she would do more prolific and substantial work than any British woman before her. Yet it is still possible to regret a major missed chance. It is ironic that the strong women's films of the 1940s were all directed by men, even at Gainsborough, even when Muriel Box was in a powerful position there. She should have begun as a Gainsborough director, not a post-Gainsborough one, and in the 1940s, the great decade of British cinema (not least for women), rather than the anti-climatic decade of the 1950s.

In any event, her own films, like Wendy Toye's, are rooted in the fifties. Like her she becomes a wry, witty commentator precisely on that grey decade and specifically on its gender relationships. The vibrant popular cinema of the 1940s had become attenuated as had the energies and opportunities of women within the society. Few British directors of the fifties worked so sensitively within that changed context as Muriel Box.

Her films are notable mainly for their variety, rather than any specific commitment or point of view, in a way that is typical of the British postwar film industry. Any impulse to make "statements" with her films was inhibited by her employers. As she has stated:

We were not under contract with Rank to make films with overt statements on social problems or those with strong propaganda themes. We were expected to produce a programme of films that would interest the general public and encourage people to go to the cinema more frequently and enjoy well-made dramas and amusing comedies. We were not engaged to indulge our own political or socialist views, however much we should have found satisfaction in doing so. (Aspinall and Murphy 1983)

What is remarkable is the extent to which she was able, nonetheless, to express intelligent tame generic materials. For Rank, she made several "women's films," including *Street Corner, The Truth About Women,* and *The Passionate Stranger.* At the time, these were received by most critics as merely formula pictures of no great merit, but, seen today, they very clearly reflect her concern with feminism in a way that must have been, at some level, read positively by women audiences of the time. Then there are the social realist films like *Too Young to Love,* a film that ran into trouble with the censor for presenting facts about prostitution and venereal disease. Even an apparently very minor comedy of 1958, *This Other Eden,* one of the few Irish-location films of the time, has recently been rescued from obscurity by nationalistic Irish critics who celebrate it as not a victim, but an acute analysis, of racial stereotyping.

That offers a key, perhaps, to Muriel Box's directing career: her films are by no means so simple as they may at first have appeared. They make deceptively subtle demands on their audience. Through all of them there runs a strong sense of humor. Even in an essentially serious film like *Rattle of a Simple Man,* she pokes fun very successfully at the ideology of the male group and its crude sexism. Indeed, *Rattle of a Simple Man* can be seen as a woman's reply to the eulogies of the northern working-class male made famous in the social realist dramas of writers like John Osborne in the 1960s and in their film adaptations. It was the commercial and critical failure of this film that ended Muriel Box's career. Ironically, it stands up rather better today than many of its male social realist counterparts. Muriel Box died in June 1991, aged 86.

Any national cinema is born out of some form of tension between popular, generic materials and the contributions of the avant-garde in touch with movements in the other arts. If Muriel Box's work is in the first category, Wendy Toye's is in the second. In her own way, she represented an infusion of artistic energy into the British cinema of the fifties comparable to, but different from, that of the more celebrated Free Cinema group (Lindsay Anderson, Tony Richardson et al.— in fact, directors of the social realist films referred to above). Wendy Toye was distinctive in two clear ways. First, she came, very unusually for a filmmaker, from the world of ballet. Second, her gender placed her definitively at a distance from the masculinity (indeed misogyny) of the Free Cinema group, and her films are characterized by the way they gently and humorously puncture male conceit.

Unlike Muriel Box, Wendy Toye did not serve an apprenticeship either in popular cinema or in instructional documentary. She was born in London on 17 May 1917, and by the age of seven she had begun training for a career as a ballet dancer. After dancing for the Sadler's Wells ballet, she decided that ballet alone was too constricting and diversified into choreography and dancing in cabaret and musicals. In 1947 she formed her own company of dancers, Ballet Hoo de Wendy Toye (a pun on the word *ballyhoo*, meaning publicity) and took it on tour abroad. She had already appeared in several films as a dancer, including *Dance Pretty Lady* (1931) and *Invitation to the Waltz* (1935), as well as choreographing and directing dance sequences in films for Alexander Korda (e.g., *The Thief of Baghdad*, 1940). And by the time she came to direct her first film, *The Stranger Left No Card*, in 1952, she was already established as a successful director of West End shows.

In fact, Wendy Toye says she never had a particular ambition to direct films, and she might never have done so had it not been for the encouragement of Korda, the most civilized and artistic, as well as the most extravagant, of British film producers. After the spectacular success, at Cannes, of her short film *The Stranger Left No Card*, it was Korda who put her under contract and gave her the chance to make features. Although the international critical success of *The Stranger* was never quite repeated in the films she made subsequently, they were certainly popular with audiences. By her own admission, Wendy Toye knew virtually nothing about the technical processes of making a film when she made *The Stranger*. Indeed, she ascribes much of that film's freshness and spontaneity to the fact that she did know so little: "I did some things in *Stranger* which I probably, two or three years later, wouldn't have attempted." And unlike Muriel Box, who sometimes had quite a struggle to prove that a woman was capable of directing, Wendy Toye appears not to have suffered any discrimination. "If I'd come up through the technical ranks in the studio, I probably wouldn't have been treated in the way I was. I might have been patronised. But because I'd reached a certain level outside the film world in opera, ballet, plays and musicals, I suppose they thought—she must know about *something*. I knew a lot of people I worked with through having done the dances in such a lot of films, and I think they were pleased to see me doing something else."

Although Wendy Toye was to return definitively, after a decade, to the world of theater and dance—with occasional forays into television—the films she made in that decade, five features and four shorter pieces, add up to a striking and personal *oeuvre* that has recently been the focus of renewed critical attention, particularly from feminist writers: see, for instance, the essays brought together in two successive issues of the British Film Institute's *Monthly Film Bulletin* (August and September 1986). Toye's films fall into two broad categories: whimsical fantasy (mainly the short films) and light comedy (mainly the feature films). Significantly, her most cherished project was one that would have broken

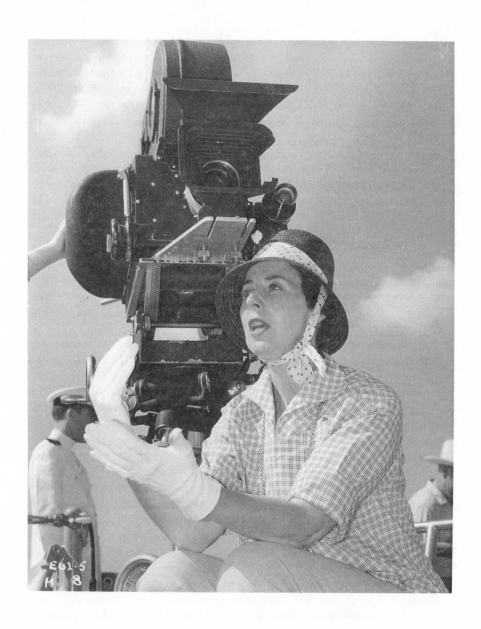

Figure 10.1. Wendy Toye in 1962. Courtesy: Wendy Toye.

down this division—a longer fantasy, set in Paris ("a wonderful idea, and I'd have given my eye teeth to do it")—but it was impossible for the British cinema of the period to accommodate such a project. Therefore, in her feature films, she worked within the generic constraints of British film comedy, subordinating her impulse to fantasy to the demands of "realistic" comedy narratives; she did not, however, abandon this impulse altogether, and it is this double personal input—of fantasy, and of the woman's point of view—that makes her comedies so distinctive.

Writing in the *Monthly Film Bulletin*, Sylvia Paskin notes the consistent way in which Wendy Toye's comedies "foreground the helplessness of men," and she goes on to make this very pertinent comment: "It is, of course, extremely tempting to read this as not simply a personal but a specifically female viewpoint. However, the situation is complicated by the fact that male uncertainty is a recurrent feature of 50s British films of all genres" (1986). In other words, it was not only Wendy Toye (and Muriel Box) who dwelt upon the failings of men and the hollowness of patriarchy; their male colleagues were doing so, with a certain masochism, at the same time. Nevertheless, Wendy Toye gives a special intensity to this familiar undermining of masculine confidence. Her two best comedies, *Raising a Riot* and *All for Mary*, contain almost surreal scenes of humiliation, of loss of potency, for their male stars. And it is significant that she turns her attention in particular, in her two biggest-budget films, to the most "typically British" of male film stars of the 1950s—Kenneth More.

More was the dominant male star of that decade, together with Dirk Bogarde. But where Bogarde had an international appeal that would deepen as time went by, More's appeal was short lived and confined to Britain and its imperial outposts. In contrast with Bogarde's dangerous androgynous appeal, More was resolutely "masculine" in a conventional quasi-military British style. It is this confident image that Wendy Toye so tellingly calls into question in the role-reversal strategies of *Raising a Riot*; these push to an extreme the analysis of male vulnerability hinted at by other British films of the time—films that may use less positive actors than More. (When she herself uses one of these weaker actors, David Tomlinson, in *All for Mary*, the results are devastating, as the all-powerful British Nanny reduces Tomlinson to the level of a four-year-old child.)

Since 1963 Wendy Toye has not directed a film, although she has worked in television, as a director and producer of opera, drama, and arts programs and in advertising. Indeed, she was one of the first well-known cinema directors to work in advertising, long before names like Alan Parker and Hugh Hudson came on the scene. She has not entirely given up the idea of making another film, however. "I would like to do another film. One of the reasons I haven't worked on more films is because, if you want to get something off the ground, you've got to concentrate on that alone. They take such a long time to set up. And the other reason is that a film is *there*, whatever you do, forever. I would only do something that I approved of, that I'd be sure I still believed in in another 10 years' time, and it's difficult to find the right subject."

When *The Stranger Left No Card* was shown at Cannes, it was described as a masterpiece by no less a figure than Jean Cocteau, and Wendy Toye went on to develop projects in collaboration with such artists as Ronald Searle; not for nothing has she been compared with the team of Michael Powell and Emeric Pressburger for her exuberant exploitation of the cinema's powers of fantasy, and her openness to the links between cinema and the other arts of painting, music, and ballet. By juxtaposing examples of her avant-garde fantasy with her mainstream popular comedies, we can appreciate the *oeuvre* of Wendy Toye in its full perspective; and when this work is juxtaposed with the more prolific, perhaps less celebrated, but equally serious films of Muriel Box, it gives an even more radically new perspective on British cinema of the postwar years and of the role within it of these two important filmmakers.

FILMOGRAPHIES

Muriel Box (1905-91)

The Happy Family (1952)
A Prince for Cynthia (1953)
Street Corner (1953)
The Beachcomber (1955)
To Dorothy, a Son (1956)
Simon and Laura (1956)
Eyewitness (1956)
The Passionate Stranger (1957)
The Truth About Women (1958)
This Other Eden (1959)
Subway in the Sky (1959)
Too Young to Love (1960)
The Piper's Tune (1960)
Rattle of a Simple Man (1964)

Wendy Toye (b. 1917)

The Stranger Left No Card (1952)
Three Cases of Murder (1953; Toye directed one segment
    of this three-part film, *In the Picture*)
The Teckman Mystery (1954)
On the Twelfth Day (1955)
Raising a Riot (1955)
All for Mary (1955)

True as a Turtle (1956)
A Life to Be Lived (1961)
We Joined the Navy (1962)
The King's Breakfast (1963)

WORKS CITED

Aspinall, Sue, and Robert Murphy, eds. *Gainsborough Melodrama: BFI Dossier 18*. London: BFI Publishing, 1983.

Box, Muriel. *Odd Woman Out*. London: Leslie Frewin, 1974.

Paskin, Sylvia. "A Delicate but Insistent Trail of Confetti . . ." *Monthly Film Bulletin* 53.632 (1986).

CHAPTER ELEVEN

AN INTERVIEW WITH WENDY TOYE

Wheeler Winston Dixon

IN 1992, WENDY Toye was awarded the Order of the British Empire, and she directed a touring company of *The Sound of Music*. Though she has not been able to direct a feature film in some time, she still enthusiastically pursues her individual creative vision. I was fortunate to have the chance to interview Wendy Toye in the summer of 1992 and found her "very chirpy and full of life," as my friend Nigel Arthur commented. It was Nigel who introduced me to Wendy Toye and thus made this conversation possible. If Wendy Toye seems somewhat sad about "what might have been" in her career as a filmmaker, she still does not dwell in the past. Clearly what she relishes most is the challenge of film and theater producing and directing, and it is this work that she continues to tackle with zeal and good humor. This interview was conducted on 6 June 1992.

Wendy Toye: It's an awful thought having to talk about myself. I've done so many things and started so young. I *am* bored with talking about myself. I think to myself, "Oh, God do we have to go all through *that*," you know? But you're here now, and I'm here, so let's talk. I came into movies through dancing, in a very roundabout way. I started dancing when I was very little, 3 years old, and because I suppose I was fairly good, I was suggested to appear at performance at 3 1/2 at the Albert Hall in London. And so I did a solo dance there and was almost immediately named by the press "the pocket wonder" because I was so small. And then I went on to doing various different charity shows with very famous variety artists.

One of them, a man called Hayden Coffin, was a very famous musical comedy star in those days. He was very impressed with me and asked if my mother would let me be his "stooge" or assistant, on stage. So I did a lot of work with him, but it wasn't what you would strictly call professional, because I was only about 5 years old. I just went on doing all sorts of things as a child, and winning millions of competitions and cups and medals. In the end, other schools wouldn't let their children in the competition if I was in it. It got as bad as that! (Laughs.)

Wheeler Dixon: Did you actually choreograph a ballet at the Palladium when you were 10 years old?

WT: Nine. It was a ballet that I had the idea of myself, and I had to use a lot of children. It came out of the school I went to, where I danced with the great ballerina Ninette de Valois. She was always encouraging me, because she had seen dances that I had arranged when I was a child. I called the dance the *Japanese Legend of the Rainbow.*

I knew nobody would take much interest in it if it was just a story by me, so I just sort of added on the "Japanese legend" part! The idea was that when flowers die, their colors all got to Heaven to make rainbows. The music that I chose was Scarlatti, which was a rather funny choice for a child.

WD: The first film that I have you as an actor in is Anthony Asquith's *Dance Pretty Lady* in 1931.

WT: Oh my goodness, yes that's right! I was a member of a ballet company at the time, and we all worked in the film, and that's how I got involved in that.

WD: How did you make the jump into films?

WT: Well, there were many jumps in between, because I was an actress as well as a dancer. I was in serious ballet, but my mother always insisted on me doing everything else as well—modern stuff, tap, and the like—which upset the ballet companies that I was with; but while I was in the ballet with Ninette de Valois at Covent Garden, I was also dancing in cabaret with a man named Frederick Franklin. He was my partner—we danced together.

We danced at the very famous Café de Paris and in lots of musicals in London. And we went on together until the Markova-Dolin Ballet Company was formed, and we were both in that. I choreographed ballets for them as well. I did a lot of commercial shows as well. Wherever I could get work, money! And then at about 18, I was quite ill with appendicitis, and I wasn't allowed to dance for quite a while, so I choreographed. I needed the work, I need *to* work. I started choreographing dances in commercial shows—like at the Palladium with the Crazy Gang.

WD: Was your mother a dancer as well?

WT: No, nothing to do with the profession at all. Nor was my father. But my mother was a very clever lady. She loved dancing herself. I think she would have loved to be a dancer herself. She was a good violinist, but not a professional one, because in those days there were very few professional women of anything. So she took me to a very good school to start with, and the lady who played the piano for us there was Glynis Johns' mother. And Glynis Johns was in the class as well!

But in the second school I went to, they suggested that my mother should take me to the Serge Diaghilev Ballet Company, the Ballet Russe, when they were in London to the rehearsals. So, when I was about 8 or 9, I was watching the rehearsals of the Diaghilev Company in London. I was really very lucky to get all that kind of experience.

WD: Did you run into Cocteau during this period?

WT: Yes, during the Diaghilev rehearsals—Cocteau was there. Constantly talking. He was brilliant. Many years later, he was the chairman of the council that was judging the films in Cannes, and he awarded me a prize for my film *The Stranger Left No Card.*

So I went from dancing/acting to choreographing all these different shows, and I learned a lot that helped me to choreograph dances in films. I was actually in the films, as well. I was in a film which they've just shown in London within the last week, called *Invitation to the Waltz.* It was a ridiculous film actually, but it was extremely lavish.

WD: Yes, *Invitation to the Waltz,* 1935, directed by Paul Herzbach. Were you picking up technical information during this period, when you were on the set?

WT: Well, not exactly that. But I used to go into the cutting room all the time. I was really very interested in the way they made films, and I was always watching what happened in the camera. And I loved being in the cutting room, seeing how they put it together. I did learn technically what you must *not* do, because when you are choreographing something, you have to learn about camera angles and coverage in the same way as if you are directing a film. If you've got suggestions for camera angles for the director, you have to know a bit about it. So I suppose I did try to learn as much as I could because I was interested.

I remember one film I worked on, and there was one section of the film that was in color. It was a terrible mime sequence which I had staged for them. And it wasn't good because the leading lady, Steffi Duna, wasn't a very good dancer and didn't move very gracefully; it simply wasn't working out. So the director was very unhappy, and he asked me if we could work together to improve it. He said, "will you watch this, Wendy? Just watch the cameras and see that we've got the covering shots, because I've got to watch the lights and the color and see what happens on that side." And so there I was about 14 years of age, actually in control of one of the whole scenes of the film.

WD: Can you remember any of the particular technicians whom you worked with?

WT: I knew you would ask me that. The very first person I worked with—when Alexander Korda put me under contract, was Georges Perinal, the lighting cameraman. And it was quite extraordinary because he was a hero to me. My mother had taken me to see all the Korda films when I was a child, and I couldn't believe that I was working with this same legend of a man.

WD: He photographed Cocteau's *Blood of a Poet*, as well.

WT: The one Georges Perinal shot for me was *In the Picture*, one of the episodes of the omnibus film *Three Cases of Murder* [1953].

WD: Did you run into David Lean in the cutting room when you were a choreographer?

WT: Oh, yes. He was the editor of a film that I did the dances for, called *The Young Mr. Pitt*. He gave me a lot of help, a lot of pointers. I met a lot of people on that film, and they were all very nice to me. People like Dickie Attenborough, who was just starting out and certainly turned into a great success later (I met him again several years ago in New York when he was directing *A Chorus Line*), and Ronald Neame, who was the camera operator, and Carol Reed, the director.

Then there was Robert Morley, who was acting in the film, and Ronnie Taylor, who was also in the camera department and has since gone on to be a director of photography himself. And David Lean was the cutter! What a lot of talent that was! It was all shot at the Gainsborough Studios. In fact, I was the one who introduced Attenborough around to the members of the company on his first day on the set . . . he was applying for a job as a runner or something!

WD: Michael Powell and Emeric Pressburger, known as The Archers, wanted to work with you, I understand.

WT: Yes, they did. I was very flattered. Emeric had seen *The Stranger Left No Card* and probably one or two other things, and I think Sir Malcolm Sargent introduced us to one another, and we used to go to the opera together, the four of us. And Emeric was very keen for me to do some work for him. I would have loved to have done it, but it just never worked out. When they were doing something that I could have perhaps been involved in, . . . like *The Red Shoes*, or *A Matter of Life and Death*, I was doing some other film, or I was busy doing something in the theatre. It's too bad. It would have been fun.

WD: On *The Stranger Left No Card* [1952], your breakthrough film, how did you get the financing?

WT: Well, I did during the war a show called *Skirts* for the American Eighth Army Air Force. The show as produced by a man named George K. Arthur. He went to all the different stage producers then working in London, like George Black at the Palladium, asking advice for somebody to choreograph this show for him. They all said, "use Wendy." So George came to me one day and said "would I do this?" and I said "it sounds very interesting, indeed. Yes, I would love to do it," and so I did.

We stayed in touch, and then when I went to America in 1949 and directed *Peter Pan* with Jean Arthur and Boris Karloff on the stage, and I remet George Arthur and his wife. He said he was going to form a company to make short films. He got the rights to three good stories. I particularly liked one of them, "Stranger in Town."

I read it and thought it was a most wonderful story, but then I forgot all about it, because how often do these things get off the ground, really? I came back to England in May, and a year later George came over and said "Well, I've got the script all finished. Who do you suggest ought to do it?" So I suggested David Lean to direct, because it was such a wonderful story, and the leading man, the designer, the person to write the music, everything. So George said "thank you" and went away.

After a week, he came back. "I've got everybody, Wendy," he said, "but I don't have David Lean. I want you to do it." Now I hadn't ever thought of directing a film in my life.

WD: You've been quoted as saying "it was never one of my major ambitions to become a film director." Is that true?

WT: Well, yes. I've never had any real major ambitions at all. I just like doing what I'm asked to do and doing what I choose to do. You know what I mean? I've never had any tremendous ambition to *be* something. I can't say that I had a great ambition to direct—not really. I suppose my only ambition when I was young was to choreograph well. And then that sort of left me after a bit, because I got offered jobs as a director.

WD: You certainly jumped in and made the absolute most of the opportunity.

WT: Well, I chose very good people to work with, didn't I? We did it in thirteen days, and it cost something like three thousand pounds. We didn't have any money. We got expenses, plus minimum wage, and that was all. I got a fifty-pound gold coin as a bonus for finishing on time, which I've still got.

Almost the whole of *The Stranger Left No Card* I'd worked out to music before we went to shoot it. And in those days we couldn't afford audiotape for the playback on the set, so I had a little wind up gramophone on all the location sets. And we had to do it with a metronome, because I knew exactly what bits of music I wanted to fit into the shots. It was all very planned out. René Clair was certainly an influence; I loved *A Nous la Liberté*. I'm really controlled by music. I think the tempo of music is something that influences the structure of all my films.

Then George had to sell the film, which wasn't easy, because it was a two-reel short subject. George went with a copy under his arm to America to try and sell the rights, and there was one copy which we gave to London Films, Korda's distributor, just to see what he thought. We never thought they'd take it.

Figure 11.1. Wendy Toye in 1993. Courtesy: Wendy Toye.

Well, we didn't hear anything. I went on working, and did another theater show, and I really thought no more about it. I thought, "one day it will be shown in America, and I will hear about it if I'm lucky." And then suddenly one of Alexander Korda's employees, a guy named Bill, rang me up and said "You've made a great hit, Wendy, with my boss." And I said, "what do you mean?"

"Well," he said, "Alex rang me up the day before yesterday, and said he was going to show a new feature film of his to a big party of people. He asked me to find a short film to go with it. So I went through all the short films lying around at London Films, and came across *The Stranger Left No Card*. I looked at it, and liked it, and sent it along to Korda's house."

That evening, down came Alex Korda with all his glamorous guests, and they ran *The Stranger Left No Card* before his film Korda had just finished. It caused such a sensation with the audience that Korda got Bill to ring me the very next day, because he wanted to send it to the Cannes Film Festival. And so it went to Cannes under Korda's banner, London Films. And that got me in with Alexander Korda, under contract.

WD: How did your next film, *The Teckman Mystery* [1954], come about?

WT: Well, this was a pretty straightforward mystery. I really didn't want to do it, but I had said "no" to so many subjects that Korda had asked me to do. Actually, I was quite frightened of him. I mean I was pretty young, and I was scared of him.

WD: He was a rather domineering person, from what I gather.

WT: Absolutely, absolutely, yes. Even with his children. One of the excuses I used was that I thought I wasn't experienced enough to do that subject. I didn't think I could do it in six weeks. But he insisted, so I jumped in. I had a lovely cast, because Korda let me have who I wanted. Margaret Leighton played the lead. So I said yes to that at last, and shot it, and that's why I did that. But it really wasn't my kind of film—really and truly. I always liked to do things that were slightly fantasy, very popular and light and admired. And in those days nobody would touch fantasy.

WD: However, in your later films, you shifted into comedy.

WT: That happened, really, because I did *Raising a Riot* [1955] under Korda's banner, but the producer of that was a marvelous, marvelous man called Ian Dalrymple. He's a wonderful man. I owe him so much. I owe so many men so much, because they laid their head on the line for me. If I hadn't done it alright, they would have been in real trouble.

Ian found the story for *Raising a Riot* and liked it and showed it to me and said "do you think you could get Kenneth More to play in this?" I said, "well, I don't know. Do you mean with me directing?" He said yes. "Well," I said, "I doubt it. I've only made one or two films before. Why should he bother with me?" So I had lunch with Kenny, whom I didn't know at all at the time. I admired him a lot. But he knew of me and said yes straightaway.

And so that was one of the last films made under Korda's banner. But it was a slightly different sort of film than the ones I did after that, which were much more straight comedy. Then Korda died. And my contract went to the J. Arthur Rank. And they did wonderful films, but they were slightly *broader* films than Korda's. It was a much larger organization, and it certainly didn't have the family feel. And of course wide screen started, and CinemaScope. We all went through all kinds of lectures and things, trying to get into these new techniques.

WD: With *All For Mary* [1955] and *True as a Turtle* [1956], it really seems that you stayed in the comedy vein. Did you want to do more fantasy? Was this just not a possibility?

WT: Very much, yes, yes, you're quite right. But I've never been very good at selling people on things that I want to do. I'm not a good seller of either myself *or* what I want to do. Partly because, I suppose, I'm not ambitious. I know that sounds silly, or overly modest, but I think you have to have a searing ambition to barge in on people and say, "I must do this, and I want to do that" and all the rest of it. I just timidly went along doing everything I was given, really. Because I was really very *grateful* to be doing it, and it was *fascinating*. And I had lovely casts.

I love filmmaking. All the crews were so wonderful. And I think one of the reasons that they were so good to me was because of my work as a choreographer. I think I was sensitive to people. I knew how to place them, how to move them, how to keep things moving on the screen. A lot of people ask me now, "as a woman, did you find it very tricky in those times?" I didn't at all. Some of the women who worked in films in Britain—I mean even Muriel Box—she hated every minute of what she was doing. Where I had a blazingly happy time in my career and absolutely enjoyed every moment of it, she really had a rotten time. And she was brilliant. She's a very good writer.

WD: Yes, no question.

WT: But because she had come from the writing side of films and hadn't gotten a career outside of films, I think the crew decided to give her a bad time of it. Or not respect her as much as they should have done. You know. Perhaps she didn't have enough experience working on the floor with actors. When you come from the editing or the writing room, that is the one thing that you miss out on. And of course I was so lucky in that way, because I had worked with actors a lot.

WD: Would you say that later in the 1950s and up to your last film, *The King's Breakfast* in 1963, that you were more or less typed as a comedy director against your will?

WT: Oh yes, I would think so. I'm also typed in the theater. I mean I've done a lot of straight things, but most of the things that I've done have been amusing. I enjoy comedy. I think people think of me as more comedy than not. I don't mind that.

WD: To what degree do you inject your own personal commentary into your comedies work?

WT: I'm not aware of it at all. But I've got a play on tour at the moment, a very old comedy called *See How They Run.* It was at a theater that I work at a lot, the Watermill Theatre, which is just outside of London. And I thought I had just done a fairly workmanlike job of it. It was very funny, and the actors were very good, they were enjoying themselves. Then one of the regular theatergoers happened to see me in the bar one evening.

He came over and said "Oh, Wendy, I would have known you had directed that anywhere!" I said, "Now, now—come on!" He said, "Well, I don't know, but just the chases and everything was so funny. There was no question that you had done it." So I suppose without knowing it at all you do leave your mark a little bit.

WD: You've also been doing a lot of television. You did a remake of *The Stranger Left No Card* for Anglia Television in Britain in 1981.

WT: I did, and I didn't want to. I really *didn't* want to.

WD: Was that shot on video tape?

WT: Yes, with Derek Jacobi. The man who bought the rights to it rang me up, because we're old friends. He said, "will you do it?" And I told him, "I don't want to do it again. I don't think I would ever do it as well as it was done originally. And it's better in black and white. That's one of the qualities of it. "Well," he said, "I'm going to do it. Do think about it for a few days, because if you don't do it, somebody will." So I thought, "well, I must do it. I can't let somebody else do it."

WD: What are your feelings about shooting on film, versus tape?

WT: I don't really like it. But I think that in a funny sort of way, it's much more practical—tape. You can see it right back, and the editing seems to go easier, but the thing about tape to me is that it strips everything down visually. It seems almost too real.

WD: Do you think that critics who discuss your films today read things into them that really aren't there?

WT: No, I don't think they could have done that. They were too simple, my films. There's a subtext in *Raising a Riot* in a very jokey way, isn't there? It's simply that in domestic matters, a man doesn't cope with it all quite as well as a woman, but that's because he hasn't had to do it for so long. It's not any stronger than that. And I think nowadays it's very old fashioned. I think it is so outdated, because I think men do help with everything now.

WD: Yes, but don't you think that those films helped influence society, pave the way, shape things?

WT: Well, I like to think so. I like to think that because I did my job, not necessarily very brilliantly, but well and never went over budget (which is probably very unimaginative of me, but I didn't), I paved the way for other women to work in film. I thought I had a job to do, and I had to stick to it. I like to think that because of that perhaps I did help other women get jobs. People say, "you've never been a feminist, and you never fight for women." Well I don't, really, but I think an example of doing something and getting on with it and not being a crashing bore about things is probably better than getting onto a platform and making some speech about it all. By being didactic, you alienate a large part of your audience.

WD: Do you miss the old studio system? Was the demise of the studio system the reason that you stopped directing films in 1963?

WT: No, not at all. I think they just didn't want me. I wanted to do my own projects and not what they wanted me to do. If I had stuck in with it and done one or two of the things that were offered to me at the time, instead of going back to the theater to do things I wanted to do, I might still be working away. In the sixties I took on a television show called *Chelsea at Nine*, which I produced for a year. So that was a whole year out of it. And what with that and with stage shows and operas and things—you know—I didn't get around to it again.

I think if I'd stuck with films, I could have been quite a good film director, eventually. But I've always been so interested in so many different things, that I've left films and gone back to the theater. I think if I'd stuck to films, I probably would have had a much better career. But I've had a lot of fun.

CHAPTER TWELVE

THE LAST GASP OF THE MIDDLE CLASS: BRITISH WAR FILMS OF THE 1950s

Neil Rattigan

THE PERIOD OF late 1940s and 1950s in Britain is seldom seen by film historians as a distinctive one in its own right. Most British cinema histories see the importance of the period not in the films produced but in terms of the disruptions caused to production by the various and mostly ill-advised interventions into the overall industry by the Labour government (1945-51), and in relation to the monopolistic practices of the Rank organization and the problems this caused as well as the problems caused to Rank by the government (Perry 1985, 104-44; Betts 1973, 209-25; Armes 1978, 156-73). In terms of the films, for the most part the late 1940s is a period that tends to be categorized as harbinger of the 1950s, and the 1950s themselves as little more than a hiatus before the flowering of British social realism in the 1960s. The rare exceptions are the justly praised (if critically overworked) Ealing Comedies, which bud and flower in the late 1940s and come to mellow fruitfulness in the 1950s and which are often felt to be the most substantive form of British cinema in the first decade or so after the war. The period 1946-59 deserves more attention than it has received, notably for the very way in which it is *precisely* a bridge between wartime films and those of the socially realist 1960s.

As the Second World War ended, British society, not surprisingly, began to take stock of the many changes that had, or that appeared to have, taken place during and because of the demands of six years of hostilities. The British Council, for example, undertook a series of appraisals of the state of British art and culture, and one such appraisal of British film was written by the prominent film critic Dilys Powell. Powell's summation of the radical changes undergone by British films as a consequence of the demands of the war became the accepted view of the state of British cinema of the time, and it remains largely unchallenged:

> The British no longer demand pure fantasy in their films; they can be receptive also
> to the imaginative interpretation of everyday life. The serious British film has thus

found an audience as well as a subject. If it preserves its newly-found standards of conception and technique, it will find not only merely a national, but an international audience. (1947, 40)

This analysis was repeated almost verbatim by Dennis Forman five years later:

> During the war a school of young film makers had triumphantly struck a mould of story-documentary production [in] which . . . all show[ed] a mastery of film technique which before the war had been apparent only in the work of a handful of leading (and well established) directors. (1952, 7)

A selective history of the wartime production was already being cemented into place within a year or two of the end of the war. Like most national film histories, this one argued that the British wartime film was defined by the qualities of a carefully selected group of particular films—the "cream" of the films—rather than from an overview that took the good with bad, the mediocre with the best.

Whether or not the aesthetic and social promises of wartime British films were later met, postwar British cinema did not take either Britain or the world by storm—at least not for another ten years or so. Today the 1950s is an almost entirely critically forgotten period of British cinema. It does not receive attention anything like that awarded to the two critically identified "periods" that precede and follow it: the war period (1939-46) and the period of the "new realism" (1959-early 1970s). The future that both Powell and Forman predicted from their assessment of the wartime cinema seems not to have occurred—at least, that is the conclusion the critical silence over 1950s British cinema would lead one to make. In fact, immediate postwar British films *did* continue trends and directions that had been encouraged during the war, without making any abrupt alterations to themes, concerns, ideologies, or aesthetics of wartime films other than a shift in the social class focus.

The concern of this essay is with British films made during the 1950s that deal with the British involvement in the Second World War, films that are almost totally ignored within this area of critical under-attention.[1] It may be that the 1950s war films have been ignored by recent British film scholars because they have been intent on rewriting British film history—rewriting that has been concerned to rediscover the "repressed" (i.e., social realism) within British film production, a "repressed" totally at odds to these 1950s war films and their unabashed middle-class ideology. And yet, the 1950s war films were direct descendants of the critically valorized wartime films.

British propaganda promoted the notion of a people's war by showing what looked like "old," class-bound Victorian Britain as being, in fact, the "new," democratic twentieth-century Britain. Even before the war ended, this approach was attacked by some who felt that there was a danger that illusion could become reality.

That is to say, the images of Britain that the propagandists were attempting to pro-mulgate at home and abroad were seen by some to be not enhancing or valorizing the "best of Britain" but denying or subverting it. These notions are useful as an indicator of the often unspoken beliefs that came to inform the 1950s war films: the attempts to bring about a return of the repressed middle class. There underlie these claims that British propaganda films of the war were offering false or distorted views of British society, that very concern that I detect in the 1950s British war films: the fear that the middle class had lost social and cultural centrality within British society during the war because of the demands of a people's war. The very "characteristic English institutions,"[2] which were judged to be threatened by the images of Britain (past and future) put forward in British wartime films, depended for their existence and their structures upon a fundamentally class-divided society in which the middle class took the formative role as to the meaning, function, and continuance of those insti-tutions. These notions about British propaganda do find some support in British films of the war period inasmuch as they occasionally show that the previously governed classes can and do demonstrate capacities and abilities to think, organize, and act for themselves.[3] What seems to me to be at work in the objections to wartime propaganda "images" is a specifically middle-class sensitivity to changes already abroad in the culture (maybe as yet unconsciously) and that could be detected within the film as well. The middle class were beginning to feel left out, taken for granted, and what they stood for diminished thereby. My interpretation of British war films made in the 1950s is that while many attempt to partially rewrite history, most are rather more engaged in attempts to rewrite the themes and narrative mechanisms of wartime films themselves.

Immediately following the end of hostilities, with less than a handful of exceptions, the war *as a topic* did disappear from British films. This may well be understood a simple commercial prudence. No doubt few producers saw many pounds to be made from harping on about that which the audiences for their films would rather put behind them. A few socially aware films were made that dealt with issues arising from the war (*Frieda* [1947], for example), but others used the war as a source of comedy (*Whiskey Galore* [1949]) or romance (*Picadilly Inci-dent* [1946]). This seems perfectly understandable, even logical. But what seems to have been overlooked at the time was the developing strength of the myth of wartime England, a myth the wartime films themselves had helped to foster, a myth that said in part that it was *then* that the British were at their best, when if Britannia did not rule the waves unchallenged, she certainly did not allow anyone else that privilege, that Britain and the British could and did "take it." This myth took root initially during the war, but it was not until the 1950s in a renewed cycle of production of war films that the myth came to have particular cinematic attraction.

As the wartime austerity that remained and even deepened in the late 1940s continued into the new decade of the 1950s, and as British international prestige faded with the waning of the empire, and as the bureaucracy of the welfare state became part of the new way of life of the British, two impulses served to make the war film an attractive proposition for British film makers and British audiences.

First, it was a way to instantly hark back to that mythic time when (it was believed) the British people stood alone but together, bravely faced adversity of the most fearsome type, and bested it. The corollary to this, to the benefit of film-makers, was that where during the war films had been determined to show the British not losing the war, now there was an opportunity, even a demand, to show the British actually winning it.

Second, the undercurrents of a surge of class conflict, a demand by the working class not simply for more of the nation's resources but also for more of the nation's attention was beginning to be felt. Historians accept that "overall, the war strengthened the solidarity and self-awareness of the working class" and that the material conditions of life of the working class improved because "there was a new upper-class and middle-class concern that, having played so crucial a role in the war effort, the workers should not be plunged back into the economic depression of the inter-war years" (Marwick 1982, 42). These combined with the election of a Labour government and the implementation of a vast array of welfare programs to change in substantial ways the parameters of working-class culture. The working class, it might thus be said, came to share more equally in the over-all image of the nation. But this was not immediately reflected in popular culture and certainly not on the cinema screens. Here the working class were initially "rewarded" for their "crucial role in the war effort" by narratives "about" them and sympathetic characterizations, as in, for example, *Hue and Cry* and *It Always Rains on Sunday* (both 1947). But this soon faded. The paternalism that Marwick suggests motivated the upper and middle classes after the war is reflected in these films—and its limits as well. Eventually, the working class would demand its own voice, or failing that, demand accurate representations of its actual conditions of existence in the cinema (and in other popular culture forms: theater, novels, and finally pop music). This would manifest itself in the so-called revolution in British cinema dating from about 1959. There is a corollary to this second condition, another explanation, related to changes being felt—consciously and uncon-sciously—within British society, as to why 1950s war films seem to reflect des-perate attempts to hold the wartime community spirit: "it does seem that 1951 can be seen as a pivotal year for British society, marking a shift from a period of post-war austerity . . . to the consumer boom of the 50s . . . The shift can also be characterised in terms of changing national values, *community spirit giving way to individualism* and an increasing emphasis on the private domain of home and family" (Barr 1986, 355; my italics).

These factors combined to bring about a return in some concentration (although never to the stage of that of wartime production) of war films by

British film makers. The types of films that they made during the fifties (and the "cycle" did peter out with the coming of the social realist films of the sixties) were both like and unlike those of the war period. Some looked as if they could have been made at anytime during the war (e.g., *The Gift Horse* [1952], *The Cruel Sea* [1953], *The Sea Shall Not Have Them* [1954]); some were concerned to replace the upper classes in the forefront of winning the war (e.g., *The Battle of the River Plate* [1956]). Others, picking on a minor trend of wartime films, revelled in the upper-middle-class "intellectuals" playing cunning games (e.g., *The Man Who Never Was* [1956] or *I Was Monty's Double* [1958]). And there were those few films that dared voice a certain amount of reservation about the glory of war and the particular way the British fought it (e.g., *The Bridge on the River Kwai* [1957]). Some differences in content are noticeable. It is obvious that certain types of stories could not have been made during the war in any case. For example, prisoner-of-war stories—since the actualities of conditions and activities within prisoner-of-war camps can only have been vaguely surmised, and such stories can hardly have been conducive to a positive war effort.[4] There is in the 1950s a minicycle of such films (e.g., *The Wooden Horse* [1950], *The Colditz Story* [1954]). Or again, authentic stories about real secret operations, counterespionage, secret weapons, and so on (e.g., *Odette* [1950], *Carve Her Name With Pride* [1958], and others mentioned above). Nearly all such films, except those like *The Bridge on the River Kwai*, are replete with self-congratulatory tones in keeping with an overall theme of "how we won the war." There is another minicycle of films whose narratives are concerned with the disillusionments of postwar civilian life experienced by ex-servicemen who had "a good war" and that emphasize nostalgia for the myth of the war (e.g., *The Intruder* [1953] and *The Ship That Died of Shame* [1955]).

Two issues paramount in any understanding of British wartime films—the question of class and propaganda/ideology—instead of disappearing with the conclusion of the war, return in something like full force (but with greater subtlety) in 1950s war films. T. S. Eliot, writing while the war was still on but with more than one eye to the postwar future, made an observation that turns out to be surprisingly pertinent to the question of the relations between wartime films and postwar British films dealing with the war:

> Of the advantages of administrative and sentimentalist unity we hardly need to be reminded, after the experience of war, but it is often assumed that the unity of wartime should be preserved in time of peace. Amongst any people engaged in warfare, especially when the war appears, or can be made to appear, purely defensive, we may expect a spontaneous unity of sentiment which is genuine, an affectation of it on the part of those who merely wish to escape odium, and from all, submission to the commands of the constituted authority. We should hope to find th

same harmony and docility among the survivors of a shipwreck adrift in a lifeboat. People often express regret that the same unity, self-sacrifice and fraternity which prevail in an emergency, cannot survive the emergency itself. (1968, 124)

There are other notable differences between the films of the wartime and the war films of the 1950s. At the most general level, the latter are more often than not (although not exclusively) concerned with showing the British *winning* the war as opposed to *not losing it*. This is typically expressed through small-scale, imaginatively conceived and boldly carried-out actions by small groups (e.g., in *The Gift Horse*, *The Dam Busters*, *They Who Dare* [all 1953] *Above Us the Waves*, *The Cockleshell Heroes* [both 1955], and *Sea of Sand* [1958]). The metaphor is obvious. Then again, the wartime need for examining (or burying) the question of class and the promoting of a certain ideology of social relationships is changed in the 1950s—although not all that changed: it is still rooted in the British class system. In the 1950s, however, it is not necessary to try and foster notions (credible or not) of social and cultural solidarity in order to unite the country to meet the demands of a people's war. Arguably, 1950s war films are concerned with putting the "people" back into their place (where, presumably. T. S. Eliot for one would like to see them put). So while the films *are* involved with notions of national identity—bolstering the failing image of Britain as a power both at home and abroad—they are also concerned with a revisionist history of the war—showing the British winning the war without needing to also propagandize the lower classes into helping. The lower classes, inasmuch as they are present, are "naturalized" to an extent that goes beyond that of wartime films such as *In Which We Serve* (1942), which clearly asserts the unquestioned naturalness of the division of society into discrete classes hierarchically organized. Any doubts on the unimportance of the lower classes in 1950s war films can be quickly dismissed by comparing *In Which We Serve* with *The Bridge on the River Kwai*, two films that invite such comparison on the level of the haughtiness of their respective commanding officer main characters and the blind obedience and loyalty of the lower ranks. Yet, unlike *In Which We Serve*, there is no need in *Bridge on the River Kwai* to "humanize" the men beyond that of ordinary British "Tommies." They are what they are. Is it their war? Hardly so. The postwar films are as much an exercise in "papering the gaps" of social inequality as the wartime films—indeed, even more so. By the 1950s, the gaps are wider, spreading, and in different places. Any by the 1960s, such remedial patchworking becomes, and is seen to become, futile. With the social realist films of the 1960s, the gaps become the decor.

A glance at the number of war films made in the 1940s and 1950s clearly implies that, in relation to other sorts of films, the 1950s is not statistically remarkable for its war films. But then, it is also apparent that during the war itself, there was a considerable weighing of war-film production in the first three to four years and a recognizable dropping off in the last two years. What is significant is that the downward trend began even before the war was over and that the peak of production of war films was in 1942. From 1943 onward the war provided a subject for fewer and fewer films. So while the dearth of films after hostilities ceased can be explained by straightforward war-weariness, the waning from the middle of the war (not known as such at the time of course) needs further explanation.

One explanation for the decrease in the production of war films during the hostilities can be related to the claim that the propaganda task of "converting" the people of Britain to the task of responding to the "fact" of a people's war had been accomplished by 1942. But another explanation suggests itself. The films of the first three or four years of the war, in addition to whatever else they had to say about the notions of a people's war and, advertently or inadvertently, about the class structure of Britain, also tended to concentrate on the theme of not losing the war rather than winning the war. With the increasing involvement of the U.S.S.R. and the United States, it became clear that any winning of the war that might take place would not be exclusively or even primarily British. It may then be a question of the blow to British self-generated prestige that caused them to be less concerned with making films about winning the war. But it may also be that the myth of the British at war, which had become quickly and firmly entrenched, and which emphasized the "British can take it" syndrome and a certain masochistic satisfaction in hardship was too powerful to give up. Britannia with her back to the wall but refusing to give in is, to British eyes and minds, a much more appealing national image than Britannia out in the middle of the ring beating the living daylights out of a reeling opponent with the help of several larger allies.

In light of this latter situation, it makes many of the films of the 1950s rather more interesting. Some show a very real continuity with the realist dramas of the war. *The Dam Busters*, for example, is a linear descendent of *Target for Tonight* (1941) and *The First of the Few* (1942). These, and others of a more Hollywood-ish tone, are simultaneously concerned with reversing the pattern just described and with showing Britain not simply fighting back but winning on its own terms.

Other aspects drawn from the history of the 1950s suggest themselves as possible motives for a revitalization of the myth of Britain at War, with the new emphasis of winning: the return to conservative government after the postwar Labour government; the disintegration of the British Empire, the fiasco of Suez.

It would seem then that the films that preceded the revitalization of a newly social-realistic British cinema in the 1960s represented a reflection of and a contribution to a last-ditch effort by the dominant culture to "keep the lid on" the British social revolution, an effort complicated by a middle-class "backlash" against the way in which the images of a people's war had given emphasis to the working class and taken the middle class for granted in wartime propaganda. Even so, one reason why the war as a narrative subject returned in significant quantity to the British film in the 1950s was an attempt to try and revive the mythic aspects of the war at a time (the last time?) in which the British stood together *in their various social positions*, united in common goals and communality. The war films of the 1950s then wished to reenergize and reactivate "that magic moment when all the class and social contradictions of British culture evaporated" (Britton 1989, 39) with these essential differences: this time Britain would not be winning-by-not-losing but be simply winning; and without the awkward (from the dominant ideological point of view) need to draw attention to the contribution required and attained by the working class.

Thus, the war films of the 1950s drew heavily upon war nostalgia, the "British myth of the war as a golden age" (Britton 1989, 39) but at the same time revised that myth, that history, by subtracting from it the very thing that had formed the basis of the myth-creating films of the 1940s: the notion of a people's war. Now the dominant classes of Britain could fight the war (or could be seen to fight the war) the way they had wanted to (and "believed" they had) from the first, without making concessions to the "sensitivity" of the lower orders simply to ensure that they would turn out for the match. The powerful myth of the war could be used as the very tool by which it was simultaneously and fundamentally "rewritten." The need to do so was, then, a consequence of the perception that the concessions wrung out of the dominant classes by the lower classes in return for going to war (for the second time in twenty years) were put into place (by the Labour government of 1945-51) and a sense that the changes in the class system that the lower classes expected (and the upper and especially the middle classes feared) were actually coming about. The war films of the 1950s are ironically prophetic of the social-realist films of the 1960s, not through being "a voice crying in the wilderness," but by being the reflection of the last ditch effort by the dominant class to maintain its hegemony by rewriting the history of the celluloid war in its own favor and offering this as a remembrance of the way things were.

There is, however, a complicating and contradictory spirit at work in the war films of the 1950s. One of the effects of the deliberate fostering of the notions of a people's war by and through the wartime films was to imply an alliance of interest and identity of all social classes and all subnational regions in Britain. Since the aim was to bring the working class around to sharing the ruling class view of the need to fight Germany and Nazism, founded in an arrogant belief that the working class could need to be cajoled into this, there was inevitably set up the notion that the working class and the ruling class not only had much in common but could form a "natural" alliance. Less a hatred of tyranny—since that may well raise awkward questions about the social relationship of ruling and ruled in Britain—the emphasis was on a mutually shared love of Britain (defined within the dominant mythos of Englishness). The prevalence of upper-class leaders in wartime films is one of its particular but not surprising features; so, too, is the way in which the working class representatives in those films, no matter how poorly or inadequately characterized (in terms of authenticity and understanding), shared the perceptions and goals of those upper-class leaders. The "middle" of the middle class, it could be or was safely assumed (by the ruling class), would understand the dominant perceptions of the war. Their screen presence in wartime films is generally unremarkable and usually takes the form of individual representatives who concur with the dominant ideology but show less aptitude that the upper-class representatives to conduct the war "properly"—to lead men, organize, and so on.

There are exceptions, and these will turn out to be important in relation to the direction taken by some postwar war films. The exception that proves the rule of the quiescence of the middle classes is *The Way Ahead* (1943). In the 1950s, however, more important are those films in which the middle class (almost inevitably upper- rather than lower-middle class) are shown to be taking a leading role in *supporting* and *promoting* the cause of Britain. Here, in the sphere of the combined attributes of intellect and practicality, is the "place" for the middle class to lead. They are, of course, dependent upon the ruling classes to "permit" them this role. Their intellect is also of the severely technological kind, not the lofty realms of disinterested philosophy. They are the "boffins," or in another especially telling term, "the back room boys." The exemplar in the postwar war films is Barnes Wallis in *The Dam Busters*. This trend may be perceived at the very end of the war in *The Way to the Stars* (1945), a film not concerned with a technical meritocracy, it is true, but very much centered on the way in which the middle class is able to rise to the occasion and lead and serve as well as the upper class (in matters both military and of the heart).

There is then a sort of tug-of-war in the 1950s war films. On the one hand, there are those films that show the upper class winning the war almost single handedly, thus revising the myth. On the other, there are those that emphasize the role of the middle classes. These, rather more numerous, arise partly from the perception (shared with the upper class) that in postwar Britain, and as a consequence of the Labour Government (while it lasted) and the introduction of the welfare state, the working class was getting too "uppity": they wanted not only to be looked after (a continuance of paternalism) but also to be seen and heard. But equally as important, the middle-class emphasis on these films was driven by the fear the middle class had of an alliance between upper class and working class. That great Victorian era invention, the middle class, had always affected to despise both these other classes, although remaining ready to allow the upper class to rule and the working class to work as long as its own class position as "the backbone of England" remained undisturbed. The promises made or implied by a people's war seemed to offer consolidation of that position and to have improved along with improving the conditions of the working class. But the results, in retrospect, were rather more disturbing to the middle class. The speed with which Conservative governments were elected after the initial flirtation with Labour suggests the degree to which the implications of social change became apparent to the middle class.

Postwar British cinema in general rather quickly fell into the mode of "attacking" the upper class. (The most devastating example is Ealing Studios'

Kind Hearts and Coronets [1949]). Awaking to the "danger" of the working class rather later, the British cinema was slower but eventually more determined to attack the working class through films such as *The Man in the White Suit* (1951) and *I'm All Right, Jack* (1959). These films, not being concerned with recreating the war, are outside the scope of this discussion, but they do add indirect support to the claim that, by and large, the postwar British war films are middle-class films. There is at least one war film that matches the cynical middle-class attitude toward the alliance of the working class and upper class that figures *The Man in the White Suit*. This film is *Privates on Parade* (1956). The film's view of the venality of both upper and lower classes is less surprising when one recognizes the extent to which this film is simply a variation on a theme found in a number of the films made by the Boulting brothers—*I'm All Right, Jack* and *Heaven's Above* (both 1960) rehearse this same theme.

An even more obvious example of the way in which these films, or some of them, rewrote history as it was understood from the wartime films can be found in *The Bridge on the River Kwai*, where the working class (the ordinary soldiers) are led totally astray by blind affection for their officer-leaders and where the object of the stupidity of the officer class, the bridge itself, and the misguided, even treacherous British colonel are both destroyed by a middle-class Englishman and an American working together. The reversal of the ideology of the wartime films can hardly be more complete. But to get to this point, the shape and structure of those wartime films had to be rehearsed then modified in the films of the 1950s. It was, however, a doomed attempt. The "bursting" onto the British cinema scene of the social-realist films of the 1960s drove British war films from that point away from any attempts to rewrite history in terms of realist aesthetics and the use of selected actuality (most of the war films of the 1950s are based on actual events and individuals).

The eulogy to the short-lived revisionist cinematic history of the middle class at war is found in a film that is not about the war at all but about the postwar military. *Tunes of Glory* (1960) has as a central character, a good, honest upper-middle-class colonel who is, quite literally, destroyed by a considerably less gentlemanly lower-class, up-from-the-ranks subordinate. The film is a bitter lament over the shift in social relations that by 1960 had been firmly established. The Thatcher years in Britain embodied the triumphant return of the middle class. The 1950s war film, for all their celebration of the middle class, are seen in hindsight as the swan song (for two decades at least) of that class.

NOTES

1. My concern will be with the social aspects of these films, especially as related to social class; the ways in which the transformation in the aesthetics of British film practice that took place during the war were continued and modified in postwar cinema deserve extended, but separate, discussion.

2. A phrase used by the economist F. A. Hayek in 1944 in an amazing attack on the notions of a planned society, which he further equated with both fascism and communism.

3. My reading of the wartime films I have analyzed elsewhere would not bring me to the conclusions Hayek indicates about the left wing propaganda affectivity of those films. Quite the contrary—these films seem, in one way or another, supportive of the status quo, at least as far as British class structure is concerned.

4. There is an interesting exception to this: *2,000 Women* (1944), which is an exception not only because it is a wartime film about prison camp life but also because it deals with women internees rather than male P.O.W.s.

WORKS CITED

Armes, Roy. *A Critical History of British Cinema*. New York: Oxford UP, 1978.

Barr, Charles. *All Our Yesterdays: 90 Years of British Film*. London: BFI Publishing, 1986.

Betts, Ernest. *The Film Business: A History of British Cinema, 1896-1972*. London: Allen and Unwin, 1973; New York: Pitman, 1973.

Britton, Andrew. "Their Finest Hour: Humphrey Jennings and the British Imperial Myth of World War II." *CineAction!* 18, 1989.

Eliot, T. S. *Christianity and Culture*. New York: Harcourt Brace Jovanovich, 1968.

Forman, Dennis. *Film 1945-1950*. London: British Council/Longman, Green, 1952.

Marwick, Arthur. *British Society since 1945*. Harmondsworth: Penguin, 1982.

Medhurst, Andy. "1950s War Films." *National Fictions: World War Two in British Film and Television*. Ed. Geoff Hurd. London: BFI Publishing, 1984.

Perry, George. *The Great British Picture Show: From the Nineties to the Seventies*. 2nd ed. London: Pavilion/Michael Joseph, 1985; Boston: Little, Brown, 1985.

Powell, Dilys. *Films Since 1939*. London: British Council/Longman, Green, 1947.

CHAPTER THIRTEEN

EVIDENCE FOR A BRITISH FILM NOIR CYCLE

Laurence Miller

FILM NOIR REFERS to a cycle of American films first perceived by Europeans as having cohesive and consistent themes and a distinctive style. The noir cycle ran from 1940-59 and consists of several hundred films (Selby 1984, 2-3; Miller 1989, 51-55). Appel nicely states the essence of film noir: "What unites the seemingly disparate kinds of films noirs . . . is their dark visual style and their black vision of despair, loneliness, and dread . . . In the best films noirs the visual style and narrative structure work hand-in-hand in consistent, unified ensemble" (1974, 153).

It is the explicitly or implicitly stated opinion of film scholars that film noir is an exclusively American form. For example, Silver and Ward state, "With the Western film film noir shares the distinction of being an indigenous American form" (1979, 1). According to Pendergast, "The term film noir was coined by French critics to describe a distinctive breed of American films that emerged in the 1940s and 1950s" (1986, 71). Even where such explicit statements of origin are not made, it is assumed that film noir is an American breed, because all of the films that are discussed are exclusively American. Only a couple of authors have vaguely suggested that film noir may not be exclusively American. Selby stated, "If there is such a thing as a British noir cycle or a French noir cycle (and there very well may be), it is left to others to define and list such films" (1984, 126). Ottoson more affirmatively stated that "for this study only American films noirs are examined, but they were also produced in England and France" (1981, 1). However, Ottoson provides no evidence to support this statement or to suggest that there were sufficient number of films to constitute a cycle in these countries.

A number of variables, to be discussed, have been identified as contributing to the development of film noir in America (Crowther 1988, 39-60; Hirsch 1981, 23-69; Ottoson 1981, 1-3; Polan 1986, 1-20; Silver and Ward 1979, 1-6; Telotte 1989, 1-39; Tuska 1984, 3-146). To establish the existence of an indigenous film noir in another country would require demonstration of similar causal variables, as well as causal variables that were unique to that country. The second factor necessary to demonstrate an indigenous film noir would be to identify a sufficient number of films made in that country from 1940 to 1959 that possess the requisite content and style to constitute a cycle. This paper focuses on British cinema from 1940 to 1959. It is the thesis of this paper that there was an indigenous film noir cycle in Britain that occurred concurrently with the American cycle. This British cycle was as well developed as the American cycle in terms of quantity and quality, content and style.

The major forces that gave rise to film noir in America and in Britain are: (1) cataclysmic events of the twentieth century, (2) crime and the underworld, (3) the roman noir (novels, stories and plays that were made into films noirs), (4) films of the 1920s and 1930s that were precursors or prototypes of film noir, and (5) a group of filmmakers who possessed the stylistic and experiential sensibilities that were expressed as film noir.

CATACLYSMIC EVENTS OF THE TWENTIETH CENTURY

Both Britain and America suffered the hardships of the two world wars and the depression. The experiences produced by these events graphically emphasized the capriciousness, unpleasantness, and hazards of living in this century, dominant themes of film noir.

World War I was unlike any previous one in terms of the horrors it produced: "Up until around the beginning of the century, certainly by the time of the First World War, . . . the majority of artists . . . were expecting their work somehow to give valid and non-contradictory answers about life, love, whatever . . . At the time of the war an incredible disillusion sets in, and a lot of the most interesting work stops so much looking for answers as questioning the whole idea of an Answer, taking more interest in questions than in any kind of answer at all" (Israel, quoted in Downey 1986, 37).

Britain suffered 750,000 soldiers killed—a whole generation was wiped out. "The war hit British consciousness with traumatic force, leaving bitterness and cynicism in its train . . . Due to the physical losses of war, life remains austere and grey for the bulk of British people. For most of the men who fought this trench warfare, World War I meant constant and seemingly fruitless agony of mud and blood almost impossible to describe" (Marwick 1971, 1, 8). "It is unspeakable, godless, hopeless" (Nash, quoted in Marwick 1971, 17-18).

Both America and Britain experienced a collapse of the postwar boom and the onset of a long depression that lasted until World War II. Unemployment increased in Britain from 10 percent in 1921 to almost 20 percent in 1931. The British export trade collapses. There was much labor unrest. "The depression was a time of hopelessness born of chronic economic depression and economic insecurity and poverty" (Marwick 1982, 84).

Britain was America's ally in World War II, and she suffered 300,000 soldiers killed. However, the experience of Britain was uniquely different—and far worse—than America's experience, because Britain was bombed by the German Luftwaffe. The bombing of London began in September 1940 and continued for seventy-six nights on end, followed by sporadic bombings for the next six months. The effects of these raids were devastating. Sixty thousand civilians were killed. Two of seven homes were destroyed or damaged, and over the course of the war there were sixty million changes of address—more than Britain's population (Marwick 1971, 99-100). The mood of the time is perfectly reflected in a diary entry from October 1940, which reads like a noir statement about fate: "Got accustomed to know may be blown to bits at any moment. Casual scraps of news bring this home better than statistics: Two girls go into a telephone box to send word they may be late home, as there is a raid on. Bomb falls close by. Both killed. Woman of 94 with six daughters takes shelter in basement when house is hit. Two of daughters die. What a picture! A family creeps out of its garden dugout to get supper. They sit down at table. Next minute they are all dead. We know this may happen to any of us. Yet we go about as usual. Life goes on" (Marwick 1971, 99).

Britain also experienced another type of warfare that was unexperienced in America in the twentieth century, the internal civil warfare of the Irish rebellion. When Britain executed Irish leaders following the 1916 Easter rising, Irish opinion was set aflame (Yeats: "A terrible beauty is born"). The partition of Ireland was followed by guerrilla warfare between the Irish Sinn Fein and the British Black and Tans. "Reprisals and counterreprisals, arson, and atrocities continued, . . . until in 1921 the Irish Free State was established, though still embodying the 1920 partition. But the Irish question was far from settled: the partition pleased no one, and in southern Ireland in particular, the Irish turned their fury against each other" (Marwick 1971, 31-32). This tragedy continues today and is reflected in some British films noirs (e.g., *Odd Man Out* [1947]; *Shake Hands with the Devil* [1959]).

CRIME AND THE UNDERWORLD

Criminal activity was a cause for concern in Britain as well as in America, especially after World War II. Since 1945 the number of crimes committed in Britain increased at an annual average rate of 9 percent (Lane 1971, 131), with 40 percent of all crimes involving robbery and violence. A 1959 government document stated, "It is a disquieting feature of our society that in the years since the war, rising standards in material prosperity, education and social welfare brought no reduction in the high crime rate; on the contrary, crime has increased and is still increasing" (Lane 1971, 131). Such preoccupation with crime is reflected in a steady high output of films of the 1940s and 1950s that focused on a variety of criminal acts.

THE ROMAN NOIR

Romans noirs, as exemplified in the writings of, for example, Raymond Chandler, Dashiell Hammett, Dorothy Hughes, Mickey Spillane, and Cornell Woolrich, were adapted into a significant number of American films noirs. The roman noir seems to be uniquely American, in contrast to the British mystery-detective tradition exemplified by Arthur Conan-Doyle (as Raymond Chandler observed, "Sherlock Holmes is after all just an attitude"), Agatha Christie, Dorothy Sayers, and others. However, the American roman noir was popular in Britain, and British editions were typically published by British publishing houses shortly after the books appeared in America, or sometimes even before. So, indirectly, a tradition of the roman noir did exist in Britain. In addition, some British novelists did write more in the American than in the British tradition. Their novels enjoyed wide popularity and served as the basis for both American and British films noirs; for example, Graham Greene's *Brighton Rock*, *This Gun for Sale*, *The Third Man*, and *The Fallen Idol*; F. L. Green's *Odd Man Out*.

PRECURSORS OR PROTOTYPES OF FILM NOIR

Film noir did not suddenly materialize in America in 1940. Film noir traces its lineage to a number of films made in the 1920s and 1930s whose themes were the same as those of film noir. *I Am a Fugitive from a Chain Gang* (1932), *Fury* (1936), *You Only Live Once* (1937) and *Let Us Live* (1939) are but a prominent few of the many film noir precursors or prototypes. Similarly, in Britain a number of films were released in the 1920s and 1930s whose themes were the same as those of British films noirs of the 1940s and 1950s, but they must be considered prototypes for the same reason as their American counterparts. *This Man is News* (1938), *A Window in London* (1939), and *I Met a Murderer* (1939) are but a few examples of such films.

PERSONNEL

A number of gifted European cinema artists, such as Fritz Lang, Edgar G. Ulmer, Billy Wilder, John Brahm, Max Ophuls, Robert Siodmak, John Alton, and Franz Planer, brought with them the experience of living in Europe, the temperament and sensibility, and the stylistic influence of German expressionism that so suffuses film noir. In addition, many American films noirs were the product of gifted native American film artists, such as Orson Welles, Henry Hathaway, Anthony Mann, Nicholas Ray, and Raoul Walsh.

Britain was not blessed with the influx of European artists that America was—no doubt the Europeans came to Hollywood because of the opportunities and to get safely and far away from Europe. Nevertheless, as in America, in

Figure 13.1. *Blackmailed* with Dirk Bogarde. Courtesy: Laurence Miller.

Britain there lived a number of talented and capable individuals with the sensibil-
ity and style to do film noir, so that an indigenous British film noir could develop.
For example, Carol Reed, John Boulting, Anthony Kimmins, Terence Fisher and
David Lean all directed British noirs.

Art is in part a reflection of a culture's state of existence at the time that art
is created. The series of forces that shaped and influenced American film noir
were no doubt present at the same time in Britain and no doubt exerted a strong
and similar influence on the content and style of British films made from 1940-59.
As a result, there developed in Britain a flourishing and productive cycle of films
every bit as much film noir as their American counterparts.

The largest and most comprehensive published filmography of American
film noir is Selby's (1984, 3). Counting color films noirs, his total is 499 films
noirs. Of these 499 films, 423 were made and distributed by the eight major American motion picture studies (Columbia, Fox, MGM, Paramount, RKO, United
Artists, Universal, and Warner Brothers) (211). From 1940 to 1959 these eight studios made and distributed a total of 5,392 films (Finler 1988, 280). Thus, 7.8 percent of the total output (423/5,392) of these studies were film noir. The percentages
run from a low of 5.4 percent (MGM) to a high of 12.0 percent (RKO). The
remaining 76 films noirs were made by twelve "minor" studios, such as Lippert,
PRC, Eagle Lion, Allied Artists, Monogram, and Republic. As complete data are
readily available for only about half of these studios, I have decided to include only
statistical data from the major studios. However, Monogram, Lippert, Screen
Guild and PRC (including partial output of Eagle Lion) made and released almost
1,000 films between 1940 and 1959. Since the output of two of the largest minors,
Allied Artists and Republic, is not included in this total, the total output is thus well
over 1,000 films. So, the percentage of films noirs released by the minor studios is
no doubt significantly less than that for the major studios.

The total number of films released by *all* British major and minor production and distribution companies between 1940 and 1959 is 2,033 (Gifford
1973, 7-17). The criteria, discussed by the authorities on film noir previously ref-
erenced, that define a film as film noir were strictly and scrupulously applied to my
own extensive personal collection of British films of this era and to my researches.
According to my findings, 331 of the total of 2,033 films are clearly film noir. That
is, 16.3 percent (331/2,033) of British films fall into this group—about twice the
percentage for American film noir.

Examination of these British films noirs reveals a point-by-point similarity
with their American counterparts in terms of philosophy, theme and content,
"noirish" titles, production values and techniques, and photography (flashbacks,
dream sequences, voiceovers, lighting, camera angles, location filming, wet streets,
shadows, nighttime filming, etc.). Also, as with American film noir, most of these
British films noirs were released by the major production and distribution companies (e.g., Anglo-Amalgamated, Associated British Film Distributors, British

Lion, Eros, Exclusive Films, Independent Film Distributors, etc.). This is not to say that British film noir was only a carbon copy of American film noir. Although similar to their American counterparts in many respects, the British noirs nevertheless have a distinctly British "personality" that distinguishes them from their American brethren.

The major difference between the American and British films noirs lies in their frequency of distribution by year. American film noir saw a gradually increasing output from 1940 to 1945 (5 to 22 films per year), a peak output from 1946 to 1950 (42 to 57 films per year), and then a gradually diminishing output until 1959, from 39 to 7 films per year (Selby 1984, 204-10). On the other hand, the output of British film noir was high in 1940 (11 of 77 films) but then dropped off drastically from 1941 to 1946 (1 to 6 films per year), because World War II and its aftermath drastically curtailed production. However, the number of films noirs then returned to the level of 1940 (9 to 13 films per year) from 1947 to 1950 as total output increased. From 1951 to 1955, 22 to 28 films noirs were released each year. The peak years were 1956 (32 films) and 1957 (41 films), followed by a decline to 25 films in 1958 and 25 in 1959. Thus British film noir experienced a steady growth through the 1950s, when American film noir was in decline.

It is impossible in the space remaining to provide a list of all 331 British films noirs. However, in order to place noir films in some kind of context, below are listed themes that commonly occur in American films noirs. Each theme is followed by representative American and British films noirs (of course, some of these American and British films could fit into more than one category):

1. Revenge, vengeance. American: *I, the Jury* (1953); *Red Light* (1948). British: *Appointment with Crime* (1946); *Vengeance Is Mine* (1949); *Cloudburst* (1951); *Lady of Vengeance* (1957).
2. Framed, false accusation. American: *Framed* (1947); *Railroaded* (1947). British: *Three Silent Men* (1940); *Murder in Reverse* (1945); *Take My Life* (1947); *Guilty?* (1956).
3. Obsession, femme fatale. American: *Double Indemnity* (1944); *Out of the Past* (1947); *The Pitfall* (1948). British: *Corridor of Mirrors* (1948); *Dark Secret* (1949); *Marilyn* (1953); *The House Across The Lake* (1954); *Yield to the Night* (1956).
4. Change in identity, pose as someone else, go underground, doppelganger theme. American: *Dark Passage* (1947); *Hollow Triumph* (1948); *The Street With No Name* (1948). British: *Man In Black* (1950); *The Six Men* (1951); *13 East Street* (1952); *Recoil* (1953); *Deadly Nightshade* (1953); *Breakout* (1959).
5. Amnesia. American: *Crossroads* (1942); *Street of Chance* (1942). British: *Black Widow* (1951); *The Stranger Came Home* (1954); *Fatal Journey* (1954); *The Man on the Cliff* (1955).

6. Policier. American: *T-Men* (1948); *The Naked City* (1948). British: *The Blue Lamp* (1950); *Assassin for Hire* (1951); *Death of an Angel* (1952); *Dollars for Sale* (1955).

7. Menaced, blackmailed, held hostage. American: *Gaslight* (1944); *The Dark Corner* (1946); *Sudden Fear* (1952); *The Other Woman* (1954). British: *Gaslight* (1940); *Pink String and Sealing Wax* (1945); *Murder without Crime* (1950); *Blackmailed* (1951).

8. Dilemma (help someone commit suicide, keep murderer's secret, take blame for crime). American: *Strange Bargain* (1949); *I Confess* (1953). British: *Delayed Action* (1954); *Confession* (1954); *Kill Me Tomorrow* (1957).

9. Psychopathology, mental instability. American: *Bewitched* (1945); *Possessed* (1947). British: *Wanted for Murder* (1946); *Mine Own Executioner* (1947); *Room to Let* (1950); *The Brain Machine* (1955); *Alias John Preston* (1956).

10. Pursued, on the run. American: *Dark Passage* (1947); *The Big Clock* (1948); *The Raging Tide* (1951); *Nightfall* (1957). British: *Odd Man Out* (1947); *The Quiet Woman* (1951); *Final Appointment* (1954); *The Weapon* (1956); *Whirlpool* (1959).

11. Prison life. American: *Caged* (1950); *Crashout* (1955). British: *The Weak and the Wicked* (1954).

12. Double-crossed, betrayed. American: *Out of the Past* (1947); *Too Late for Tears* (1949); *Short Cut to Hell* (1957). British: *The Good Die Young* (1954); *The Witness* (1959).

13. Bait, pawn. American: *Lured* (1947); *Trapped* (1949); *The Narrow Margin* (1952). British: *Midnight Episode* (1950); *Murder at 3 AM* (1953); *Women without Men* (1956); *The Vicious Circle* (1957).

This chapter has hopefully demonstrated the contemporary existence with American film noir of a fully developed noir cycle in Britain. Therefore, film noir cannot be considered to be "indigenous" only to America. Rather, it is likely that film noir developed in each country in response to a similar series of events that occurred at the same time. Additionally, it is likely that American and British film noir influenced each other's development. The sociocultural and artistic ties between America and Britain run deep and have a long history. All eight major American studios had their own production and distribution companies in Britain (Gifford 1973, 16-17). American film companies were no doubt encouraged to set up shop in Britain, due in part to the Quota Act of 1927, which required exhibitors to give 5 percent of their screen time to British films. American companies were encouraged to help finance such productions.

For example, Columbia's in-house British division, Columbia British, was founded in 1934 (Hirschhorn 1990, 374). For the next thirty years, Columbia

British released many low-budget British films. Most of these films were made by local production companies for local consumption, but a number were released in America, and some of these were films noirs. For example, the British film *The Long Haul* was released in 1957. Interestingly, this picture starred Victor Mature, an American, who had appeared in American films noirs (e.g., *The Kiss Of Death*, 1947). In fact, it was not uncommon for Americans with film noir experience to appear in British films.

Additionally, a British film noir may have had little connection with an American studio until it was picked up by the American studio for distribution in the United States. For example, *Man Trap* (1953), an all-British production, was produced by Hammer and released in the United States by United Artists as *Man in Hiding*. United Artists also released *The Good Die Young* (1954), distributed by Independent Film Distributors, in America in 1955. The film starred, along with British stars, Gloria Grahame and Richard Basehart, two prominent American film noir personalities (Bergan 1968, 306-7). And, of course, American films noirs were widely distributed in Britain, and British actors and actresses (e.g., James Mason and Jean Simmons) appeared frequently in American films noirs.

It is beyond the scope of this chapter to speculate to what extent America and Britain were influenced by each other's films noirs. Suffice it to say that each country developed its own noir cycle. Each cycle shares many characteristics, while at the same time being distinctly British or distinctly American.

WORKS CITED

Appel, Alfred. *Nabokov's Dark Cinema*. New York: Oxford UP, 1974.

Bergan, Ronald. *The United Artists Story*. New York: Crown, 1986.

Crowther, Bruce. *Film Noir: Reflections in a Dark Mirror*. New York: Continuum, 1988.

Downey, Roger. "A Post-Modern Ring." *Seattle Weekly* 30 July-5 Aug. 1986: 37.

Finler, Joel W. *The Hollywood Story*. New York: Crown, 1988.

Gifford, Denis. *The British Film Catalogue, 1895-1970: A Reference Guide*. New York: McGraw-Hill, 1973.

Hirsch, Foster. *Film Noir: The Dark Side of the Screen*. New York: Da Capo Press, 1981.

Hirschhorn, Clive. *The Columbia Story*. New York: Crown, 1990.

Lane, Peter. *A History of Post-War Britain*. London: Macdonald Educational, 1971.

Marwick, Arthur. *The Explosion Of British Society, 1914-1970*. London: Macmillan, 1971.

Miller, Laurence. "How Many Films Noirs Are There? How Statistics Can Help Answer This Question." *Empirical Studies of the Art* 7.1, 1989: 51-55.

Ottoson, Robert. *A Reference Guide to the American Film Noir: 1940-1958.* Metuchen, NJ: Scarecrow, 1981.

Pendergast, Alan. "A Touch Of Noir." Vi*deo* 10.8, 1986: 152-54.

Polan, Dana. *Power and Paranoia.* New York: Columbia UP, 1986.

Selby, Spencer. *Dark City: The Film Noir.* Jefferson, NC: McFarlane, 1984.

Silver, Alain, and Elizabeth Ward. *Film Noir: An Encyclopedic Reference to the American Style.* Woodstock, NY: Overlook, 1979.

Telotte, J. P. *Voices in the Dark: The Narrative Patterns of Film Noir.* Urbana: U of Illinois P, 1989.

Tuska, Jon. *Dark Cinema: American Film Noir in Cultural Perspective.* Westport, CT: Greenwood, 1984.

CHAPTER FOURTEEN

THE TRADITION OF INDEPENDENCE: AN INTERVIEW WITH LINDSAY ANDERSON

Lester Friedman and Scott Stewart

This interview took place on 8 June 1989.

Lester Friedman/Scott Stewart: In your mind, what have been the important societal influences on British cinema during the past ten years?

Lindsay Anderson: By the end of the sixties the radical impulse in British filmmaking was over. In particular, the rush to conformism which has characterized Britain during the last twenty years has deeply affected movie making here. On the positive side, television, and specifically the policy of Channel 4, has helped filmmakers in this country, since it has given some relief to the eternal economic problem. Yet, at the same time, there has been continual pressure to think of movies in terms of American distribution. The home market is not going to pay for film production, so there is the need to break into the American market. This desire has characterized British cinema since the thirties, even though it has never been fully achieved. The idea that video sales would be a help to a smaller-budgeted picture also seems to be vanishing because video sales inevitably go to the big-budget pictures.

LF/SS: Earlier you mentioned what you characterized as "the rush to conformism" in Great Britain. What are the specific effects of this "rush to conformism"?

LA: Either it creates a bad atmosphere for artists or it can sometimes create a good atmosphere. By this I mean it gives them something to think about. I'm afraid at the moment there isn't much kick left in this country. We've yet to grieve the loss of the socialist ideal—something that's happening across the world. The hard-core Communist-Socialists, particularly the people who haven't had to live under them, represent an ideal, a force that has more or less perished. If you think back into the thirties, you can't help envying the artists of the Left, hard on the Left. It's very different times now. It's really hard to be anyone. Either you go with the profit-making philosophy of Thatcher and Reagan, or you're left with a kind of anarchic despair—which is how you could characterize *Britannia Hospital*. The only substitution for a Left ideal, I suppose, is the Green ideal, which could take hold of the imagination of the people, the young particularly. It hasn't got the same force of conformism, of dedication to career and class position, of the acquisition of material goods, as other elements of British life. These forces have taken over.

LF/SS: How do you feel about the way in which contemporary British movies deal with class and race-related issues?

LA: By comparison with the traditional British cinema, today's movies demonstrate a much wide choice of subject area about almost all aspects of society; they also deal with them much more freely than directors in traditional British cinema ever would. But, of course, you've got to bring in television. One of the absurdities, really critical absurdities, if this silly division between cinema of the theaters and films for television. Film critics, if they weren't so lazy, ought to review every new film made for television. Yet they prefer to live an easy and quiet life. There is also a journalistic hierarchy now. But one must see what's being shown on television every day because it is just as relevant as the movies in the theaters which the film critic writes about. Critics enjoy being facetious at the expense of bad theater pictures, which is easy to do, rather than to cover a good film made for television. Don't forget that *My Beautiful Laundrette* was a film made for television and shot on 16mm. In fact, Stephen Frears was initially quite alarmed by the proposition that it was going to be shown in cinemas.

LF/SS: What do you feel about the exodus of so many talented British filmmakers to American and elsewhere?

LA: When you deal with the British cinema, you deal in quite a complicated subject. Economically, Britain can't support such an industry. There is also the plain fact that America represents, to many filmmakers, the chance to move beyond the barriers of class, since class is not much of a consideration in America. Ridley Scott, for example, also belongs to that generation that grew up making movies for television and are, therefore, interested in style and technique—and in little else.

I would also mention David Putnam here. The difference between say Alan Parker and David Putnam, who are friends, is that Putnam is somebody who desperately wants to become somebody, who is part of the establishment. I mean he's a snob. The greatest joy for Putnam would be to be Sir David Putnam. He no doubt will get that title if he gives enough money to this charity and that cause. So Putnam is very divided in his attitude toward America. He can't cope with it and failed terribly. It wasn't the first time. Remember this. Before *Chariots of Fire*, Putnam spent two years in Los Angeles as the head of filmmaking for some record company. He failed. Then he accepted the Columbia job, taking on the American film industry like a complete idiot. He failed again. He's not like Parker. Parker has not made the same mistakes. Parker is a fully accredited American filmmaker now. He's not a British filmmaker anymore.

LF/SS: Many of your films deal with tradition and how Britons deal with it in their daily lives. Do you think English people, in particular, are torn between tradition and movement away from it?

LA: I have an ambivalent feeling towards tradition. I have a particularly strong suspicion towards tradition when it loses its vitality and truth, when it becomes simply a politician's cliché. When Margaret Thatcher talks about the Falklands, saying we're a *Great* Britain again, that appeal to a tradition of greatness is absurd—and bad. But it's a complicated question at the moment when a decision has to be made as to whether we were going to defend the Falklands. I don't necessarily think the wrong decision was made, so I don't join in the cry of Warmonger Thatcher. On the other hand, we should have never gotten to that stage. If it weren't for our ineptitude, it would never have happened. That's what was really wrong. Then she used the whole tragic action as a royal plum to feed people's patriotic fervor, which I find disgusting. You could say the boys in *If . . .* were traditionalists, which sounded paradoxical because all the apparatus of tradition appears to be on the side of authority, but that's not necessarily true. They are part of the tradition of independence, the rights of the individual, the right to question authority and to behave freely. When traditions have become fossilized, and instances of reaction as well, then they have to be rebelled against. That act in itself is a tradition.

LF/SS: In *If . . .* , what did you have in mind when the headmaster went up in a puff of smoke?

LA: It may have been a mistake. I think it may be a mistake. I'll tell you two things about that. Very often while you're creating you have to make a quick decision. One thing I had in mind was I never ever wanted to be literal, just literal. I think that if the headmaster was just lying there it becomes just that episode. I didn't want that. At the very end of *If . . .* , it's Mick against the whole mass society, not just about the headmaster anymore. I was surprised that young people cheered that ending when it first came out. Perhaps they didn't look beyond the end, because it's very difficult for me to imagine that Mick is going to win.

LF/SS: David Sherwin (the film's scriptwriter) said that by the film's ending Mick has become a monster as bad as the system he fights against.

LA: That's idiotic. I don't know why he said that. I think that's completely untrue. Mick isn't as big a monster as the system. That's silly. He's actually not a monster at all. He's terrified, of course, although it's up to you to determine what you see on the screen. I think at the end of *If* . . . Mick is absolutely desperate. It's just him and this small band of followers. That's all he's got.

LF/SS: What was in your mind when Mick is getting his beating? You cut to the boys listening, but you end up with Peanuts looking in the microscope at what appears to be cell division.

LA: I think it's just another perspective. You know a lot of things are not always rational. It's a poetic suggestion. Make what you will of it. I think it's good to have a few things like that. I hope people will get something out of what the artist is not fully conscious of himself. By the way, David Sherwin and I are talking about doing a sequel to *If* . . . . This would be a sequel taking place at the school with many of the same characters twenty years older.

LF/SS: Is Malcolm [McDowell] interested in doing this?

LA: Oh yes! He's a wonderful actor. It's just a shame Hollywood had no idea what to do with him. He's even wonderful in *Sunset* as the villain. Very, very bad. Embarrassing actually. He seems more of a personality than an actor. I read some reviews and there wasn't really any mention of Malcolm. His wife [Mary Steenburgen] is a wonderful actress as well. Absolutely wonderful. She's a very excellent, intelligent, and charming actress.

LF/SS: What about the controversial "chaplain-in-the-drawer" sequence in *If* . . . ? Do you expect us to take this literally?

LA: Of course not! It is a clear metaphor and one of the elements that is designed to work towards the conclusion of the film. The film is not, in the end, literal. You see there were these expectations like, "Golly you shouldn't have done that." They've got these idiots who are so systematic that have this sort of expectation. People need to have respect for the artist. They need to look at things with an open mind and wait a little bit before they exercise their superiority over the artist.

LF/SS: Your films seem to present a balance between education, and by that I mean attempting to make the audience active thinkers, and entertainment. Do you look for films balanced like your own when you choose to go see a film?

LA: I'm actually very lazy about going to see movies and as you can see I'd rather collect old movies and watch them at home. I'm really very bad. You'll realize how bad I am when I tell you I haven't seen *A Fish Called Wanda*. I doubt that I will. It's a very successful picture. But the tradition of English facetiousness is not one that I respond to. My taste in humor is more satirical.

LF/SS: What are your feelings about the films of Carol Reed?

LA: The Fallen Idol is better than *Odd Man Out*. I really think so. I think *Odd Man Out* probably is a little more pretentious. I mean it's interesting from that perspective, but I think that Reed is a very curious and sad case really. He's obviously a man of immense talent who somehow went astray. He ended up in *Oliver* somewhere. It's very strange. But you should see *The Fallen Idol*—it's a very good film.

LF/SS: One critic once said about *Britannia Hospital*, in reference to its tone, that you had resorted to ranting instead of wit. What's your reaction?

LA: Rubbish! You know they really are all idiots! I think the movie is violent, extremely violent. We live in a very violent world. Another critic at the time said the movie was hopeless. Well that's what it's likely to be at a time of disaster. I can't help the bourgeoisie critic who longs to be left alone, who needs assurance. They want to be reassured. The nearer you get to the terrifying truth, the more they want not just to evade it, but to discredit you as well. So, you go off to see *A Fish Called Wanda*.

LF/SS: How did you come to direct *Whales of August*? It seems to be very different than anything else you've ever directed.

LA: Well it is, but anybody who wasn't chicken would accept the opportunity to direct Lillian Gish and Bette Davis. It is the least political of my motion pictures. But one can have different attitudes; one can make different choices for different reasons, as a theater director is likely to make different choices. I mean one might say why do you direct a play by Chekov instead of a play with contemporary social implications like *March on Russia*, which I have directed? The point is this isn't a conflict. I've made films that have strong social implications, but trying to be objective about my work, which is always difficult, I think my work has always shown an extremely strong humanistic attitude. That's the kind of film that *Whales of August* is. So think that if anyone looked at my work through the years they would see elements of lyricism in those works and in *Whales of August*. I believe *Whales of August* has a more recognizable poetic style than *On Golden Pond*. It's more lyrical. Although that, of course, was a much more popular film because it's much more schmaltzy.

LF/SS: How did you find working with Bette Davis?

LA: It's very hard work because she's a very abrasive and destructive person. I imagine she always has been. Of course, she's much more difficult now because she's been ill. She's got a demon in her, whatever that demon is. She has become this sort of sad media figure—good for TV interviews because she'll say nasty things.

By the way, I've spent the last year in Toronto making a miniseries for Home Box Office. It's called *Glory! Glory!* I took that on because, amazingly, the script turned out to be quite good. I was very astonished by it actually. That does have some relevance to some of the things I have done. But I'd say that I've taken advantage of opportunities to make films outside of Britain, mainly because the possibilities of filmmaking in Britain for someone of my temperament are very difficult, very limited. That's what I said earlier about the present conformism in Britain. The violent rejection of my last British film, *Britannia Hospital*, is evidence of this.

LF/SS: Why do you think this was?

LA: We're accustomed, to put it pretentiously, to a film culture in which absurdly grotesque horror is a part of a tradition. My film was so satirical that it demanded a sense of humor. Of course, the trouble is that people have begun to think in clichés. If they think they're going to see a satirical social film, then they're not prepared for the kind of extended satire present in *Britannia Hospital*. That in itself is actually relevant. It's satirical about the craziness of the progress of science. In the end of the film, you have this crazy doctor who is making absolute sense, but of course it's gone beyond his sense into further madness. By the end of the film, you have a film that's pessimistic about the possibility for human survival because we have science for science's sake and out of the realm of a human purpose. So the ending, of course, is extremely dark.

LF/SS: Do you think of yourself as a man of the theater or a man of the cinema?

LA: The answer is both, really. I've been extremely lucky to have been able to alternate. After I've made a film, I haven't felt an overpowering need to make another one. In that way, I'm a lot like John Ford, who at one time said, "I'm not a career man." He had a fantastic career, except towards the end of course, but in this sense he was very fortunate. He never had to sit down to scheme and plan how to get a picture made, since pictures were being made all the time. I don't think he needed to keep a career going. Being a filmmaker today is a gift I don't really have. I'm not proud of that, but I'm simply not able to fly to LA, have meetings, sell stories—all those aspects of modern filmmaking. I'm absolutely hopeless at it. In that way, I'm not sure that I am a filmmaker. I mean I'm a filmmaker in the sense that I have done some films, but I'm amazed that I've managed to do even that.

Also, I never have compromised. I think this is why, at times, people are hesitant to send me scripts. For one reason or another, I've turned down a lot of them. I don't think I've made anything that represents a compromise, so I haven't made very many films. But at least the ones I've made, I can stand by them. I think it's incredible to make a mini-series for HBO, incredibly lucky really, because I didn't even work on getting it.

LF/SS: How did *Glory! Glory!* happen?

LA: I think it happened because the producer, whose name is Bonnie Door, had this idea of a film or miniseries about evangelists on television. She had this

Figure 14.1. Lindsay Anderson directs. Courtesy: British Film Institute.

notion long before the big scandals in recent years, which are indeed more farcical than the film we made. The people in *Glory! Glory!* all behave in a rather nefarious way from time to time, but there is a certain charm about them. They are much more charming than those people you see on American television.

When I came into the project it was late, and HBO was very scared. Although they put money into it, they didn't really know whether they wanted to go through with it or not. They told Bonnie Door that she must get a director who is not just any director; he must be special. They tried Nick Roeg and others. Finally the script arrived here, and I liked it. I said yes, it's delightful, and I went to Los Angeles. We met the HBO people there. I hadn't really realized that this was crucial, that depending on what I said about the script would determine if HBO did it or not. I did quite a good sales pitch, and they went ahead. The script had been written before the writers strike, which was then in progress, so I couldn't sit down and rewrite it. Shooting had to be started and completed within two months. I thought this was great. For once I'm not going to go through this Hell! I'll take this script as it is. We did have to make some minor changes, and we did have to cut, but essentially it was the first time I basically went with a script. It was incredible luck that it coincided with my temperament.

I do think, however, there were elements there that, if I had time work on the script, I would have looked to develop more fully. Especially when you consider Jim and Tammy. If you look at them, they're much more extreme, and more obnoxious, than anything in our movie. But I think it makes the film rather nice really; it's different; it's not a satire of Tammy and Jim or anyone else. Who's that other horrible one? Jimmy Swaggart. There is nobody in it as awful as Swaggart, not even the old chap in the beginning. Oral Roberts is the one who inspired the series, because Bonnie had done research on Oral Roberts several years ago. That gave her the idea, and she got Stan Daniels to write it. Stan Daniels is a very interesting chap and a very good writer. He worked on "The Mary Tyler Moore" show and "Taxi." I think it's a superior script. It did well. It was very well received.

LF/SS: Could you elaborate on why you called Humphrey Jennings the only "British poet"?

LA: You have to see his pictures. He's very important actually. Jennings was a very interesting filmmaker who didn't make a very large number of films. He started as a painter and had a very strong feeling for tradition. He came to maturity during the war, the ideal time for him to be able to make his films, which were very patriotic without any drumbeat in the background. Working in the medium of documentary cinema, he wasn't at all commercial. He didn't have any commercial pressures on him; therefore, he was freely able to express his strong, personal, patriotic feelings about his country. It's interesting he didn't survive the war. He tried to go on, but he didn't make it. Somehow that particular time inspired him, and then very sadly he died young.

I guess that one could say what does one mean by the word *poetic*? We don't want to get into a long discussion about lyricism and all that. I would say Humphrey Jennings is a poet in a way that you could say David Lean is not a poet, in my view. I think he has a very, very personal style in the handling of the film, a poetic use of the medium. You should see *Listen to Britain, Fires Were Started,* and *Diary of Timothy.* That's all you need to see. The great confusion, of course, is between documentary cinema and journalism. Documentary through television has more or less become journalism. So what I call the "poetic documentary" is hardly made now. It's more or less dead today. I've made one or two. You know I often think of that remark about Jennings rather ruefully. I wrote that, of God, twenty years or more ago. It always seems to be quoted, and I'm waiting, of course, for someone to ask the next logical question: does Anderson consider himself a poet?

LF/SS: Well, do you regard yourself as a poet?

LA: I would rather be regarded by others as a poet. When I do say poet in that sense, I mean something particularly personal, a lyrical feeling in cinema, consistency in personality with an integration of style and content. You get that with John Ford, of course; the way he uses the camera displays an easily recognizable style.

LF/SS: How do you feel Thatcherism has affected the films of contemporary British filmmakers like Stephen Frears and Derek Jarman?

LA: We unfortunately seem to have fallen completely for what we call the "auteurist" philosophy of filmmaking, that being the absurd notion that the director is responsible for the entire picture. This leads to errors, particularly in the case of someone like Stephen Frears. What you're thinking about are a couple of films written by Hanif Kureishi. Whatever you think of Hanif Kureishi—I don't like Hanif Kureishi myself—that's Hanif Kureishi, not Frears. The two films written by Hanif Kureishi that Stephen, being an intelligent fellow, took on don't imply any thought to anti-Thatcherite policy on the part of Stephen Frears. Before that, Stephen directed other things on television by Alan Bennett, who is not in any way a radical; he also directed *Gumshoe* in 1971, an Albert Finney film. That was the first thing he directed before he found his feet, so to speak. There's another film he made, *The Hit,* and he's just directed *Dangerous Liaisons.* What do these films tell you about the personality of the director?

I think you'll find that Stephen chose *My Beautiful Laundrette* because it's a lively kind of script, intelligently written. It was something contemporaneous. It had a visceral kick to it. It's not particularly anti-Thatcherite is it? I never thought it so, and, of course, *Prick Up Your Ears* has very little social content as well. So I'm really cautioning you not to be too journalistic in your thinking. A journalist will make a trend out of two pictures, and they do need more analyzing than that.

Derek Jarman. Again, there isn't any real consistency there. I don't know how you rate Derek Jarman's work. *The Last of England. Caravaggio. The War Requiem.* There really is not a consistent attitude in any group of English film-makers, British filmmakers, as to compare with, say, the group of the Free Cinema, a related group of the sixties, and the films made in the first half of the sixties. Here you did have a fairly consistent social point of view, class point of view, and partly because of that reason we were scorned and rejected by English middle-class critics and intellectuals who all strongly resisted radical filmmaking. You will find, of course, isolated or lonely examples of people working in that viewpoint. I certainly didn't feel a part of any intellectual group. Also I must caution you, as happens when one gets older, you get lazy, you get less interested. Unfortunately, I don't religiously go to all these movies, and I don't go to movies the way I would if I were a critic.

LF/SS: One critic claimed, about Stephen Frears, that you can trust him to take a piece of work and not muck it up.

LA: Well that's a charming thing to say. By contrast Stephen was being very kind to me while he was doing a five-part series based on Alan Bennett's books for television. He only directed two of them, and he very kindly got me to do one. I said to him and to Alan Bennett: "Look this is tricky for me. As a film director I'm used to working on the scripts (and the script they showed me wasn't fully complete). I'd like to work on this with Alan, if he's prepared to, in a way one would work on a movie." Alan Bennett said, "I'd love to," and we actually worked on it together very happily. We made a one-hour television piece called "The Old Crowd." This piece was extremely criticized. One critic even noted that I was the first director who's been able to make Alan Bennett unfunny. Now, in a sense, I take this as a compliment, because what we produced was not just a very good transcription of an Alan Bennett script, but something else. It was more like a movie.

I'm not taking anything from Stephen at all. He's been very, very clever, intelligent, and good in his selection of material; he's put it on the screen very, very well. The only thing I would say is that he has not yet, and perhaps he won't, develop into a director whose films belong to him rather than to the scriptwriter. There's no reason why he should. If it wasn't for the snobism of the *auteur* theory, we wouldn't think twice about it because what actually matters is what is up there on the screen. Stephen can now do more or less what he wants now. He is a very interesting case. He's very independent, very individual in his choices. But how far he wants personally to commit himself is another matter. He's been blessed and also been very intelligent. One of Stephen's qualities is intelligence and choosing to do good material.

LF/SS: You've done a lot of writing on John Ford. Yet he's certainly not a social critic is he?

LA: No, no, no, he wasn't. But I would say that the conflict in Ford between traditionalism and individuality was extremely strong. The sense of the independence of the individual makes him an individualist and also a traditionalist. You see Ford was a great artist, but an artist with whom there is a great danger to intellectualize about too much. Read some of the commentary by some of the latter day, what you would call "auteurists." There is a book by Tag Gallagher with a lot of good research in it, but it's absolutely idiotic. It shows the need of the "intellectual" critic to try to construct some intellectual conception that will actually justify their existence, so they sit down and write a paper about it and about the pessimism of Ford. *My Darling Clementine* is not a pessimistic film, nor is *She Wore a Yellow Ribbon.* They would try to make out, like Peter Bogdonavich, that there is a progression to pessimism.

What happened to Ford was that he got old and, of course, old age brings different insights. He got old in a world in which he felt increasingly alienated, but he was not a person who would ever discuss that in an interview. The only time he would be able to talk about something like that with someone was if he knew them well enough to get drunk with them. Of course, he's not to betray himself, and he was absolutely right. We're all interviewed absolutely too much, and it's a very dangerous mistake to be honest. Most interviews filmmakers give are going to be used one way or another for the films they have made. You have to be aware that you're making publicity at the same time. So a lot of these interviews you can't take too seriously.

There are only two books you should read about Ford. Mine, and John Ford's son's book called *Pappy,* which isn't an academic book. But it's good. I think the trouble is that, as the whole, the academic study of cinema has developed people who have to make jobs for themselves. So they fabricate. Academicians have to fabricate to justify the fact that you may be paid so much a year to be a professor of cinema or something. None of these things should exist. They become an end in themselves. I don't think they enlighten people.

LF/SS: Do you think we should study the history of cinema?

LA: The history of cinema—that's a different matter. You see you slipped in that word there. I think the history of cinema is essential to study, but a history of cinema not nearly dealing so much with aesthetic differences. It should be much more involved with the social implications and the economic problems of cinema. There's a great deal to discuss before one gets on to deconstruction. Aesthetics don't have anything to do with the experience of art. They are an end in themselves. To write about style is a tremendously difficult thing to do, but it's a very valuable thing to do if anybody did it right.

This is another reason why you ought to read my book about John Ford. It has much more to do with the experience of seeing John Ford's films than these theoretical books. I mean that idiotic thing by Peter Wollen, *Signs and Meanings* or some such thing. I don't know how anybody can really get through that stuff. You still find academic studies that seem to be totally infected by auteurism. I remember going to a seminar in Italy about John Ford and listening to all that academic nonsense. One contribution I made was to say you've got to understand that some of Ford's films were written by Dudley Nichols, some were written by Frank Nugent, and some he took on because he had nothing else to do. You have to make these differentiations. These are supposed to be academics after all. Yet none of them were capable even of mentioning a writer. So most of what they were talking was rubbish, actually. They were constructing an image of this John Ford they found appropriate. That's why Ford, during one interview, told Peter Bogdanovich to shut up.

LF/SS: So how do you make an audience think?

LA: Now there's a fatal assumption. You can't make them all think, though I have tried to. I try not to satisfy an audience's expectations. Maybe that's the defect of a lot of filmmaking: that it's careful to remain in the audience's expectations with the hope of getting a distribution deal. I suppose if you want to become a professional filmmaker, it would be wise for you to adapt your work to your market. If you want to become what I call a "film artist," you're apt to go the other way.

CHAPTER FIFTEEN

THE SIGHT OF DIFFERENCE

Ilsa J. Bick

INTRODUCTION

I BEGIN THIS analysis with the aim of shedding new light on a troubling and troublesome film, Michael Powell's deeply psychological, perverse, and grim depiction of voyeurism and sexual sadism, *Peeping Tom* (1960). Haunted by Kaja Silverman's reading and appropriation of this film to bolster a highly dubious argument, I find myself compelled to expand upon the core of her assertions while highlighting my own difference (all puns intended).

My difference alters my voice of *Peeping Tom*'s mystery. The mystery at the heart of *Peeping Tom* is not exclusively centered around lack but the "un-scene"— that which meets the reciprocal gaze, what it is that is the "seen" scene. At one level removed, this is the primal scenario repetitively and compulsively reconstructed as identified with the look of the father and of the son as the excluded third-person viewer. While I would agree with Silverman that the mystery of the female genital is central to *Peeping Tom*'s trajectory, I look behind the mirror to the face and the voice—to the ultimate recuperation of the maternal gaze and the mutual affirmation of mother and infant looked upon by the father, the sight of difference.

CITING DIFFERENCES

As a woman and an analyst, I am continually amazed at efforts that ground femininity in phallocentrism, as if all women must first highlight that the fact of their womanliness rests upon their lack of manliness (and vice versa). I am troubled by a tenacious emphasis upon my visible "lack," since this obscures the fact that I have an inner space that fills, develops, and become a living being. I cover a space of potentials. And I resist equating a baby with a (hidden) penis, if only because the experience of one's baby is so totally different from the experience— I would presume—of one's penis. This is not to say that such fantasies do not exist nor that children cannot be used in a "phallic" way.

But I anticipate myself. There is a time when potentials, both real and imagined, exist in abundance—specifically in the look of the mother and her infant. Such a look does not exclusively exist outside the realm of what might be imagined to be desire, as Olivier contends, nor must it be devoid of fantasy informed by gender and sexuality. For that matter, Chodorow has convincingly demonstrated that mothering need not be gender-specific. I would argue, however, that there is a fundamental state of being of a mother and infant—a bubble of potential space—that is filled by the looking, touching, smelling, vocalizing, tasting of primal experience. To this, Freud gave the name "oceanic feeling" (1953, 21: 72), a sense of merging and timelessness; Mahler called it the infantile "symbiosis" (1975, 290-91); Lacan extrapolated his emphasis upon recapturing a (fantasied) state of mirroring perfection (1977, 1-7); and so on. Informing the experience is the longing for reunion with the primal mother, the reinscription of infinite potential.

In her analysis of *Peeping Tom*, Silverman asserts that the film's trajectory and *modus vivendi* are representative of the "verbal and auditory defenses by means of which Hollywood fortifies the male subject against his own losses" (1988, 41). Following a Lacanian paradigm inclusive of a misreading of Freud (and misremembering this particular film), Silverman presents the theoretical premise for her argument involving her placement of the (lost) female voice in cinema—that a *symbolic* castration predates that more widely and consciously acknowledged, informed, and inscribed by more traditional (psychoanalytic) gender and sexual distinctions. This "castration" is symbolic only in the sense of a rendering, a forcible separation "from the mother and the entry into a linguistic order which anticipates and exceeds the subject. And the positive Oedipus complex [yields] theoretical priority to its 'feminine' counterpart, the negative Oedipus complex, site both of desire for and identification with the mother, and thus generative not only of narcissism, but . . . feminism as well" (234). Although space does not permit my recounting her arguments in detail, what Silverman stresses is that the classical derivation of the Oedipus complex is the *organizing principle*, the mediating stratum in psychic development through which a subject passes and is irrevocably transmuted by his/her incorporation of and entry into language, symbolic thought, mature gender sexuality, and Law (the latter usually defined as synonymous with phallic, patriarchal authority). Central to Silverman's formulations is the notion that development does not *commence* with the subject's entry into the Oedipal era but that a subject's intrapsychic life is a continuously dynamic formation, strongly influenced by his/her association with and longing for the idealized oneness with the pre-Oedipal, preverbal mother. For Silverman, dominant Hollywood cinema's persistently phallocentric focus upon female lack defends against "man's" own inutterable loss, his castration/splitting from the mother. Films such as *Peeping Tom* that persistently focus upon female lack cover a more pervasive terror of male lack cloaked beneath a celluloid veil of perverse sexuality.

As intriguing and persuasive as Silverman's premise is, I find her argument troubling. What astounds me in my reading of Silverman is that film theory should have taken so long to arrive here at all. Captivated by the signification of sexuality, sexually based inequities, and recriminative accusations, feminist psychoanalytic film theorists have continued their debate while consistently ignoring the vast amount of psychoanalytic theory and clinical practice and observation extrinsic to film that explores the preverbal, preoedipal, and Oedipal epochs in detail.[1]

What is disturbing about Silverman's premise is not her emphasis on pre-Oedipal determinants requisite to cinematic experience.[2] There are, however, three points with which I take issue. First, Silverman expands a reading of selected films to encompass an entire medium (and, I would add, Powell's film is definitely "outside" Hollywood). Second, she dismisses crucial determinants in the etiological epigenesis and functions of the perversions. Lastly, informed by Lacanian thought, she proposes the equation of castration with separation.

Of the first assertion, I am constrained to point out that my own approach is of an eclectic psychoanalytic bent—sometimes "Freudian," at other times "Winnicottian," and so on until I encompass a veritable panoply of "creatures." I am wedded to no particular theory or approach other than a motivation to apply my associations to the moments of the film as a narrative process[3] and as part of an historical continuity of which its and my moments intersect. While I adhere to no "political" basis, I am in agreement with Noel Carroll's views, which find attempts to institute one grand, overarching, universal theory of cinema or spectatorship to be inherently reductionistic, although I do *not* agree with his dismissal of psychoanalytic thought as a critical tool.

Silverman's exclusive focus upon castration anxiety ignores the manifold functions of the perversions, a "lack" that her late work on masochism seems at pains to cover.[4] In her formulations regarding the relationship between creativity and the perversions (specifically fetishism), Janine Chassequet-Smirgel proposes that the pervert is continually "trying to free himself from the paternal universe and the constraints of the law" (1984, 12) by the creation of devices that level difference—not solely the difference between the sexes but also those manifest in generational distinctions. Realized in the creative production of the "anal" phallus, the pervert "attempts to exclude the genital penis from the sexual stage . . . Genitality represents the major obstacle between the son and his mother because of the differences it includes between the sexes *and the generations*, that is, reality itself" (87; italics mine).[5]

Most troubling of all, however, is the equivalence Silverman gives to castration and separation. Any emphasis upon castration per se—symbolic or actual—is to detract from and diminish the importance with which Silverman rightly views the subject's pre-Oedipal relationship to and with the mother. For many theorists (even "hateful" ones such as Chassequet-Smirgel), the power of this relationship resides in ambivalence. Simply put, Silverman does an injustice to the very mother and feminism she seeks to recuperate by continually casting her argument in terms of sexual and gender distinctions. Part of her difficulty in extricating separation from castration lies in her reliance upon a Lacanian paradigm elaborated upon by Christian Metz equating the splitting from the mother in the mirror stage of development with castration. Any argument evolving from such an equivalence must *automatically* look backward at separation through the filtering rubric of sexuality. I do not totally disagree with this approach. In many senses, this is developmentally appropriate, since any backward glance involves a sifting through the layering topsoil of sexuality superimposed upon the bedrock of early mother-child and father-child interactions.[6] But this is ultimately limiting if sexuality remains the *first assumption.*

In his 1926 paper "Inhibitions, Symptoms and Anxiety," Freud equated separation and castration only to the extent that they were dangers heralded by signal anxiety; the affect he was tracing was *anxiety*, not an idea nor the homonomy of the (threatened) loss of a penis with separation from the mother.[7] As Leo Rangell argues, "Perhaps in this pain, of separation and castration, we have approached the duality of unity of the body-mind continuum. Loss of Love means lack of protection of the body, the sensorially felt, vulnerable half of the self . . . a mind can not be without a body" (8).

To say that something is *like* something else is not to state that it *is* that something. Castration is castration, not a metaphor or analogy. Freud insisted that "it would be very satisfactory if anxiety, as a symbol of a separation, were to be repeated on every occasion on which a separation took place . . . [however] we know what the affective reactions to a separation are: they are pain and mourning, not anxiety" (1953, 20: 130-31). Rangell expands upon this to assert that castration "is a pathological belief operative in the unconscious which originated during the period of childhood sexuality . . . castration leads to terror, separation to depression and quieter states of lonely isolation and despair . . . *The opinion of some that castration is a defense against preoedipal conflicts, a form of resistance upwards, suggests that the defense against anxiety can be terror*" (3, 9). Castration is not separation, anymore than the loss of a penis can be equated to the rending apart of perfectly united, mutually interdependent Siamese twins. To lose a part of oneself is not the same as the loss of self ideally reflected in the mirroring and affirming gaze of the mother, the jarring discontinuity of separateness, and the frustration inherent in a longing for return. What if a baby looked and its mother did not?

Where does that leave us with *Peeping Tom*? I am not in agreement with Silverman's assertions that the film depicts the closest approximation a man can achieve to being a woman—that is, the "embrace" of his own castration in a reenactment of the negative Oedipal complex—nor do I see Helen's history as inseparable "from that of the male subject" (1988, 41). If anything, I hope to show that Helen is the *agent* of history. What I do find striking about the film is its emphasis upon the recuperation of the lost maternal voice (frequently displaced to the paternal) coupled with the reinvocation of her affirming gaze with primal scene elements as *secondary elaborations*, the topsoil upon the bedrock.

In the beginning there is the word, however it is not the Word of the Father but the song of the mother and the cries of the infant. With sound, smell, taste, and touch, the infant first experiences himself at one with his mother. In sight, the infant perceives not only his mother but also himself, as D. W. Winnicott so eloquently states, "In individual emotional development, *the precursor of the mirror is the mother's face* . . . the mother is looking at the baby, and *what she looks like is related to what she sees there*" (1971, 111, 112). Kenneth Wright observes that the baby exists in a "positively amplifying circuit mutually affirming both partners" (1991, 12).

To this mimetic circuit is added the gaze of a third—that of the father. Thus, an infant is not just found in and formed from his attachment to his mother but structured by the look of his father. In vision and the recognition of his father as separate from his mother, the child also sees difference, but I would hasten to emphasize that this difference is, at least initially, predicated not upon sexuality but upon *exclusion*. As Kenneth Wright elaborates:

> Up until now, the child had related separately to the mother and the father . . . But now he sees them together . . . He has become the observer of them as a couple. He is now forced to take the position of the third person in the threesome, which was originally, from the baby's point of view, the father's and to look at what the other two, the mother and father, are doing together. Looking at what the other two are doing—this parental "intercourse" which the child sees is the core of the oedipal problem that has to be resolved . . . it is the child's *attachment* to the mother that is being threatened . . . What this new oedipal structuring of the earlier space provides, which are not there before, is a more radical underpinning . . . a space, the boundaries of which must not be broached, a NO ENTRY space, within which objects can only be looked at or observed, but never touched. (115, 121; my italics)

Thus, it is the look of the father—and the child's identification with this look—that enforces separation. I would suggest that, in *Peeping Tom*, Mark's project is not to seek his own castration—to become a woman in order to become fused with her—but to first identify with the look of the father, both the father of sexuality *and* as displacement for the mother (the discovery of the mother in recreation with the father of "the lost fusional state" [Wright 1991, 114]). Recreating this fusion leads to the rediscovery of the lost maternal voice as it exists both inside and outside the subject (in this case, Mark Lewis).

The thrust of my analysis will, like Silverman's, focus first upon the sexualized expression of this quest and subsequently upon the structuring pre-Oedipal elements. Unlike Silverman, however, I suggest that, when Mark finally turns his mirror on himself, he rediscovers himself not as a woman but first as a participant in a mutually affirming and thence ultimately destructive maternal and narcissistic circuit.

A SITE OF DIFFERENCE

As we look backward in *Peeping Tom*, the look of the father is initially that in and of the primal scenario—a look identified with father as participant and as son-observer and that privileges "un-seen" scenes. Within the film's prologue, crucial elements of the primal scenario are well delineated—so much so that the argument could convincingly be made that much of what follows merely elaborates and expands upon this material. The prologue's allusions to primal-scene motifs, ingredients of sexual sadism synonymous with auteurial control,[8] considerations of voyeurism, and the play upon eyes, sight, and castration all figure prominently in the ideological and psychological landscapes of the cinematic text.

Whether intentional or serendipitous, the juxtaposition of the first two sequences—the bull's-eye and the human eye—seems more than fortuitous. Although Powell's association with Archer productions made the bull's-eye trademark inevitable, the metonymy presented between an arrow piercing the bull's-eye following into the human eye seemingly startled into wakefulness (accomplished with a jump cut that "opens" the eye) appears to privilege many underlying motifs. The shapes even echo one another—the dark center of the target paralleling the pupil of the eye and so on.

First and foremost, one might expect a similar assault upon the human eye—to literally "have it in the eye."[9] In a sense, the violent murder that follows is, for the audience, to "have it in the eye," to be assaulted by the activity of the director (consistently parodied throughout the film as approaching varying degrees of sadism).

Furthermore, the opening of the eye is designed in such a way as to suggest that sleep has been disturbed. This disturbance is equated in some measure to the activity of the film audience while also implying that something has occurred or will occur that is startling. In contrast to the immediacy of the preceding sequence (the human eye), the first murder sequence opens with a shot from a great distance. The juxtaposition of the open eye with the quick cut to the night scene implies that the latter is the point-of-view shot of the former. The abruptness of the cut, coupled with the long shot, initially renders the scene barely discernible or decipherable. I find myself straining to both understand and orient myself to the scene much as I might expect a child to react when, abruptly awakened from sleep, she stares into the darkness of her parents' bedroom. (This is reiterated in Helen's own re-view of the primal scene near the end of the film, as she penetrates Mark's forbidden projection room, settles down into Mark's director's chair, and watches Mark's films with horrified fascination, attempting at one point even to see *around* the screen.)

In addition, the movie camera, coupled with the male hand that activates it, is positioned in such a way as to suggest the powerful phallus (at waist level). In the film's emphasis upon the carefully precisioned cross-hairs, the camera also reiterates the penetrating power of the arrow in the first sequence—the camera moves forward in the frame until it is almost a blackened, amorphous blob (penetrating my eye) and, at prologue's end, plunging down into the cavernous darkness of the prostitute's screaming, gaping mouth . . . "bull's-eye."[10] By extension, the eye is alternatively given the equivalent power of the phallus—seeing = penetration = intercourse = death—while implying that my participation as observer is to become receptive to this penetration. In other words, I occupy both sides of the same circuit, just as the film places me in the roles of partner(s) and observer(s). Particularly interesting in the murder's reprise is the fact that the observer, Mark, slowly straightens as the prostitute removes her clothes; he rises from the chair as the camera pulls in to her terrified face; and he is totally erect, his head positioned precisely in her gaping mouth, as his film ends. He then collapses into his chair, seemingly exhausted. In his slowly intensifying state of arousal—Mark's body as erect penis—the entire sequence becomes an obvious metonym for and allusion to sexual intercourse.

The wide gaping mouth of the prostitute in which Mark is metaphorically engulfed and the clear implication that her bedroom expands to include the whole of Mark's projection room (and, by extension, the theatre within which I sit) point to the importance of oral incorporative and projective fantasies as they relate to or are activated by the primal scene. Bertram D. Lewin's formulations regarding the oral triad (as manifested at the maternal breast) and the primal scene are particularly apropos as motivational and sustaining imagery in *Peeping Tom*. Lewin stipulates that the primal scene, in disturbing the child's sleep, leads to a "triad of wishes . . . : a wish to eat, a wish to be eaten . . . and a wish to go to sleep" (1950, 137) originally hallucinated at the mother's breast/dream screen by the nursing infant. Implicit from the opening sequence, the disruption of sleep is a recurrent theme throughout the film, as the young Mark is traumatically and repetitively awakened from sleep by his scientist-father and filmed (enhancing the identification of the camera with the father and the intrusive, powerful paternal phallus). Further, Mark murders via "oral" incorporation (the knife through the throat; the camera down the screaming mouth). The argument might be made that penis and breast are here interchangeable, presaging what appears to be another of the film's primary concerns in the pre-Oedipal roots of an "unconscious reenactment of the mother-child role via the breast-penis equation . . . to under separation" (Socarides 1988, 241). (This parallel is offered again when, much later in the film, Mark caresses the long, phallic lens of his camera with his lips after Helen kisses him.)

In addition, the film's first closeup view of the prostitute is juxtaposed to a store window filled with what are essentially female body parts. This appears to reflect themes of traumatic dismemberment, castration through oral incorpora-

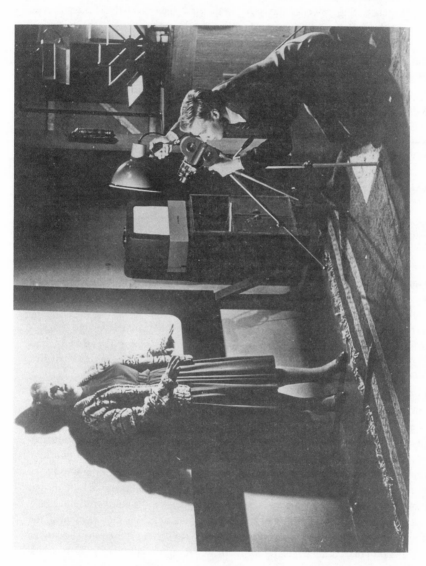

Figure 15.1. Anna Massey and Carl Boehm in *Peeping Tom*. Courtesy: British Film Institute.

tion, and oral sadistic assault—that is, woman as the ultimate "terror-object" against which, as Robin Wood puts it, a sexuality "totally perverted from its functions into sadism, violence, and cannibalism" is perpetrated (32).

Other key, recurrent elements include the ticking of the prostitute's clock that precedes, is augmented in, and accompanies her murder. This ticking is principally reiterated in those sequences involving the darkroom (as synonymous with the parental bedroom) and is wildly exaggerated in the pounding rhythm's of Viv's dance sequence as she undulates and makes love to Mark ('s camera). The emphasis given to such rhythmicity recalls the perception of rhythmic, repetitive sounds as auditory equivalents of parental intercourse.[11] The superimposition of this upon images of breasts and buttocks (the mannequin parts) recalls interchangeable elements in the preliminary phase of beating fantasies inspired by primal-scene material; and this appears to be particularly important, given the traumatically repetitive nature of A. N. Lewis's "assaults" upon the young Mark.

Finally, the red light, which invariably accompanies the murder sequences (either as a solitary focus or as background lighting) and is quite exaggerated during and after Viv's murder, suffuses Mark's darkroom and projection theatre. While this light is an obvious reference to danger and sensuality (in cinematic and cultural tradition), the red light and the play given to light as an accompaniment to sight recall Andrew Peto's assertions regarding archaic superego forerunners expressed as somatic derivatives. Peto writes of the visual origin of the superego agency as representative of the (red) glaring paternal eye turned toward the child as he intrudes upon the primal scene. Within dreams that feature self-observation, such visual representations constitute "the struggle (between ego and archaic superego) . . . as a relationship between the body ego and the archaic superego symbolized by the onlooking eyes. The phenomenon functions in the face of 'being looked at' on the part of the regressed archaic superego representation . . . The looking, glaring eyes represent the threatening destroying superego in one of its archaic somatic forerunners" (1969, 204). Given this, the awakened eye of the prologue takes on additional meaning—perhaps I have stumbled into the primal scene that is this film and am now subject to the rage and hostility of the enraged parent/director, just as I become a horrifically fascinated participant. Certainly, Mark captures his murder victims with light, just as his father repetitively awakened him with a flashlight. The light Mark employs to photograph his female subjects is clearly what Silverman would call an "externalizing displacement which converts the paternal flashlight into the son's projector lamp, and the image into the gaze" (1988, 35). Having been previously identified with the father, the flashlight, *now in the hands of the police*, seeks out Mark after Viv's murder (the police as synonymous with "law"/superego). Each murder is equated with a trespass against the (paternal) superego, as the police are habitually figured or appear after each murder sequence. Thus, retribution by the superego is implicit and the

Figure 15.2. Carl Boehm and Anna Massey in *Peeping Tom*. Courtesy: British Film Institute.

result of Mark's assumption of the role previously held by his father in his repetitive, vengeful identification with the humiliator (in an homoerotic sense)[12] and aggressor (the reinforcer of taboo).

THE SIGHT OF DIFFERENCE

Until now, I have drawn attention to the ways in which the look of the father recaptures a genitally informed sight and site of difference and the repetitive restructuring of this experience in Mark's use of the camera in a predominantly penetrative, phallic fashion and reduplication of elements of the primal scenario in the film—the topsoil upon the bedrock. Yet, if we accept identification with the father in a genital sense as a structuring look, then we must also examine the look of the father as third-party observer prior to such identification—in other words, as disruptive to the bonded attachment and look between mother and infant (since any identification with father includes his look at this pair, not just his look from his pairing with the mother).

I have repeatedly pointed to an underlying motif to all the primal scene imagery in this film; and such a motif is consistently foregrounded in the assumption that, in Henry Edelheit's view, central to mythological reversals are the child's (principally oral) incorporation of both parents of the primal scene. For Edelheit, this results in the formation of a "double-identification," manifested by a tendency for the child to "de-differentiate and to produce fused forms" (232). The composite creatures of the mythologies are representative of these "hybrid images." Thus, fusions of male/female *and* mother/child (or, for that matter, father/child) may *coexist*, particularly in light of the *oral* incorporative and projective fantasies constituting these images. Edelheit adds that "mother/child fusions superimposed upon the male/female ubiquity of the typical primal scene fantasy accounts for the frequent oral or polymorphous elaboration of these fantasies . . . Remarkably often, primal scene fantasies exploit the *visual*, thus emphasizing the polarity of *viewer/exhibitor*" (213, 214).[13]

Mother/child fusions, awakening from sleep, hallucinating at the breast/dream screen, a regression to orality—if oral incorporation promotes identification (and, working backward, with such identification a reinstitution of imitation as prelude to this and thence ultimately to attachment and fusion), then the camera—and, by extension, the eye—is one of the chief means through which a maternal identification is enhanced for Mark, one that is not solely infused with genital aims. By capturing the woman's stare, Mark is so reflected. The tenacity of his need for such identification and imitation is pointedly underscored by Mark's mimicry of Helen's and Millie's movements.

As the sustaining, "unseen" set piece of *Peeping Tom*, the mirror and the theme of mirroring/identification might be said to be the "mystery" of *Peeping Tom*. The mirror serves as an extension of the camera—the immutable gaze through which one is beheld and defined. As an artistic and psychological metaphor, mirrors may represent equivalent and contradictory variables simultaneously.[14] In the context of *Peeping Tom*, the mirror appears alternately as representative of the mysterious female genital (the look of the father) and the mystery of the mother's face (the look of the infant). While obsessively preoccupied with the woman's face, Mark is even more enamored of the defective female face—distorted either by fear or physical deformities. This is pointedly underscored in the first photographic sequence involving Dora, whose harelip appears to be a source of erotic fascination for Mark. As Silverman observes, "the facial contortion caused by Dora's harelip makes her look very much like the twisted faces reflected in the mirror attached to Mark's camera" (1988, 34). Significantly, he exchanges his usual camera for his "documentary" camera and, in this highly erotic encounter, uses his camera in a primarily seductive manner as he caresses Dora with his words—on one level, he assumes the look of the genital father.

Also of significance, however, is the fact that Mark does *not* comment on Dora's harelip per se, but states that this is the *first time* he is in front of *"eyes . . . eyes* such as *. . . eyes* so full of *. . ."* I would suggest that, behind the mystery of the female genital looms, what is for this film, an even greater mystery in the search to recapture the reciprocal gaze of the mother. Donald Silver contends that the appearance of the mirror in dreams "symbolizes in the unconscious of the dreamer the specular image of the mother's face" (256). Such is the case in this film, particularly when one considers that the face of Mark's dead mother is never directly visualized. Mark is similarly unfocused in the eyes of her successor. In fact, the one mother who comes closest to approaching Mark in an empathetic and understanding way, Mrs. Stevens, is blind[15]—Mark is literally part of an "un-scene." Furthermore, only through the touch of her *hands* is Mark "seen," just as Mark is filmed *by his father* touching his dead mother's hands—and yet, her *face* remains hidden from the father's camera/sight. The father's film focuses on the emptiness of Mark's gaze and the lack of a reciprocal gaze (the "un-seen") marred by his (the father's) exclusion from this circuit. I would further suggest that the repetition of this exclusion—the fact that Mark is consistently on the "other" side of the mirror—is representative of the look of the father gazing upon the mirroring looks of mother and infant.

Seeing and being seen, touching and being touched—in his efforts to recapture the look of the mother, Mark looks and touches from a distance; and his apparatus forecloses the possibility of being seen or touched. So, too, does his apparatus take away the sound of the mother's voice—his films are as silent as Mrs. Stevens is blind.

Helen becomes the agent of Mark's reconstituted history, verbal and visual, identified with all participants at once. She simultaneously levels the barriers of exclusion; on the one hand, by entering Mark's projection room—the No Entry space—and insisting upon knowledge (as she herself states earlier in the film, "I like to understand what I'm shown"), she reduplicates the look of the genital father and the look of son-observer. More importantly, however, she reclaims a maternal No Entry space for Mark by consistently existing outside the mirror. Mark refuses to capture her stare in it (and consistently fails to film her), while she closes her eyes to her own mirrored reflection, insisting only upon her emotional, feeling relationship *to* Mark—for example, she is frightened *for*, not *of*, him. (At one point, she even reclaims his distracted look away at a [sexual] couple.)

Thus, Helen "sees" Mark, not the Mark as identified with the father, but as the child—literally in her visualization and verbal reconstitution of Mark's narrative/filmic history and solidified in her wish to work with Mark to find the face of the child hidden beneath that of the adult for her children's book, *The Magic Camera*. The fact that Helen is posited as the one who *writes* also places her in the position of mother and father *simultaneously*, just as I pointed out earlier that a substitute for regaining the lost, idealized oneness with the mother can be had in a fusional state with the father. *Helen* is the one who initially "hears" the whispers of the father, as she bends to read A. N. Lewis's dedication to his opus on fear—a dedication to Mark himself.[16] Thus, Helen reconstitutes the voice and allows for the integration of sight with sound, touch with feeling, crying with being heard. For when Helen truly "sees," Mark truly "hears" and is heard, as he plays tapes of his recorded cries (startlingly similar to the screams of the woman he murders).

This very search for reunion, for being mirrored in the mother's gaze, is the final regression—the thrust toward death, just as Lewin asserts that to sleep is to die. For Mark is not content with being seen and seeing; he insists upon being the sole arbiter of the seen scene. While he says to Helen that he wishes he could have found her children's faces for her, he ultimately excludes her by insisting that his is the only face which can be seen. In the instant before he plunges the tripod-knife into his throat, Mark exclaims rapturously, "Helen, Helen, I'm afraid! And I'm glad I'm afraid!" If one accepts that, for the infant, one of the functions of the mirroring gaze of the mother is to both validate and redefine the infant's existence and affect—to match and confirm the emotions of the infant—then Mark has finally discovered and effaced his "lack." By allowing himself to be reflected in the mirror—confronting his own face—Mark rediscovers himself in a reciprocal gaze and gazing that meets his own. In the assumption of his capacity to feel anything at all (something he has been unable to do earlier, even as he leaves unfinished his yearning in his statement, "Helen, I feel . . . never mind") and thus reconstitute the dialogue of the "seen," Mark rediscovers the meaningful reciprocal dialogue of subject and object, of mother and infant.

Bedrock . . . this is the meaning I attribute to Mark's suicide run, elaborately orchestrated to the multiple flashes of camera bulbs and tape recordings of his own terrified cries—and his ultimate tragedy. In a remarkable paper, Rene Major develops Lacan's allusion to a "pulsion invocante" (calling instinct) as a form of internal talking recorded as a "pure bodily experience of sounds. This subsumes the idea that the infant's first coenaesthetic impressions are linked to sounds" (460). Mark's tragedy, as with Narcissus, is in the "absence of difference" achieved by a "self-vision obliterating the capacity to hear oneself and the notion of all differences . . . to become the connexion between object and subject . . . Narcissus becomes the fantasy itself" (461).

Peeping Tom began with sleep disturbed by the sounds of the primal scene, with the solitary cry of the frightened child, with an identification with the look of the father. The film ends with sleep restored, with death, with the look and the whispered words of the father as he gazes upon the perfectly united pair of mother and infant captured in the narcissistic fantasy reconstituted in Mark—"There, there now. Don't be a silly boy. There's nothing to be frightened of."

Dry your eyes. And sleep.

NOTES

1. Some representative examples are Robert N. Emde, "The Affective Self: Continuities and Transformations from Infancy," in *Frontiers of Infant Psychiatry*, vol. 2, ed. Justin D. Call, Eleanor Galenson, and Robert L. Tyson (New York: Basic Books, 1984), 38-54; Henri Parens, "On the Girl's Psychosexual Development: Reconsiderations Suggested from Direct Observation," *Journal of the American Psychoanalytic Association* 38 (1990): 743-72; and Daniel N. Stern, *The Interpersonal World of the Infant: A View from Psychoanalysis and Developmental Psychology* (New York: Basic Books, 1985).

This, of course, raises the intriguing question as to whether or note there are *two* psychoanalyses—one of theoretical criticism and the other of theory and practice.

2. I would point out, however, that Silverman's essentialist view negates the importance of situation—for example, the dynamics of viewing a documentary are vastly different from those of viewing the melodrama.

3. For examples of this approach to literature and art, respectively, see Meredith Anne Skura, *The Literary Use of the Psychoanalytic Process* (New Haven: Yale University Press, 1981).

4. See Silverman 1988.

5. While I do not agree that *all* perversions are grounded in anality, Chasseguet-Smirgel's essential point—that they level the differences imposed by reality and most specifically the reality separating a child from his/her mother—is largely substantiated on the basis of clinical experience (see, for example, Elaine V. Siegel, *Female Homosexuality: Choice without Volition* [Hillsdale: Analytic Press, 1988]). Further, Silverman herself arrives at this point in her later work while characterizing Chasseguet-Smirgel as "hateful" (1988, 33).

6. For an example of his approach, see Ilsa J. Bick, "The Look Back in *E.T.*," *Cinema Journal* 31.4 (Summer, 1992), 25-41.

7. Freud did speculate, however, that the "high degree of narcissistic value which the penis possesses can appeal to the fact that the organ is a guarantee to its owner that he can be

once more united with his mother—i.e. to a substitute for her—in the act of copulation. Being deprived of it amounts to a renewed separation from her, and this in its turn means being helplessly exposed to an unpleasurable tension due to instinctual need" (1953, 20: 139).

8. Throughout the film, there are recurrent allusions to the sadistic pleasure inherent in auteurial, directorial control juxtaposed against (disguised) masochistic surrender to the agents of own's own drama—perhaps as commentary upon Powell's own relationship to his film. Certainly one could read the film as an Odysseyian voyage—that is, Mark's tenacious identification with his father as defense against regression, just as Wright observes that Odysseus subjects himself to torment and "gets his men to strap him to the mast [the upright phallus] and plug his ears against the sweet siren voices so that he is not lured into their fatal, devouring embrace" (1991, 114). These concerns are explicitly addressed during what are the film's establishing shot (the archery target/production credits), the end of the prologue (the movie projector over which the directorial credits appear), Mark's carefully orchestrated, methodically directed murder of Viv on a film set, the film-within-a-film's director's sadistic treatment of his starlet, the producer's manipulation of tiny, doll-like figures representative of the film's actors, the taunts Mark endures from Millie, and so on. For an interesting discussion of sadomasochism as figurations within a cinematic text, see Krin Gabbard, "The Circulation of Sado-Masochist Desire in the *Lolita* Texts" (Paper delivered at the Workshop on Sadism and Masochism in the Film Narrative, American Psychoanalytic Association, New Orleans, 9 May 1991).

9. This recalls similar preoccupations in an equally infamous film, Bunuel's *Un Chien Andalou* (1929). Among its more memorable sequences, this film's prologue equates the moon and the female eye with images of castration and death just as one emphasis in *Peeping Tom* is upon viewing the mystery of the castrated woman.

10. The prostitute's mouth becomes an obvious parallel to the *vagina dentata*, reiterating preoccupations with castration fears.

11. For example, see William Niederlund, "Early Auditory Experiences, Beating Fantasies and Primal Scene," *The Psychoanalytic Study of the Child*, 13 (1958): 471-504.

12. This is a particularly compelling reading since, by his compulsive repetitions, Mark seeks to reestablish a negative Oedipal constellation in his identification with his female victims, as Silverman rightly concludes.

13. Mark's creative solutions—his camera-mirror-tripod/knife apparatus, his documentary film, and his manipulation of his female victims—are all representative of what Chasseguet-Smirgel might term as distillates of the anal universe in defensive substitutions and replacements for the genital phallus. Informing another developmental level, however, such creations and creativity might also represent Edelheit's primal scene condensations—for example, the camera as identified with the paternal phallus, the "mirroring" eye of the mother, the "phallic" nature of the tripod/knife. Leonard Shengold paraphrases Kanser's (1950) discussion of the significance of the unspoken, hostile relationship between Jocasta and Oedipus, equating Jocasta's brooch with the talons of the Sphinx and postulating that the Sphinx and Jocasta are synonymous. If the camera/knife/mirror configuration in *Peeping Tom* is a representation of an orally composed composite creature, could the knife then be alternately equated with the talons of the Sphinx? The mirror with Perseus's golden shield? The knife kills by piercing the women's throats; and, perhaps not surprisingly, the name of the Sphinx means "the strangler." Henry Bunker has written of the female voice as equivalent to the female phallus—thus, the knife both castrates (by pierc-

ing the throat and depriving the women of voice—their films are "silent") and, like the Sphinx, penetrates/orally incorporates (the camera plunging down into the women's open mouths just as the Sphinx strangles and then devours its victims. Then, too, Perseus slew the Medusa by reflecting back to her her own horrific visage and mesmerizing eye in the mirroring sheen of his golden shield, just as Mark transforms the woman's hidden genital into its visual equivalent and, with this sight, transfixes his monsters and slays them.

14. Laurie Scheider, "Mirrors in Art," *Psychoanalytic Inquiry* 5, no. 3 (1985): 283-324.

15. Her blindness is also equated to castration as she has allowed herself to be "operated on by a man in whom [she] had no confidence." Furthermore, in keeping with the mythological subtext to the film, the blind, prescient Mrs. Stevens could very well double for the blind prophet Teresias. Both prophets "see" what is plainly visible; both are doubles for the protagonist (the one for Oedipus, the other for Mark).

16. I can not help but wonder whether the similarity between the bound volumes of Lewis's work and those of Freud is accidental. Punctuated by the episode with the ludicrously uncomprehending psychoanalyst and the overt indictment of psychological theory, Powell seems more than intent upon directing part of his hostility toward psychoanalysis as a "violating," penetrating, directorial "art."

WORKS CITED

Bunker, Henry. "The Voice as (Female) Phallus." *Psychoanalytic Quarterly* 3 (1939): 391-429.

Carroll, Noël. *Mystifying Movies: Fads and Fallacies in Contemporary Film Theory.* New York: Columbia UP, 1988.

Chasseguet-Smirgel, Janine. *Creativity and Perversion.* New York: Norton, 1984.

Chodorow, Nancy. *The Reproduction of Mothering: Psychoanalysis and the Sociology of Gender.* Berkeley: U of California P, 1978.

Edelheit, Henry. "Mythopoesis and the Primal Scene." *The Psychoanalytic Study of Society* 5: 212-33.

Freud, Sigmund. "Civilization and Its Discontents." *The Standard Edition of the Complete Psychological Works.* Vol. 21. Trans. James Strachey. London: Hogarth, 1953. 59-148.

———. "Inhibitions, Symptoms, and Anxiety." *The Standard Edition of the Complete Psychological Works.* Vol. 20. Trans. James Strachey. London: Hogarth, 1953. 77-178.

Lacan, Jacques. "The Mirror Image as Formative of the Function of the 'I.'" *Ecrits: A Selection.* Trans. Alan Sheridan. London: Tavistock, 1977. 1-7.

Lewin, Bertram D. *The Psychoanalysis of Elation.* New York: Norton, 1950.

Mahler, Margaret S., Fred Pine, and Anthony Bergman. *The Psychological Birth of the Human Infant.* New York: Basic, 1975.

Major, Rene. "The Voice Behind the Mirror." *The International Review of Psychoanalysis* 7.4: 459-68.

Metz, Christian. *The Imaginary Signifier: Psychoanalysis and Cinema*. Trans. Celia Britton, Annwyl Williams, Ben Brewster, and Alfred Guzzetti. Bloomington: Indiana UP, 1982.

Niederlund, William. "Early Auditory Experiences, Beating Fantasies and Primal Scene." *The Psychoanalytic Study of the Child* 13 (1958): 471-504.

Olivier, Christine. *Jocasta's Children: The Imprint of the Mother*. Trans. George Craig. London: Routledge, 1989.

Peto, Andrew. "Terrifying Eyes: A Visual Superego Forerunner." *The Psychoanalytic Study of the Child* 24 (1969): 197-212.

Rangell, Leo. "Castration." *Journal of the American Psychoanalytic Association* 39: 3-24.

Scheider, Laurie. "Mirrors in Art." *Psychoanalytic Inquiry* 5.3: 283-324.

Shengold, Leonard. "The Parent as Sphinx." *Journal of the American Psychoanalytic Association* 11: 725-51.

Silver, Donald. "Mirror in Dreams: Symbol of Mother's Face." *Psychoanalytic Inquiry* 5.3: 253-56.

Silverman, Kaja. *The Acoustic Mirror: The Female Voice in Psychoanalysis and Cinema*. Bloomington: Indiana UP, 1988.

———. "Masochism and Male Subjectivity." *Camera Obscura* 17 (1988): 31-68.

Socarides, Charles W. *The Preoedipal Origin and Psychoanalytic Therapy of Sexual Perversions*. Madison: International Universities P, 1988.

Winnicott, D. W. *Playing and Reality*. London: Tavistock, 1971.

Wood, Robin. "The Return of the Repressed." *Film Comment* 14: 24-32.

Wright, Kenneth. *Vision and Separation: Between Mother and Baby*. Northvale: Aronson, 1991.

CHAPTER SIXTEEN

TWILIGHT OF THE MONSTERS: THE ENGLISH HORROR FILM 1968-1975

David Sanjek

THROUGHOUT THE GLOBE, 1968 was a cataclysmic year. Social unrest proliferated as distraught populations protested against the Vietnam War, repressive government policies, and a rising tide of racism and sexism. Simultaneously, a motion picture made on a shoestring budget was released that not only fed off the international zeitgeist of pessimism and anxiety but also brought about a radical transformation of the horror genre. That film was George Romero's *Night of the Living Dead*. Made for only $114,000, it broke any number of rules that heretofore had governed the form. Violence that once was implied or briefly demonstrated now was shown in all its visceral details. The film's victims in several cases became themselves monsters, thereby muddying the distinction between the monstrous and the normal as well as locating terror in the everyday world. Critic Roger Ebert saw the picture at a Saturday matinee largely attended by children. They were stunned, and as a nine-year-old girl began to cry, he realized, "I don't think younger kids really knew what hit them. They had seen horror films before, but this was something else" (Hoberman and Rosenbaum 1983, 111-12).

For a time thereafter, the horror genre itself did not seem to know what to do with this new development. The overt subversion of Romero's work had inaugurated the modern horror film. From this time forward, "the genre became increasingly reflexive and allusive, flaunting its generic inheritance and its own identity as horror and as film" (Waller 1987, 2). A principal part of that inheritance was the rich and substantial body of horror films produced in England from the 1950s onward, particularly but not exclusively those released by the Hammer Studios. For all their groundbreaking alteration of generic rules and taboos—it is well to recall that the company's first full-fledged horror production, *The Curse of Frankenstein* (1957), was labelled by one critic "among the half-dozen most repulsive films I have ever encountered" and brought another to call for a new film certificate, "SO" or "For Sadists Only" (Pirie 1974, 40)—the company's releases had become by 1968 increasingly safe and formulaic. The ambiguity of Romero's film underscored the increasingly inoperative moral allegory of Hammer's output, and Hammer's predilection for dramatizing the intrusion of the "abnormal" monster into a "normal" human community. This allegorizing reflects what David Pirie has called "the innate Manicheanism of the English" (1974, 11), which, until 1968, had supported the creation of "the only stable cinematic myth which Britain can properly claim as its own" (1974, 9).

The bullet that entered the brain of Romero's protagonist at his film's conclusion helped set in motion the decline of the British horror film and the myth it embodied. When monsters and human beings could no longer easily be distinguished, the tidy universe of the English horror film was in jeopardy. To some degree, the creators of that national myth recognized its near moribund condition but attempted nonetheless to resuscitate the form in an increasingly anxious and often frantic manner. They tried making its sexual dimension ever more explicit and salacious, escalating the level of gore and blood, engaging in out and out parody of generic conventions, and grafting incongruous materials, including hard driving bikers and Far Eastern Kung Fu. This period certainly had its share of outrageous attempts to combine genres into novel constructions. Two especially memorable additions were 1973's *The Legend of the Seven Golden Vampires* a.k.a. *The Seven Brothers Meet Dracula* and 1971's *Psychomania*. In the former, Hammer collaborated with the veteran Hong Kong filmmaker Run Run Shaw in a futile attempt to integrate martial arts and horror. The director was a veteran Englishman, Roy Ward Baker, while a Chinese technician, Liu Chia-Liang, handled the fight scenes (Hardy 1968, 278). Needless to say, their styles clashed. The latter film, on the other hand, is a particularly memorable piece of strange cinema in which a set of young bikers, led by a young man whose mother is a witch, discover that if they kill themselves, they will return from the dead, immortal. The scenes of the young people gleefully committing suicide have to be seen to be believed, and the film is "one of the very few black comedies to derive from British horror thanks largely to Don Sharp's refusal to resort to blatant comic effects" (Pirie 1974, 187). All was to no avail. By 1975, Hammer Studios was a bit player in the film industry, as were such smaller but noteworthy operations as Amicus, Tigon, and Tyburn.

The reasons for these studios' demise and the virtual abandonment of the cinematic myth they supported are many, but chief among them is the exhaustion of what James B. Twitchell has called "artificial horror," which he defines as "what a audience searches for in a verbal or visual text when it wants a particular kind of *frisson* without much intellectual explanation or sophistication," and its replacement by "real horror," verbal or visual imagery that is repellent in actuality (1985, 8). Noel Carroll has proposed an alternate set of terms, the replacement of "art-horror" by "natural horror," yet whatever the chosen terminology, it is altogether clear that the opposition of British sedateness and extra-human forces appropriate to the construction of a British national cinematic myth no longer terrified audiences when human actions superseded any creations of the imagination. The transformation British society was undergoing during the period 1968-75 demanded that viewers as well as creators address the "disquieting intimation not only that there are latent possibilities for frightfulness in a great many people, but that relatively small shifts in social structures can permit those possibilities to realize themselves" (Fraser 1974, 85). To remain worthy of attention, the British horror film would have to embrace the monstrous in audience and viewer alike. Few horror films produced in England between 1968 and 1975 achieved this goal.

To assess why this is so and what few films met these requirements, we must first examine the tumultuous social, cultural, and economic conditions existent in Britain at the time, then turn to a brief analysis of certain of the principal horror films produced during this period—especially those featuring the most long-lasting horror characters (Frankenstein's monster and the vampire), parodies of generic conventions (the Dr. Phibes films, *Theater of Blood*, and *Horror Hospital*) and antiestablishment paranoid narratives (the work of Peter Walker, Gordon Hessler's *Scream and Scream Again*, and Robin Hardy's *The Wicker Man*)—and conclude with a more detailed discussion of two films that most tellingly embrace the monstrous in viewer and creator alike: Michael Reeves's *The Witchfinder General* a.k.a. *The Conqueror Worm* and Gary Sherman's *Death Line* a.k.a. *Raw Meat*.

The British film industry was in particularly dire shape during the period under review. Throughout the 1960s, the number of theaters fell precipitously from 3,034 to 1,530, as did the sale of tickets, from 500 to 116 million (Hewison 1978, 289). British film companies were financially beholden to foreign sources of capital, particularly from the United States. By 1967, 90 percent of production money came from this source, and when American companies themselves suffered substantial losses, principally due to overcapitalization of big-budget white elephants, and were taken over by nonfilm conglomerates, the figure remained high, as 50 percent of financing still came from abroad (Murphy 1986, 64-66). Many complained that British talent was being exploited for the benefit of foreigners, but in truth opportunities were bleak for all filmmakers. This can sadly be demonstrated by David Pirie's 1971 article "New Blood." He highlights the financial crisis in the British film industry as well as the limited opportunities open to those individuals ready to work within the established rules of the horror genre. The harsh truth, however, is that the four directors he spotlights—Stephen Weeks, Peter Sasdy, Gordon Hessler, and Peter Sykes—all fell prey to the "sadly vast record of [British] film-makers who have sunk without a trace after one or two promising pictures," (75) a fate Pirie hoped they might avoid.

If the financial structure of the British film industry was unstable, so too was the society as a whole. Harold Wilson's Labour government that promised technocratic solutions to systemic social ills had benefitted from the economic boom of the mid 1960s, but then it broke apart when financial markets fell. Under Conservative leadership, unemployment rose steadily, reaching its first million in 1975; inflation took off beyond control; property prices doubled; and labor unions fought aggressively for their share of a diminishing pie, 1970-71 having the worst record for strikes and stoppages since the unrest of 1926 (Hewison 1987, 182-83). The period climaxed with a particularly bitter election in 1974; the first ballot gave neither party a majority and the subsequent ballot gave Wilson's Labour party only a three vote majority. The Conservatives proceeded to elect Margaret Thatcher their leader the following year, the first sign of more traumatic changes to come.

Clearly not a time to engage in outlays of speculative capital for film production nor a stable society in which to create imaginative myths, British society continued to rupture as individual constituencies fought over whatever vestiges of power or symbols of order they could salvage. The least successful were those connected to the cultural revolution of the young and disenfranchised. The government and police perceived them as pernicious malcontents, while the Far Left denigrated their cultural platform as nothing more than the "stifling haze of hashsmoke and Amerikan hipculchur" (Hewison 1987, 168). Representatives of the Far Right, principally embodied by that paragon of cultural conservatism Mary Whitehouse, engaged in a moral panic over collapsing values, while the Left stagnated in sectarian disputation, climaxing with the bombings, arrest, and conviction of the "Angry Brigade" in 1972 (Fountain 1988, 178). It should come as no surprise that British society began to turn inward, retreating to the exploration of inner space rather than issues of external social realities.

This mood of reactionary solipsism is reflected by a 1969 British Arts Council Report that warned: "The so-called permissive society may have its casualties; the repressive society almost certainly has a great deal more. Repressed sexuality can be toxic both to the individual and to society. Repression can deprave and corrupt" (Hewison 1987, 171). British society increasingly exhibited a schizophrenic facade: consumed by the desire for affluence yet disturbed by money's effect upon the culture; anxious to hold onto the signs of social discourse yet committed to actions and policies that guaranteed anomie. The film industry likewise engaged in schizophrenic behavior, nowhere better seen than in the forlorn attempt to resuscitate the Gothic archetypes that had dominated the horror genre in Britain from the start. The loosening of censorship laws and the advance of the sexual revolution permitted an expansion of permissible content in films, but the results were often heavy handed. Rather than reanimating the horror genre, many individuals merely grafted overt sexual material with liberal doses of gore to a preexistant framework. It should come as no little surprise that the results were incompatible, for, as David Pirie argues, "Much of [British art's] didactic power is ultimately derived from the way it permits the audience to enjoy virtue in principle and vice in practice" (1974, 52). The removal of the clear demarcation between virtue and vice obscured the essential emotions and attitudes upon which these films depended.

Take away the hypocrisy and all one has left is a somewhat hapless attempt to update a set of conventions whose time has past. In most instances, the effort met with dismal failure. However, much as the Baron himself was repeatedly able to resurrect lifeless matter, the final additions to the Hammer Frankenstein cycle directed by Fisher, *Frankenstein Must be Destroyed* (1969) and *Frankenstein and the Monster From Hell* (1973), manage to reinvigorate the form by blurring the line between the Baron and his creation, particularly in the earlier film, which features "one of the most overly pathetic and moving Frankenstein monsters in the history of the cinema" (Pirie 1973, 80). By contrast, the baron's excessive brutality, which ranges from the murder of innocent bystanders to the rape and eventual murder of his assistant's wife, raises the question, Who is the monster and who ought to be destroyed? The "real horror" of the baron's demented behavior in the film only increases in the sequel, Fisher's *envoi* to the cinema and Peter Cushing's to the character. Here, the baron, imprisoned in a madhouse and crippled by the fire into which his creature had carried him at the conclusion of the previous film, attempts once more to perfect his experiments. However, the patchwork nature of the result parallels, Wheeler Winston Dixon asserts, the patched-together nature of the film (Dixon 1991a, 282). Drained by age, the scientist stitches together portions of various asylum inmates, much as the film's director, himself in his late sixties and ailing, cobbles together the Gothic conventions to which he had devoted the past eighteen years with the excessive gore (graphic brain removals, eyeball graftings, and the eventual tearing asunder of the eponymous creature) requisite to the transformed cinematic climate. The result evidences a "despairing end-of-the-road" (Newman 1988, 18) that only makes the baron's final speech all the more evocative: "We've a long work ahead of us. We must get this place tidied up so we can start afresh . . . Next time, we will need fresh material" (Dixon 1991a, 286). But there would not be next time, nor would there be fresh material. There would be only Hammer's other misguided addition to the cycle: *The Horror of Frankenstein* (1970), a ham-fisted remake of *The Curse of Frankenstein* that lacked any of the subtlety and nuance Fisher brought even to a film as hopelessly at odds with itself as his final release. Raymond Durgnat described Hammer's earlier output as a "blend of Technicolor elegance and cold savagery" (1970, 223), but devoid of that elegance, all that can result is a vapid display of dispassionate violence.

The vampire, the most consistently filmed and financially remunerative character in Hammer's horror pantheon, figures in at least ten films produced during the period under review. However, those that feature Bram Stoker's Dracula most often reduce him to a one-dimensional parasite. The diminution of his personality went so far that in several instances he was denied the power of speech, leaving only a snarling, inarticulate presence. Even his once-powerful adversary, Dr. Van Helsing, was replaced by a sequence of drab romantic couples. Production values suffered too, as the voluptuous Technicolor canvas of Fisher's *Horror of Dracula* (1958) gave way to pasteboard faceless European villages. About the only point of interest in the succession of mediocre resurrections of a once-vital set of symbols and images represented by *Dracula Has Risen From the Grave* (1968) and *The Scars of Dracula* (1970) is the unusual manner in which Dracula is dispatched in the final reel: thrown upon an impaling cross or struck by lightning. At a loss for novelty to beef up their diminishing revenues, Hammer proceeded gratuitously to augment the sexual dimension of the vampire's powers, parading across the screen a succession of nubile, half-naked or fully naked female victims, and pointlessly updated the myth to the twentieth century in the final installments: *Dracula AD 1972* (1972) and *The Satanic Rites of Dracula* (1974). At the conclusion of the latter film, the count is ignominiously skewered on a hawthorne bush. Previously he attempted to spread a plague throughout the world by means of bacteriological warfare. However, the operating metaphor of the vampire myth is the paradoxical attractiveness of the vampire's kiss of death. To equate his contagion with environmental catastrophe offers a metaphor that is novel but too shallow to sustain significant alteration of the myth.

A more substantial although equally unsatisfying attempt to renovate the vampire narrative was Hammer's introduction of lesbianism and female antagonists in the "Karnstein Trilogy": *The Vampire Lovers* (1970), *Lust for a Vampire* (1970), and *Twins of Evil* (1971). These films shamelessly drew upon the redefinition of women as active agents of their own destiny, brought about by the women's movement as well as by the sexual revolution's renegotiation of notions of gender and sexual orientation. One might wish the trilogy had used the image of a female vampire to subvert hegemonic definitions of femininity, but each instead incorporates a number of voracious female characters possessed of unhealthy lusts and appetites. The loosening of the censorship codes in 1968 permitted the near-pornographic display of female bodies that the fantastic narrative structure rendered "safe." Even more dismaying, the eventual destruction of the villainous women allowed audiences implicitly to condemn at one and the same time vampirism and lesbianism, equating the two as crimes against nature. As Bonnie Zimmerman has written, "The function of the lesbian vampire is to contain attraction between women within the safe boundaries of sexual violence, to force it into a particular model of sexuality. By showing the lesbian as a vampire-rapist who violates and destroys her victims, men alleviate their fears that lesbian love could create an alternate model, that two women without coercion or morbidity might prefer one another to a man" (1984, 156).

The singular exceptions to these weak resusitations of a once vital generic form are Peter Sasdy's *Taste the Blood of Dracula* (1969) and *Countess Dracula* (1970) and Brian Clemens's light-hearted parody, *Captain Kronos, Vampire Hunter* (1974). Sasdy moves ahead of his predecessors by refusing to transform his subsidiary characters into mere fodder for the vampire's appetites. Instead, he not only recaptures but also reformulates the strength of Stoker's original vision "in the way he uses the spectre of Dracula to subvert the facade of Victorian society, or more precisely the facade of the Victorian family" (Pirie 1979, 80). Even though Dracula plays a minor role in the overall narrative of *Taste the Blood of Dracula*, he is the precipitating factor that brings about the literal consumption of a set of fathers by their children. Influenced, perhaps, by the anti-psychiatric theories of R. D. Laing popular at the time, this film virtually dramatizes the therapist's statement, "Only by the most outrageous violation of ourselves have we achieved our capacity to live in relative adjustment to a civilization apparently driven to its own destruction" (Hewison 1987, 134). Sasdy continued this sophisticated exploration in *Countess Dracula*, a retelling of the story of Countess Bathory, the female counterpart of Vlad the Impaler, the inspiration for the character of Dracula. Here he inverts the gender orientation of his other film by focusing upon a vampiric mother who, albeit unsuccessfully, attempts to consume her own daughter in an effort to prolong her youth. By combining elements of the Gothic myth with a sophisticated understanding of the potentially schizophrenic composition of the family unit, Sasdy redefines the vampire myth without debasing its components.

Countess Dracula is not alone in its exploration of the schizophrenic nature of family life. A number of horror films of the period took this as their subject and constitute some of the most interesting work in the genre. They include Viktors Ritelis's *The Corpse* a.k.a. *Crucible of Horror* (1969), in which a mother and daughter kill her husband only to have the corpse reappear, thereby allegorically dramatizing the seeming inescapability of patriarchy; Peter Skye's *Demons of the Mind* a.k.a. *Blood Will Have Blood* (1972), an exceptional return to the best Hammer Gothic style and a devastating narrative of how a mad father's attempt to keep his children from the influence of the blood of his ancestors leads only to incest, madness, and death; Seth Holt's *Blood from the Mummy's Tomb* (1971), an adaptation of a Bram Stoker novel in which an Egyptologist's daughter is the murderous reincarnation of the spirit of a dead princess; Peter Sasdy's *Hands of the Ripper* (1971), in which the daughter of the murderer inherits her father's compulsions; and Freddie Francis's *The Creeping Flesh* (1972), which dramatizes how a scientist, eager to keep his daughter from inheriting her mother's insanity, injects her with the flesh of an excavated corpse that turns out to be incarnated evil, leading the daughter to insanity and murder. In addition, virtually all these films incorporate critiques of the psychiatric establishment and dramatize how the fine line between sanity and insanity can be drawn to the benefit of the dominant order.

Brian Clemens, on the other hand, expands upon the horror genre through parody, but without cheapening that which he satirizes. His hero, Captain Kronos, is a novel construction, a combination of Sergio Leone's "Man With No Name," a kung fu warrior, and the archetypical vampire fighter. His exploits are a farrago of

Figure 16.1. Christopher Lee in *Taste the Blood of Dracula*. Courtesy: British Film Institute.

serial anticlimaxes, Grand Guignol gore, and romantic high adventure whose vitality cause one to wonder why Clemens's film, especially considering its competition, remained on the shelf for two years before theatrical release. It is a parodic example of "artificial horror" at its best, without any condescending critique of its constituent parts.

While *Captain Kronos* good-naturedly toys with generic conventions, several other films engage in wholesale mockery of the horror form, most noteworthy among them Robert Fuest's *The Abominable Dr. Phibes* (1971) and *Dr. Phibes Rises Again* (1972), Douglas Hickox's *Theatre of Blood* (1973), and Anthony Balch's *Horror Hospital* a.k.a. *Dr. Bloodbath* (1973). Each presents a calculated exercise in camp that, as Susan Sontag defines the term, "converts the serious into the frivolous" (1969, 278) and reduces the symbols and situations appropriate to the horror genre into entertaining, albeit one-dimensional, narratives. Vincent Price is a ubiquitous presence in all but Balch's film, as are a plethora of guest stars from the English stage and screen, and Balch's self-regarding theatricality emphasizes style at the expense of content, a tendency typical of camp. Fuest's two films also subordinate action to decor, for their over-the-top art deco set designs overwhelm the narrative, turning it at times into a series of stillborn tableaux. Balch, on the other hand, as one might expect from one who distributed films by such disparate figures as Robert Bresson and Tod Browning, as well as producing a short subject, *Towers Open Fire* (1963) in collaboration with William Burroughs, engages in parody that is at once sophisticated and sleazy. Much like Burroughs' cut-up literary forms, Balch provides the requisite shocks but also includes a low-budget allusion to Cocteau's *Orpheus* (1950) in the form of a troop of motorcycling killer zombies. And yet, what dismays one most about these enjoyably trashy films is their reduction of what was once a coherent and deliberate narrative form into a series of elaborately staged executions. One feels hurried from atrocity to atrocity, each guest star victim serving little function other than participating in their appointed demise. The intricacy of their ends (in Fuest's films based upon the plagues of the Old Testament and in Hickox's adapted from deaths in Shakespearian plays) takes precedence over characterization or plot construction. The result is a set of ingenious contrivances, as if the creators were admitting the hollowness of all horror conventions that would no longer serve for anything more than cheap gallows humor.

Another form popular during the period that too often descends to trivial, albeit amusing, gallows humor is the anthology picture. Created in the model of the classic 1945 *Dead of Night*, these films were principally produced by the Amicus studio, starring with *Dr. Terror's House of Horrors* (1964). Each uses a narrative link to connect episodes of quite "artificial horror," and a number of them were direct adaptations of the American EC horror comics of the 1950s. Due to the short length of individual episodes, characterization was often dim or nonexistent, and plots centered on the final image, usually one in which the villain of the piece received her or his just desserts. Some of the better films in this group, such as *Torture Garden* (1968) and *Tales From the Crypt* (1972), were directed by cinematographer Freddie Francis. Yet even Francis admitted the constrictions of the form when he stated, "One of the satisfactions I've gotten out of doing the horror films is that I think on every film that I did, I transcended the script visually" (Dixon 1991b, 18).

A number of other films substitute shock for substance but at the same time engage in explicit anti-institutional critique. Each affords the opportunity for a systematic discourse upon the abuses of the hegemonic culture but casts it aside in order to obliterate another set of undeserving victims. The principal culprit in this regard is Pete Walker. An early proponent of "splatter," Walker produced *Whipcord* (1974), *Frightmare* (1974), and *The Confessional* a.k.a. *House of Mortal Sin* (1975), which take on the institutions of the prison system, the mental health and psychiatric establishments, and the Catholic Church, respectively. But each one does little more than "adopt a brutally cynical approach loosely related to the sixties, anti-authoritarian ideologies and ruthlessly exploit the theme for all the gore and sex it can possibly yield within a commercially saleable format" (Hardy 1986, 302). Walker does assert, "I like the idea of taking people who are in a position of authority and showing that they had either murderous or peculiar quirks about them" (Hallenbeck 1983, 43), yet the results too often descend to crude shocks and displays of exposed viscera. Nonetheless, *Frightmare* remains a particularly disturbing and bleak instance of a family literally consuming itself, as the cannibalistic matriarch, whose husband guiltily indulges her voracious appetites, is joined in her compulsion by her equally unstable daughter.

A more successful instance of institutional analysis is Gordon Hessler's *Scream and Scream Again* (1970). It audaciously joins together a series of seemingly discontinuous plot threads, all of which converge in the revelation that the English and other international governments are directed by a conspiracy of murderous humanoids. In David Pirie's view, "one of the finest SF movies ever written" and "an absolute *tour de force* of directional excitement," the film also constitutes one of the rare instances in the period of a nonlinear fragmented narrative that at one and the same time provides the requisite frisson and alludes to a society led by those literally without soul (Pirie 1974, 158). An equally impressive depiction of a world without security is provided by Robin Hardy's *The Wicker Man* (1973). In it, a middle-aged, virginal, conservative police officer is sent to an isolated island community to investigate the reported disappearance of a young girl. There his whole way of life is called into question, as the island is populated by a community of nature-worshipping pagans. The mystery, however, proves to be a red herring, for the girl is alive and the policeman has been sent on a wild goose chase whose aim is his sacrifice to insure the island's and its practices' continued survival. However, Hardy and his scriptwriter Anthony Shaffer make the drama a complex one. We find it hard to sympathize with the policeman's smug, foolish behavior but mourn his loss and are terrified by his fate. The islanders, on the other hand, though vital in their practices and secure in their beliefs, alienate us by the ferocity with which they celebrate a human being burnt alive. *The Wicker Man* may allow us to embrace the monstrous, but we wish to relinquish it almost immediately.

The most compelling and successful examples of embracing the monstrous are Michael Reeves's *The Witchfinder General* a.k.a. *The Conquerer Worm* (1968) and Gary Sherman's *Death Line* a.k.a. *Raw Meat* (1972). Both films permit us empathy for the victim but at the same time present their violators in such a way that we understand, perhaps even confirm, their psychopathological vision. Furthermore, both blur the line between violator and victim and the latter turns into the former at the films' conclusion, making it difficult, if not impossible, to conceive of clear boundaries to our ethical process. Reeves and Sherman created insistently violent films. David Pirie has isolated a strain in British culture he calls "Selwynism," so named for a sadistic eighteenth-century nobleman who sought out atrocities (Pirie 1974, 17-8). A number of English films, most notably Arthur Crabtree's *Horrors of the Black Museum* (1958), have been analyzed by Pirie as needless and titillating sadism, yet one could not accuse either Reeves or Sherman of such practices. It can be argued that the violence their films portray is problematic; part of the films' intent is to embrace the monstrous and force the viewer to retheorize his assumptions about victimhood and victimization. John Fraser has stated, "the most meaningful . . . and the most daring . . . kind of violence . . . involves a penetration into and empathy with other consciousnesses in action" (1974, 53). These two films, more than any of the others under review, meet his test.

The Witchfinder General is the fourth and final film of Reeves, who died, seemingly a suicide, at the age of twenty-four (see Kelly 1991; Paul 1971; Wood 1969-70). That so young a man could produce such an accomplished film is miraculous in itself, but that it would be released by the American exploitation film company like American International is even more impressive. As several lines of verse from Edgar Allan Poe were tagged onto the start of the narrative and the film starred Vincent Price (the leading actor in Roger Corman's series of Poe adaptations), it was marketed as yet another in a series of such works. However, the story is drawn from historical fact and set in Cromwell's England during the Civil War; it concerns the brutal activities of one Matthew Hopkins, an actual hunter of witches. However, its true subject is the sickening futility of violence. Hopkins is a monster in human guise who uses the name of the Church in order to molest attractive young women, kill innocent people, and profit from his labors in the name of God and Country. If nothing else, Reeves managed to make Price treat the role seriously and not descend to camp flourishes. Despite Price's protestations about Reeves's youth and inexperience, the young man prodded, even bullied the American star into creating "a superb presence of inexorable vindictiveness around which the other characters move with fascinated repulsion" (Pirie 1974, 154).

At the film's conclusion, a young English soldier manages to escape Hopkins's clutches and, just as Hopkins is torturing the soldier's bride-to-be, the soldier attacks the witchfinder with a axe and literally chops him to pieces. The film ends with the scream of the mad young woman. The young soldier has become, during the course of the film's narrative, so morally outraged that he has fallen to virtually the same moral depths Hopkins inhabits. This horrific conclusion helps convey, as Robin Wood has written, "the disturbing sense throughout that sanity and goodness are powerless against the all-pervading corruption and violence" (Wood 1969-70, 6). Wood further states how the film seems more to spring to life in scenes that involve excessive cruelty and horror, but it must be added that the genuine commitment between the young couple colors, even if it does not mitigate, their eventual fate. The degree to which Reeves integrates the physical landscape of the English countryside into the narrative, creating, as William Paul has stated, a synchronism between character and setting, is rare in English horror films, giving an extra dimension to this unsettling work. Nonetheless, *The Witchfinder General* remains a rare instance of a film that examines and critiques our response to violence by simultaneously appearing to justify it, while showing it in its least appetizing light. Reeves's loss at so young an age is truly a shame, as he was "the kind of film-maker which the English cinema needed (and still needs) so desperately . . . someone who could merge the popular tradition of the horror film with more avant-garde concerns without rearing the curious bastard, which so often results from such experiments" (Pirie 1974, 155).

An equally expressive but less well known motion picture, Gary Sherman's *Death Line* a.k.a. *Raw Meat*, like Reeves's film, was also released in the United States by American International Pictures. It differs by being set in contemporary London and having as its monster not a sadistic true believer but a middle-aged cannibal who is the descendent of a group of underground workers trapped and then abandoned following a tunnel collapse. Also, unlike Matthew Hopkins, the "Man" is a sympathetic figure, perhaps the only truly human figure in the film, despite the rotting bodies littering his subterranean home and his savage killing in the middle of the film of three subway workers. In *Death Line*, Sherman addresses above all other considerations the theme of the futility of violence. These contrasts extend beyond the obvious distinction between above and below ground. First, there is the less than fine line between the "monster" and the "hero." The latter is a young American exchange student, depicted more often than not as a surly, solipsistic lout. Parallels can be made to Peckinpah's *Straw Dogs* (1971), which also focussed upon the violence within one and all and featured a disaffected expatriate; Sherman goes so far as to permit his "hero" to own, as did Peckinpah's, a toy composed of hung-up ball bearings. He deigns to help others only at the film's conclusion, remaining apart and verbally abusive of any collaboration until then. Like Orpheus searching after Eurydice, he descends into the subway tunnels in search of his girlfriend, whom the "Man" has kidnapped, and then virtually kicks the "Man" to a bloody pulp. He is stopped only by the young woman's protestations. At this point, the victim becomes the victimizer, and our sympathy, even our pity, is with the "Man," who only wanted a companion to replace the dead "Woman" whom he interned earlier in the film. Sherman also introduces a class component to his narrative. The English policeman investigating the "Man's" crimes is a lower-class boor who verbally abuses the young American as well as his upper-class superior from the Secret Service. He never really solves the crimes, he only cleans up the mess at the end and, it is implied, will aid and abet a cover-up of the preceding events and the tunnel collapse that led to them. However, the significant focus of Sherman's film is the "Man." His underground world is privileged by Sherman, as shown in a long, graceful tracking shot when the character is first introduced; it amply indicates that this environment, despite his practices, possesses greater visual detail, what with its chiaroscuro shadows and grisly testaments to its inhabitants' appetites, than the pale, dull institutional surfaces of London aboveground. The sympathy we end up feeling for this character is certainly well laced with disgust, but one must recognize he kills out of need, not for the love of violence. When the "Man" mournfully intones the only English he can speak, "Mind the doors," as he chases the American's girlfriend, Sherman makes clear that the compartmentalization of the monstrous from the normal is no simple matter. Too often we mind the doors ourselves rather than embracing the synchronities that, much to our dismay, join us with that which we loathe.

The years following 1975 have been only occasional achievements to equal Reeves' and Sherman's. One might look to Neil Jordan's *The Company of Wolves* (1984), Clive Barker's *Hellraiser* (1987) and *Nightbreed* (1989), or Bernard Rose's *Paperhouse* (1988) to find comparably sophisticated examples of the horror genre, but the field is a fallow one. The British horror genre is truly moribund. Few films produced in Britain, or elsewhere for that matter, respond with any substance to the issues raised by Dana Polan: "part of the sophistication of recent horror films lies in the way they reject or problematize this simple moral binary opposition to suggest that horror is not something from out there, something strange, marginal, ex-centric, the mark of a force from elsewhere, the in-human" (1984, 202). The forces that gave rise to the English cinematic myth that the horror film represented may be behind us, but, as we continue to grapple with our own horrific behavior, Polan and others realize that the true monster of the modern cinema is within the viewer, rather than within the confines of the cinema frame.

WORKS CITED

Arkadin (pseud.). "Film Clips." *Sight and Sound* 38.2 (Spring, 1969): 104-5.

Britton, Andrew, Richard Lippe, Tony Williams, and Robin Wood. *American Nightmare: Essays on the Horror Film*. Toronto: Festival of Festivals, 1979.

Carroll, Noel. *The Philosophy of Horror; or, Paradoxes of the Heart*. New York: Routledge, 1990.

Davis, Colin. "Eros Exploding: The Films of Anthony Balch." *Shock Express* 2.4 (Summer, 1988): 9-10.

Dixon, Wheeler Winston. *The Charm of Evil: The Life and Films of Terence Fisher*. Metuchen: Scarecrow, 1991a.

———. *The Films of Freddie Francis*. Metuchen: Scarecrow, 1991b.

Durgnat, Raymond. *A Mirror for England: British Movies from Austerity to Affluence*. London: Faber and Faber, 1970.

Fountain, Nigel. *Underground: The London Alternative Press 1966-74*. London: Comedia-Routledge, 1988.

Fraser, John. *Violence in the Arts*. Cambridge: Cambridge UP, 1974.

Hallenbeck, Bruce G. "From Gore to Gothic." *Fangoria* 27 (May, 1983): 42-45.

Hardy, Phil, ed. *Encyclopedia of Horror Films*. New York: Harper, 1986.

Hewison, Robert. *Too Much Art and Society in the Sixties 1960-75*. New York: Oxford UP, 1987.

Hoberman, J., and Jonathan Rosenbaum. *Midnight Movies*. New York: Harper, 1983.

Hoffman, Eric C. "Hammer's Frankenstein Series." *Bizarre* 4 (1974): 35-51.

Kelly, Bill. "Michael Reeves: Horror's James Dean." *Cinefantastique* 22.1 (August, 1991): 33-45.

Murphy, Robert. "Under the Shadow of Hollywood." *All Our Yesterdays: 90 Years of British Cinema*. Ed. Charles Barr. London: BFI Publishing, 1986. 47-71.

Newman, Kim. *Nightmare Movies: A Guide to Contemporary Horror Films*. New York: Harmony, 1988.

Paul, William. "Michael Reeves Revisited." *Village Voice* 3 Mar. 1971.

Pirie, David. *A Heritage of Horror: The British Gothic Cinema 1946-1972*. New York: Avon, 1974.

———. "New Blood." *Sight and Sound* 40.2 (Spring, 1971): 73-75.

———. *The Vampire Cinema*. London: Gallery, 1977.

Polan, Dana. "Eros and Syphilization: The Contemporary Horror Film." *Planks of Reason: Essays on the Contemporary Horror Film*. Ed. Barry Keith Grant. Metuchen, NJ: Scarecrow, 1984. 201-11.

Ringel, Harry. "Terence Fisher: The Human Side." *Cinefantastique* 4.3 (1975): 5-16.

Sontag, Susan. *Against Interpretation*. New York: Dell Laurel, 1969.

Twitchell, James B. *Dreadful Pleasures: An Anatomy of Modern Horror*. New York: Oxford UP, 1985.

Waller, Gregory, ed. *American Horrors: Essays on the Modern American Horror Film*. Urbana: U of Illinois P, 1987.

Wood, Robin. "In Memoriam Michael Reeves." *Movie* 17 (Winter, 1969-1970): 2-6.

Zimmerman, Bonnie. "Daughters of Darkness: The Lesbian Vampire On Film." *Planks of Reason: Essays on the Horror Film.* Ed. Barry Keith Grant. Metuchen, NJ: Scarecrow, 1984. 153-63.

CHAPTER SEVENTEEN

RE-VIEWING THE LOSEY-PINTER *GO-BETWEEN*

Edward T. Jones

THE LATE JOSEPH Losey, the American director who had a Marxist bent and was once blacklisted in Hollywood, expatriated himself to Britain, where he made such films as *The Servant* and *Accident*, in 1963 and 1967, respectively, and other films that have acquired a reputation for their quintessential "Englishness." His *The Go-Between*, released in 1971, had a screenplay by his frequent collaborator, Harold Pinter, and was based on L. P. Hartley's delicate minor masterpiece of novel writing with the same title (1953). It received the Grand Prize at the Cannes Film Festival and has been considered an epitome of a species of traditional British cinema whose familiar and stylish ambience endures in the literary adaptations much loved in the United States, that are shown on "Masterpiece Theatre" and the Arts and Entertainment cable channel. Such programs are replete with the handsome production values associated with the BBC, Granada, and Thames Television. Nevertheless, to an extent not hitherto adequately noted or appreciated, Losey and Pinter deconstruct the Hartleian source material and subvert the world of the English country house nostalgically celebrated by Anglophiles on this side of the Atlantic. To be sure, there is more than a hint of this process in Hartley's novel itself, but the novelist does not throw the order and values of his presented world into question to the degree that the film does.

Hartley chose a Jamesian technique of narration by a participant who looks back at events fifty years earlier, to the summer of 1900 when the narrator, Leo Colston, turned, unluckily, thirteen and underwent a trauma that affected the rest of his life. Moreover, the novel also used a frame structure of prologue and epilogue to secure the double articulation of time. Pinter and Losey more fluidly manage this component with occasional flashes forward, confusing at first but gradually lengthening as the film unfolds, until the shadowy glimpses of Leo grown old (played well by Michael Redgrave), obviously separate from the turn-of-the-century scenes, demonstrate that the child was lamentably father of the man. As time goes by in the film, these moments of forward illumination become sharper and more explicit until they reach the ending, which is set in the present.

This cinematic method of establishing continuity proves considerably more flexible and economical than the narrative of the diary, which Hartley employed in his novel.

As a novel, *The Go-Between* has become a favorite text for school examinations in Britain and the Commonwealth nations, probably because of formalist perspectives on the novel's constituent parts, especially its symbolism and images. In addition, its initiation theme presumably exerts upon Britons a similar appeal as *Huckleberry Finn* and *Catcher in the Rye* do in the American secondary-school curriculum.

A major symbolic construct of the novel, largely and wisely omitted from Pinter's screenplay, is the zodiac, which appears briefly in the film on the cover of Leo's diary. In Hartley's novel, young Leo relishes the symbolic possibilities of the zodiac applied to the denizens of Brandham Hall, where he goes as a guest of his classmate, Marcus Maudsley. Amid a cast he sees as larger than life, minimized Leo assigns maximal, even celestial, roles to the adults around him. The Archer is represented by Hugh, the ninth viscount Trimingham, a disfigured veteran of the Boer War and ancestral owner of the hall itself. The Water carrier, appropriately enough, is identified with the virile tenant farmer on the estate, Ted Burgess; and the family's nubile daughter, Marian, who befriends Leo as go-between in her covert amatory relationship with Ted, the youngster sees as the apex of the whole structure—as the Virgin. Trimingham supplies Leo with a forging link between the boy's imaginative constructions and his social role when the viscount names him Mercury, not only the smallest planet but also the messenger of the gods. This last attribution Losey and Pinter retain in the film. While the film shows the rising temperature of a hot summer on several occasions, it is doubtful the viewing audience connects this aspect of Mercury with Leo as Hartley's trope in the novel would have it. Gerry Fisher's evocative photography, however, does capture a certain mercurial quality in Leo. Indeed, the camera work, pacing, and editing realize concretely on film much that is achieved with rather labored metaphors in the novel.

Leo's imaginative response to the deadly nightshade, the symbolic *Atropa belladonna* found on the estate, tends to be oppressive both in the novel and in the film. Leo's first encounter with the plant in the novel is ambivalent:

> It looked the picture of evil and also the picture of health; it was so glossy and strong and juicy-looking: I could almost see the sap rising to nourish it . . . I knew that every part of it was poisonous. I knew too that it was beautiful, for did not my mother's botany book say so? I stood on the threshold, not daring to go in, staring at the button-bright berries and the dull purplish hairy, bell-shaped flowers reaching out towards me. I felt that the plant could poison me, even if I didn't touch it, and that if I didn't eat it, it would eat me, it looked so hungry, in spite of all the nourishment it was getting. (Hartley 1954, 38)

Pinter and Losey make the symbolic connection between the plant and Marian Maudsley, whom Leo has first observed lying in a hammock. In the published screenplay, Marcus remarks as a literal translation of the belladonna, "My sister is very beautiful," to which Leo replies affirmatively. Then the screenplay specifies:

> They [Leo and Marcus] approach a roofless outhouse. In it is a large glossy shrub with bell-shaped flowers. They stop. The camera goes before them and stops, regarding the shrub. Their voices over. (Pinter 1978, 289)

Leo explains to his friend the salient details about *Atropa belladonna* derived from Hartley's novel. This explanation is followed by a cut back to Marian in the hammock to complete visually the symbolic parallel. Admittedly, the effect is more literal in the film than it is in the novel, but it suffices. This symbolism reminds one of Hawthorne's "Rappacini's Daughter," doubtless an influence on Hartley, and its intricacy may require more than mere visualization and juxtaposition of person and plan for true comprehension. The film's approach instead emphasizes the discontinuity between what is intended and what is expressed.

The film is surely less concerned than Hartley about showing Leo's inflated thoughts and mythic constructs and not simply because the medium cannot "tell" in quite the way the novelist does. Dominic Guard, playing the young Leo with superb and understated veracity, expresses a great deal by facial expression and gesture that is consistent with the character as Hartley presents him. To some degree, Losey and Pinter reverse Hartley's handling of Leo, often with surprisingly happy results. Hartley shows how Leo invests the people of Brandham Hall with larger-than-life size, considering them immortals, inheritors of the summer and heirs to the coming glory of the twentieth century. Yet in the film Leo's first view of Marian and the entourage at the Hall comes from high up on the balcony of the manor house as he looks down upon the greensward.

The director and screenwriter emphasize throughout the film the absolute smallness and detachment of Leo in the midst of the adults or amid the dizzying verticality of Norwich cathedral. This aspect of Leo receives its best realization as the camera follows Leo in his traversing the immense horizontal Norfolk countryside he must negotiate as go-between, carrying messages from Brandham Hall to Black Farm and vice versa. Losey and Pinter crystallize a central relation between Hartley's novel and the film medium with these sequences, rendering kinetic what is often only static and aesthetic in Hartley's novel, despite or maybe because of his reliance on symbolism and literary devices.

By the same token, again without words, Michel Legrand's musical score for the film achieves with its relentless rhythms and eerie effects of a solo piano the anxious, nervous, sad, yet curiously numinous mood Hartley less economically produces in his verbal descriptions.

We often look down with Leo in point-of-view shots or down upon him in crane shots. This depiction of Leo derives from the novel and may take its cue from a casual remark made by Leo about midway through *The Go-Between* that has great significance for the concluding trauma of the novel. Leo associates "spooning," incomprehensible adult sexuality to him, with the ribald postcards he has seen at English seaside resorts: "I still conceived the act of spooning visually, comic-post-card fashion: an affront to the eye and through the eye to the mind. Silliness, silliness, a kind of clowning that made people absurd, soft, soppy . . . Pitiful at the best, but who wanted pity? It was a way of looking down on people, and I wanted to look up" (120).

The ultimate degradation for Leo comes when, dragged by Mrs. Maudsley, he discovers with her in the outbuilding, formerly protected by a thick cover of deadly nightshade that he has destroyed, Marian, the Virgin of his zodiac visions, *in flagrante delicto* with Ted Burgess. Losey's preparation for this traumatic scene may be seen in the downward camera angles and shots so often associated in the film with Leo's point of view. L. P. Hartley's telling cannot be transferred seamlessly or faithfully to the film medium: "and it was then that we saw them, together on the ground, the Virgin and the Water-carrier, two bodies moving like one. I think I was more mystified than horrified; it was Mrs. Maudsley's repeated screams that frightened me, and a shadow on the wall that opened and closed like an umbrella" (1954, 290). Hartley takes Leo out of the stars and violently back to earth and a nervous collapse. As Seymour Chatman notes in *Coming to Terms: The Rhetoric of Narrative in Fiction and Film*: "Film gives us plentitude without specificity. Its descriptive offerings are at once visually rich and verbally impoverished" (1990, 39). Narratively, film's ability is to show rather than to tell.

The cinematic showing in Losey's *Go-Between* is textually full and rich, even baroque. We see how people of a privileged class organize their lives in a period where manners and caste have not yet been seriously questioned, except surreptitiously in the liaison between Marian and Ted. Like Leo himself, we as viewers are enchanted by the vistaed lawn, the family's deer herd, not mentioned in the novel but a splendid and apt visual referent for the family's wealth, the quantity of the liveried servants, the grand staircases with their gallery of portraits, and the abundant silver—all of which the camera lovingly embraces in slow pans and traveling shots to such an extent that the subtext seems implicitly political and critical. Early in the film, Marcus informs Leo that he would advise against wearing cricket togs, a solecism new to the Pinter screenplay and not present in the novel: "Only cads wear their school clothes in the holidays. And another thing. When you undress you mustn't fold your clothes and put them on the chair. You must leave them lying wherever they happen to fall. The servants will pick them up. That's what they're for" (Pinter 1978, 293). The Maudsley family receives Leo with the patronizing graciousness reserved for poor but well-

bred little boys. Losey and Pinter capture this quality with more subversive bite
and detail than Hartley provides in the novel.

The essential snobbery of the Maudsleys is most often articulated by young
Marcus, who is, of course, to the manor [manner] born. After Leo's triumph in the
cricket match between Brandham Hall and the village in which Leo catches out
Ted Burgess and later also bests him in singing following an obligatory shared dinner between members of the Hall and the village, Pinter has Marcus comment:
"Well, thank goodness we've said good-bye to the village for a year. Did you
notice the stink in that Hall?" (Pinter 1978, 334). Leo, less cultivated in his olfac-
tory perceptions, replies negatively. This sequence ends with Marcus suddenly
confiding to Leo that Marian is engaged to marry Lord Trimingham.

Convincing himself that he is restoring social and even universal order,
Leo falsifies the meeting time between Marian and Ted in Hartley's novel to pre-
cipitate the final tragedy of summer 1900. Perhaps because neither Losey nor
Pinter believes in that nostalgic past, this action is far less clear in the film version.
We see Leo incant a curse over the belladonna leaves and roots he has brought to
his room and then flushes down an especially decorative loo. The poisonous weed
is not so easily destroyed in its metaphoric and symbolic extension.

Leo suffers a nervous breakdown as a result of his traumatic encounter in
the outbuilding of Brandham Hall. He vaguely recalls in the novel that somehow
he learned of the self-inflicted death of Ted Burgess. Perhaps Marian had, indeed,
been the intense passionate heat of summer, and Leo became the embodiment of
Icarus, flying too near the sun. Ted, who once seemed to the boy like a wheat field
ripe for reaping, had been cut down and left in the sun. Pinter retains the reference
to Icarus in a voice-over from the aged Leo, and Losey dutifully includes numerous shots, now rather cliched, of waving grass and wheat as emblems of what
Hartley describes.

Julie Christie's performance in the role of Marian Maudsley, as Pauline
Kael noted in her *New Yorker* review of the film, "makes hypocrisy villainously
beautiful" (1971, 56). The film version retains, via a voice-over spoken by the aged
Leo, the famous opening line of Hartley's novel: "The past is a foreign country:
they do things differently there" (1954, 3). Much of the difference has to do with
deference and the contrast between appearance and reality. Perfidious Albion has
always traded on alluring surface—as does Losey's film itself, thanks to Carmen
Dillon's evocative art direction. If Hartley found this past strangely secure, Losey
and Pinter suggest otherwise, challenging the seemingly socially constructed reality as appearance only. They question, as Hartley does not, the meaning and value
such constructions give to human existence. Hartley himself comes close to anticipating Michel Foucault's concept of the relationship of power to discourse in
the following passage that may have influenced the filmmakers in their choices: "It
hadn't occurred to me that just as we changed our language and vocabulary when
we went into polite society, so we changed our nature—or at least our expression

of them" (25). As R. E. Pritchard has explained, "Leo composes fictions; and Hartley's fiction in turn parades its fictional devices and echoes, so that this almost seems the real subject: the fictionalization of experience into art" (Pritchard 45). Through the film medium Losey and Pinter attempt to return art to experience.

In Hartley's novel, Leo as an old man opens the last piece of undisturbed evidence from summer 1900, the final undelivered letter from Marian to Ted wherein she wrote she would be at their rendezvous at six, "and wait until seven or eight or Doomsday—darling, darling" (Hartley 1954, 297). With the first tears he thinks he has shed since he left Brandham Hall so many years earlier, Leo learns that his birthday bicycle, a present from Marian he never received, was presumably intended to facilitate his carrying messages between the hall and Black Farm. To be sure, he feels used again, but he recognizes that Marian used all the men in her life. Lord Trimingham obligingly married her and accepted Ted's child as his own without reproach; he always said that nothing is ever a lady's fault. Likewise, Ted's suicide represents the triumph of his peasant scruples over decadent aristocratic license. Both men in Marian's love triangle attempted to serve her honorably.

Visiting Marian fifty years later, Leo finds himself confounded by her self-deception, which has been sustained by the sacrifice of so many. Hartley specifically links the actions of summer 1900 to the carnage of the wars that have followed in the twentieth century. Once more this symbolic connection does not yield easily to film portrayal, and the filmmakers wish to give a different emphasis anyway. Losey and Pinter underscore further the role hypocrisy, class-inspired, played in the events shown as a period love story. Alexander Walker in *Hollywood UK: The British Film Industry in the Sixties* articulates the principles and effects in the film *Go-Between* with fairness and precision:

> The county family pay lip service to ideals of love, marriage and responsibility which they do not hold intellectually at all, but only use emotionally to cling to their privileges. The deceit infects everyone and, as in *Accident*, people never learn their lesson till it is too late—and sometime not then. Patterns repeat themselves, post-mortems are never held into the true reasons, but only to provide veiled excuses. The Losey-Pinter universe holds out no indulgence to its trapped characters, only sad inevitability. (1974, 438)

The actress who best captures the well-bred suspicion and hypocrisy of the great house is Margaret Leighton, who was scheduled for the role of Marian when, in the mid-fifties, Hartley's novel was first planned to be shot as a movie but was abortively shelved. The natural man who disturbs this world is likewise realized forcefully on the screen in Alan Bates's Lawrentian Ted Burgess. Leighton's Mrs. Maudsley distills the essence of dangerous gentility.

Obviously Losey and Pinter manifest less respect for the station of Hartley's characters than the novelist does. If one part of L. P. Hartley believed that a vision of splendor can excite people to rise above themselves, Losey and Pinter display no such faith. That may be why, at the end of their film, the aged Leo seems more a norm and standard, more a reliable judge of what has preceded, than he does in the novel. Celibate Leo, a bibliographer working on other people's books as he once disastrously worked on other people's lives, has committed himself to the truth of facts, finding, as Hartley brilliantly expressed it, "facts that existed independently of me, facts that my private wishes could not add to or subtract from . . . Indeed, the life of facts proved no bad substitute for the facts of life" (Hartley 1954, 280). Leo notes that after what he observed in the exposed out-building during the summer of his thirteenth year, the activity of spooning held no more interest to him. To be sure, his formula of seeking only the life of facts has proved as inadequate as his earlier romantic fantasies vis-à-vis an abundant life. We as viewers of the film participate in Leo's disillusionment with what he experienced at Brandham Hall. By extension, the confirmation, identity, enlargement, refinement, and substantiality we seek in visiting the stately homes of England—in person or vicariously in traditional British cinema—may never be quite the same. Losey and Pinter offer a way to understand and criticize the ideological assumptions behind the culture of the stately home.

On film, the ending of *The Go-Between* borders on the undecidable, as deconstructionists might have it, in its meaning as the aged Leo is asked to carry a last message to Marian's grandson, the new Lord Trimingham but also the biological descendant of Ted Burgess, to the effect that there is no curse but an unloving heart. The assumption of unity and coherence found in the Epilogue of Hartley's novel becomes considerably more problematic at the end of the film. Interestingly enough, just before the Epilogue and its leap in time, Hartley has the reflection of the young Leo suggest the impossibility of the wholeness advanced later:

> I did not realize that this attempt to discard my dual or multiple vision and achieve a single self was the greatest pretence I had yet embarked on. It was indeed a self-denying ordinance to cut out my consciousness the half I most enjoyed. To see things as they really were—what an impoverishment! Chafed in my flesh, chafed in my spirit, I wandered aimlessly about with Marcus, half wishing that he would barge into me, or call me names, or practice his superior French on me, instead of wrapping me in the cotton-wool of his society summer. (1954, 278)

Losey and Pinter consistently undercut the hierarchial principles of Brandham Hall and the spiritual transcendence that Hartley implies at the end of the novel to supply a measure of unity.

Hartley often uses apotheoses to secure closure in his novels, and his ending of *The Go-Between* approximates this effect, as Anne Mulkeen explains in *Wild Thyme, Winter Lightning: The Symbolic Novels of L. P. Hartley*:

At the end, after reading and thinking it through, after seeing Marian again, after seeing and hearing the aftermath of the tragedy, suddenly he [Leo] sees spring into view "the south-west prospect of the Hall, long hidden from my memory." It is a symbol of the attaining of a true vision which has all along been lacking. At last he can see the thing whole. (1974, 99)

We can contrast the novel with the final montage taken from the published Pinter screenplay:

> Exterior. Road. Day   Present
> The southwest prospect of Brandham Hall springs into view.
> The elms have been cut down.
> The car stops.
> Brandham Hall.
> A cloud of dust from the slightly obscures the view. (1978, 367)

Hartley's novel suggests that Leo, in maturity, has mastered the moral and aesthetic distance necessary for a favorable response to the lofty facade— he can see Brandham Hall steadily and whole, now like life itself. If Leo is still the go-between, he accepts the role at this point out of free choice, informed by self-knowledge and knowledge of others. He perceives the human frailty behind Marian's message of love and her curious plea to him. He responds to that plea with compassion and humanity, without zodiacal constructs, in much the same spirit with which he views the southwest prospect. Joanne Klein in *Making Pictures: The Pinter Screenplays* comes to a similar conclusion of the basis of the film:

> The view, still obscured, but now by dust rather than by leaves, at once encloses the work and symbolizes its themes. The imperious facade of Brandham Hall, so rich with its history and so inscrutable, so altered by time and so immutable, presides as the ultimate figuration of the relationship between past and present . . . we leave the story on the verge of its telling. What we have witnessed has not just been told, but is about to be told, here to Marian's grandson. (1985, 101)

If Hartley makes a portion of Brandham Hall once more a principal signifier in *The Go-Between*, I argue, in contrast to Joanne Klein, that Losey and Pinter reveal a final lack on the part of the signifier that is consistent with their critique of the social system all along. This effect may well constitute "a cruder art," as Neil McEwan would have it in his chapter on Hartley's novel in *The Survival of the Novel: British Fiction in the Later Twentieth Century* (1981, 146). The filmmakers end *The Go-Between* in a kind of freeplay that disrupts both the presence and the transcendence Hartley assumes.

Hartley's *Go-Between*, like a number of his novels, moves Prufrock-like toward some overwhelming question—about love, identity, good and evil, fantasy and fact—that is never quite phrased, let alone answered. Through symbol and metaphor, his artistry often gives the illusion of beautiful integration. Similarly, the "look" of the Losey-Pinter film, like other novelistic British films that are so strong on period background complete with authentic settings, seems to duplicate that unity. Hartley's southwest prospect of Brandham Hall does not serve as the full signifier in the movie that it does in the novel. What we admire in Losey and Pinter are the discontinuities, ambiguities, and internal self-cancellations of their film against the essentializing projects of authoritarians of right and left. The filmmakers have explored in their own film medium a significant feature of Hartley's novel, namely, the difficulty of harmonizing outward institutions and inward constitutions, which goes well beyond the reproduction of British social existence at the turn of the century as the most notable quality of the filmed *Go-Between*. Years before the term *poststructuralism* emerged, Losey and Pinter deconstructed a venerable twentieth-century British novel to create a spare, pure, exigent—and even prophetic—film.

WORKS CITED

Chatman, Seymour. *Coming to Terms: The Rhetoric of Narrative in Fiction and Film*. Ithaca: Cornell UP, 1990.

Hartley, L. P. *The Go-Between*. New York: Knopf, 1954.

Kael, Pauline. Rev. of *The Go-Between*. *New Yorker* 31 July 1971: 55-56.

Klein, Joanne. *Making Pictures: The Pinter Screenplays*. Columbus: Ohio State UP, 1985.

McEwan, Neil. *The Survival of the Novel: British Fiction in the Later Twentieth Century*. Totowa, NJ: Barnes and Noble, 1981.

Mulkeen, Anne. *Wild Thyme, Winter Lightning: The Symbolic Novels of L. P. Hartley*. Detroit: Wayne State UP, 1974.

Pinter, Harold. *Five Screenplays*. New York: Grove, 1978.

Pritchard, R. E. "L. P. Hartley's *The Go-Between*." *Critical Quarterly* 22: 45-55.

Walker, Alexander. *Hollywood UK: The British Film Industry in the Sixties*. New York: Stein and Day, 1974.

CHAPTER EIGHTEEN

KEEPING HIS OWN VOICE:
AN INTERVIEW WITH STEPHEN FREARS*

Lester Friedman and Scott Stewart

INTRODUCTION BY LESTER FRIEDMAN

"YOU OBVIOUSLY EXPECTED a somewhat younger man," chided Stephen Frears as he gently shook my hand, "everybody does." He was right. We suspiciously surveyed the rather scruffy middle-aged man who stood before us on the steps of the Syracuse University London Centre. Dressed in a rumpled brown corduroy jacket and a pair of baggy gray pants, his hair disheveled and waistline creeping over his belt buckle, Frears knew precisely what we were thinking: where was the fire-breathing young radical who had directed *My Beautiful Laundrette* (1986), *Prick up Your Ears* (1987) and *Sammy and Rosie Get Laid* (1988)? "After all," he continued with an almost embarrassed smile, "I've had quite a long career, though few people outside England know anything about it." Right again. For most of us, Frears did indeed burst, seemingly out of nowhere, into prominence on the strength of the most interesting trilogy of British films made during the 1980s.

These films resonated so deeply within my consciousness that I scoured video stores to find other films made during the Thatcher era. My explorations ultimately gave way to further research in England, where, during the summer of 1989, I taught a class called "Contemporary British Cinema." Though I greatly admired films by other British directors like Derek Jarman and Peter Greenaway, Issac Julien and Sally Potter, Terence Davies and Mike Leigh, I remained most touched by Frears. So, being "a cheeky American," I found Frears's number in the London directory, rang him up, and invited him over for a chat. Much to my delight, not to mention surprise, he quickly agreed, and the following interview represents a distillation of that conversation, which I conducted with my colleague, Scott Stewart.

---

*This interview was conducted on 7 June 1989.

Frears quite correctly called my attention to the fact that he did have "quite a long career" before making his celebrated trilogy. Born in Leicester (England) in 1941, Frears, like many other British filmmakers, began his career in the theater, eventually directing plays at the Royal Court (home to Joe Orton). He also started dabbling in the cinema, working for Karel Reisz on *Morgan* (1966) and Lindsay Anderson on *If . . .* (1969). His first feature-film directing assignment was *Gumshoe* (1972), a wry detective yarn starring Albert Finney, which appeared on the scene and quickly sank from view. Frears spent the next twelve years working on BBC and ITV television. While there, he joined other notable directors like Michael Apted, Mike Newell, and Ken Loach, and he collaborated with some of the finest writers of the period, including David Hare, Alan Bennett, and Christopher Hampton. He remains proud of this work, claiming that television "gave an accurate account of what it's like to live in Britain . . . something not found in many countries." In 1984, Frears completed his second theatrical feature, *The Hit*, the story of a small-time criminal (Terence Stamp) who testifies against his superiors and lives in constant fear of their retaliation. Like *Gumshoe*, *The Hit* was a critical success and a commercial failure.

One cannot overstate the profound impact Frears's extended internship in television had on the three films (all financed, at least in part, with television funds) he made during the 1980s as well as on his subsequent movies. First, his experiences with outstanding writers gave him tremendous respect for the written word. As he says, "I start from a collaborative (with the writer) point of view." To put it another way, part of his success comes from the fact that good writers trust him "not to muck up" their work. Second, his years in British television also informed his work habits; he quickly acquired a reputation as an efficient director who brings projects in on time and within the budget—two traits that endear him to the businessmen who finance films. Third, as his television films usually dealt with "men and women who go to work and lead rather desperate lives," so his theatrical films concentrate on the gritty realism of daily existence, focusing on the position of marginalized outsiders. To this stratified cultural context, he applies the British television tradition of social criticism, a point of view that endows his pictures with a class consciousness absent in most American movies. Finally, Frears's "invisible" style remains indebted to the unobtrusive techniques that characterize television aesthetics; consequently, he overtly situates himself in the tradition of such "I go to work" directors as Vincente Minnelli and Billy Wilder, rather than the self-conscious artistry of more flamboyant auteurists. So, unlike his flashier contemporaries (like Alan Parker, Tony Scott, Adrian Lyne, and Ridley Scott) who gravitated to feature films from advertising, Frears favors story over style. As he puts it, sometimes you find "by standing back things come out more clearly."

This interview took place right after Frears's spectacular success with *Dangerous Liaisons* (1988) and just before he left England to make *The Grifters*

(1990), for which he received an Academy Award nomination as best director. Yet, given the subject matter, characters, tone, social milieu, and themes of *The Grifters*, one can easily trace the connections between Frears's latest film and his 1980s trilogy. Any critical assessment of filmmaking must rank Frears's work among the foremost achievements in world cinema during the last decade.

Lester Friedman/Scott Stewart: In a January 10 [1988] article in the London *Sunday Times* entitled "Through a Lens Darkly," Norman Stone characterized two of your films (*My Beautiful Laundrette* and *Sammy and Rosie Get Laid*) and four by other directors as being "depressing," "dominated by left-wing orthodoxy," and "generally disgusting." How do you respond to this type of attack?

Stephen Frears: It's the official line coming from Downing Street. That's what you'd expect someone like Stone or Jonathan Miller to say, particularly in the *Sunday Times*. One of the problems with the Thatcher government is they could never find any evidence of an economic miracle. The fact that the evidence contradicts this is rather embarrassing to them. One of the things that upset them at the time, and still upsets them, is that they could never find any novelist or painter or other artist who would actually put their finger on this triumph, except Sir Andrew Lloyd Webber. So, this eventually became rather embarrassing to them, particularly since the arts are rather successful in Great Britain. Also, they're a big earner—about our fifth biggest export. So, the government finds themselves connected with these people they dislike who make money for them, people who are actually quite seriously saddened by the state of the country. The Thatcher government wants someone to tell the world how beautiful they are, and the only people they can find are journalists, of whom I have no regard, and that is naturally depressing to them. They find this right-wing historian, who is this known quality, and they set him up to it. Of course, he made a fool of himself because he didn't know what he was actually writing about. When people write or film what it's really like in England today, you have to expect that kind of response from people like Norman Stone. That is what that's all about.

LF/SS: What would you say are the common themes that pervade your film work?

SF: Well, I suppose you start off noticing things that are going on at deeper levels. *Dangerous Liaisons*, for example, isn't clearly about the conditions in Britain, although people try to suggest it is. It may well be, however, that my interest in the material, in the novel, is due to these deeper interests. When the play came out it was a huge success. Somehow it captured the spirit of the times: when very rich people behaved very selfishly. Some people think that's the way we are now, which may be some of the reason behind its success. But we didn't make it because of that reasoning.

It seemed to me that the idea of people enjoying a story set in the 1780s was very bizarre. People were wearing funny clothes and speaking funny. To make people realize what was actually going on underneath was very interesting and enjoyable. Seeing the same ways we all behave, that was what we were really after. It was actually quite the opposite of trying to construct a portrait of the society. At the time, you start to notice certain things going on underneath the basic information, attitudes between people that are very similar, things you're more interested in than to merely reconstruct. I suppose when we make films about Britain we make them with such profound knowledge. You make films about things you know about as if you were walking across the street—an accurate photograph of the world.

LF/SS: That doesn't seem to be the case with *Sammy and Rosie Get Laid*. There you seem to construct a rhetorical situation when you say different things to different audiences.

SF: Quite right. That film is entirely bound up in the politics of Britain. That's to say at the time, 1987. Right up to election night, Mrs. Thatcher thought she would lose the election. She actually thought she was going to lose. They broke down and started having a row in the Tory party, and somebody said the following day they had been screaming at each other all up and down Downing Street. They thought they were going to lose, and it seemed there was going to be some change. It didn't come off, of course. So *Sammy and Rosie* was made in the spirit of an account, of what it as like to live here in 1987.

Before I made *My Beautiful Laundrette*, I'd made films like that in my previous ten, fifteen years working in television. It's part of the tradition of television. It has nothing to do with upper-class men running around a track as in *Chariots of Fire*. It's actually about men and women who go to work and lead rather desperate lives. That is what Mrs. Thatcher is trying to prevent us from saying. She's trying to destroy television because television embraces the concept of social criticism, not at a particularly ferocious level, but simply by giving an accurate account of what it's like to live in Britain. If you were to look at the record of British television the last twenty-five years, it would be a very, very accurate record—and quite unique.

It's something not found in many countries. People actually describing how people lived as though it were a part of the British character to record what life was really like. So we go on doing that. Then I made *My Beautiful Laundrette*, which actually seemed to be another TV film, and it became very popular in America, France, Australia, and all over the world. That was a complete surprise to all of us. We had just done the same thing we had been doing for the last fifteen years. It was, therefore, quite hard to absorb why people should suddenly find my work so interesting. I still don't know the answer.

LF/SS: You mentioned that Thatcher is trying to destroy television because it embraces the concept of social criticism. How exactly is she going about that?

SF: The government regards the BBC as a bunch of Communists. They think they're actually subversive. We, on the other hand, think it's a rather right-wing organization and that it's our responsibility to attack the BBC. Both positions are absurd, really, because the BBC somehow walks the middle road. There are two ways she is using to get at the BBC. The BBC is funded not by advertisements but by license fees which the government controls and doles out at their whim. She is trying to destroy this old system and replace it with the American system of advertisement support. Presently, the BBC is run by responsible middle-class groups which support educational shows, religious shows, and other such shows of high quality. Advertisement supported shows, like game shows, cheapen television. This is precisely what Thatcher wants to do. She is also trying to turn it away from being so tightly regulated. She says this is part of her philosophy—not to regulate people's lives—but in fact it all becomes an ill system. In the end it has to do with process. Mrs. Thatcher claims that she is instinctively against regulation. The market will sort it out she tells us. Nonsense. It just means the BBC will be destroyed.

LF/SS: What kind of effect do you feel this would have on the cinema?

SF: First, you must understand that there is no British cinema. It doesn't exist; it is gone. What happened is that we've been hiding behind television money. Using it to make films. Thatcher would like to give the money to her friends rather than to people she dislikes, people who criticize her government. She would rather give it to people who write editorials for the *Sunday Times. My Beautiful Laundrette, Prick Up Your Ears, Sammy and Rosie Get Laid*—they all had television in there helping with the budget. That was because of a loophole that allowed some people to get a tax relief. You become rather adroit at taking advantage of things like that. You become very good at surviving in a quite tightly regulated society. People do it in all areas of life. It's like the nation has never really recovered from the war. During the war, there was a huge black market. People were rather happy selling nylons, chewing gum, and things like that. We never really recovered from that mentality. I have learned I'm very, very good at that. I can work my way through a film keeping a lot of people in the dark about what's going on. As me and my friends would say, we'll figure it out when we can get in there and that's how you learn to do it. If you try to do it the official way, it's sort of impossible.

LF/SS: In *My Beautiful Laundrette* there were a lot of times when we see the characters through windows or glass of some sort. People come and go through glass or windows. Is that thematic?

SF: It's more technical that thematic. Think about it. If you sit in this room, a window is sort of depth, sort of like a graphic slide. In other words, if I shoot a young lady sitting against the wall, all there is, really, is her face. If, however, I shoot through the window over there, there's a window across the street, so immediately there's a depth to the shot. It's as simple as realizing the second shot is more interesting than the first. A brick wall behind a head is not very interesting. After a time, you start to play with the perspectives. You put the window there and the camera there because you can see there and there, so you can get endless perspectives, or a much longer perspective. What's interesting is everybody in relation to each other. It's always interesting seeing what's going on through the window on the other side of the window. I've spent my life walking down streets looking through other people's windows. It's always interesting. It's sort of natural. It's there to be used. It's part of the perspective. It puts everyone in relation to one another.

In *My Beautiful Laundrette*, I was always intrigued with the window shots. In one shot, for example, you see Johnny, while Omar is sitting in the car thirty to forty feet away. There he gets out of the car and walks over to Johnny. I realized I had done similar shots through windows in the rest of the film. Here I realized someone was crossing over from alienation to being white, written by someone with a white English mother and a Pakistani father. It's about the journey from one side to another. So I realized the shot that arrived quite intuitively perfectly expressed what the film was doing, what the film was about; crossing over and integration through separation.

LF/SS: How much do you think about theme when choosing your shots?

SF: Not at all. When I first looked at the script for *My Beautiful Laundrette*, the thing that I most liked was the economics. That's right, economics. It seemed to be very funny. It seemed to be very, very good. Down the line, the idea of saying this Pakistani is a rich entrepreneur and the embodiment of Mrs. Thatcher's values seemed brilliant. Such a wonderful idea. Such a funny, outrageous idea. That's what I really liked. When I started reading it and realized it was about Asians, my heart was in my boots because I didn't want to make the movie. But then I saw how radical a film it was. The sexual anarchy came out, and the sexual was as radical as the rest of it. The jokes were funny. I was really very, very happy. So when I say I don't think about the themes, It's because films don't present themselves like that.

That tracking shot with Omar from Asians to white, the one we just discussed, is what I mean. I didn't actually think about the themes, but I actually noticed that shot perfectly expressed the theme. Again you're trying to find out what happens when it comes to life, and you are trying to record that. Of course, you're choosing to underline certain things. By underlining, I mean by saying we need a close-up here. Instinctively I think we need to emphasize that line, or make that line clearer. I think rather unconsciously, or not, it's saying this film is about that. It's quite practical, and it's not a very complicated thing. It's more to do with emphasis, isn't it? But out of it certain themes emerge.

You can either emphasize things or stand back. You might find by standing back things come out more clearly. What you are trying to do is make sense of it. After a while, you begin to notice that you can take the images and that they add up to something that sort of means something. You'll get people who will criticize it. You can't stop that. But when you take all this mess, and you shape it like that, it will add up to something. If you don't get the shape right, then it won't mean anything. How you do that is your affair. I can see that's what people want to know, but I don't know the answer. But that's what you learn as you get more experienced and maybe you can get better. Of course, you do it without really thinking about it because what you are really trying to do is to tell a story.

LF/SS: In both *My Beautiful Laundrette* and *Sammy and Rosie Get Laid*, there are homosexual relationships that work out better than the heterosexual relationships. Is this a comment on straight vs. gay relationships?

SF: It was so right that the boys were in love with each other in *My Beautiful Laundrette*. It's so poetically right. I remember when I shot it. I shot it, quite literally, like *Rebel without a Cause*. Actually, I shot it as a parody of that film. But, of course, if you think about it, that's what the film is about: It is about taking an image, taking something people understand, and showing them it isn't like that at all. That's two boys kissing, not a boy and a girl, so the world isn't quite the way everybody thinks it is in the movies. You effortlessly create a subversive image. Most films that deal with homosexual relationships deal with them as problems. One of the things I liked about these two films is that they didn't treat homosexuality that way. Now most homosexuals I know are probably as straight-forward as I am. They don't have these sort of terrible problems hanging over them. So it seemed to me to be quite lifelike and quite funny that they were the happier couple, and that all men and women were having a terrible time.

I remember a boy in Britain saying how pleased he was, how grateful he was, that the film didn't conform to the typical film stereotypes about homosexuals. I said, "I don't know what you mean," and he said, "The two gay boys don't end up mad or dead." I said, "I'm about to make a film about Joe Orton. Do you want me to leave the death out because clearly it confirms people's worst prejudices in the film?" Yet it's nice that things could end happily for Johnny and Omar.

LF/SS: My Beautiful Laundrette has been criticized because the conclusion's upbeat tone doesn't match the bleak outlook of the rest of the film. Why did you feel you needed this happy ending?

SF: Because it would be too depressing without it. Like everybody else, I want the world to be happy and cheerful. It's only at the very end that there is this flicker of happiness, and there isn't much happiness at the end. Actually, it's not a completely bleak film. It seems more cheerfully defiant. I think if it had been a bleak film it wouldn't have been as well received. To the contrary, it is rather spirited. People sort of shouting back and sticking their fingers out. It was one of the reasons why it was so successful. I don't think of it as a bleak film. Any film with that sort of cheerfulness about things isn't very bleak. I think *Sammy and Rosie Get Laid* is a much bleaker film, but then times were worse.

LF/SS: I see Omar, say ten years later, as becoming Salim. In fact, I have no problem seeing him betraying Johnny later on down the line.

SF: Yes, that's quite right.

LF/SS: Is there anybody in the film, then, who functions as a kind of moral center?

SF: I think that Johnny, who goes to defend his mate, does. That shot of him when he's pausing, well that's like Gary Cooper isn't it. When he takes his watch off, it's like Gary Cooper when he's going to rescue someone. I think it's a very American thing that you want to have someone positive. I don't think we English quite understand this. If they're terrible, why not say they're terrible. It's really peculiar, and something I don't really understand. Some people blame it on television because the actors say "give me something good to do" because if they actually do something terrible or act as terrible as people in real life, people will switch them off. So I think it's sort of a rather American characteristic to look for some type of silver lining. *My Beautiful Laundrette* does not avoid moral responsibility, but I don't see why the film should do the work for you. That's to say, you show it and allow the audience to form its own opinion.

I just don't think you need to tell people everything's going to be all right, largely because it generally isn't all right. It's true you get fed up making films about how ghastly everything is. But there *is* something wrong. The system doesn't work, and people are being penalized. Thinking about that seems to be a tremendously positive thing. It's infinitely more positive than saying everything will come out all right or that individuals can defeat the system, although some individuals can defeat the system. But still it's the system that should be changed; it's the cracks in the system that need mending. I don't necessarily mean in some revolutionary way. I simply mean if people are being penalized by it, or are suffering by it, it should be changed on that level. In fact, the people in *Sammy and Rosie Get Laid* are working out quite complicated relationships, aren't they?

LF/SS: Because *Prick Up Your Ears* was an adaptation of a biography of somebody's life, did you feel any responsibility to do your own research?

SF: Well, they're dead aren't they, so you really can't get at the stuff you would want to. I think that John Lahr must have got it right. I knew people who knew Joe Orton, and I've also met his sister. It's quite difficult making films about real

Figure 18.1. Frances Barber and Ayub Khan Din in *Sammy and Rosie Get Laid*. Courtesy: British Film Institute.

people. It's actually a pain in the ass, to be quite honest with you, because you can never actually make up your mind if it's fiction or not. Then you get people who endlessly say, "Well he didn't always wear these kind of shoes." You say, "Well that's not very, very important." But you can never quite convince anyone.

It was really a horrible story, a really terrible story, and it seemed to have things buried in it, things I recognized as being true growing up in Britain. Joe was really sort of a funny fellow. I liked the idea that people who were funny and entertaining had all these other things going on underneath. Besides his dying, I remember seeing the plays while he was still alive. So in that I can identify with him. It also seemed to be very sensational. I remember that when Joe's book first came out people had no idea about Orton's life. People knew accounts of homosexual life, but if you had said this bloke, this famous playwright, had actually all this going on, I just don't think anybody would have believed it. So this whole story was going on that nobody knew anything about, this secret life. It intrigued me. Secrecy is very important. It's a story based around secrecy. It's a very secretive society really. We don't have a lot of openness. You seem to live in an open society compared to us, although I'm sure it's closed in many ways with many secrets. But it's definitely not in the same league with us.

LF/SS: Is it true you were asked to direct *Scandal* and turned it down?

SF: Yes. They came and asked me if I'd make the film. The Profumo scandal was one of the two great events that happened during my life. Watergate, of course, was the best. The televising of the trials was quite wonderful. It was like a holiday. It went on for weeks. Little people like Sam Ervin just emerged from this drama that was running on. The other great event in Britain during 1963 was the Profumo scandal. But I turned it down precisely because of that. I would try to make the film the way it really happened because I was alive at the time and conscious of the events. I'd try to make it accurate and get trapped between fact and fiction. I thought it was smart of them to get someone who was barely alive when it all happened. To get someone who wasn't really aware of it when it all happened, someone who would say, "Who are these people and what was so interesting about them?" was a good notion.

LF/SS: Do you feel that England thinks of itself as a culturally mixed society?

SF: No. But if you live down my street, well, it's like New York; it's great. It seems to me the single best thing that's happened to England. We've been brought up in a very closed society, and now we're a very mixed society. It's complicated, but it's got something that a lot of sections of British people like. Look at the British economy. When the Jews arrived before the war, they regenerated British industry, and, of course, the arrival of the Asians has done the same. So England's success in the last forty or fifty years is due largely to immigration. Then there's this whole thing with China. Mrs. Thatcher fears that if it continues all those people in Hong Kong will be coming here. Trouble in Peking and three and a half million people show up at your door with passports to live here. That's what she's worried about. What do you do with all of them? Do you say no to them and not make them feel welcome? It's extraordinary having a colonial past, which is what all my films are about.

LF/SS: The role of Rosie is an extraordinarily interesting woman's role. How was it conceived?

SF: I come from a very repressed background, and it has taken a long while for women to appear in my films. For a long time, they simply didn't appear. They were just off there somewhere. I think that *Dangerous Liaisons* is about weak men and strong women. I see this as progress. Anyhow, most of Rosie was there in the script. We just went the whole way. It was terrific.

LF/SS: What do you think of Clause 28, which limits the representation of homosexuals?

SF: I think Clause 28 was actually a mistake. It's very, very odd. As it was going through Parliament, nobody was paying any attention. Then, suddenly, the actors said, "Well, there's this law going through." Nobody really noticed until somebody said "Do you realize what this law really means?" To be truthful, I don't think the government actually realized what it said. They hadn't really read the writing. Then suddenly it became an issue, and they don't like to be seen as backpedaling. Yet there haven't been any cases brought; there hasn't been any sort of big row. I don't think, however, I could make *Prick Up Your Ears* now. I'm not even sure if you could make *My Beautiful Laundrette* now for a combination of both economic reasons and morals. But nobody's been prosecuted yet under the clause.

LF/SS: Do you find that it leads to some form of self-censorship in many artists in one form or another?

SF: Yes, it seems to me that self-censorship is much more prevalent. The BBC comes under attack from the government and is vulnerable in the ways that I was saying. The government periodically threatens to change it all. There is legislation on the Irish subject and direct restrictions on broadcast issues. But I don't think Clause 28 was part of some deliberate conspiracy. One thing it is influencing, to some extent, is this libel law. Recently the libel cases that have come up have affected the BBC. They had something come up that was based, rather loosely, on someone's life. It ran into some problems because they actually shot some stuff around his house. They also suggested that this character wore ladies panties. They were actually rather stupid about it.

LF/SS: The casting of *Dangerous Liaisons* seemed to get the most critical attention. What were you thinking when you cast John Malkovich in the lead role?

SF: Christopher Hampton, who wrote the play, had seen John Malkovich on Broadway. He thought John was so wonderful he went to him and asked if he would make a film of his play. John, who knew of the play, read it and said, "Yes, this is wonderful." So when I was hired, they said to me, "John Malkovich would like to do it. Do you want him?" I can remember saying to various friends of mine in New York at the time that he might do it. And, well, they were very rude about it. But anyway, I really started to think about it. I wondered if there was anyone I thought could do it better, and I couldn't think of a better American actor; I still haven't. No one has come up with a better idea.

I thought of casting an English actor, and Daniel Day Lewis came to mind; but, I didn't want to make a film of British actors behind glass. I wanted to make a film that was about emotion rather than about manners. British actors are very good about playing manners, but if you cast a lot of British actors it would be perceived as being a fashionable play, something behind glass, and it would become a piece of culture, something I didn't really want it to be. I wanted the film to be vulgar, so I gradually began to see that casting British actors would be less interesting and less irreverent, in a way more respectful to customs practiced. It would be more outrageous with a cast of American actors. So I started to go with American actors.

Now it's true it also had to do with economics. If you make a film that costs as much as *Liaisons* did, you have to bring in people to see it. There is no doubt that casting American actors makes it more accessible to larger audiences. Particularly, it's more appealing to American and European audiences. Even British audiences, for some unjust reason, really like American films. So one has to make some sort of economic equation, particularly if you are spending a certain amount of money. I didn't want to be caught making a film for a lot of money where the possibility of earning the money back would be less than good. All these things made it seem sensible to cast the Americans. It was both an artistic and realistic decision.

John got through because nobody came up with anyone better. I think John is a wonderful actor. I think he's wonderful in the film. It was easy for me. When it opened, I was shocked by how many people wrote about John. A lot of critics said that casting John was appalling. Then they had the grace to say he was actually very good in the role. I noticed one thing during a preview. The audience filled in forms, and they always ranked John higher than Glenn. I had always assumed that Glenn would be the one audiences would like because she was a bigger attraction. I found that none of the audiences had a problem with John, just the critics. I then started noticing that men were more nervous about John than women were; women liked John, even though he projected an image of selfishly sexual men in life. He is now, by the way, a very good friend of mine, and a wonderful actor whom I was lucky to have in the film.

LF/SS: For each particular picture, do you have a strong sense of your audience?

SF: It always seemed to me that *Liaisons* would be very popular. I thought that if it could actually make it to the cinema, people would enjoy the film. The story was so wonderful. If you could get people interested in the story, then they would have a wonderful time because it was so extraordinary. You know the audience is going to be filled with mostly middle-class people. You can't escape that. But within that limit, it seemed to me that audiences would really enjoy it very much. *Sammy and Rosie Get Laid*, on the other hand, was an attempt to bring Margaret Thatcher down. It clearly failed. It's actually very overt in its attempts to rally the troops. I don't think I have a sense of who the audience is other than people like me, but I think I've become much more aware of the audience, much more concerned with the audience than I used to be.

Look at *My Beautiful Laundrette*. Nobody had any idea that this world existed. When Hanif wrote it and gave it to me, I was the first person, really, to have a look at it. I thought if I could make that clear to the audience, then they would enjoy this as much as I do. The truth is before Hanif appeared in my life, I had actually been rather gloomy. I didn't think I could make a film career. Then Hanif turned up, and the impact was overwhelming. Nobody has ever done this before. Nobody had ever written from that perspective before. It was astonishing because he got it so right. That someone could be so right, so confident about it, make the jokes, be so on the inside. So the arrival of Hanif in my life was a tremendous event.

LF/SS: Do you see yourself as part of a new resurgence in British films?

SF: There are enormous problems about being a British film director. It's sort of a contradiction in many respects because, in the end, people go and see American films. Just look at the financial figures here. It's particularly difficult to be a British film director because it's a very small market. It's also a small market for cars or steel or whatever, and we in films are just the same. If you make a film in America, I imagine you can get your money back by showing it to large groups of Americans. Over here, you can make a decent film and not get your money back. So I've depended on fiddling with government regulations, getting a bit here and a bit there. You also depend on becoming an export. I've become an export, like Scotch whiskey or something. I can now get my money because my films have sold in France and America. The economics are as simple as that. I can talk about money for two hours.

LF/SS: For all your gloomy talk about this country's lack of a film industry, it does seem that British cinema is getting a lot more attention these days.

SF: It's only been in the last eighteen months or so. It's been close to death most of the rest of the time. You can chart it rather nicely. It started in 1987, and last

November I remember saying to someone, "it's all over." Filmmakers are trained in where to get the money, so the number of films have dropped very dramatically recently. I think all that crop of films have come out including *High Hopes* and *Distant Voices, Still Lives*. They've all come out and had their sort of acclaim, but they haven't generated any money.

My *Beautiful Laundrette* came out and made money. It actually made Orion Pictures a lot of money. I think if you can guarantee four times the rate of return, they'll give you money. It's just very peculiar that at the time it came out, people like me were unlikely to have made twenty films. It's almost embarrassing when I walk into a room, and they see this middle-aged man who's been around. They didn't know about it. But it's funny. Someone will come along and make a film that will make a lot of money, and the financing will come back somehow.

LF/SS: Why don't you go to America then?

SF: That's a very difficult question to answer because it is so logical. The Americans have an industry, and it's so much easier to make movies there. It makes sense. In Britain, everyone is caught halfway in the middle between thinking they're part of an industry and thinking they're independent. Television here in Britain is an industry, so I worked a lot in television because I could find jobs there. If you make a film in England, nobody actually needs you because they'd rather watch a film from America. So, you end up constantly fighting the system. What you have is one sort of rebel after another telling you how they fought the system. Now we could say that those who've gone to America didn't actually fight the system, but they actually wanted to make films. It comes down to what you want to make films about. If you want to make films about life in Britain, then the Americans aren't very sympathetic to it.

LF/SS: Let's talk about your relationship to writers. You've had some of the best—Kurieshi, Bennett, Hampton.

SF: Well, of course, they're enormously important. One of the reasons *Liaisons* wasn't any different than the other films was that the writer was a friend of mine. Writers were always my friends because I've grown up with writers. I've come from a theater where the writers were regarded as what was important. There the job of the director was to realize the work of the writer. In the cinema, it's not quite like that. I start from a collaborative point of view, which is considered rather odd nowadays. I have great respect for the writers, but they do their job and I do mine.

LF/SS: In your relationship to writers, you said, "they do their job and I do mine." What do you see as your job?

SF: In relation to the writer, I might say "that bit's not very good" or "why don't you do that instead of this." I don't exclude the writer's opinions, just as I would expect the writer to have opinions on what I was doing. I can talk most about

Liaisons. That one seems to be the clearest. I remember hiring people to do the costumes, which required very specialized knowledge. I quickly realized I should leave them alone, so I have them take the responsibility. I'd talk to them about what I wanted to see, but I couldn't really say "that's wrong!" I can only say that in sort of a broad sense. I can only *do* what I'm supposed to do, which has to do with narrative, which has to do with acting, which has to do with the human values around the whole edge of the film. So, in the end, that's what I did. But, you end up taking responsibility for everything. Still, I didn't think it was my job to find new furniture or places to shoot.

LF/SS: So you don't take a traditional auteur approach to your direction?

SF: Auteurism was only just mentioned in the sixties, so it's not all that traditional. Before auteurism there was a more traditional way, where some fat producer put it all together. No, I don't think of myself as an auteurist, but I think of myself as traditional. Of course, a lot of people when they identified auteurism said that directors like Alfred Hitchcock were authors. Well, Hitchcock didn't write his films. They were actually trying to classify a lot of the American directors whose work had consistent themes in it, but who didn't write their films. These men didn't say "I'm an artist, I'm an auteurist." They just said, "I go to work every morning." Here I mean people like Minnelli, who made twenty-five films for MGM. He didn't really have control over much of what he was doing, but his work was consistent with identifiable themes. Because I can find some identical themes in my films, I'm more classical than auteurist. You have to be precise.

LF/SS: Is *Dangerous Liaisons* your transition film, the start of your move to Hollywood?

SF: No. Well, yes. But it's not that. It isn't like I'm going to move to Hollywood or anything like that. When you make a film that has the success of *Dangerous Liaisons*, you become a part of a list of directors that the studios will employ. They now think "he's alright." "We can trust him with that sort of money." So I've gone from this bloke who made these little films to someone who can handle slightly bigger films. British directors like me are very, very experienced—to the point where very few American directors in my position have done as much work as I have. It's not like in the old days. Then they'd make four or five films a year, so they'd become very experienced. They'd make "B" films, than they'd go on to make "A" films. By going to television, I choose the path to continuity and stability and regularity. I didn't actually come under contract to anybody, but I did go on and on working. I thought I could learn that way. So actually, I'm rather experienced. I'm also experienced through the sense of economy and, of course, that is quite an attractive quality to the American studios.

Now there is one certain film which I would like to make in America, which if all thing go well, I'll make at the end of the year. But it doesn't seem to involve going over to live there. It also depends on what material there is at any given time. None of my friends are writing scripts right now, so I can't find anything to make here. Plus, I found the whole situation of making a film in another place, with other people, very stimulating. It's also what you read. You read about something you want to make. If it's set in America, that's that. You make it in America.

LF/SS: So you don't see yourself, as you said in one interview, going to America and sitting around a pool in Beverly Hills?

SF: Well, I can see that sort of life. A lot of my friends did that to get work. I didn't have to do that, or I refused to do that. I didn't make those films. I don't want to live like that. I really don't like it there. I get rather bored. Although at the moment, I'm treated rather well there. I lived there when my filming was there, like I'm living here when my filming is here. My family is here. That's the end of it. Anyway, it's only ten hours away. Most evenings nowadays I'm on the phone trying to set up the next film.

LF/SS: What are you working on?

SF: It's a novel by Jim Thompson [*The Grifters*]. It's set in Southern California. I've actually been waiting on it for several years. He wrote it in 1963. It was the thing I most liked, the thing I most wanted to do. I don't think there's any more to it than that. Now I've found that California seems to be the place for it to get done. When I get there, the people I run across seem to be rather vigorous. It's really rather fast and productive. Here, there's no work. There might be one film going, or there's one about to start. That's it. It's really terrible here when you've got a mortgage and a family. It's a really difficult way to run your life when there's only one film being made. California will be like my office or a boarding school. It'll be like when I was eight and went away to school for six months. I'll do the film and come back here afterwards.

LF/SS: So are you going to make larger Hollywood movies instead of smaller British movies with British subjects?

SF: I don't think it's like that. In fact, the story I'm about to make is sort of in the middle. It isn't like a Hollywood film because it's much too dark. But it's true that I can't find anything in Britain that I'm quite interested in right now. Maybe I ran out of steam making those three films. I really don't have anything else to say about England right now. I know that must sound rather pompous, but what I mean to say is that if someone shows me something good, I want to do it.

LF/SS: Who are some of the directors whose work interests you? How about Lindsay Anderson and Karel Reisz?

SF: Those men surely don't agree with what I'm doing. What happened with Karel and Lindsay is that they changed the world. They actually rode through it.

They introduced realistic films. In the 1960s, television took it over, so it just advanced way beyond what they had been doing. I was really influenced by the American cinema, mostly the classic cinema. When I made *Dangerous Liaisons* it seemed to me to be like a forties film. I watched mostly films by European filmmakers in Hollywood: Hitchcock, Wilder, lots of others. So, I think of myself in that tradition really. I know there are some British directors in Hollywood, Alan Parker and Ridley Scott, for example, but I don't particularly identify with them. They come from different backgrounds. I identify with Billy Wilder, of course. He was a man who went to Hollywood and made a very, very elaborate range of films; yet, he kept his own voice. That's what I'd like to do.

LF/SS: What about contemporary American filmmakers like Woody Allen?

SF: Woody Allen is the most wonderful man, though I don't think he would consider himself a contemporary filmmaker. He's really the previous generation, isn't he? I don't want to speak rudely, because he's absolutely wonderful. What's really good about Woody Allen is that as the years go by, he's gotten better and better. What I mean is that he made all those films, and then he made *Annie Hall*. When you make all those films over a period of time, you do get better.

LF/SS: What is your attitude towards the direction of your actors?

SF: I think actors are very, very skillful, generous people. They do something that I couldn't. They're the ones that actually stand up and make fools of themselves. They, in a sense, get the roughest end; they get the most brutal treatment. The rest of us can sort of hide while they stand up and make fools of themselves. I take a lot of trouble when I cast people. Then again, I think I cast people rather well. But having cast them, I let them get on with it. It seems to me what we're trying to do is bring something to life. I'm just the opposite of an Alfred Hitchcock. He drew it all out beforehand, and that's what he found interesting. He wasn't really interested in what was happening during the shooting and didn't care what the people were doing, since he had exercised his imagination when he did the drawing. I'm not like that. I can sort of make things up as I go along because I've solved it all at the point of casting. The actors always know far more than I know about the characters. They're full of ideas, and they do things. Then you say, "I like that," or "I don't like that," and you gradually accept their contribution. Sometimes you can add to it, and sometimes you can make it worse. Sometimes an actor will do something that is absolutely wonderful and will then get gradually worse. Often I say something because I feel like I should say something, when I probably shouldn't have said anything at all. You're actually much better off keeping your mouth shut. They're very skillful people.

LF/SS: When you refer to handling things "as you go along," are you referring to shots, plot, and shooting at locations as well?

SF: Well that's very complicated, isn't it? For example, say I was making a film in the street there and someone came to me and asked, "Where do we park this?" I'd say, "Alright, you can park over there." What you're really saying is, I won't shoot in that direction because there are five hundred trucks over there. So you sort of mentally say, Let's shoot this way because the sun is coming in this direction and this and this and this. Whatever it is, the story makes sense here. So you've begun to actually exercise a director's decision because you've said, "I won't shoot that way." If you did want to shoot that way, you'd say, "Go park on another street because I want to shoot all around here." Alright, so that may have been a decision that was preplanned, or I may have come and given that one limitation, or various other limitations. I would have then started to work out what I was going to do. Maybe you should come down there or maybe the camera should be over there.

LF/SS: So there is really no preset plan or storyboard?

SF: You do have a preset plan. Some of it's preplanning whether you like it or not. Placement of the vehicle can be preplanning whether you like it or not. When we did the riot in *Sammy and Rosie Get Laid*, the fires and all, we had to do a storyboard because there was so much work to be done and we didn't have too much time. So there was no question. We had to light those fires and put a camera there. It seems to me certain things dictate themselves. For instance, in this room you'd probably want to light through the windows. Well, to light through the windows, you'd probably have to put up big rigs. You'd also put up scaffolding towers with a light on the top of it. If you put your camera there, you're going to put your lights coming in from that angle. So you see, you are endlessly making decisions on a very practical level. Whether the camera was there or there or what lens you put on was decided at the time. What you're looking for is a sort of moment of grace, aren't you? You're looking for the moment it comes to life. What I want is some sort of growth, something to flower. If you are lucky, you photograph that moment; you gradually strip things away to get at that moment.

LF/SS: You've worked a lot with both the professional and nonprofessional performers. Frances Barber, from *Sammy and Rosie Get Laid*, said she had a hard time working with nonprofessionals in that film. I was wondering what you prefer?

SF: I don't quite know what Frances means. If you make a film with a lot of black or Asian actors, generally speaking they've had few opportunities to act. So there aren't many good English speaking Asian actors. To find the boy who plays Sammy, well there really wasn't much of a choice. So you end up with someone quite inexperienced. If I had been casting a white person, there probably would've been a choice of ten. So that's what happens when you make films about groups of people who haven't been in films with other people. That's just part of the deal. There's nothing you can do about it unless you change the names or paint people's faces. It's as simple as that. The working conditions don't change, except some people are more experienced than others. You make films about minorities, at least partially, to advance that situation.

LF/SS: You said that with *Sammy and Rosie*, you did the riot in one take. In *My Beautiful Laundrette*, the fight between Johnny and his friends didn't look very staged at all. Was it also done in one take?

SF: It wasn't one take. It was a lot of takes. But, then again, we sort of made it up. What happens is you have this thing called stunt arrangers. Since they're usually in James Bond films, they think everybody has got to be John Wayne and slug it out. It's choreographed as if everything looks like a Western. If you've seen a street fight, it's not like that at all. It's messy. So, gradually, you take what people offer and you subvert it. You turn it to your own purposes. Fights are quite interesting because they're like set pieces.

When I made *Gumshoe*, it had a very, very good killing in a tunnel, an awful sadistic killing. But it was a gangster film. Eventually, I began to realize if you make a gangster film, you may have to do these killings. They're sort of like a big number in a musical. They have to satisfy people because that's what they're there for. These stunt arrangers would come and say, "Well, how do you want to kill 'em?" I thought that was beyond discretion. But then I began to realize that was the whole point of it. So I had to ask myself, What kind of film do I want to make? Eventually, I worked out one that I was actually very, very proud of. It was very, very good. You realized that that was part of it. In *Liaisons*, the duel was the same thing. The fight was messy and awkward and grubby.

So that's what happens, and it's strange how it happens. It takes some kind of identifying. By the end of *Liaisons*, the bits I really liked were every time there would be a horse and carriage; it seemed to be very authentic. If you're making a film about the eighteenth century, you have to have scenes with a horse and carriage. I started thinking that we didn't have to shoot anything with a horse and carriage. It's kind of ridiculous. But by the end, I came to realize it's part of the language of it. I just loved it when those people in the coach would come around. You become very attached to those little details which you don't think you care about. You realize the film is made up of things like that.

LF/SS: What does British realism mean to you?

SF: That sometimes you can create material that contains some accurate aspects of life. It's hard. I'm increasingly sort of confused by it. When you are making films about England, you are making films about a way of life that is easily identified. In America, it seems different, because there isn't a consistent way of life, because life on the East Coast is so different than life on the West Coast. So it's hard to say this is what life in America is like. Directors like Hitchcock, Lean, and Reed worked a lot from the written word and were able to extract a lot out of it. A lot of arguing goes on in Britain about television and cinema—which is more visual. It's a whole issue I find very uninteresting. As you can see, I find it very difficult to answer your question.

When I made *Dangerous Liaisons*, I felt like making it in the studio. All my life I've been trying to get back to the studio. It's funny. At the same time people like Lindsay and Karel have been trying to get back on the streets, I've spent my whole life on the streets and want to get to the back lot of MGM. I'd love to do car scenes with back projection. Once I made a documentary when I was younger, and I thought it would be easier if I had actors who could say what they want to say. These real people are getting in the way. You're just trying to take diverse elements and make them coherent. I think that I do prefer it when the film process all starts with a basis in something believable. I think *Dangerous Liaisons* is a wonderful story about living in Paris, but the truth is that I would have rather have made *Dangerous Liaisons* in Paris, Paramount than in Paris, France.

CHAPTER NINETEEN

THE POLITICS OF IRONY: THE FREARS-KUREISHI FILMS

Leonard Quart

IN A *NEW YORK Times Magazine* profile, Martin Amis, author of the best-selling and angrily satirical *London Fields*, stated that "London is a pub. Not the pub with the jolly butcher and the smiling grannies; it's the pub of nine alcoholics, a handful of hustlers and nutcases and a few token regular people" (Stout 1990, 32). His piece goes on to declare that England is in "a gentle, deep decline," one "not as frenzied as America's, but perhaps even more poignant, more tragic" (32).

This vision of ominous decline has ironically coincided with, or been caused by (dependent on one's point of view), the prosperity of the Thatcher era. During Thatcher's eleven years in power, the ruthless unleashing of market forces may have helped a majority of English people to prosper materially during much of her reign (it began to unravel in 1990-91 with a deepening economic recession and double-digit inflation) but at the same time turned England into a more morally callous, crude, and desperate society where a falling quality of life was covered over by a rising standard of living. She helped create an England where the rich got richer and consumed more conspicuously, while the ethic of social responsibility began to unravel. Her policies, which included cuts in public spending, tax reductions weighted toward the affluent, and, where possible, the privatization of social services, have led to the growth of a visible, embittered underclass—20 percent of the people living under the poverty line, the number of the homeless up to 1,000,000 (150,000 under the age of twenty-five) and the highest per capita prison population within the European community. Clearly, one of Thatcher's prime legacies was to produce a more impoverished life for a sizeable portion of the population.

Until recently, one had a feeling that Thatcher and the Tories would remain in power interminably. Of course her forced resignation in November 1990 and replacement by the much less ideological and abrasive John Major (after the Labor

Party showed a 15 percent lead in the opinion polls), has changed the political climate. But during Thatcher's years in power, the English left was both divided and self-destructive, a large segment of the skilled working class bought into the Tory vision of an enterprise culture, and much of the traditional political opposition to Thatcher—the Labor party leadership, the unions, and Liberals and Social Democrats had been neutralized. In fact, it sometimes seemed that in their savage critiques of Thatcherism, the English films of the eighties produced one of the few effective political weapons against the Thatcher tide. In films like *The Ploughman's Lunch*, *Letter to Breshnev*, and *High Hopes* the meanness, greed, and absurdity of much of contemporary English life during the Thatcher era was corrosively skewered.

Two of the most original, ambitious, and complex films about eighties English society were products of the collaboration of director Stephen Frears (*Gumshoe* and *Prick Up Your Ears*) and Anglo-Pakistani playwright Hanif Kureishi—*My Beautiful Laundrette* and *Sammy and Rosie Get Laid*. The two films explored themes built around issues of race, class, and gender with a passion for ambiguity and contradiction. The works were ironic, literate, and unpredictable—made by men sympathetic to the left who consciously avoided allowing their films to become either politically didactic or schematic. In fact, in both films victims of racial prejudice and economic deprivation can, at the same time, be either exploiters or barbaric racists; idealistic leftists can espouse politics that are essentially rhetorical or futile, or become, with their ascent to power, murderers and torturers; and feminists, whose point of view they are clearly sympathetic to, can become shrilly judgmental and self-righteous. Frears and Kureishi maintain an ambiguous and ironic perspective on society, and most of the characters inhabiting the films are people of conflicting and contradictory parts; the only true villain in the two films is Margaret Thatcher herself.

The Frears-Kureishi films eschew left sectarianism and puritanism for a commitment to an anarchic, impulsive, and sexual life (though even here there is a touch of irony)—a sympathetic variation on the values of the sixties' counterculture. Kureishi has written "that openness and choice in sexual behavior is liberating . . . that ambition and competitiveness are stifling narrowers of personality; and that all authority should be viewed with suspicion and constantly questioned" (Kureishi 1987, 77). He imagines "the desire for more freedom, more pleasure, more self-expression to be fundamental to life" (77). It's his belief in a life of spontaneity—free of guilt and crass self-interest—which the films set in opposition to all that is respectable, repressive, and calculating in society. Frears' directorial style reinforces this vision by making use of a split screen, rapid, rhythmic cross cutting, shock cuts (e.g., cutting from the police killing a middle-aged black woman to the bare, tattooed behind of a nubile woman photographer), swish pans, tracking with a hand-held camera, overlapping dialogue, vivid color (a use of blue light and red filters)—a barrage of visual and aural fireworks to help disrupt our sense of order and affirm a life lived without conventional constraints.

In *My Beautiful Laundrette* (1986) the film's narrative centers around a young, unformed Anglo-Pakistani, Omar (Gordon Warnecke), his white working class friend and lover, Johnny (Daniel Day Lewis), and Omar's family of successful, rapacious entrepreneurs. Omar, adrift and on the dole, suddenly finds direction by going to work for his wealthy, hustler uncle, Nasser (Saeed Jaffrey), and becomes totally committed to the Thatcherite ethic of making big money. For the family, that means amorally wheeling and dealing in slum housing, porn-video cassettes, narcotics, and a host of other businesses. Adaptable Omar learns quickly and is not adverse to illegal dealings, but he focuses his drive for success on transforming a squalid, graffiti-ridden South London launderette into a glittery Ritz of poor people's fantasies—a launderette replete with a fish tank, video screens, potted plants, and piped-in music.

My Beautiful Laundrette consistently succeeds in subverting the predictable and stereotypical. The once colonial Pakistani, who, in London, are often victims of racial prejudice and violence, live well in large suburban homes and luxury flats. While their tormentors—lumpen white punks and skinheads—have only the dole and gratuitous street violence to console themselves with. In fact, the whites are seen as the real victims of Thatcherism in *Launderette*. The Pakistani also may wax nostalgic about their past privileged life in Karachi, but they are not put off, despite the racism, by Thatcher's England. They know "there is money in the muck" and display murderous contempt for those English who lack the energy and drive "to squeeze the tits of the system." They, in turn, have passionately embraced the opportunities open in the new business culture. Nasser declaring "that we're professional businessmen not professional Pakistani."

The Pakistani characters are not seen as figures of virtue. The film directly confronts the fact that immigrant success, on arrival in a new and alien world, is often built on overstepping the fine line between shrewd business practice and criminality. Frears and Kureishi's Pakistani exploit other Pakistani, and in their scramble for money are devoid of any semblance of social concern; the only Pakistani who has political ideals turns out to be Omar's embittered and alcoholic, socialist intellectual father, who hates England.

However, for Frears and Kureishi, the idealistic and self-pitying father, who rarely leaves his bed, is much less sympathetic and seductive than the exploitative and materialistic Nasser. Omar's father's life and politics are mired in defeat—the working-class boys he once tried to reach have repudiated him and marched to the rhetoric of the National Front rather than the ideals of socialism—while Nasser is warm, generous, sexual, and life loving. The film is clearly critical of Nasser's whole ethos—he is not only corrupt but also a domestic autocrat and totally insensitive to his daughter's desire for sexual and intellectual independence. However, though most of Nasser's values may be repellent, he is also capable of being emotionally expansive and caring—he genuinely loves his poignant, dignified English mistress Rachel (Shirley Anne Field) as well as Omar.

Figure 19.1. Gordon Warnecke and Daniel Day Lewis in *My Beautiful Laundrette*. Courtesy: British Film Institute.

He has an appetite for living, and in Frears and Kureishis' vision that human characteristic can be as, or more, important than adhering to a more acceptable set of right-thinking political principles.

The most sympathetic figure in the film is Johnny, who embodies many of the values the film perceives as unequivocally positive. Johnny is a complex figure who sees working with Omar as a means of escape from squatting and living an aimless life on the streets. Johnny's new life does involve a modest amount of criminal activity, but the drive for success does not take him over. It's his love of Omar that is his consuming passion, but despite that commitment, he still maintains some loyalty to the group of racist punks he once belonged to. In different instances, he can convey quiet strength and decency, human concern and high spirits—riding with Omar's daughter Tania on a bicycle in a scene reminiscent of *Butch Cassidy and the Sundance Kid* or licking Omar's neck with his tongue in front of his old friends.

The relationship between Johnny and Omar is spontaneous, natural, and even tender at times. There are suggestions of darker elements lying underneath— a strong possibility that Omar, who likes his new social status and power, will ultimately betray or dispense with Johnny as he becomes even more deeply committed to making big money. These strains aside, their relationship is evoked on the screen without a hint of sexual self-consciousness or any suggestion that their sexual commitment is in any way psychologically problematic. In a scene that takes place on the day of the launderette's opening, Johnny and Omar are seen in a medium two shot in their back office making love, while in the background, one can see, through a one way mirror, Rachel and Nasser amorously waltzing. The scene uses deep focus to embrace what it sees as parallel kinds of sexual passion, without making anything special of the homosexual link between Omar and Johnny. What is strongest about their relationship is seen here and in the film's concluding scene, where, after Johnny is beaten by his old gang, Omar tenderly soaps him and washes his cuts and bruises.

Their second collaborative work, *Sammy and Rosie Get Laid* (1987) is a riskier, more frenetic and stylized film than *Laundrette*. Like *Laundrette* it is ironic and satiric in tone, and it juggles, through fluid crosscutting, a melange of narratives and themes. But though *Laundrette* contains scenes shot in film noir style—Omar renewing his relationship with Johnny, who is back lit in the inky blackness under an ominous railroad overpass with graffiti-scarred walls— most of the film avoids stylization. *Sammy and Rosie* is much more expressionistic in form. Its *mise en scène* contains a one-eyed, Pakistani, cab driver-ghost; a group of omnipresent buskers; and a Felliniesque group of squatters living on waste ground that has been turned into an aestheticized, giant-size collage. In addition, there are both a number of self-reflexive scenes (i.e., Sammy's Woody Allen-like homage to London, Rosie's discourse on kissing) and literary monologues that suspend the narrative and detach the audience from the emotional life of the characters. These are two films where language plays as significant a role as the *mise en scène* and editing.

Sammy and Rosie is a work of excess, a carnival of sensation, an ambitious film that touches on a variety of themes: the nature of third-world revolution; the turbulent state of contemporary London; and sex and marriage among the radical chic. It's a much less focused film than *Laundrette*, but if it has a center, it's Rafi (Shashi Kapoor), a brutal, Pakistani cabinet minister and wealthy factory owner who has returned to London to recapture his abandoned relationships with his son Sammy (Ayub Kahn Din) and his English upper-middle-class love of thirty years before, Alice (Claire Bloom).

Rafi exemplifies Frears and Kureishi's gift for creating multidimensional characters and for seeing the ambiguities and ironies involved in political commitment. Rafi is a man of conflicting parts: a callous sexist ("Alice is a good woman, she's got another ten years wear in her") who is repelled by feminists and lesbians; a conventional patriarch who attempts to bribe his son to have a grandchild and buy a house in the suburbs; a hedonist who takes great pleasure in food, drink, and sex; a tyrant and murderer who justifies torture and repression as political necessities with elegant Kureishi one liners ("a man who hasn't killed is a virgin"); and a former revolutionary who still has some residual sympathy for squatter and rioters.

Like Nasser, Rafi is a man who can both be detested for his values and actions and still be charming and seductive; he is also the most singular and developed character in the film. Frears and Kureishi like characters in size and panache, and they take aesthetic and intellectual pleasure in Rafi—allowing him to overwhelm an earnest Rosie and her decent political values in a raging, overly rhetorical argument about his use of torture when in power.

Frears and Kureishi, however, are clearly ideologically on the side of the Left rather than with Rafi in *Sammy and Rosie*: their sympathies lie with the inner-city rioters rather than with police; with beatific squatters rather than sleazy property developers; and with feminists and radicals rather than with sexists and Thatcher. They view as a given that contemporary England is a country dominated by racism and social injustice—and underline that idea in an ironic precredit long shot of a muddy waste ground accompanied by a voice over of the plummy, arrogant tones of Thatcher welcoming a Tory election victory and speaking complacently of the party's program for transforming the inner cities. They make their perspective even clearer when the traditional hymn "Jerusalem" and a Thatcher speech declaring "that out of discord will grow harmony" are heard on the sound track as the squatters are bulldozed off their grounds, so it can be turned into luxury housing by speculators.

Nevertheless, Frears and Kureishi are not interested in constructing a traditional Left critique. Their film satirizes Left positions, knowing exactly how chic leftists, like chartered accountant Sammy and social worker Rosie, are trapped by their own language and contradictions. Rosie indulges in politically inane comments, as when, viewing the rioting, says it is "an affirmation of the human spirit" and, at the same time, walks through the heart of the riot oblivious to what is happening around her. Sammy passively agrees with her Left sentiments until his car is demolished by the rioters. Sammy and Rosie top it off with a self-consciously sardonic and hip one-liner about a party they're throwing for Rafi—"we can't let a bit of torture get in the way of a party." They're the apotheosis of radical chic—characters who can mouth leftist positions but have never really examined their substance or how their lives relate to their politics. The rioters themselves enact Keystone Cop routines with the London police and pose for photographs while burning cars blaze around them. None of the rioting seems to be truly serious—a great deal of posturing and performing with little political design or effect. And a lesbian couple whose politics are exemplary are treated with more than a touch of irony—the more assertive of the two, Rani (Meera Sayl), tending to be self-righteously anti-heterosexual and cruelly manipulative of her lover. And feminist Rosie is obviously, with more than a tinge of subtle sadism, coolly controlling of the callow, masochistic Sammy.

The film's deepest commitment lies in a rejection of bourgeois life and an affirmation of sexuality and disorder. In one striking scene, Frears cuts rapidly between three interracial couples having sex in very distinctive locations—one of them a flat lined with candles overlooking the Thames and another in a room with a blazing red background in a caravan on the squat site. The cutting accelerates as the sex becomes more intense—an overhead shot of a nude Rosie moving her tongue across Danny's (Roland Gift) body—culminating in the screen splitting in three horizontally when they all reach orgasm. It is an ecstatic affirmation of sex for its own sake, revved up even further by intercutting a Rastafarian singing group, accompanied by the buskers, serenading the couples with Motown's "My Girl."

And though both works take pleasure in rogues like Nasser and Rafi, neither of the films conclude on a triumphant note for them: Rafi, whose life has lost direction, commits suicide, while a close up of Nasser, at the film's climax, sees him melancholy and puzzled—"finished," he says—left by both his mistress and daughter. Kureishi has written that he still likes to think in sixties' terms, seeing "businessmen as semi-criminals, and the more innocent and lively standing against the corrupt and the stuffy" (Kureishi 1987, 77). So it's a squatter like Danny; sweet, sexual, politically uncertain, and questing, who exists totally outside bourgeois convention or Thatcherite avarice, that comes closes to the Frears-Kureishi ideal.

The two films, however, are too subtle to merely turn the world into some Manichean conflict between the virtuous hip and the odious straight. Danny may be a sentimentalized figure, but seemingly traditional and genteel Alice turns out to be much more intricate than what is conveyed by her respectable, suburban surface. She may hate the "ignorant clangor" of the times and pay homage to a culture based on Chopin and Constable, but she can also eloquently articulate a growing feminist resentment of family life and the men who took her for granted.

Frears and Kureishi's works are "skeptical, questioning, doubting," undermining notions of political correctness, affirming spontaneity, and shaped by a style of choreographed discord. Both films are critical of the social inequity and brutalization of life in Thatcher's England, but neither one posits nor intellectually explores an alternative political vision. (That absence of political certainty is in itself an eloquent statement of where the Left stands in the late eighties and early nineties.) What Frears-Kureishi films project is a radical perspective where all our social categories—oppressor-victim, black-white, male-female, and hip-straight—can be ironically subverted. Where, despite the film's leftist and counterculture sympathies, no social group has a monopoly of virtue or wisdom. That vision makes Frears and Kureishi somewhat unusual, artists of the Left who not only acknowledge the ambiguous nature of the social and political world but also revel in its ironies and contradictions.

NOTE

Portions of this essay appeared in a different form in *Cineaste* Fall 1986 and Spring 1988.

WORKS CITED

Kureishi, Hanif. "Film Diary." *Granta* 22 Autumn 1987: 77.
Stout, Mira. "Down London's Mean Streets." *New York Times Magazine*, 9 Feb. 1990.

CHAPTER TWENTY

THE LONG DAY CLOSES:
AN INTERVIEW WITH TERENCE DAVIES

Wheeler Winston Dixon

BORN IN 1945, Terence Davies survived a terrible childhood composed of equal parts of economic and social privation, as well as beatings at the hands of a brutish and uncomprehending father. A child of the Liverpool blitz era, Davies's strongest memories of his childhood are those of escape: escape to the cinema, to a singalong at a pub, to brief holidays away from home. Subjected to a vigorously Catholic upbringing, Davies originally trained to be an accountant, but soon drifted into theater as a way to express the alienation of his own existence.

In a series of 16mm shorts begun in 1976, Davies created a five-part autobiography, tracing his life up until his most recent film, *The Long Day Closes*, completed in 1992. By that time, Davies was working in 35mm, with a budget of $1,750,000; his first film had a budget of £8,000. The first three shorts, *Children* (1976), *Madonna and Child* (1980), and *Death and Transfiguration* (1983), all financed by the BFI Production fund, led to the production of his first film in 35mm, *Distant Voices, Still Lives* (1988), which won numerous international awards and established Davies as a major figure of the modern British cinema.

Davies's work is spare and austere; his framing recalls the minimalist rigor of Jean-Marie Straub, or Davies's own contemporary, Derek Jarman, although, as he notes, Davies's sensibility is very much his own. Having come up in the ranks of the BFI's production program, Davies is now at work on the script of an contemporary "thriller" set in New York; it is to be financed by a combination of British and French production funding. Quiet, reserved, and yet very definite in his views, Davies consented to give this telephone interview from a small cottage in the English countryside, where he was completing the screenplay for his new film and "listening to Saint-Saëns."

Davies is privileged, in that he has never had to work on a project that was not wholly personal, self-scripted, designed to meet his expectations alone. Although his childhood and early professional career informed the structure and content of his first five films, he is now moving toward the "thriller" genre as a vehicle for his ideas, rather than starting out as a genre artist who longs to create an entirely individual project. Like Eric Rohmer, who continues to turn out gorgeously personal (and, it must be said, resolutely noncommerical) films, Davies absolutely refuses to sacrifice any aspect of his personal vision to the whims of executive producers and/or distributors, while simultaneously remaining resolutely practical in the matter of budgets and shooting schedules, in the manner of any journeyman filmmaker.

Yet for all his individuality of vision, Davies is deeply concerned with the public reception of his work, and the personal pain that he exorcises in his films is never far from the surface of his discourse. Although the grim physical world of *Distant Voices, Still Lives* is punctuated with a series of seemingly inappropriate show tunes that simultaneously mirror and offer sardonic commentary on the bleak lives of Davies's protagonists, in his lush pictorial continuity, severely sculptural lighting, and deeply felt sense of color, Davies sees mundane life as something that continually seeks release and transmogrification through the redemptive quality of escapist entertainment. "There's nothing *wrong* with *Tootsie*, you know," he admonished me at one point in our conversation. Davies seeks to please, then, both himself *and* his audience, no matter how much the precise crafting of his films belies this fact.

Perhaps the most telling indication of all this is that, speaking before the first public presentation of *The Long Day Closes* at the Society for Cinema Studies Conference in Pittsburgh in 1992, Davies was characteristically modest and even deferential in speaking of the work we were about to see. Once the lights dimmed, however, Davies left the screening room, and could be seen throughout the performance seated on a stone stool in the lobby of the theater, staring at the rain falling outside, wondering how the audience was accepting his film and yet seemingly afraid to view its reception firsthand. Terence Davies takes his work and his audiences seriously; his upcoming New York "thriller project" seems, more than anything else, an attempt to move beyond the confessional confines of his own existence and reach out to a wider audience. This interview was conducted on 23 July 1992.

Wheeler Dixon: Where do you see yourself in the continuum of British Cinema?

Terence Davies: I don't see myself in it at *all*, really. It's very difficult to say, really, because I was brought up on the American musical. That's what my sisters took me to see when I was a child. "Real" sorts of films, Hollywood films, were made by people who didn't come from my background. I'm from a large working-class Catholic background. People in England who were making films were all middle class, and they'd all gone to university, and I never thought I'd get the chance to make films myself. I still can't quite believe that I *do*, you see what I mean?

WD: Your films offer a much more honest, and certainly a *different*, vision of working-class life in than Britain has been previously been shown. Could you speak a little bit on that?

TD: Well, I'm trying to be truthful to the audience in my background. My background was very similar to that of lots of people in this country, and certainly of my class. It was, in many ways, a very *constricted* culture, but a very rich one. All we had was the radio and the cinema, the pub, and the dance hall and for men, the football match on a Saturday. But that culture was very *rich*, because you had to make your own entertainment, which was why when you went to the pub you sang, and then when you came back to the house with some beer you sang *again*, and then you listened to some records, and they were always American pop records.

American popular music was dominant in Britain, you know, up until the early sixties. So that was the way it was when I was growing up, and I tried to be truthful to that. What was extraordinary, for me anyway, was that so many people said that the vision in my films was sort of universal. I tried to be honest to that background and to my family, because they are films about my family and about that culture, which is really long gone now. I mean, the England of the mid-fifties, to modern young British men and women, is as remote as ancient Egypt. It's completely gone.

The downside of this life was that if you were born in the working class, you were brought up to know your place, and to "touch the forelock," metaphorically speaking. It kept you in your place, and that was wrong. But there was a lot more social discipline than there is now, for instance, and that was a given. If you were told by someone in authority what to do, or that this was the way it was, you accepted what they said. They were in authority, and you believed them. That's not necessarily a good thing. I tried to be absolutely honest to the experiences of myself and my family, which was what I think I achieved. What was extraordinary for me, as I say, was people all over the world saying *their* lives were like that. That was astonishing. It was *my* life, and *my* films came out of that, but somehow it seems that I've touched a chord that transcends national boundaries.

WD: You were born in 1945. When did you close in on the fact that it would be possible for you to make films? Many people here in America say that they've wanted to make films all of their lives. Was this true of you?

TD: Well, absolutely not. I grew up, as I say, on the American musical and I never thought I'd get a chance to do one of my own. My first film, which I saw at seven, was *Singing in the Rain*. Then I saw the first CinemaScope film ever made, which was *The Robe*, made in 1953. The bloke who played Caligula in *The Robe* was fabulous. He had all the best lines! It was terribly camp, and I thought he was wonderful, and so I immediately wanted to be an actor. My sisters had encouraged me from when I was seven or eight to dance and sing with them, so now I really wanted to act. Then I left school at fifteen in 1960. I began to act with amateur companies in Liverpool, and I also started to write, mostly prose.

It wasn't until I was twenty-seven, when I was still working as an accountant, which I hated, that I got into drama school. That was 1973. I had written the first part of my trilogy, *Children*. I took it all over England and everybody had turned it down. I still don't know where that script "came from," so to speak, because that wasn't specifically what I wanted to do. But I wrote it, and I kept sending it out.

I sent it off to the British Film Institute Production Board. A year later, I was told to go down to London. There I was told that I had eight and a half thousand pounds, not a penny more, to do the film, and I was to direct it. I said, "well, I've never directed before," and the head of the Production Board said, "now is your chance," and that's how it happened.

WD: What was your response to the Tony Richardson and Karel Reisz "kitchen sink" films of the early 1960s? Did you find them utterly inauthentic because the people who were making them were doing it from the outside of the culture, rather than from the inside?

TD: You didn't realize that back then. You're right, of course, but they looked authentic at the *time*. The one that looked most authentic at the time, which now looks *least* authentic, is *A Taste of Honey*. For the first time in a film, people were speaking with Northern accents. Up to that time, established British stars wouldn't do accents, in case their fans might think they talked like that in real life! These films started out as plays, plays or novels, and they were made into films, shot on the real locations, with people doing proper accents for that particular part of Manchester, or whatever, and that was a revelation.

But you look at them now, and you realize just how *contrived* they are. At the time they seemed rather legendary; it seemed like a huge change was going to happen. What is sad about them is that there isn't an ounce of sentiment in any of them. Perhaps the best one is *This Sporting Life*, simply because of Rachel Roberts's performance, rather than that terrible sub-Brando performance that Richard Harris gave in the lead role. But what these films did for the first time, like what Beckett and Pinter did for the English stage, was open up areas which never, never had been looked at in English cinema or English theater. Most British films then were drawing-room comedies with a French window in them; these *feeble* middle-class comedies which were just *terrible*.

Yet the era between 1944 and about 1956 was the best era for British screen comedy because we had the best actors. We had people like Margaret Rutherford, Alastair Sim, Alec Guinness, people like that. And we had them in depth, even the minor characters, like Cecil Parker, and Richard Wattis; they were just *deeply* gifted. The wonderful Terry-Thomas, people like that. The films of the late fifties and early sixties, which are now called "Kitchen Sink," did seem rather revolutionary. But if you look at them now, you realize that they are drawn from the middle class point of view. And they're relentlessly *dreary*. Those constant shots of canals with stuff floating in them. Working-class life was difficult, but it had great beauty and depth and warmth.

WD: Having seen your most recent film, *The Long Day Closes*, the visual style is very elegant, and the color is very muted, and yet deeply saturated. It almost seems like you're copying the look of Michael Powell and Emeric Pressburger's films for their production company, The Archers.

TD: Well, content always dictates form. A film will tell you how it wants to be made and therefore how it wants to be shot and therefore what sort of color to use. In the recreation of the fifties, what you can't use is modern color, because modern color is not right for it. It's too garish. Actually I was trying to reproduce were two things: one was three-strip Technicolor, and in one or two scenes we've actually achieved that, though it's very difficult to reproduce. But what I also wanted to do was to shoot the film in tonal ranges of brown, sort of muted colors. That means that you have to make sure that you light it in a certain way and use certain filters, because otherwise primary color will change drastically. Reds will go purple or black, that kind of thing, and black will lose all texture in it.

For *The Long Day Closes*, I saw some still photographs which had been taken in Manchester in the late fifties and early sixties. There were some beautiful color ones; they have this wonderfully rich, but quite restricted, tonal range. That's because a lot of them were made before the Clean Air Act, so there's a lot of soot in the air because of people burning coal fires. Everything's actually seen through a haze of coal/smoke, or it's backlit through the sun. That's what I was trying to recreate.

WD: So it's somewhat like fifties Kodachrome, in a sense.

TD: Well, not Kodachrome exactly. You'd have to see the photographs, because they are absolutely unique. I'd have to say the look of *The Long Day Closes* was a combination of those photographs and the film *The Red Balloon*, which is a wonderful use of Technicolor and, of course, all the great Technicolor musicals as well. Take *Young at Heart*, for example. Look how glowing *that* is.

WD: How did you arrive at your style of camera work? It seems, in all your films, that the action proceeds as almost a dreamlike series of still life compositions, as opposed to having the camera move more aggressively about the set. There's something very sculptural and austere about the way that the camera is used in your films. Do you agree?

TD: Well, I don't know, because it's very difficult to talk about style. I don't know how style evolves. I think it has to evolve from content dictating form, as I

Figure 20.1. Terence Davies, writer and director of *The Long Day Closes*, with Leigh McCormack. Courtesy: Terence Davies.

said. Content always dictates form—never the other way around—and so I see the images in the film in that way. But I've no idea where my style comes from! I've not studied painting, I've not studied sculpture, it's all just visual intuition, learning by doing. I mean, "that's how it looks right to me," you know? That's a pretty feeble answer, I realize, but that's the best I can come up with.

WD: Do you feel a link to the work that Derek Jarman is doing in *Caravaggio*?

TD: No, I don't. I feel his style is completely different. I think his films are much more overtly "painterly," I think. Mine aren't. At least I don't *think* so, but then I'm the *last* person to know, because it's very difficult to actually analyze one's style. Yet I think they're different. I mean, as beautiful as I think *Caravaggio* is, it's *much* too florid for my taste.

WD: With your films, you have been very fortunate, it seems to me, because you've been able to do exactly what you wanted to within certain economic constraints. Rather unusual, wouldn't you say?

TD: It's *very* unusual, but when I started out I didn't realize how unusual it was, to be truthful. But by the same token, if you write the script and say, "that's what I'm going to do," and they give you the money for it, whether that money is adequate or not, *that's* what you do, *that's* what you shoot. And I make a point of doing that, sticking completely to the script, just as I make a point of coming in on budget and on time. Those are things that are your moral obligation. It's not *your* money, it's somebody else's. I guess that's my Catholic working-class background coming out.

I *am* lucky. But at the same time, I do say, "look, this is the way I'm going to do it. If it takes a year for me to write a script, you'll have to wait until I'm done with it." Every track, every pan, every bit of dialogue, *everything* is in it, and that's what I shoot. I don't improvise at all. I mean, I may add an odd close-up here, or a pick-up shot there, but that's *very* rare.

This process gives me a great degree of control. People know exactly what they're getting, and if they turn around and say, "you can't do that," you say, "but I'm sorry, it's in the script. I *told* you I was going to do that." And with it being so detailed, I can say, "I will track on these days, I will crane on those days, on that day we need twenty extras, on this day we only need four," I mean, you can do all that then. I never do a story board, you see. But you don't need to if everything's all written out.

WD: What is your feeling about shooting in the studio versus shooting on location? The studio gives you so much more control over lighting, and it seems you use that beautifully. Is that why you shoot inside so much?

TD: Well, the area that you don't have any control over, because this is England and not California, is the bloody weather! Sometimes it just rains the very day you want it to be sunny, and when you *want* it to rain, it's sunny! Completely unpredictable! So we have great problems with the weather, *terrible* problems. In *The Long Day Closes* we had one and a half days of sunshine in *eight* weeks of shooting. But you learn to adapt. And if you shoot inside, you can make it do anything you want. So it's economic *and* aesthetic. In one of the scenes in the film, it was supposed to be a bright and sunny sports day outside, with children gamboling around in the sunshine like frisky little lambs. Well, they can't gambol around in weather that looks like something out of Tennessee Williams! But we have to keep going, so we shot it anyway.

WD: On *The Long Day Closes*, you used Mick Coulter as your director of photography, as opposed to William Diver, who shot all of your earlier films. Is there any particular reason for that?

TD: William wants to edit, and I think he's a brilliant editor, but also there were problems with the union. They wouldn't allow someone to be director of photography and then edit it as well. They just won't allow it, and that was all there was to it. And also, by the time I got to *The Long Day Closes*, there was the other disadvantage of William not being that experienced as a director of photography. He's really only shot *my* films, nobody else's, and obviously if people are putting up $1.75 million, they want someone with a name and more experience, which is fair enough. I was lucky enough to find someone as gifted as Mick Coulter.

WD: Yes, he did a superb job with it.

TD: He was fabulous.

WD: And Christopher Hobbs, the production designer, was just marvelous.

TD: He's a genius. I'm very lucky to be working with people like that. Hobbs also worked on Derek Jarman's *Edward II*, incidentally.

WD: Are there any directors today whom you particularly admire?

TD: Well, there are one or two *films* by people that I like. But I'm not really an "auteur." I like individual films far more than individual directors. I know he's not making films anymore, but I couldn't live without *Fanny and Alexander*, and I think that Ingmar Bergman is one of the greatest directors who ever lived. I do like Derek Jarman's *War Requiem*—I think it's his best. I love *My Life as A Dog*—I think they're all lovely, just lovely. But then, you see, I'd also say that I think, as a piece of entertainment that *Tootsie* is *terrific*. There's nothing *wrong* with *Tootsie*, you know. It's like *When Harry Met Sally*, which is another good film. They're not great art, they do nothing for the art of cinema, but they're just bloody good pieces of entertainment, and you come out thinking, "I've had a really good time!" That's no bad thing. *Sunday in the Country* I think is wonderful, and parts of Alain Resnais's *Providence*. I don't think *Providence* works as a whole, but sections of it are superb.

WD: Derek Malcolm has said of your work, "If there had been no suffering, there would be no films." Do you think now that with *The Long Day Closes*, the autobiographical section of your work has come to a conclusion? You end the film in 1956, so it *could* conceivably go forward. Will you pursue this?

TD: Well, no, that's the last bit of my autobiography. I shan't do anymore. I've said it all now. But I do think it's true that if there hadn't been all that misery in my life and in my family's lives, there would have been nothing to write about. I suppose one is the product of one's background. I can't conceive writing about something which is just simply happy. It's very difficult to write about that; I just don't think that way. I *do* think that it's true; *without* all that suffering, there wouldn't have been any films, 'cause I wouldn't have anything to say. But I don't want to do any more autobiography. I've done enough. I've been doing it for eighteen years, and it's an awfully long time.

WD: Your first film, *Children*, made in 1976, was forty-six minutes long. The next part of the initial trilogy, *Madonna and Child*, was thirty minutes in length. *Death and Transfiguration* was twenty-five minutes long. All of these films were shot in 16mm, as opposed to 35mm. How were they shown? How did you get these films out before the public? Was it through BFI Distribution?

TD: Well, they took ten years to make, and they were shown at the ICA here in London to tiny audiences, literally *very* tiny audiences, and that started it. Then they were taken for the New York Film Festival, and they showed them, and then they got little showings here and there and started to win prizes. But they weren't shown on a massive scale. Not only are they 16mm black and white, but they're also *incredibly* depressing—there isn't a "gag" anywhere in them! They were my apprentice work, and you can tell.

WD: What are you working on now?

TD: Well, on my table right at the moment, I'm writing a thriller set in New York, in the present day.

WD: That surprising. Do you see yourself now doing genre films?

TD: Well, I shouldn't think so, but I *will* do this particular story. I mean, *thriller* is a very loose term. When I think of thrillers, I think in terms of film noir of the late forties, particularly, *Gilda* and *Laura*, which are my touchstones. I don't think of modern thrillers. They're rather boring, it seems to me.

WD: Is this going to be produced by the BFI?

TD: No, but we've got some money from two companies, one in England and one in France. We've only got development money at the moment. I'm just starting to write the script. I shall be going to New York in September, just to stay in New

York and get the feel of New York. I also want to get a feel for the *rhythm* of American English, because it's not the same as British English—it has its own rhythm, and one has to listen to that.

WD: Can you tell me anything about your new film?

TD: Well, it's very difficult to talk about because it's still in embryonic form, but it's basically about someone driven by intense loneliness. That doesn't tell you very much, but I really don't know myself what's going to happen. But that's the broad theme.

WD: Are there any actors that you would particularly like to work with?

TD: Well, there are some American actors I'd like to work with. I think that even *bad* American actors are so much *better* than English actors, because they always know what to do with their eyes! I like quirky actors. I like people like Christine Lahti, Pamela Reed, and Aidan Quinn. I think Jeff Bridges is a wonderful actor. But it's difficult to know who you'll be able to get. Jeff Bridges is a big star, for heaven's sake!

But, no, it's just that American actors always do little things with their eyes, or other bits of business, that are always interesting for a director. The drawback to American films for me, as an Englishman, is that so much of the time the acting, and indeed the films, are ruined by this dreadful sentimentality, where everyone cries all the time and tells each other that they love one another, and this is supposed to mean something. I *do* find that kind of sentimentality really quite repellent. It's very tedious, I must say. And the crashing music cues that tell you when to emote, that's another weakness. So I don't know what the new film will be, but I guarantee you it won't be like that! That's not the sort of film I want to make. I'm after something altogether different. It will be interesting to see what happens.

THE FILMS OF TERENCE DAVIES

Children   1976/46 mins/b&w/16mm
Producer: Peter Shannon; Script: Terence Davies; Director of Photography: William Diver.

Madonna and Child   1980/30 mins/b&w/16mm
Producer: Mike Maloney; Script: Terence Davies; Director of Photography: William Diver.

Death and Transfiguration   1983/25 mins/b&w/16mm
Producer: Claire Barwell; Script: Terence Davies; Director of Photography: William Diver.

Distant Voices, Still Lives 1988/85 mins/col./35mm
Producer: Jennifer Howarth; Script: Terence Davies; Director of Photography:
William Diver, Patrick Duval; Cast: Freda Dowie, Pete Postlethwaite, Angela
Walsh, Lorraine Ashbourne, Dean Williams.

The Long Day Closes 1992/92 min/col./35mm
Producers: Colin MacCabe, Ben Gibson; Director of Photography: Mick Coulter;
Costume Designer: Monica How; Production Designer: Christopher Hobbs; Editor: William Diver. Released in Britain on May 22, 1992. Premiered at the Cannes
Film Festival, and at the Society for Cinema Studies Conference, Pittsburgh, PA;
Spring 1992.

CONTRIBUTORS

Ilsa J. Bick is a child and adult psychiatrist and psychoanalyst in private practice in Fairfax, Va. She is also a candidate at the Washington Psychoanalytic Institute in Washington, D.C. She has presented widely on applied analysis to film and is the author of numerous articles in both film and psychoanalytic journals.

Stephen Bottomore is a a freelance television producer and historian of early cinema based in London. He is currently working on a book about the filming of warfare before 1914.

Wheeler Winston Dixon is Chairperson of the Film Studies Program at the University of Nebraska, Lincoln, Nebraska; his most recent book is *The Early Film Criticism of François Truffaut* (Indiana University Press).

Lester Friedman, editor of *Fires Were Started: Thatcherism and The British Cinema* (University of Minnesota Press, 1992), teaches film at Syracuse University and humanities at the SUNY Health Science Center.

Andrew Higson is Chair of Film and Cultural Studies at the School of English and American Studies, University of East Anglia, United Kingdom.

Edward T. Jones, Professor of English and Chair of the English and Humanities Department at York College of Pennsylvania, has written books on L. P. Hartley and Peter Brock and numerous articles on literature and film for such journals as *Literature/Film Quarterly*. He teaches courses on Shakespeare, theater, and film.

Brian McFarlane is an Associate Professor of English at Monash University Melbourne, Australia. He is the author of many articles and books on film and literature. His two most recent books are (coauthored) *New Australian Cinema: Sources and Parallels in American and British Film* (Cambridge) and *Sixty Voices: Celebrities Recall the Golden Age of British Cinema* (British Film Institute).

Brian McIlroy is an Assistant Professor of Film Studies in the Department of Theatre and Film at the University of British Columbia, Vancouver, Canada. He is the author of *World Cinema 2: Sweden* (1986), *World Cinema 4: Ireland* (1989), and numerous articles on Irish studies in journals such as *Irish University Review*, *Studies, Mosaic, Eire-Ireland, The Canadian Journal of Irish Studies, Film Criticism*, and *Literature/Film Quarterly*. Presently, he is working on contemporary British and Irish Cinema.

Caroline Merz is a freelance journalist and film historian with a particular interest in British women filmmakers.

Laurence Miller is a professor of psychology at Western Washington University. His research interest is psychological influences in film and literature. He has published articles in both psychology and film journals and presented papers at both psychology and film and literature conferences.

Leonard Quart is an Associate Professor of Cinema Studies at The College of Staten Island & The Graduate Center/CUNY, an editor of *Cineaste*, author of the revised and expanded edition of *American Film and Society Since 1945* (Praeger) and coauthor of *How the War Was Remembered: Hollywood and Vietnam* (Praeger).

Neil Rattigan is the author of *Images of Australia: 100 Films of the New Australian Cinema* (Southern Methodist University), and a member of the faculty of the School of Politics and Communication Studies, University of Liverpool, England.

David Sanjek's articles on film, popular culture, and contemporary literature have appeared in *Literature/Film Quarterly*, *American Quarterly*, *Post Script*, *Film Criticism*, *Cardozo Arts & Entertainment Law Journal*, *Journal of Popular Culture*, *Popular Music and Society*, *Trackings: Popular Music Studies*, the newsletters of the Institute for Studies in American Music and the Rhythm & Blues Foundation. He is coauthor with his late father, Russell Sanjek, of *The American Popular Music Business in the 20th Century* (New York: Oxford University Press, 1991).

Scott Stewart, who is currently completing his master's degree at Wesleyan University, has done a wide variety of freelance film and video productions.

Tony Williams is Associate Professor of Cinema Studies at Southern Illinois University at Carbondale in the Department of Cinema and Photography. He has contributed articles to *Movie*, *CineACTION!*, *Wide Angle*, *Jump Cut*, *Science Fiction Studies*, *From Hanoi to Hollywood* (1990), and *Inventing Vietnam* (1991) and is author of *Jack London: The Movies* (1992).

Cynthia Young, an instructor of English at Southern Illinois University, is working on her doctoral dissertation on Virginia Woolf and Cinema.

BIBLIOGRAPHY

This bibliography contains works directly consulted in the creation of this volume, as well as works of related interest. Where two editions of the same work are cited, both editions are listed within one citation.

Adair, Gilbert, and Nick Roddick. *A Night at the Pictures*. Bromley, Kent, Gt. Brit.: Columbus, 1985.

Addison, Paul. *The Road to 1945: British Politics and the Second World War*. London: Jonathan Cape, 1975.

Aldgate, Anthony. *Cinema and History: British Newsreels and the Spanish Civil War*. London: Scolar, 1979.

Aldgate, Anthony, and Jeffrey Richards. *Britain Can Take It: The British Cinema in the Second World War*. Oxford: Blackwell, 1986.

Anderegg, Michael. *David Lean*. Boston: Twayne, 1984.

Anderson, Benedict. *Imagined Communities: Reflections on the Origin and Spread of Nationalism*. London: Verso, 1983.

Anstey, Edgar. Rev. of *This Happy Breed*. *Spectator*, 2 June 1944, n.p..

Appel, Alfred. *Nabokov's Dark Cinema*. New York: Oxford UP, 1974.

Arkadin (pseud.). "Film Clips." *Sight and Sound* 38.2 (Spring, 1969): 104-5.

Armes, Roy. *A Critical History of British Cinema*. New York: Oxford UP, 1978.

Ashliman, D. L. "Symbolic Sex-Role Reversals in the Grimms' Fairy Tales." *Forms of Fantasy*. Ed. Jan Hokenson. New York: Greenwood, 1986. 193-98.

Aspinall, Sue, and Robert Murphy, eds. *Gainsborough Melodrama: BFI Dossier 18*. London: BFI Publishing, 1983.

Balcon, Michael. "The British Film during the War." *Penguin Film Review* 1 (Aug. 1946).

Balcon, Michael, Ernest Lindgren, Forsyth Hardy, and Roger Manvell. *Twenty Years of British Film, 1925-1945*. London: Falcon, 1947.

Barker, Felix. *The Oliviers*. London: Hamish Hamilton, 1953.

Barker, Martin, ed. *The Video Nasties: Freedom and Censorship in the Media*. London: Pluto, 1984.

Barnes, John. *The Beginnings of the Cinema in England*. Newton Abbot: Charles, 1976.

Barr, Charles, ed. *All Our Yesterdays: 90 Years of British Cinema*. London: BFI Publishing, 1986.

——— . *Ealing Studios*. London: Cameron and Tayleur/David and Charles, 1977; Woodstock, NY: Overlook, 1980.

——— . "Introduction: Amnesia and Schizophrenia." *All Our Yesterdays: 90 Years of British Cinema*. London: BFI Publishing, 1986.

——— . "Projecting Britain and the British Character: Ealing Studios Part I." *Screen* 15.1 (1974): 87-121.

Barthes, Roland. *Mythologies*. New York: Hill and Wang, 1957.

Bergan, Ronald. *The United Artists Story*. New York: Crown, 1986.

Bergstrom, Janet. "Alternation, Segmentation, Hypnosis: Interview with Raymond Bellour." *Camera Obscura* 3.4: 70-103.

Betts, Ernest. *The Film Business: A History of British Cinema, 1896-1972*. London: Allen and Unwin, 1973; New York: Pitman, 1973.

Bogarde, Dirk. *Snakes and Ladders*. London: Chatto and Windus, 1978.

Bommes, Michael and Patrick Wright. "'Charms of Residence': The Public and the Past." *Making Histories: Studies in History-Writing and Politics*. Ed. Richard Johnson. London: Hutchinson, 1982.

Box, Muriel. *Odd Woman Out*. London: Leslie Frewin, 1974.

Bragg, Melvyn. *Laurence Olivier*. London: Hutchinson, 1984.

"Brian Desmond Hurst." *Sight and Sound* Autumn, 1958: 257.

Britton, Andrew. "Their Finest Hour: Humphrey Jennings and the British Imperial Myth of World War II." *CineAction!* 18, 1989.

Britton, Andrew, Richard Lippe, Tony Williams, and Robin Wood. *American Nightmare: Essays on the Horror Film*. Toronto: Festival of Festivals, 1979.

Brown, Geoff, Lawrence Kardish, and Michael Balcon. *The Pursuit of British Cinema*. New York: Museum of Modern Art, 1984.

Bunker, Henry. "The Voice as (Female) Phallus." *Psychoanalytic Quarterly* 3 (1939): 391-429.

Butler, Ivan. *The War Film*. South Brunswick, NJ: A. S. Barnes, 1974.

Calder, Angus. *The People's War: Britain, 1939-1945*. New York: Pantheon, 1969. New York: Ace, 1972.

Carroll, Noël. *Mystifying Movies: Fads and Fallacies in Contemporary Film Theory*. New York: Columbia UP, 1988.

——— . *The Philosophy of Horror; or, Paradoxes of the Heart*. New York: Routledge, 1990.

Chatman, Seymour. *Coming to Terms: The Rhetoric of Narrative in Fiction and Film*. Ithaca: Cornell UP, 1990.

Chambers, Iain. *Popular Culture: The Metropolitan Experience*. London: Methuen, 1986.

Chanan, Michael. *The Dream That Kicks: The Prehistory and Early Years of Cinema in Britain*. London: Routledge, 1980.

——— . *Labour Power in the British Film Industry*. London: BFI Publishing, 1976.

Chasseguet-Smirgel, Janine. *Creativity and Perversion.* New York: Norton, 1984.

Chodorow, Nancy. *The Reproduction of Mothering: Psychoanalysis and the Sociology of Gender.* Berkeley: U of California P, 1978.

Christie, Ian. *Arrows of Desire: The Films of Michael Powell and Emeric Pressburger.* London: Waterstone, 1985.

———, ed. *Powell Pressburger and Others.* London: BFI Publishing, 1978.

Cooper, Susan. "Snoek Piquante." *Age of Austerity.* Ed. Michael Sissons and Philip French. London: Hodder and Stoughton, 1963. 33-54.

Coultass, Clive. *Images for Battle: British Film and the Second World War, 1939-1945.* London: Associated University Presses, 1989.

Cross, Robin. *The Big Book of British Films.* London: Sidgwick and Jackson, 1984.

Crowther, Bruce. Film Noir: *Reflections in a Dark Mirror.* New York: Continuum, 1988.

Curran, James and Vincent Porter, eds. *British Cinema History.* London: Weidenfeld and Nicolson, 1983; Totowa, NJ: Barnes and Noble, 1983.

Darlington, William Aubrey. *Laurence Olivier.* London: Hazell Watson and Viney, 1968.

Davis, Colin. "Eros Exploding: The Films of Anthony Balch." *Shock Express* 2.4 (Summer, 1988): 9-10.

Deleuze, Gilles. *Cinema 1: The Movement-Image.* Minneapolis: U of Minnesota P, 1986.

Dickinson, Margaret, and Sarah Street. *Cinema and State: The Film Industry and the British Government, 1927-84.* London: BFI Publishing, 1985.

Dixon, Wheeler Winston, ed. *British Cinema 1900-1975. Film Criticism* 16.1-2: 1992.

———. *The Charm of Evil: The Life and Films of Terence Fisher.* Metuchen, NJ: Scarecrow, 1991.

———. *The Films of Freddie Francis.* Metuchen: Scarecrow, 1991.

Doane, Mary Ann. *The Desire to Desire: The Woman's Film of the 1940s.* Bloomington: Indiana UP, 1987.

———. *Femmes Fatales: Feminism, Film Theory, Psychoanalysis.* London: Routledge, 1991.

Dockray, Keith. *Richard III: A Reader in History.* Gloucester, Gt. Brit.: Sutton, 1988.

Downey, Roger. "A Post-Modern Ring." *Seattle Weekly* 30 July-5 Aug., 1986: 37.

Downing, David B., and Susan Bazargan, eds. *Image and Ideology in Modern/Post Modern Discourse.* Albany: State U of New York P, 1991.

Durgnat, Raymond. *A Mirror for England: British Movies from Austerity to Affluence.* London: Faber and Faber, 1970.

Dyer, Richard. *Now You See It: Studies on Lesbian and Gay Film.* London: Routledge, 1990.

Eagleton, Terry. *Raymond Williams*. Boston: Northeastern UP, 1989.

Edelheit, Henry. "Mythopoesis and the Primal Scene." *The Psychoanalytic Study of Society* 5: 212-33.

Eliot, T. S. *Christianity and Culture*. New York: Harcourt Brace Jovanovich, 1968.

Ellis, John. "Art, Culture and Quality: Terms for a Cinema in the Forties and Seventies." *Screen* 19.3 (Fall, 1978): 9-49.

——— . "Made in Ealing." *Screen* 16.1 (Spring, 1975): 78-127.

——— . *Visible Fictions: Cinema: Television: Video*. London: Routledge, 1982.

——— . "Watching Death at Work: An Analysis of *A Matter of Life and Death*." *Powell, Pressburger and Others*. Ed. Ian Christie. London: BFI Publishing, 1978. 79-104.

Eyles, Allen, Robert Adkinson, and Nicholas Fry, eds. *The House of Horror: the Complete Story of Hammer Films*. New York: Lorrimer, 1984.

Falk, Quentin. *The Golden Gong: Fifty Years of the Rank Organisation, Its Films and Its Stars*. London: Columbus Books, 1987.

Finler, Joel W. *The Hollywood Story*. New York: Crown, 1988.

Forman, Dennis. *Film 1945-1950*. London: British Council/Longman, Green, 1952.

Foucault, Michel. *The Order of Things: An Archaeology of the Human Sciences*. New York: Random House, 1970.

Fountain, Nigel. *Underground: The London Alternative Press 1966-74*. London: Comedia-Routledge, 1988.

Fraser, John. *Violence in the Arts*. Cambridge: Cambridge UP, 1974.

Freedman, Carl. "England as Ideology: From 'Upstairs Downstairs' to *A Room with a View*." *Cultural Critique* 17: 70-106.

Freud, Sigmund. "Civilization and Its Discontents." *The Standard Edition of the Complete Psychological Works*. Vol. 21. Trans. James Strachey. London: Hogarth, 1953. 59-148.

——— . "Inhibitions, Symptoms, and Anxiety." *The Standard Edition of the Complete Psychological Works*. Vol. 20. Trans. James Strachey. London: Hogarth, 1953. 77-178.

——— . *The Interpretation of Dreams*. New York: Signet, 1965.

——— . *Introductory Lectures on Psychoanalysis*. New York: Norton, 1977.

Freud, Sigmund, and Josef Breuer. *Studies in Hysteria. Vol. 3 of The Pelican Freud Library*. London: Penguin, 1974.

Friedman, Lester D., ed. *Unspeakable Images: Ethnicity and the American Cinema*. Urbana: U of Illinois P, 1991.

Furman, Nelly. "The Politics of Language: Beyond the Gender Principle?" *Making A Difference: Feminist Literary Criticism*. Ed. Gayle Green and Coppelia Kahn. New York: Routledge, 1985. 59-79.

Gifford, Denis. *British Cinema: An Illustrated Guide*. New York: A. S. Barnes, 1968.

———. *The British Film Catalogue, 1895-1970: A Reference Guide*. New York: McGraw-Hill, 1973.

Gledhill, Christine, and Gillian Swanson. "Gender and Sexuality in Second World War Films: A Feminist Approach." *National Fictions: World War Two in British Films and Television*. Ed. Geoff Hurd. London: BFI Publishing, 1984.

Gloversmith, Frank, ed. *Class, Culture and Social Change: A New View of the 1930s*. Sussex: Harvester, 1980.

Gorak, Jan. *The Alien Mind of Raymond Williams*. Columbia: U of Missouri P, 1988.

Gramsci, Antonio. *Selections from the Prison Notebooks*. Ed. Quintin Hoare and Geoffrey Nowell-Smith. London: Lawrence and Wishart, 1970.

Hallenbeck, Bruce G. "From Gore to Gothic." *Fangoria* 27 (May, 1983): 42-45.

Hardy, Phil, ed. *Encyclopedia of Horror Films*. New York: Harper, 1986.

Harwood, Ronald. *Sir Donald Wolfit*. New York: St. Martin's, 1971.

Hartley, L. P. *The Go-Between*. New York: Knopf, 1954.

Heath, Stephen. *Questions of Cinema*. Bloomington: Indiana UP, 1981.

Hewison, Robert. *In Anger: British Culture in the Cold War, 1945-1960*. New York: Oxford UP, 1981.

———. *Too Much Art and Society in the Sixties 1960-75*. New York: Oxford UP, 1987.

Higson, Andrew. "Addressing the Nation: Five Films." *National Fictions: World War Two in British Films and Television*. Ed. Geoff Hurd. London: BFI Publishing, 1984.

———. "'Britain's Outstanding Contribution to the Film': The Documentary-Realist Tradition." *All Our Yesterdays: 90 Years of British Cinema*. Ed. Charles Barr. London: BFI Publishing, 1986.

———. "Constructing a National Cinema in Britain." Diss. University of Kent at Canterbury.

Hill, John. *Sex, Class and Realism: British Cinema 1956-1963*. London: BFI Publishing, 1986.

Hirsch, Foster. Film Noir: *The Dark Side of the Screen*. New York: Da Capo Press, 1981.

———. *Laurence Olivier*. Boston: Twayne, 1979.

Hirschhorn, Clive. *The Columbia Story*. New York: Crown, 1990.

Hoberman, J., and Jonathan Rosenbaum. *Midnight Movies*. New York: Harper, 1983.

Hoffman, Eric C. "Hammer's Frankenstein Series." *Bizarre* 4 (1974): 35-51.

Hogenkamp, Bert. *Deadly Parallels: Film and the Left in Britain 1929-1939*. London: Lawrence and Wishart, 1986.

Hoggart, Richard. *The Uses of Literacy: Aspects of Working-Class Life with Special Reference to Publications and Entertainment*. London: Chatto and Windus, 1957; New York: Oxford UP, 1957.

Holden, Anthony. *Laurence Olivier*. New York: Athenaeum, 1988.

Horrox, Rosemary. *Richard III: A Study of Service*. New York: Cambridge UP, 1989.

Houston, Penelope. *Went the Day Well?* London: BFI Publishing, 1992.

Howard, Ronald. *In Search of My Father: A Portrait of Leslie Howard*. London: William Kimber, 1981.

Hurd, Geoff, ed. *National Fictions: World War Two in British Film and Television*. London: BFI Publishing, 1984.

————. "Notes on Hegemony, the War, and Cinema." *National Fictions: World War Two in British Films and Television*. Ed. Geoff Hurd. London: BFI Publishing, 1984.

Hurst, Brian Desmond. "Hurst [Travelling The Road]." Unpublished ms. British Film Institute, 1986.

Jackson, Rosemary. "Narcissism and Beyond: A Psychoanalytic Reading of *Frankenstein* and Fantasies of the Double." *Aspects of Fantasy* 19: 43-53.

Jameson, Fredric. *The Political Unconscious: Narrative as a Socially Symbolic Act*. Ithaca: Cornell UP, 1981.

Johnson, Richard, et al., eds. *Making Histories: Studies in History-Writing and Politics*. London: Hutchinson, 1982.

Johnson, Rosemary. *Fantasy: The Literature of Subversion*. London: Methuen, 1981.

Jones, Stephen G. *The British Labour Movement and Film, 1918-1939*. London: Routledge, 1987.

Kael, Pauline. Rev. of *The Go-Between*. *New Yorker* 31 July 1971: 55-56.

Kaplan, E. Ann. *Psychoanalysis and Cinema*. London: Routledge, 1990.

————, ed. *Women in Film Noir*. London: BFI Publishing, 1980.

Kelly, Bill. "Michael Reeves: Horror's James Dean." *Cinefantastique* 22.1 (August, 1991): 33-45.

Kiernan, Thomas. *Sir Larry: The Life of Laurence Olivier*. New York: Time Books, 1981.

Kinlaw, Dennis C. *Developing Superior Work Teams: Building Quality and the Competitive Edge*. San Diego: Lexington, 1991.

Klein, Joanne. *Making Pictures: The Pinter Screenplays*. Columbus: Ohio State UP, 1985.

Klein, Michael, and Gillian Parker, eds. *The English Novel and the Movies*. New York: Frederick Ungar, 1981.

Korda, Michael. *Charmed Lives: A Family Romance*. New York: Avon, 1979.

Kuhn, Annette. *Women's Pictures: Feminism and Cinema*. London: Routledge, 1982.

Kureishi, Hanif. "Film Diary." *Granta* 22 (Autumn, 1987): 77.

Lacan, Jacques. "The Mirror Image as Formative of the Function of the 'I.'" *Ecrits: A Selection*. Trans. Alan Sheridan. London: Tavistock, 1977. 1-7.

Landy, Marcia. *British Genres: Cinema and Society 1930-1960.* Princeton: Princeton UP, 1991.

Lane, Peter. *A History of Post-War Britain.* London: Macdonald Educational, 1971.

Lant, Antonia. *Blackout: Reinventing Women for Wartime British Cinema.* Princeton: Princeton UP, 1991.

Larsen, Egon. *Spotlight on Films.* London: Max Parrish, 1950.

Lejeune, Caroline. Rev. of *This Happy Breed. Observer*, 27 Aug. 1944, n.p..

Lewin, Bertram D. *The Psychoanalysis of Elation.* New York: Norton, 1950.

Longmate, Norman. *How We Lived Then: A History of Everyday Life During the Second World War.* London: Arrow Books, 1977.

Low, Rachael. *The History of the British Film: 1914-1918.* London: Allen and Unwin, 1949.

――――. *The History of the British Film 1929-1939: Film Making in 1930s Britain.* London: Allen and Unwin, 1985.

MacCabe, Colin. *Tracking the Signifier: Theoretical Essays—Film, Linguistics, Literature.* Minneapolis: U Minnesota P, 1985; Manchester: Manchester UP, 1985.

McEwan, Neil. *The Survival of the Novel: British Fiction in the Later Twentieth Century.* Totowa, NJ: Barnes and Noble, 1981.

McFarlane, Brian. *60 Voices: Celebrities Recall the Golden Age of British Cinema.* London: BFI Publishing, 1992.

McFarlane, Brian, and Geoff Mayer. *New Australian Cinema: Sources and Parallels in American and British Films.* Cambridge: Cambridge UP, 1992.

McIlroy, Brian. "Appreciation: Brian Desmond Hurst 1895-1986: Irish Filmmaker." *Eire-Ireland* Winter 1989-90: 106-13.

McLaine, Ian. *Ministry of Morale: Home Front Morale and the Ministry of Information in World War II.* London: Random House, 1979.

Mahler, Margaret S., Fred Pine, and Anthony Bergman. *The Psychological Birth of the Human Infant.* New York: Basic, 1975.

Major, Rene. "The Voice behind the Mirror." *The International Review of Psychoanalysis* 7.4: 459-68.

Manvell, Roger. *Film.* Rev. ed. London: Penguin, 1946.

Manvell, Roger, and R. K. Neilson Baxter, eds. *The Cinema, 1952.* Harmondsworth: Pelican, 1952.

Marwick, Arthur. *Britain in the Century of Total War: War, Peace, and Social Change, 1900-1967.* Boston: Little, Brown, 1968.

――――. *British Society since 1945.* Harmondsworth: Penguin, 1982.

――――. *Class: Image and Reality in Britain, France, and the USA since 1930.* New York: Oxford UP, 1980.

――――. *The Explosion of British Society, 1914-1970.* London: Macmillan, 1971.

Mayer, J. P. *British Cinemas and Their Audiences: Sociological Studies.* London: Dobson, 1948.

Medhurst, Andy. "1950s War Films." *National Fictions: World War Two in British Film and Television*. Ed. Geoff Hurd. London: BFI Publishing, 1984.

Metz, Christian. *The Imaginary Signifier: Psychoanalysis and Cinema*. Trans. Celia Britton, Annwyl Williams, Ben Brewster, and Alfred Guzzetti. Bloomington: Indiana UP, 1982.

Miller, Laurence. "How Many Film Noirs Are There? How Statistics Can Help Answer This Question." *Empirical Studies of the Art* 7.1 (1989): 51-55.

Minney, R. J. *The Films of Anthony Asquith*. South Brunswick, NJ: A. S. Barnes, 1976.

Modeleski, Tania. *Loving with a Vengeance: Mass Produced Fantasies for Women*. New York: Methuen, 1982.

Morgan, Kenneth. *Labour in Power: 1945-1951*. New York: Oxford UP, 1984.

———. *The People's Peace: 1945-1989*. New York: Oxford UP, 1990.

Morley, Sheridan. *Tales of the Hollywood Raj: The British, the Movies, and Tinseltown*. New York: Viking, 1983.

Mulkeen, Anne. *Wild Thyme, Winter Lightning: The Symbolic Novels of L. P. Hartley*. Detroit: Wayne State UP, 1974.

Mulvey, Laura. *Visual and Other Pleasures*. Bloomington: Indiana UP, 1989.

Murphy, Robert. *Realism and Tinsel: Cinema and Society in Britain, 1939-1948*. London: Routledge, 1989.

———. "Riff-raff: British Cinema and the Underworld." *All Our Yesterdays: 90 Years of British Cinema*. Ed. Charles Barr. London: BFI Publishing, 1986.

———. "Under the Shadow of Hollywood." *All Our Yesterdays: 90 Years of British Cinema*. Ed. Charles Barr. London: BFI Publishing, 1986. 47-71.

Nairn, Tom. *The Break-Up of Britain: Crisis and Neonationalism*. London: New Left, 1977; London: Verso, 1981.

Newman, Kim. *Nightmare Movies: A Guide to Contemporary Horror Films*. New York: Harmony, 1988.

Niederlund, William. "Early Auditory Experiences, Beating Fantasies and Primal Scene." *The Psychoanalytic Study of the Child* 13 (1958): 471-504.

Oakley, C. A. *Where We Came In: Seventy Years of the British Film Industry*. London: Allen and Unwin, 1964.

O'Connor, Alan. *Raymond Williams: Writing, Culture, Politics*. New York: Blackwell, 1989.

Olivier, Christine. *Jocasta's Children: The Imprint of the Mother*. Trans. George Craig. London: Routledge, 1989.

Olivier, Laurence. *On Acting*. London: Weidenfeld and Nicolson, 1986.

Orwell, George. *The Collected Essays, Journalism and Letters of George Orwell*. Vol. 2. Ed. Sonia Orwell and Ian Angus. London: Secker and Warburg, 1968.

———. "Raffles and Miss Blandish." *The Collected Essays, Journalism and Letters of George Orwell*. Vol. 3. Ed. Sonia Orwell and Ian Angus. London: Penguin, 1971. 246-60.

Ottoson, Robert. *A Reference Guide to the American Film Noir: 1940-1958.* Metuchen, NJ: Scarecrow, 1981.

Park, James. *Learning to Dream: The New British Cinema.* London: Faber and Faber, 1984.

Paskin, Sylvia. "A Delicate but Insistent Trail of Confetti . . ." *Monthly Film Bulletin* 53.632 (1986).

Paul, William. "Michael Reeves Revisited." *Village Voice* 3 Mar. 1971.

Penley, Constance. *Feminism and Film Theory.* New York: Routledge, 1988.

Pendergast, Alan. "A Touch of Noir." *Video* 10.8 (1986): 152-54.

Perry, George. *Forever Ealing: A Celebration of the Great British Film Studio.* London: Pavilion, 1981.

——— . *The Great British Picture Show: From the 90s to the 70s.* New York: Hill and Wang, 1974.

——— . *The Great British Picture Show: From the Nineties to the Seventies.* 2nd ed. London: Pavilion/Michael Joseph, 1985; Boston: Little, Brown, 1985.

Petley, Julian. "The Lost Continent." *All Our Yesterdays: Ninety Years of British Cinema.* Ed. Charles Barr. London: BFI Publishing, 1986.

Peto, Andrew. "Terrifying Eyes: A Visual Superego Forerunner." *The Psychoanalytic Study of the Child* 24 (1969): 197-212.

Petrie, Duncan. *Creativity and Constraint in the British Film Industry.* New York: St. Martin's, 1991.

Pettigrew, Terence. *British Film Character Actors: Great Names and Memorable Moments.* London: David and Charles, 1982.

Pinter, Harold. *Five Screenplays.* New York: Grove, 1978.

Pirie, David. *A Heritage of Horror: The British Gothic Cinema 1946-1972.* New York: Avon, 1974.

——— . "New Blood." *Sight and Sound* 40.2 (1971): 73-75.

——— . *The Vampire Cinema.* London: Gallery, 1977.

Polan, Dana. "Eros and Syphilization: The Contemporary Horror Film." *Planks of Reasons: Essays on the Contemporary Horror Film.* Ed. Barry Keith Grant. Metuchen, NJ: Scarecrow, 1984. 201-11.

——— . *Power and Paranoia.* New York: Columbia UP, 1986.

Polhemus, Ted, and Lynn Proctor. *Fashion and Anti-fashion.* London: Thames and Hudson, 1978.

Powell, Dilys. *Films Since 1939.* London: British Council/Longman, Green, 1947.

——— . Rev. of *This Happy Breed. Sunday Times,* n.d. (probably 1944); collated on microfiche at BFI.

Powell, Michael. *A Life in the Movies: An Autobiography.* London: Heinemann, 1986; New York: Knopf, 1987.

Pratley, Gerald. *The Cinema of David Lean.* South Brunswick, NJ: A. S. Barnes, 1974.

Pritchard, R. E. "L. P. Hartley's *The Go-Between.*" *Critical Quarterly* 22: 45-55.

Quinlan, David. *British Sound Films: 1928-1959*. Totowa, NJ: Barnes and Noble, 1984.

———. *British Sound Films: The Studio Years*. London: Batford, 1984.

———. *The Illustrated Guide to Film Directors*. London: Batford, 1983.

Quinn, Bob. *Atlantean*. London: Quartet Books, 1986.

Rangell, Leo. "Castration." *Journal of the American Psychoanalytic Association* 39: 3-24.

Rev. of *The Tell-Tale Heart*. *Variety* 19 (June 1934): 27.

Rev. of *Theirs is The Glory*. *Variety* 28 (Aug. 1946): 14.

Richards, Jeffrey. *The Age of the Dream Palace: Cinema and Society in Britain 1930-1939*. London: Routledge, 1984.

Richards, Jeffrey, and Anthony Aldgate. *British Cinema and Society, 1930-1970*. Totowa, NJ: Barnes and Noble, 1983.

Richards, Jeffery, and Dorothy Sheridan. *Mass-Observation at the Movies*. London: Routledge, 1987.

Ringel, Harry. "Terence Fisher: The Human Side." *Cinefantastique* 4.3 (1975): 5-16.

Robertson, James C. *The British Board of Film Censors: Film Censorship in Britain 1895-1950*. London: Croom Helm, 1985.

Robinson, David. *The History of World Cinema*. New York: Stein and Day, 1974.

Russo, Vito. *The Celluloid Closet: Homosexuality in the Movies*. New York: Harper and Row, 1987.

Salt, Barry. *Film Style and Technology: History and Analysis*. London: Starword, 1983.

Sarris, Andrew. *The American Cinema: Directors and Directions, 1929-1968*. New York: Dutton, 1968.

Scheider, Laurie. "Mirrors in Art." *Psychoanalytic Inquiry* 5.3: 283-324.

Selby, Spencer. *Dark City: The Film Noir*. Jefferson, NC: McFarlane, 1984.

Sellar, Maurice, Lou Jones, Robert Sidaway, and Ashley Sidaway. *Best of British: A Celebration of Rank Film Classics*. London: Sphere Books, 1987.

Shengold, Leonard. "The Parent as Sphinx." *Journal of the American Psychoanalytic Association* 11: 725-51.

Short, K. R. M., ed. *Feature Films as History*. Knoxville: U of Tennessee P, 1981.

Silver, Alain, and Elizabeth Ward. *Film Noir: An Encylopediac Reference to The American Style*. Woodstock, NY: Overlook, 1979.

Silver, Donald. "Mirror in Dreams: Symbol of Mother's Face." *Psychoanalytic Inquiry* 5.3: 253-56.

Silverman, Kaja. *The Acoustic Mirror: The Female Voice in Psychoanalysis and Cinema*. Bloomington: Indiana UP, 1988.

———. "Masochism and Male Subjectivity." *Camera Obscura* 17: 31-68.

Sinfield, Alan. *Literature, Politics, and Culture in Postwar Britain*. Berkeley: U of California P, 1989.

Socarides, Charles W. *The Preoedipal Origin and Psychoanalytic Therapy of Sexual Perversions.* Madison: International Universities P, 1988.

Sontag, Susan. *Against Interpretation.* New York: Dell Laurel, 1969.

Stallybrass, Peter, and Allon White. *The Politics and Poetics of Transgression.* London: Methuen, 1986.

Stam, Robert, Robert Borgoyne, and Sandy Flitterman-Lewis. *New Vocabularies in Film Semiotics: Structuralism, Post-Structuralism and Beyond.* London: Routledge, 1992.

Stevenson, John. *British Society, 1914-1945.* Harmondsworth: Penguin, 1984.

Stout, Mira. "Down London's Mean Streets." *New York Times Magazine* 9 Feb. 1990.

Swann, Paul. *The British Documentary Film Movement, 1926-1946.* Cambridge: Cambridge UP, 1989.

————— . *The Hollywood Feature Film in Post-War Britain.* London: Croom Helm, 1987; New York: St. Martin's, 1987.

Tabori, Paul. *Alexander Korda.* London: Oldbourne, 1959.

Tanitch, Robert. *Olivier: The Complete Career.* New York: Abbeville, 1985.

Taylor, Philip M., ed. *Britain and the Cinema in the Second World War.* New York: St. Martin's, 1988.

Telotte, J. P. *Voices in the Dark: The Narrative Patterns of Film Noir.* Urbana: U of Illinois P, 1989.

Thomson, David. *England in the Twentieth Century.* Harmondsworth: Penguin, 1979.

Tudor, Andrew. *Monsters and Mad Scientists: A Cultural History of the Horror Movie.* London: Blackwell, 1989.

Tully, Montgomery. "Boys in Brown." Unpublished screenplay, 1949.

Turner, E. S. *The Phoney War on the Home Front.* London: Quality Book Club, 1961.

Tuska, Jon. *Dark Cinema: American Film Noir in Cultural Perspective.* Westport, CT: Greenwood, 1984.

Twitchell, James B. *Dreadful Pleasures: An Anatomy of Modern Horror.* New York: Oxford UP, 1985.

Veeser, H. Aram, ed. *The New Historicism.* London: Routledge, 1989.

Vermilye, Jerry. *The Great British Films.* Secaucus, NJ: Citadel Press, 1978.

Walker, Alexander. *Hollywood UK: The British Film Industry in the Sixties.* New York: Stein and Day, 1974.

————— . *National Heroes: British Cinema in the Seventies and Eighties.* London: George G. Harrap, 1985.

Walker, John. *The Once and Future Film: British Cinema in the Seventies and Eighties.* London: Methuen, 1985.

Waller, Gregory, ed. *American Horrors: Essays on the Modern American Horror Film.* Urbana: U of Illinois P, 1987.

Whitebait, William. (a) First review of *This Happy Breed. New Statesman*, 27 May 1944, n.p.; collated on microfiche at the British Film Institute.

————. (b) Second review of *This Happy Breed. New Statesman*, 21 Oct. 1944, n.p.; collated on microfiche at the British Film Institute.

Williams, Raymond. "Base and Superstructure in Marxist Cultural Theory." *Problems in Materialism and Culture*. London: Verso, 1980. 31-49.

————. "Literature and Sociology." *Problems in Materialism and Culture*. London: Verso, 1980. 11-30.

————. *Marxism and Literature*. London: Oxford UP, 1977.

Williams, Raymond, and Terry Eagleton. "The Politics of Hope: An Interview." *Raymond Williams*. Ed. Terry Eagleton. Boston: Northeastern UP, 1989. 176-83.

Williams, Tony. "Remembering and Forgetting History: *The Ploughman's Lunch*." *Jump Cut* 36, 1991.

Winnicott, D. W. *Playing and Reality*. London: Tavistock, 1971.

Winnington, Richard. Rev. of *This Happy Breed. News Chronicle*, 27 May 1944.

Wood, Alan. *Mr. Rank: A Study of J. Arthur Rank and British Films*. London: Hodder and Stoughton, 1952.

Wood, Robin. "In Memoriam Michael Reeves." *Movie* 17 (Winter, 1969-1970): 2-6.

Wright, Kenneth. *Vision and Separation: Between Mother and Baby*. Northvale: Aronon, 1991.

Yacowar, Maurice. *Hitchcock's British Films*. Hamden, CT: Archon Books, 1977.

Zavarzadeh, Mas'ud. *Seeing Films Politically*. Albany: State U of New York P, 1991.

Zimmerman, Bonnie. "Daughters of Darkness: The Lesbian Vampire on Film." *Planks of Reason: Essays on the Horror Film*. Ed. Barry Keith Grant. Metuchen, NJ: Scarecrow, 1984. 153-63.

INDEX

A Nous la Liberté 137
Abbey Theatre 28, 37
Abominable Dr. Phibes, The 203
Above Us The Waves 148
Accident, The 211
Addinsell, Richard 36
Age of the Dream Palace, The 25
Aldgate, Tony 26
Alias John Preston 162
Alibi 36
Alibi Inn 124
All for Mary 129, 140
All Our Yesterdays 2
Allen, Lewis 54
Allen, Woody 237, 245
Allied Artists (Studio) 160
Alton, John 158
American International Pictures
    (Distributor) 205, 206
Amicus (Studio) 8, 196
Amis, Martin 241
Anderson, Hans Christian 114-115, 118
Anderson, Lindsay 7, 8, 126, 168-176,
    222, 236, 240
Anglia Television 141
Anglo-Amalgamated (Distributor) 160
Annakin, Ken 58, 125
Annie Hall 237
Appel, Alfred 155
Appointment With Crime 161
Apted, Michael 222
Archers, The (Studio) 182, 253
Arliss, Leslie 56
Armes, Roy 2
Arthur, George K. 136, 137
Arthur, Jean 137
Arthur, Nigel 133
Arzner, Dorothy 121

Ashliman, D. L. 109
Askey, Arthur 58
Asquith, Anthony 2, 53, 56, 92n.1, 123,
    134
Assassin for Hire 162
Associated British Film Distributors 160
Associated British Pathé 11
Associated British Picture Corporation
    (Studio) (*See also* British International
    Pictures) 26
Atlantean 28
Attenborough, Sir Richard 36, 43-44, 136

Baddeley, Hermione 102
Baker, Roy Ward 57, 58, 196
Bakker, Jim and Tammy 172
Balch, Anthony 203
Balcon, Sir Michael 25, 26, 67, 121, 125
Balkan Wars 20-21
Ballet Russe. *See* Serge Daighilev Ballet
    Company.
Barber, Frances 238
Barker, Clive 207
Barnes, Barry K. 33, 61
Barnes, John 2
Barr, Charles 2, 96, 97
Barthes, Roland 108, 110-111, 116
Basehart, Richard 163
Bateman, Anthony 59
Bates, Alan 216
Batley, Ethyl 121
Battle of the River Plate, The 147
BBC. *See* British Broadcasting
    Corporation.
Bedelia 58, 60, 61-62
Beginnings of the Cinema in England, The
    2
Bellour, Raymond 111-112, 116

Bennett, Alan 173, 174, 222, 234
Bennett, Compton 58
Bennett-Stanford, John M. 19
Bergman, Ingrid 256
Best, Edna 33
Betts, Ernest 2
Bewitched 162
Bête humaine, La 61
BFI Productions 9, 249, 251, 257
Bicycle Thief, The 42
Big Clock, The 162
Bioscope Company 20
Bird, Norman 57
Black and White 11, 12
Black Widow 161
Black, George 136
Blackmailed 162
Blackton, J. Stuart 11
Blattner's Studio 27
Blood From the Mummy's Tomb 201
Blood of a Poet 136
Blood Will Have Blood. See *Demons of the Mind.*
Bloom, Claire 246
Blue Lamp, The 100, 162
Boehm, Karl 7
Boer War 19-20, 22-23
Bogarde, Dirk 43-44, 129
Bogdanovich, Peter 176
Bohne, Louise 20
Borthwick, Jessica 18
Boulting, John 160
Box, Betty 53
Box, Muriel 2, 3, 6, 122-127, 128, 129, 130, 140
Box, Sydney 50, 122, 124, 125
Boys In Brown 5, 43-44, 48-49, 51
Brady, Matthew 4
Brahm, John 158
Brain Machine 162
Breakout 161
Bresson, Robert 203
Bridge on the River Kwai, The 147, 148
Brief Encounter 100
Brighton Rock 158
Britain Prepared 18

Britannia Hospital 166, 169, 170
British and Dominion (Studio) 26
British Broadcasting Corporation 48, 103, 211, 222, 225, 231
British Cinema History 2
British Council 124, 143
British Film During The War 67
British Film Institute 28, 127
British Institutional Films (Studio) 123
British International Pictures (*See also* Associated British Picture Corporation) 28-29, 31
British Lion (Studio) 161
British Ministry of Information 26, 35, 83, 92n.4, 124
British politics 95-96, 98, 100, 143, 146, 149-152, 165-167, 197-198, 241-242, 246
British society 5-9, 25, 67-76, 79, 83-92, 143-153, 198, 230-231, 251
Broadway Melody 78
Browning, Tod 203
Brownlow, Kevin 18
Bull, René 11, 13, 23n.1
Bullard, F. Lauriston 12
Burgoyne, Robert 3
Burleigh, Bennet 12, 19
Burroughs, William 203
Butch Cassidy and the Sundance Kid 245
Byron, Kathleen 57

Caesar and Cleopatra 37
Caged 162
Cahiers du Cinéma 121
Call for Arms, A 35, 38
Cannes Film Festival 127, 130, 139, 211
Canterbury Tale, A 63
Captain Kronos, Vampire Hunter 200-203
Caravaggio 174, 255
Cardiff, Jack 54
Carroll, Noel 179, 196
Cartier, Rudolph 103
Carve Her Name With Pride 147
Cash on Demand 56
Cass, Henry 125

Castration 179-180
Catcher In The Rye 212
Catling, Daniel 43
Catto, Max 60
Cavalcanti, Alberto 88
Cellier, Antoinette 29
Censorship 21-22, 30, 103, 126, 200
Censorship Board 25
Chambers Journal for 1900 19, 23n.4
Chamberlain, Neville 35, 99
Chandler, Raymond 158
Charge of the Twenty-first Lancers 19, 23n.4
Chariots of Fire 166, 224
Chase, James Hadley 100
Chassequet-Smirgel, Janine 179, 190n.5, 191n.13
Chatman, Seymour 214
Chekov, Anton 169
Chelsea At Nine 142
Chia-Liang, Liu 196
Children 249, 252, 257
Chodorow, Nancy 178
Chorus Line, A 136
Christie, Agatha 158
Christie, Ian 107
Christie, Julie 215
Churchill, Winston 19-20
CinemaScope, 140, 251
Cinematic apparatus, 41-45, 47-51
Clair, René 137
Clark, Robert 29
Clarke, T. E. B. 96, 104
Class structure 83-92
Class and race 166
Clemens, Brian 200-203
Clifton, Henry Talbot de Vere 27
Close, Glenn 232
Cloudburst 161
Cockleshell Heroes, The 148
Cocteau, Jean 130, 135, 136, 203
Coffin, Hayden 133
Colditz Story, The 147
Cole, George 56
Columbia (Studio) 160, 167
Columbia British (Studio) 162-163

Combat Naval en Grèce 15
Comfort, Lance 2, 5, 58-62, 63, 65
Coming to Terms: The Rhetoric of Narrative in Fiction and Film 214
Company of Wolves, The 207
Conan-Doyle, Sir Arthur 158
Confession 162
Confessional, The 204
Conqueror Worm, The. See *Witchfinder General, The.*
Cooper, Gary 228
Corman, Roger 205
Cornelius, Henry 96
Corpse, The 201
Corridor of Mirrors 161
Coulter, Mick 256
Countess Dracula 200, 201
Coward, Nöel 43, 67, 70
Crabtree, Arthur 53, 54, 56, 205
Craigie, Jill 3, 122, 124
Crashout 162
Crawford, Anne 61
Creeping Flesh, The 201
Cripps, Sir Stafford 99
Critical History of the British Cinema 2
Cronin, A. J. 58
Crossroads 161
Crucible of Horror. See *Corpse, The.*
Cruel Sea, The 147
Curran, James 2
Curse of Frankenstein, The 8, 195, 199
Cushing, Peter 56-57, 199

Dalrymple, Ian 139
Dalton, Hugh 99
Dam Busters, The 148, 149, 151
Dance Pretty Lady 127, 134
Dangerous Liaisons 8, 173, 222, 223-224, 231-233, 234, 235, 239-240
Dangerous Moonlight 35
Daniels, Stan 172
Dark Corner, The 162
Dark Passage 161, 162
Dark Secret 161
Daughter of Darkness 59, 60-61
Davies, Terence 4, 9, 221, 249-258

Davis, Bette 7, 169
de Marney, Derrick 36
de Valois, Ninette 134
Dead of Night 103, 203
Deadly Nightshade 161
Dean, Basil 25, 26
Dear Murderer 61
Dearden, Basil 53
Death and Transfiguration 249, 257
Death Line 197, 205, 206-207
Death of an Angel 162
Debussy, Claude 27
Defense de Bazeille, La. See *Episodes de Guerre.*
Defiant Ones, The 56
Delayed Action 162
Demi-Paradise, The 5, 69, 83-92
Demons of the Mind 201
Denham Studios 31-32
Derniéres Cartouches, Les 15-16
Desperate Hours, The 57
Diary of Timothy 173
Dickson, W. K. L. 19
Dietrich, Marlene 32
Difference in cinema 177-190
Dillon, Carmen 215
Din, Ayoub Khan 246
Displacement 42, 185
Distant Voices, Still Lives 9, 234, 249, 250
Diver, William 256
Dixon, Wheeler Winston 199
Dockers, Eugene 104
Documentary cinema 2-4, 11-23
Dollars for Sale 162
Donald, James 38, 57
Door, Bonnie 170-171
Doppelganger in cinema 161
Double Indemnity 161
Dr. Bloodbath. See *Horror Hospital.*
Dr. Phibes Rises Again 203
Dr. Terror's House of Horrors 203
Dracula 8
Dracula A.D. 1972 200
Dracula Has Risen From The Grave 200
Dryden, Norman 27

du Maurier, Daphne 37
Duna, Steffi 135
Dupuis, Paul 102, 103
Durgnat, Raymond 37, 51, 199

Eagle Lion (Studio) 160
Ealing (Studio) 26, 53, 96, 97, 98, 99-100, 121, 125, 143, 151
Ebert, Roger 195
Edelheit, Henry 187, 191n.13
Edward II 256
Eighth Army Air Force (U.S.) 136
Eliot, T. S. 147
Ellis, John 100, 107
Ellis, Mary 31
Elstree Studios 27, 28
Elvey, Maurice 2
English, Inn, The 124
Episodes de guerre 15
Eros (Studio) 161
Ervin, Sam 230
Esmond, Jill 57, 61
Exclusive Films (Studio) 41, 161
L'Execution d'un espion 15

Falklands Conflict 95, 167
Fallen Idol, The 158, 168-169
Famous War Correspondents 12
Fanny and Alexander 256
Farmer, David 64
Fatal Journey 161
Female authorship 117-119
Female body 183
Female castration 115
Femme fatale as construct in cinema 161
Fetishism 179
Field, Shirley Anne 243
Fields, Gracie 28
Film 67
Filmic Dialogism 119
Film Business, The 2
Film Criticism 1
Film Noir 7, 60, 62, 114, 155-163, 257
Final Appointment 162
Finney, Albert 222
Fires Were Started 173

First of the Few, The 84, 149
First World War 16, 21-22, 75, 76-77, 156
Fish Called Wanda, A 168-169
Fisher, Gerry 212
Fisher, Terence 42, 160, 199, 200
Flanagan, John 28
Flitterman-Lewis, Sandy 3
Forber-Robertson, Sir Johnston 27
Ford, John 27, 53, 170, 174-176
Forman, Dennis 144
Forsyte Saga, The 48
49th Parallel 63
Foucault, Michel 3, 215
Fox Films (Studio) 27, 160
Framed 161
Franchise Affair, The 63
Francis, Freddie 54, 201, 204
Franco-Prussian War of 1870 16, 21
Frank, Charles 53, 54
Frankenstein and the Monster From Hell 199
Frankenstein Must Be Destroyed 199
Franklin, Frederick 134
Fraser, John 205
Frears, Stephen 3, 8, 166, 173, 174, 221-240, 242-248
Freeman, Carl 96
French, Harold 58
Freud, Sigmund 97-98, 178, 180, 190n.7, 192n.16
Frieda 145
Frightmare 204
Front Page, The 30
Fuest, Robert 203
Furman, Nellie 111, 115, 117
Fury 158

G & S Films (Studio). *See* Gilbert and Sullivan Films (Studio).
Gainsborough (Studio) 26, 36, 48, 50, 54, 63, 69, 124, 125, 136
Gallagher, Tag 175
Gaslight (British version) (1940) 54, 162
Gaslight (American version) (1944) 162
Gaumont-British/Gainsborough (Studio) *See* Gainsborough (Studio).

Gentle Sex, The 71
Gift Horse, The 147, 148
Gift, Roland 247
Gilbert and Sullivan Films (Studio) 26, 33
Gilda 257
Gish, Lillian 169
Glamorous Night 29, 31, 33, 38
Glory! Glory! 169, 170-171
Go-Between, The 8, 211-219
Good Die Young, The 162, 163
Good Time Girl 125
Gordon, Kenneth 11, 23n.5
Gordon, Major Stevely 17
Goring, Marius 63, 64, 65, 109
Grahame, Gloria 163
Gramsci, Antonio 96
Gray, Alan 64
Gray, Sally 36, 38
Great British Picture Show, The 2
Great Day 58, 61, 62, 63
Great Expectations 54
Greco-Turkish War 12-16, 17, 23n.4
Green, Max 59
Green, F. L. 33, 158
Green, Guy 54
Greenaway, Peter 221
Greene, Graham 158
Granada (television channel) 211
Grierson, John 124
Griffith, D. W. 16
Grifters, The 8, 222-223
Guard, Dominic 213
Guilty? 161
Guinness, Sir Alec 105, 252
Gumshoe 173, 222, 239, 242
Guy, Alice 121
Gynt, Greta 64

Halifax, Lord 99
Hamer, Robert 96, 97, 98, 102, 105
Hammer (Studio) 8, 41, 42, 96, 101, 163, 195-196, 199, 201
Hammett, Dashiell 158
Hammond, Paul 15
Hampton, Christopher 222, 232, 234

Hands of the Ripper 201
Hardy, Robin 197, 204
Hare, David 222
Harris, Richard 252
Hartley, L. P. 211-219
Hathaway, Henry 158
Hatter's Castle 58-59, 60, 62
Havelock-Allan, Anthony 57
Hayes, Joseph 57
HBO 169, 170-171
Hearts of the World 16
Heaven's Above 152
Heller, Otto 63
Hellraiser 207
Hepworth, Cecil 2
Hero 8
Herzbach, Paul 135
Hessler, Gordon 197, 204
Hickox, Douglas 203
High Hopes 234, 242
Hill, John 51
Hillier, Erwin 64
Hinton, Mary 59
History of the British Film 1929-1939
    23n.4, 29
Hit, The 173, 222
Hitchcock, Alfred 2, 4, 5, 115, 121, 122,
    235, 237, 239
Hitler, Adolf 35
Hobbs, Christopher 256
Hobson, Valerie 57
Hodgson, Pat 12
Hoggart, Richard 85
Hollow Triumph 161
Holloway, Stanley 101, 104
Hollywood Feature Film in Post-War
    Britain 3
Hollywood U.K.: The British Film
    Industry in the Sixties 3, 216
Holt, Patrick 38
Holt, Seth 201
Home Box Office. *See* HBO.
Hordern, Michael 101
Horror fims 8, 96, 195-207
Horror Hospital 197, 203
Horror of Dracula, The 200

Horror of Frankenstein, The 199
Horrors of the Black Museum 205
House Across the Lake, The 161
House of Mortal Sin. See Confessional,
    The.
Howard, Leslie 91
Howard, Ronald 91
Huckleberry Finn 212
Hudson, Hugh 129
Hue and Cry 146
Hughes, Dorothy 158
Hundred Pound Winner, The 36
Hungry Hill 37, 39
Hunter, Ian 61
Huntington, Lawrence 2, 5, 58, 62-64
Huntley, Raymond 65, 99
Hurst, Brian Desmond 2, 3, 4, 25-39
Hutchinson, Walter 27
Hylton, Jane 56, 102

I Am A Fugitive From A Chain Gang
    158
I Confess 162
I Met A Murderer 57, 158
I, The Jury 161
I Was Monty's Double 147
I'm All Right, Jack 152
Ibbetson, Arthur 62
If ... 167-168, 222
Illustrated London News, The 11, 12, 16,
    22
In The Picture 136
In Which We Serve 43, 148
Independent Frame Method 5, 41-51
Independent Film Distributors 161, 163
Interpretation of Dreams, The 97
Introductory Lectures on Psychoanalysis
    98
Intruder, The 147
Invitation to the Waltz 127, 135
Irigaray, Luce 116-117
Irish Hearts 27, 28
It Always Rains on Sunday 54, 146
It's Not Cricket 56
ITV 222
Ivy 61

Jackson, Rosemary 98
Jacobi, Derek 141
Jaffrey, Saeed 243
Jane Shore 104
Japanese Legend of the Rainbow 134
Jarman, Derek 4, 173, 174, 221, 249, 255, 256
Jassy 125
Jennings, Humphrey 124, 172-173
Jerrold, Mary 65
Jig-Saw 124-125
John, Rosamund 63, 64
Johns, Glynis 134
Johnson, Celia 70
Johnston, Denis 29
Jordan, Neil 207
Jory, Victor 31
Julien, Isaac 221

Kael, Pauline 215
Kapoor, Shashi 246
Karloff, Boris 137
Keel, Howard 57
Kellino, Roy 57
Kent, Jean 38
Kerr, Deborah 59, 62
Khartoum Campaign 1898 19
Kill Me Tomorrow 162
Kimmins, Anthony 160
Kind Hearts and Coronets 96, 97, 98, 152
Kinematograph and Lantern Weekly 21
King Lear 59
King's Breakfast, The 140
Kinlaw, Dennis 48
Kipling, Rudyard 12
Kipps 56
Kiss of Death, The 162
Klein, Joanne 218
Kneale, Nigel 103
Knight Without Armour 32
Knowles, Bernard 54, 56
Korda, Alexander 2, 6, 25, 26, 31-32, 35, 127, 135-136, 137, 139
Korda, Michael 32
Korean War 100
Kramer, Stanley 56

Kruger, Otto 31
Kureishi, Hanif 3, 8, 173, 233, 234, 242-248

La Chienne 61
Lacan, Jacques 111, 178, 189
Lachman, Harry 27
Lady of Vengeance 161
Lady Vanishes, The 56
Lahr, John 228
Lahti, Christine 258
Laing, R. D. 201
Landy, Marcia 54, 56, 62
Lang, Fritz 158
Larsen, Egon 45, 47-48
Last of England, The 174
Laura 257
Lavender Hill Mob, The 104-105
Lawrence, Quentin 54, 56-57
Le Fanu, Sheridan 54
Le Prince, Augustin 2
Leacock, Philip 58
Lean David 5, 43, 53, 67, 136, 137, 160, 173, 239
Legend of the Seven Golden Vampires, The 196
Legrand, Michel 213
Leigh, Mike 221
Leighton, Margaret 139, 216
Leone, Sergio 201
Let Us Live 158
Letter from Ulster, A 35
Letter to Brezhnev 242
Lewin, Bertram D. 183, 189
Lewis, Daniel Day 232, 243
Lewton, Val 50
Life and Death of Colonel Blimp, The 107
Light That Failed, The 12
Lindsell, Stuart 59
Lion Has Wings, The 35, 36
Lippert (Studio) 160
Liscomb, W. P. 26
Listen to Britain 173
Loach, Ken 222
Lockwood, Margaret 36, 37, 60, 61
Loder, John 30
Lodge, John 29-30

London Fields 241
London Films (Studio) 6, 26, 31, 137, 139
London Globe, The 16, 18
London Graphic, The 12
London Morning Post, The 13, 19
London Standard, The 12, 13
London Sunday Times 223
London Telegraph, The 12
Long Day Closes, The 9, 249-250, 253, 256-257
Long Haul, The 163
Look of the father 190
Losey, Joseph 8, 211-217, 219
Lost Weekend, The 50
Low, Rachael 19, 29, 31
Lowell, Raymond 36
Luchaire, Corinne 33
Lupino, Ida 121
Lured 162
Lust for a Vampire 200
Lyne, Adrian 222

McDonald, David 58
McDonell, Fergus 54, 57
McDowell, Malcolm 7, 168
McEwan, Mel 218
McKenna, Siobahn 60, 61
MacGinniss, Niall 29
MacQuitty, Bill 35
Mackay, Barry 31
Mackendrick, Alexander 96, 97, 102, 105
Madonna and Child 249, 257
Madonna of the Seven Moons 69
Magic Lantern Journal Annual 16
Mahler, Margaret 178
Major, John 241
Major, Rene 189
Make Mine a Million 58
Making Pictures: The Pinter Screenplays 218
Malcolm, Derek 257
Malkovich, John 231-232
Malthete-Méliès, M. 15
Mamoulian, Rouben 27
Man In Black 161
Man In Hiding. See *Man Trap*.

Man In The White Suit, The 152
Man On The Cliff, The 161
Man Trap 163
Man Who Finally Died, The 56
Man Who Never Was, The 147
Mander, Kay 122, 124
Mann, Anthony 158
March on Russia 169
Marilyn 161
Mark of Cain, The 38
Markova-Dolin Ballet Company 134
Marvellous Méliès 15
Marwick, Arthur 146
Mary Tyler Moore 172
Masculine desire 115
Mason, James 63, 125
Massacres de la population Crètoise 15
Masterpiece Theatre 211
Mathewson, Tracy 18
Matter of Life and Death 107, 136
Mature, Victor 163
Maugham, Somerset 29, 30
Metz, Christian 180
Méliès l'Enchanteur 15
Méliès, Georges 15
MGM (Studio) 27, 160, 235, 240
Midnight Episode 162
Milland, Ray 54
Miller, Jonathan 223
Million and One Nights, A 18
Millions Like Us 69, 71, 73
Mimicry 116
Mine Own Executioner 162
Minnelli, Vincente 222, 235
Mirror stage 187, 188, 191n.13
Monogram (Studio) 160
Monthly Film Bulletin 127, 129
Moon In The Yellow River, The 29
More, Kenneth 129, 139-140
Morell, André 56
Morgan 222
Morgan, Kenneth 100
Morley, Robert 136
Mosley, Oswald 31
Mr. Perrin and Mr. Traill 63, 64-65
Mrs. Miniver 70

Mulkeen, Anne 217
Murder At 3 A.M. 162
Murder by Proxy 42
Murder In Reverse 161
Murder Without Crime 162
Murphy, Robert 3, 25, 38, 51, 56
Murray, Barbara 101
My Beautiful Laundrette 8, 166, 173, 221, 223-228, 231, 233, 234, 239, 242-245
My Brother's Keeper 56
My Darling Clementine 175
My Life As A Dog 256
Mycroft, Walter 26, 28-29, 31
Myth in the cinema 108-111, 114-119

Nairn, Tom 76
Naked City, The 162
Narrow Margin, The 162
National Film Theatre 28
NATO 100
Neame, Ronald 54, 136
New Historicism, The 1
New Vocabularies in Film Semiotics 3
New York Times Magazine 241
New York Film Festival 257
New Yorker, The 215
Newell, Mike 222
Newton, Robert 58, 59, 63
Nichols, Dudley 176
Night Boat to Dublin 63
Night of the Living Dead 195
Nightweed 207
1984 100
No Orchids For Miss Blandish 100
Norman, Leslie 103
Norman, Montague 99
North Atlantic Treaty Organization. *See* NATO.
North By Northwest 115
Notorious 115
Novello, Ivor 29, 31
Nugent, Frank 176

Oberon, Merle 35
Odd Man Out 157, 158, 162, 168
Odd Woman Out 123

Odette 147
Oliver 169
Oliver Twist 54
Olivier, Christine 178
Olivier, Sir Laurence 2, 53, 104
Omdurmann, Battle of 11, 13, 16-23, 23nn.1,4
On Golden Pond 169
On The Night Of the Fire 33, 38-39
Open City 50
Ophuls, Max 158
Optical Magic Lantern Journal 18
Orion Pictures (Studio) 234
Orpheus 203
Orton, Joe 222, 227, 228, 230
Orwell, George 87, 100
Osborne, John 126
Oscar, Henry 33
Other Woman, The 162
Ottoson, Robert 155
Ourselves Alone 28-30, 33, 37, 38
Out of the Past 161, 162

Paperhouse 207
Pappy 175
Paramount (Studio) 160
Parker, Alan 129, 166-167, 222
Parker, Cecil 37, 252
Pascal, Gabriel 37
Paskin, Sylvia 129
Passionate Stranger 126
Passport to Pimlico 2, 6, 96-105
Patriarchal Law 110-112
Paul, Robert W. 2
Paul, William 206
Pavlow, Muriel 63
Peeping Tom 2, 7-8, 177-178, 180-192
Pelissier, Anthony 58
Pendergast, Alan 155
Penis 183
Perinal, Georges 135-136
Perry, George 2, 48, 49-50
Peter Pan 137
Peto, Andre 185
Phallus 183, 191n.8
Picadilly Incident 145

Pinewood Studios 43
Pink String and Sealing Wax 162
Pinter, Harold 8, 211-219
Pirie, David 196, 197, 198, 204, 205
Pitfall, The 161
Place of One's Own, A 54
Planer, Franz 158
Ploughman's Launch, The 242
Poe, Edgar Allan 27, 205
Point-of-view 182
Polan, Dana 207
Pollock, Wilfred 13
Porter, Vincent 2
Portman, Eric 38, 62, 63
Possessed 162
Post-Modernism in cinema, 163
Potter, Sally 221
Powell, Dilys 143
Powell, Michael 7-8, 35, 53, 63, 107-108,
    114, 119, 123, 130, 136, 177, 191n.8,
    192n.16, 253
PRC (Studio) 160
Prelude to Fame 57
Pressburger, Emeric 107-108, 114, 119,
    130, 136, 253
Price, Dennis 37
Price, Vincent 203, 205
Prick Up Your Ears 173, 221, 225, 228-
    231, 242
Prior, Melton 12, 22
*Prise de Tournavos par les troupes du
    Sultan* 15
Prison Without Bars 32, 38
Pritchard, R. E. 216
Private Information 57
Privates on Parade 152
Profumo, John 230
Providence 256
Psycho 115
Psychoanalysis and cinema 97-98, 111-
    117, 119, 177-192
Psychomania 196
Putnam, David 166-167

Quatermass and the Pit 103
Queer Cinema 2-4, 9, 25-39, 221, 241-258

Quiet Woman, The 162
Quinlan, David 56, 58
Quinn, Aidan 258
Quinn, Bob 28

Racial marginalization, 241-248
Radford, Basil 100
Raging Tide, The 162
Railroaded 161
Raising A Riot 129, 139-140, 141
Ramsaye, Terry 18
Rangell, Leo 180
Rank Organization (Studio) 5, 26, 33, 41-
    45, 48, 50-51, 126, 140, 143
Rattle of a Simple Man 126
Raw Meat. See *Death Line.*
Rawnsley, Frank 43, 48
Ray, Nicholas 158
Reagan, Ronald 166
*Realism and Tinsel: Cinema and Society
    in Britain 1939-1948* 3, 25
Realism, "Kitchen Sink" 251-253
Rear Window 115
Recoil 161
Red Balloon, The 253
Red Light 161
Red Shoes, The 2, 6, 108-119, 136
Redgrave, Michael 211
Reed, Carol 53, 56, 136, 160, 168-169,
    239
Reed, Pamela 258
Reeves, Michael 197, 205-206, 207
Reisz, Karel 222, 236, 240, 252
Relph, Michael 53
Renown (Studio) 41
Republic (Studio) 160
Resnais, Alain 256
Reville, Alma 122
Richard III 105
Richards, Jeffrey 25, 38
Richardson, Ralph 33, 38
Richardson, Tony 126, 252
Ride With Uncle Joe 124
Riders To The Sea 28, 38
River War, The 20
RKO (Studio) 160

RKO British (Studio) 26, 36
Robe, The 251
Roberts, Oral 172
Roberts, Rachel 252
Robson, Flora 62
Robson, Mark 50
Roc, Patricia 63
Roeg, Nicholas 172
Rohmer, Eric 250
Romero, George 195-196
Room To Let 162
Roome, Alfred 54, 56, 57
Rope 45
Rose, Bernard 207
Rose, W. K. 13
Rosenthal, Joseph 20
Rotha, Paul 124
Russo-Japanese War 20
Rutherford, Dame Margaret 104, 252

Sammy and Rosie Get Laid 8, 221, 223,
    224, 228, 233, 238-239, 245-248, 285
Saraband for Dead Lovers 100
Sargent, Sir Malcom 136
Sarris, Andrew 53
Sasdy, Peter 197, 200, 201
Satanic Rites of Dracula 200
Saville, Victor 2
Sayers, Dorothy 158
Scandal 230
Scarlet Street 59
Scott, Ridley 222
Scott, Tony 222
Scream and Scream Again 197, 204
Screen Guild (Studio) 160
Scrooge 26
Sea of Sand 148
Sea Shall Not Have Them, The 147
Searle, Ronald 130
Second World War 35, 41, 67, 76-77, 83-
    85, 88-89, 91-92, 143-153, 156-157,
    161
Secret of Blood Island 56
See How They Run 14
Selby, Spencer 155, 160
Sensation 29, 30-31, 32, 38

Serge Diaghilev Ballet Company 135
Servant, The 8
Seven Brothers Meet Dracula, The. See
    Legend of the Seven Golden Vampires,
    The.
Seven Days to Noon 54
Seventh Veil, The 125
Sex, Class, and Realism 51
Sexual difference 110, 112
Shaffer, Anthony 204
Shake Hands With the Devil 157
Shakespeare, William 53, 59, 104
Sharp, Don 196
Sharpe, Edith 57
Shaw, Run Run 196
She Wore A Yellow Ribbon 175
Shearer, Moira 109, 117
Sherman, Gary 197, 205, 206-207
Sherwin, David 167-168
Ship That Died of Shame, The 147
Shoeshine 42
Short Cut To Hell 162
Shurey, Dinah 121
Sight and Sound 26
Silver, Alain 155
Silver, Donald 188
Silverman, Kaja 177-181, 188, 190n.2,
    191n.12
Sim, Alastair 252
Sim, Sheila 62
Simmons, Jean 54
Simon, Simone 59
Simpson, Wallis 31
Singin' In The Rain 251
Siodmak, Robert 158
Sistrom, William 26
Six Men, The 161
Skirts 136
Slater, John 103
Sleeping Beauty 113
Small Voice 57
Smith, Albert E. 11
Smith, George Albert 19, 23n.4
Snakes and Ladders 44
So Evil My Love 54
Society for Cinema Studies 9, 250

Somlo, Josef 26
Sontag, Susan 203
Sound of Music, The 133
Spaceways 42
Spanish-American War 11, 23
Spectacle in the cinema, 119
Spillane, Mickey 158
Stam, Robert 3
Stamp, Terence 222
Stanton, Philip 102
Steenburgen, Mary 168
Steevens, George 12, 22
Stewart, Hugh 26
Stoker, Bram 199, 201
Stone, Norman 223
Strange Bargain 162
Stranger Came Home, The 42, 161
Stranger Left No Card, The 127, 130,
    135-140
Straub, Jean-Marie 249
Straw Dogs 206
Street Corner, The 126
Street of Chance 161
Street With No Name, The 161
Sudden Fear 162
Summers, Walter 29
Sunday in the Country 256
Sunday Times of London 223, 224
Sunset 168
Survival of the Novel: British Fiction in
    the Later Twentieth Century 218
Swaggart, Jimmy 172
Swan Lake 113
Swann, Paul 3, 43
Sykes, Peter 197
Synge, J.M. 28

T-Men 162
Take My Life 161
Tales From The Crypt 204
Target For Tonight 149
Taste of Honey, A 252
Taste The Blood of Dracula 200, 201
Taxi 162
Taylor, Ronnie 136
Tchaikovsky, Peter I. 27

Teckman Mystery, The 139
Tell-Tale Heart, The 27
Temptation 61
Temptation Harbour 58, 59-60, 62
Tenth Man, The 29, 30, 32, 33
Thalberg, Irving 27
Thames Television 211
Thatcher, Margaret 8-9, 95, 100, 152,
    166-167, 173, 198, 221, 223-226, 230-
    231, 233, 241-243, 246-248
Theatre and the cinema, 140-142
Theater of Blood 197, 203
Theirs Is The Glory 37
There Was A Young Lady 63
They Walk Alone 60
They Who Dare 148
Thief of Baghdad, The 127
Third Man, The 158
13 East Street 161
Thirty-Nine Steps, The 54
This Gun For Sale 158
This Happy Breed 5, 67-79
This Man Is News 158
This Other Eden 126
This Sporting Life 252
Thomas, Ralph 53
Thompson, Edward 98
Thompson, Margaret 124
Thompson, Jim 236
Three Cases of Murder 136
Three Silent Men 161
Tigon (Studio) 196
Today's Cinema 79
Todd, Ann 54
Tom Brown's Schooldays 26
Tomlinson, David 129
Too Late For Tears 162
Too Young To Love 126
Tootsie 250, 256
Torture Garden 204
Towers Open Fire 203
Toye, Wendy 2, 3, 6-7, 122, 125, 126-
    130, 133-142
Trapped 162
Travelling the Road 27
Trollenberg Terror, The 56

Trottie True 38
True As A Turtle 140
Truth About Women, The 126
Tully, Montgomery 2, 5, 43, 48-51
Twins of Evil 200
Twitchell, James B. 196
Two Cities Films (Studio) 26, 36, 37, 92n.1
Tyburn (Studio) 196

Ulmer, Edgar G. 158
Uncle Silas 53, 54
Under the Frozen Falls 43
Uninvited, The 54
United Artists (Studio) 160, 163
Universal (Studio) 160
Upturned Glass, The 63, 64
Urban, Charles 18, 21, 23

Vampire Lovers, The 200
Variety 27, 37
Varley, Beatrice 56, 59
Veeser, H. Aram 1
Vengeance Is Mine 161
Verity Films (Studio) 161
Vernon, Richard 57
Vicious Circle, The 162
Video aesthetics, 141-142
Vietnam War 195
Villiers, Frederic 2-4, 11-23
Voyeurism 177

Walbrook, Anton 6, 36, 110
Walker, Alexander 3, 216
Walker, Peter 197, 204
Walpole, Hugh 64
Walsh, Dermot 38
Walsh, Raoul 158
Wanted for Murder 63, 162
War and a Wheel 13
War in the cinema 11-23
War Illustrators, The 12
War Requiem, The 174, 256
War, the West, and the Wilderness, The 18
Ward, Elizabeth 155

Warnecke, Gordon 243
Warner Brothers (Studio) 41, 160
Warner, Jack 26, 43, 56
Warren, Betty 101
Warsaw Concerto 36
Warwick Trading Company 20
Watergate 230
Wattis, Richard 252
Way Ahead, The 151
Way to the Stars 151
Wayne, John 239
Wayne, Naunton 99, 100
Weak and the Wicked, The 162
Weapon, The 162
Webber, Sir Andrew Lloyd 223
Weber, Lois 121
Welles, Orson 158
Went the Day Well? 88-89
Whales of August, The 169
When Harry Met Sally 256
When the Bough Breaks 63-64
Whipcord 204
Whirlpool, The 162
Whiskey Galore 96, 98, 145
Whitehouse, Mary 198
Wicker Man, The 197, 204-205
Wilcox, Herbert 25, 26
Wild Thyme, Winter Lightning: The Symbolic Novels of L. P. Hartley 217
Wilder, Billy 158, 222, 237
Williams Raymond 95, 96-97, 98, 99
Williams, Tennessee 256
Wilson, Donald 48
Wilson, Harold 197-198
Window In London, A 158
Winnicott, D. W. 181
Witchfinder General, The 197, 205-206
With The Greeks In Thessaly 13
Witness, The 162
Wolff, Philipp 16, 18
Wollen, Peter 7, 175
Women Aren't Angels 63
Women in British Film Industry 121-142
Women Without Men 162

Women's Institute 123
Wood, Robin 185, 206
Wooden Horse, The 147
Woolrich, Cornell 158
World War I. *See* First World War.
World War II. *See* Second World War.
Wright, Kenneth 181, 191n.8
Wyler, William 57
Wynward, Diana 33

Yield to the Night 161
You Only Live Once 158
Young At Heart 253
Young Mr. Pitt 136
Young, Terence 35, 36
Youth Runs Wild 50

Zavarzadeh, Mas'ud 4, 44
Zimmerman, Bonnie 200